Building Sanctuary

Building Sanctuary

The Movement to Support Vietnam War
Resisters in Canada, 1965-73

Jessica Squires

UBCPress·Vancouver·Toronto

21 20 19 18 17 16 15 14 13   5 4 3 2 1

Printed in Canada on FSC-certified ancient-forest-free paper
(100% post-consumer recycled) that is processed chlorine- and acid-free.

Library and Archives Canada Cataloguing in Publication

Squires, Jessica, author
Building sanctuary : the movement to support Vietnam war resisters
in Canada, 1965-73 / Jessica Squires.

Includes bibliographical references and index.
Issued in print and electronic formats.
ISBN 978-0-7748-2524-5 (bound). – ISBN 978-0-7748-2526-9 (pdf).

1. Vietnam War, 1961-1975 – Draft resisters – United States. 2. Vietnam War, 1961-1975 – Draft resisters – Canada. 3. Vietnam War, 1961-1975 – Draft resisters – Government policy – Canada. 4. Vietnam War, 1961-1975 – Protest movements – Canada. 5. Peace movements – Canada – History – 20th century. 6. Canada – Emigration and immigration – Government policy – History – 20th century. 7. Canada – Politics and government – 1963-1984. I. Title.

FC628.D73S68 2013   971.064'4   C2013-904231-8
                                                  C2013-904232-6

Canadä

UBC Press gratefully acknowledges the financial support for our publishing program of the Government of Canada (through the Canada Book Fund), the Canada Council for the Arts, and the British Columbia Arts Council.

This book has been published with the help of a grant from the Canadian Federation for the Humanities and Social Sciences, through the Awards to Scholarly Publications Program, using funds provided by the Social Sciences and Humanities Research Council of Canada.

UBC Press
The University of British Columbia
2029 West Mall
Vancouver, BC V6T 1Z2
www.ubcpress.ca

Contents

Preface

The first decades of the twenty-first century witnessed a surge of interest in the "long sixties."[1] The sixties continue to hold meaning for those who lived through them and for a new generation of Canadians seeking fresh interpretations of later developments that bear a striking resemblance to the events of that famous decade. While researching this book, when I was asked about my research topic, I frequently replied that it was about Canadian support for Vietnam-era American war resisters. Often – in fact, almost always – upon hearing this, the questioner would tell me that he or she had known a draft dodger while growing up or had been acquainted with a war resister. Similarly, people whom I have talked to about this book and who later describe my project to someone else tend to say that it is about "draft dodgers." They transformed my analysis of Canadian support for resisters into a study of the war resisters themselves. This may seem like a minor distinction, but I think it says a lot about the strength of the myth of Canada as a haven for war resisters. This myth is so strong that the support dimension of the story is easily dismissed; after all, part of the myth is that Canada has always been such a haven. There is an assumption that support for the war resisters would have been automatic, homogeneous, and unproblematic from all levels of society and that no movement to support resisters should have been necessary. I share Daniel Francis's view that to interrogate and question myths is not to suggest that there is no truth to them.[2] Rather, the aim is to unravel, question, and fill in the gaps – to make the picture of the myth as complete as possible. This research shows that the experience of war resisters in Canada in the late 1960s and early 1970s, during which time the haven myth was entrenched, was actually the product of a complex and varied set of relationships, actions, and interactions by and among various individuals, institutions, and groups.

In addition to the government and private fonds and contemporary and movement publications reviewed here, this research uses archived interviews as well as interviews that I conducted with several anti-draft activists and war resisters. The interviews help to provide an accurate picture of the culture of the anti-draft movement. Indeed, the interviewees discussed a range of motivations, experiences, and perceptions. They recounted different experiences crossing the border and within Canada, different perceptions of the interaction between Canadians and Americans, and different depths of involvement in anti-draft work. The interviews also serve as an effective means to fill in the gaps in the record. They corroborate, or interrogate, the documentary record of the development of the anti-draft movement, presenting a personal counterpoint to the more general political dimension of the story and providing a voice to those directly involved.[3]

Decisions about terminology had to be made, especially for two significant elements of this study. These decisions were rendered more complex by their relationship to the hegemonic tensions present in the very history I am telling. First, I use the term "anti-draft movement" throughout the work. I decided to use this term for several reasons. Primarily, it serves to differentiate the movement to support American war resisters from the antiwar movement. It is also, in large measure, how the movement described itself, as several groups named themselves "anti-draft programmes." The term "anti-draft" provokes certain questions. By 1965, Canada had not seen conscription for twenty years, and "draft" was largely an American term for conscription. Did the notion of a Canadian anti-draft movement imply that the movement was an importation, or an imitation, of an American idea? The earliest use of the term "anti-draft" to describe a group in Canada was in 1965, by the Student Union for Peace Action (SUPA)'s Anti-Draft Programme. American war resister Mark Satin's involvement in this group largely explains the use of the term. However, their use of the term also implies that SUPA activists perceived that it was useful to oppose a policy of the American government as part of general activities in favour of peace. The term describes a movement whose unstated goal was to undermine the American Selective Service Program – the legal name of the program that ran the American military draft – by helping young American men avoid its talons.[4] Additionally, its explicit self-identification as a Canadian "anti-draft" movement seeking to have an impact on American government policy is a reminder of the international linkages within the movement and the internationalist outlook of many of its activities.

The second question of terminology revolved around the use of the expressions "war resister," "draft dodger," and "deserter." During my research, I encountered many Vietnam-era war resisters, especially at two "Our Way Home Reunion" conferences in Castlegar, British Columbia, in July 2006 and 2007. Some of them advocated rejecting the terms "deserter" and "draft dodger" because of their negative connotations. Instead, they advocated the use of "war resister." Others, however, wanted to use the terms "deserter" and "draft dodger" as an act of reclaiming the terms and changing their connotation. Some pointed out that the terms describe fairly well what the men were doing. "War resister," on the other hand, is more inclusive of the many women (and men) who came to Canada in the period not to avoid the draft or military service but out of a more general rejection of American policy and life.

The fact that the Canadian government treated draft dodgers and deserters differently in the immigration regulations until May 1969 complicates this discussion. Government officials probably profited from the negative connotations evoked by the words "dodger" and "deserter." War resisters at the time also contested the terms they used to describe themselves. Furthermore, anti-draft groups treated deserters and draft dodgers differently because they had different needs, both perceived and real, upon arrival and later as they required continued immigration counselling. These terms help account for important historical distinctions.

I use all three terms. I use "war resister" when the draft status does not matter to the story and when discussing war resisters as a larger group, including women and others whose decision to emigrate was not related to military status. I use "draft dodger" and "deserter" when discussing individual experiences, approaches anti-draft groups took to various kinds of immigrants, and political campaigns and debates centred on the question of deserter status in particular. "Draft dodger" refers to Americans who evaded the American Selective Service Program in some way, either by leaving the United States and going to Canada or Sweden, or by some other method. A deserter in this work is someone who has enlisted in, or been drafted into, the American military forces and subsequently decided to leave his post. I have avoided the terms "draft resister" and "draft evader" both because of the vernacular use of the term "draft dodger" in the period and because the terms "draft resister" and "draft evader" are mainly useful to differentiate between anti-draft tactics in use in the United States, an issue that does not form a part of this study. A war resister, for the purposes of this volume, is any American immigrant who came to Canada to avoid complicity in, or out of opposition to, their government's actions in Vietnam.

A final consideration: some of those interviewed for this work were part of a present-day war resister support movement with which I have been involved, albeit peripherally.[5] Does this connection cast doubt on my objectivity as a researcher of this story? Or does it make me an ideal person to do the research? Like Bernard Cohn, who interrogated his role as an anthropologist able to "pass" as a historian, I sometimes wondered if I was a war resister "passing" as a historian, or the other way around.[6] Similarly, the question of the past as colonized territory came up in my interpretation of the actions of figures, both living and dead, from this history. David Lowenthal's preoccupation with the misuses of memory also shapes my approach. Lowenthal is concerned with "how memory establishes personal identity; the links between personal and communal memory; how recollections are verified; ... the function of forgetting; how time alters old and invents new memories." He notes, "[W]e brainwash ourselves into believing that we simply reveal the true past – a past which is unavoidably, however, partly of our own manufacture."[7] To this, I would add that we are partly of its manufacture and that, as Cohn would say, culture is historically constructed as much as history is culturally constructed.[8] I thus justify my presumption to interpret the actions of others in the past and to thereby use bits of their stories to make a new story.

Accordingly, this is a story with which many will not agree. During the research process, when I presented portions of my work, formally and informally, people who "were there" sometimes challenged the truth of my findings. I had to remind myself that documents are not the ultimate source of truth; but neither, of course, is memory. I have tried to be as honest as possible with the evidence. I hope I have fairly acknowledged the understandings of those whose stated recollections of the story differed from my retrospective compilation and selective emphasis, whether or not

I came to agree with them. Here, it is useful to recall the words of David Lodge: history is the judgment "of those who were not there on those who were."[9] I hope that my attempts here are more in line with Donald Ritchie's caution to remember that "oral history is a joint product," shaped by both the researcher and those she interviews.[10] Furthermore, I value the contributions of those I interviewed, not for their ability to shed light on the facts, although they certainly did so, but for their memory of their experience of this movement.[11] The value is in their lived experience and its interaction with my own as a researcher.[12]

When American forces invaded Iraq in 2003, Canada was not a direct participant – just as Canada did not participate in the war on Vietnam. A few Americans have made their way over the border as deserters from the war on Iraq. Of course, the specific circumstances have changed. But a study of the war resisters and anti-draft activists of the late 1960s and early 1970s provides both knowledge and inspiration for those who want to make sense of the almost eight-year occupation of Iraq.[13] I believe this story will contribute significantly not only to our understanding of the past but also to our understanding of the present and the future.

Acknowledgments

This research would not have been possible without the support and guidance of a great many people: friends, family, colleagues, and acquaintances. I cannot possibly name them all; I hope those I omit will forgive me and know that I nonetheless thank them sincerely.

I would particularly like to thank my primary mentor, Dominique Marshall, for her superb capacity to undertake this journey with me, despite the seemingly tenuous connections between her interests and mine. The importance she places on theory allowed us to find a remarkably large amount of common ground. Her unwavering encouragement and ability to push me to take one more analytical step were both inescapable and essential.

Encouragement from other Carleton University colleagues, both faculty and graduate students, has been crucial for this work's completion. There are too many to name, but, in particular, I would like to thank Kristina Guiguet, who helped keep me focused and convinced that the finish line really was in view. Norman Hillmer's almost offhand remark about historians and nationalism resulted in the development of one of the core conceptual frameworks of this book. I would also like to thank my colleagues Marcel Martel, Laura Macdonald, Andrew Johnston, Joanna Dean, and Michel Gaulin for their thoughtful consideration of this work.

Carleton sociology professor Bruce Curtis's rigorous questioning of my theoretical ponderings was indispensable to my articulation of the theoretical framework that informs both this volume and my other research. Shirley Tillotson of Dalhousie University was responsible for setting me on the path of exploration of state-society theory and its applicability to historical research. Lara Campbell of Simon Fraser University, Lori Olafson of the Department of Educational Psychology at University of Nevada, and other scholars working in this area have offered constructive criticism and mutual encouragement.

I would especially like to acknowledge archivists for their contributions. In particular, Laura Madokoro and the Access to Information and Privacy analysts at Library and Archives Canada have my warmest thanks, not least for the reams of formal requests I made to consult the records of the RCMP. The staff at the archives of the University of Toronto, University of British Columbia, York University, McMaster University, and Dalhousie University were always professional and helpful. Their dedication attests to the fact that, just because something is old does not mean it is useless. As Arthur G. Doughty, dominion archivist from 1904 to 1935, observed, "[O]f all our national assets, Archives are the most precious; they are the gift of one generation to another and the extent of our care of them marks the extent of our civilization."

Financial support from Carleton University and a Social Sciences and Humanities Research Council Doctoral Fellowship made this research possible.

The former activists and war resisters I interviewed for this project were unerringly generous in their answers to my questions. Participants in the "Our Way Home Reunion" conferences always offered new perspectives and new ways of emphasizing various aspects of the story. I would especially like to thank Vietnam War resisters Joseph Jones and Lee Zaslofsky, whose consistent interest in the story I am telling went well beyond their own involvement in these events. Special thanks also go to Hans Sinn, who kindly agreed to read certain sections of the manuscript dealing with his own involvement in the early establishment of the movement. I certainly hope this work meets the expectations of all those I met and interviewed, and if I have written anything they disagree with, I hope we will have other opportunities to continue the conversation.

I would most like to thank my partner, Benoit Renaud. His unwavering faith in me allowed me to keep focused, even at the most difficult moments in the process. He has accepted sacrifices we have made to this project in time and resources with absolutely no resentment, and he only ever offered me positive encouragement and constructive criticism. Should he ever wish to change careers, he could certainly make a living as a combination counsellor and copy editor!

Finally, I would like to honour the new generation of war resisters and those who work to support them. No matter how one feels about a particular war, and no matter their individual reasons for coming to Canada, the actions of young people seeking to avoid the soul-killing effects of fighting wars can, I think, only really be understood as courage. Their courage is inspiring us now, as those resisters in the sixties and early seventies inspired an earlier generation to imagine a world without war.

Abbreviations

ADC	American Deserters Committee
AID	Ottawa AID: Assistance with Immigration and the Draft
BRO	Black Refugee Organization
CALCAV	Clergy and Laymen Concerned about Vietnam
CARM	Committee to Aid Refugees from Militarism, Toronto
CATWO	Canadian Assistance to War Objectors
CCC	Canadian Council of Churches
CCCO	Central Committee for Conscientious Objectors
CFIP	Toronto Committee for a Fair Immigration Policy
CNVA	Committee for Nonviolent Action
CUS	Canadian Union of Students
MCAWR	Montreal Council to Aid War Resisters
NSCAAWO	Nova Scotia Committee to Aid American War Objectors
RCAD	Regina Committee of American Deserters
RCMP	Royal Canadian Mounted Police
RITA	Resistance Inside the Army
RWB	Red White & Black
SAC	University of Toronto Students' Administrative Council
SDS	Students for a Democratic Society
SNCC	Student Nonviolent Coordinating Committee
SUPA	Student Union for Peace Action
TADC	Toronto American Deserters Committee
TADP	Toronto Anti-Draft Programme
UAE	Union of American Exiles
VAEA	Vancouver American Exiles Association

VCAAWO	Vancouver Committee to Aid American War Objectors
VOW	Voice of Women
VVAC	Vancouver Vietnam Action Committee
WILPF	Women's International League for Peace and Freedom
WRL	War Resisters League
WSP	Women Strike for Peace

Chronology

1959	Vietnam War begins
1966	Earliest articles regarding war resisters appear in mainstream newspapers in Canada and the United States
1966	Hans Sinn compiles fact sheet for war resisters, Montreal
1966	Toronto Anti-Draft Programme (TADP) begins as Student Union for Peace Action (SUPA) Anti-Draft Program
1966	Nova Scotia Committee to Aid American War Objectors founded, Halifax
1966	Montreal Council to Aid War Resisters founded
1966	Vancouver Committee to Aid American War Objectors (VCAAWO) founded
1966	VCAAWO publishes "Immigration to Canada and Its Relation to the Draft"
1967	Points system introduced by Government of Canada, Ottawa
ca. 1967	Ottawa Assistance with Immigration and the Draft founded
1967	University of Toronto Students' Administrative Council gives money to Toronto Anti-Draft Programme
1967	SUPA publishes *Escape from Freedom, or, I Didn't Raise My Boy to Be a Canadian*
1967	Students for a Democratic Society (US) issues a statement in qualified support of emigration to Canada

1967	VCAAWO brief "A Note on Fugitives from Justice" released
1967	VCAAWO brief "A Note on the Handling of Draft-Age Immigrants to Canada" released
1968	TADP publishes *Manual for Draft-Age Immigrants to Canada*
July 1968	Operational Memo (Ottawa) secretly issued to exclude deserters from Canada
1968	TADP publishes *Manual for Draft-Age Immigrants to Canada,* 2nd edition
1968	War resister Howie Petrick addresses Vietnam Mobilization Committee Conference, Toronto
1968	Canadian Union of Students considers becoming a contact point for war resisters
ca. 1969	TADP publishes *Manual for Draft-Age Immigrants to Canada,* 3rd edition
ca. 1969	War resister Melody Killian addresses Canadian Union of Students congress
1969	TADP publishes *Manual for Draft-Age Immigrants to Canada,* 4th edition
1969	VCAAWO brief "A Further Note on the Handling of Draft-Age Immigrants to Canada" released
1969	Tom Faulkner, pro-draft dodger candidate for University of Toronto Students' Administrative Council, re-elected
22 May 1969	Minister of Manpower and Immigration Allan MacEachen announces open border to deserters and issues revised operational memorandum to immigration officers
Dec. 1969– early 1970	Canadian Council of Churches Ministry to Draft-Age Immigrants established
January 1970	Voice of Women issues public statement in support of war resisters
May-June 1970	Pan-Canadian Conference of US War Resisters held in Montreal

1970	TADP publishes *Manual for Draft-Age Immigrants to Canada,* 5th edition
1970	Black Refugee Organization founded, Toronto
1970	Red White & Black founded, Toronto
1971	TADP publishes *Manual for Draft-Age Immigrants to Canada,* 6th edition
July-August 1972	Administrative Measures Program (Government of Canada) allows relaxed criteria for the consideration of appeals
3 November 1972	Section 34 of the Immigration Regulations repealed (Government of Canada); landing at the border or from within Canada no longer allowed
June 1973	Bill C-197 debated and adopted, eliminating universal right to appeal and announcing Adjustment of Status Program (Government of Canada)
15 August-15 October 1973	Adjustment of Status Program (Government of Canada) implemented

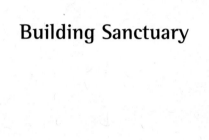

Building Sanctuary

Introduction
War Resisters in Context

Je viens de recevoir
Mes papiers militaires
Pour partir à la guerre
Avant mercredi soir.

Monsieur le président
Je ne veux pas la faire,
Je ne suis pas sur terre
Pour tuer de pauvres gens.

– Boris Vian, "Le Déserteur," 1954[1]

Wars are divisive. They divide countries from one another, and they also divide populations and families. As the Vietnam War took hold of the American consciousness, opposition to the war became more and more widespread. At first, the opposition was mainly expressed by youth. Later, people from a variety of ages and political, economic, and social backgrounds voiced opposition.[2] The question of military service increasingly became a focus of debate and acrimony.[3] The debate continued throughout the duration of the conflict and into the years following its end in 1975. The 1976 US election was partly about the issue of amnesty for Americans of draft age who had emigrated.[4]

The war also had a considerable impact on people living in Canada. Many Canadians still remember the protest movements against the Vietnam

War. The image of Canada as a harbour for Americans of conscience, "draft dodgers," to a lesser extent "deserters," and their families and friends has become an important Canadian legend and part of Canadian identity.[5]

The exact number of American war resisters to immigrate to Canada between 1965 and 1973 was a matter of some debate, and remains so.[6] The consensus appears to be that forty to fifty thousand young men came to Canada to escape the draft during this period. Women also came, and many of them saw themselves as part of the same group. Estimates of the number of American war resisters in Canada suggest that this group represented a fairly large percentage of the American men who took various actions to beat the draft. To compare, a quarter million young Americans are estimated to have avoided the draft by omitting to register on their eighteenth birthday.[7] The numbers of war resisters who came to Canada were also small compared to the number of Canadians who participated in the wider opposition to war in Vietnam. But the size of this movement remains significant and helps explain the prevalent idea of Canada as a haven for draft dodgers.

In general, the draft dodgers phenomenon is one of the events to which Canadians often point, uncritically, to emphasize the differences between Canadians and Americans. But this idea of Canada as a peaceful nation is an oversimplification. The myth is that Canada, a more peaceable country than the United States, allowed American draft dodgers and deserters to find refuge from militarism across our border, which, while true, overlooks how that refuge was achieved – through the efforts of a social movement.[8]

This myth, which began to take hold in the sixties, was not always as persistent as it became. The history of war resisters is as old as the history of modern wars. According to a British study conducted after the First World War, "50,000 Englishmen pledged never to take part in another war"; sixteen thousand men refused to participate between 1916 and 1918; and 1,300 went to jail, declining alternative service provisions for conscientious objectors.[9] Furthermore, public fascination with the phenomenon of war resisters is almost as old as the phenomenon itself.

The myth represents an important part of the larger image of Canada as a peaceful nation, which, in turn, is often attributed to the government of the day, the Liberal administration of Pierre Trudeau. Trudeau's supposed sympathy for war resisters is also legendary, and the tenacity of the myth of Canada as a haven for war resisters remains linked to the former prime minister. Trudeau is often quoted as saying, "Those who make the conscientious judgment that they must not participate in this war ... have my complete sympathy, and indeed our political approach has been to give them access to Canada. Canada should be a refuge from militarism." This quotation appears in two of the important works on war resisters in Canada: Renée Kasinsky's 1976 work, *Refugees from Militarism: Draft-Age Americans in Canada,* and John Hagan's 2001 book, *Northern Passage: American Vietnam War Resisters in Canada.*[10] The left alternative press also used the quotation in support of the campaign to allow American war resisters from the Iraq conflict to stay in Canada.[11] Archivist and Vietnam-era war resister Joseph Jones has traced the origins of this quotation to erroneous newspaper reports and concluded that the quotation is actually an amalgam of two statements by Trudeau, one in 1970 and one in 1971. Jones argues that Trudeau's statements about war resisters were limited to these two disparate declarations made to religious groups in the context of what Trudeau may have perceived as theological discussion. He goes on to point out that Trudeau also made at least two statements in 1969 that suggest that he believed deserters should be treated differently from draft dodgers.[12] The notion that the Trudeau government and, indeed, Trudeau himself unequivocally supported the US war resisters of the Vietnam era is, therefore, overstated.

It is true that, in a series of speeches in early 1969, Prime Minister Trudeau and Minister of Manpower and Immigration Allan MacEachen instructed immigration officials that military service was not a matter for interrogation at the border or in immigration offices when considering applications to move to Canada.[13] But the Trudeau quotes came after the 1969 announcement concerning the border. The events leading to that decision were more complicated than the myth leads us to believe. The experience of war resisters and their supporters was far from uniform as they interacted with government officials, police, and one another, both before the announcement, while the majority of American war resisters coming to Canada were draft dodgers, and after, when the balance shifted towards deserters. The Canadian anti-draft movement's interaction with government officials and police varied from openly antagonistic to fully cooperative. The interactions between activists and resisters were equally complex.

There was a broad and vibrant movement to support American war resisters who came to Canada either to avoid the draft or to avoid the war in Vietnam. The support for these immigrants, however, was neither monolithic nor unanimous. Many of the contentious issues in the war resisters' movement and in the broader antiwar movement reflected domestic debates about relations between the United States and Canada, which were also being played out at the level of the federal government. For example, cabinet discussions regarding the treatment of deserters at the Canadian border considered the relative wisdom and potential political impact of applying American law within Canada. The war resisters and their supporters contributed to the debates about nationalism and Canada's relationship to the United States that pervaded this period. Accordingly, in one sense, this story is a part of the history of international relations from the bottom up.

Americans arrived in a Canada that was in many ways similar to the United States they had left. In Canada, as in the United States, the movements for civil rights and against the war in Vietnam mingled with burgeoning feminist movements, and with those for Black Power, Red Power, and gay rights. Many of these social movements were influenced by activity in the United States. They were also developing at the same time as important ideas, such as Trudeau's "Just Society" and Quebec separatism, were being debated. Questions about Canadian sovereignty and Canada's place in the world were also circulating. Of this mix, the Canadian anti-draft movement was both a part and a separate ingredient. The American movement against the draft as it existed in the late 1960s had roots in the civil rights movement and cold war pacifism, conscientious objection movements of the First World War, and the "peace churches."[14] The Canadian movement had seemingly congruent origins but also incorporated the immigrants themselves into the work.

By considering merely one of the more obvious contextual issues, cross-border relations, the complexity of this movement is immediately apparent. Cross-border relations are often seen as a reflection of diplomatic history.[15] But perhaps the question to be answered is: how do Americans and Canadians talk to each other? What factors need to be considered in asking such a question – and how does one go about researching them? The literatures on nationalism, immigration history, bureaucracy, policing, and the Gramscian theories of hegemony and consciousness underlie my approach to writing the story of Canadian support for Vietnam-era American war resisters.

This work has several objectives. By presenting an account that is as complete as possible of the development of the anti-draft movement in Canada, this book accounts for the transnational nature of the story. It replaces the common assumption that Canadian social movements merely imitate or are part of American ones with a picture of homegrown autonomous social movements that had mature and complex relationships with sister movements in the United States.[16] The ideas, ideals, and mutual perceptions of anti-draft activists and war resisters interacted in interesting and often unexpected ways. Describing this interaction sheds new light on the tensions that existed between Canadians and Americans of the time. These tensions can neither be reduced to Canadian nationalism nor to anti-Americanism – and neither should one be conflated with the other.

The campaign to open the border to deserters in May of 1969, which shows how the haven Canada became was the result of concerted and conscious pressure by the movement, is a central narrative of this story. The decision to open the border came about, in large part, because of a campaign by the anti-draft movement that mobilized public pressure and the mainstream media in a hegemonic skirmish for the dominant perception of war resisters in Canada. The ideas consciously promoted in this campaign remain resonant in debates about Canada's global identity. A competing force in this skirmish, the coercive activity of the government, took the form of police and RCMP surveillance of the war resisters and their supporters. Although this surveillance reflected a segment of Canadian public opinion and the opinions of some government actors, it also exposed some of the divisions among both the government and the public, which illustrates the contingent nature of hegemony. In the end, a particular confluence of events – namely, a simultaneous increase in unemployment and a rapid increase in immigration – combined to make strange bedfellows of civil society groups, such as the anti-draft movement, and government agencies, such as immigration offices, who worked together to achieve temporarily shared ends.

While the experiences and events of war resisters are taken up by scholars across various disciplines, the literatures of the twentieth-century historiography of war resisters, United States–Canada relations, and the Vietnam War are particularly important in this work. I also draw from the broader literature on pacifism and American history as well as immigration history because of the prominence of nationalism in the 1960s in Canada. Because this work weaves together social, cultural, and political histories, the state and relations between state and society are also important factors. In effect, the relationships between ideas, movements, and politics; nationalism in Canada; the nature of American immigrants; and the interactions of state and civil society, bureaucracy, and policing all form a part of the picture.[17]

The movement to support American war resisters in Canada was a social movement with multifaceted and layered relationships to the state and its institutions. What is a social movement? Movements, which often include both pressure groups and individuals,[18] can be understood as "collectivities acting with some degree of organization and continuity outside of institutional or organizational channels for the purpose of challenging or ending extant authority, whether it is institutionally or culturally based, in the group, organization, society, culture, or world order of which they are a part."[19] Such was the Canadian anti-draft movement. It played a role in, and was influenced by, hegemonic processes buffeting around ideas such as the changing role of immigration, the legacy of old movements and the rise of new ones, and nationalism and national identity. The interaction of actors from government officials to police, from anti-draft groups to individual activists and war resisters, calls for framing that can account for this complexity without reducing it to the realm of either material experience or cultural practice.

As political scientist Robert Cox points out, "[T]heory is always for someone and for some purpose."[20] A history of the Canadian anti-draft movement should analyze the policing and surveillance of its proponents, the effects of individuals on movements, the movement's effects on politics and on ideas, and the interaction of individuals and groups across borders to gain an understanding of the entire picture of international relations both horizontally and, more importantly, vertically. A view of how the state and society interact, intersect, and overlap both physically and culturally is necessary for understanding. The result is a history supported by theory. Taking an interdisciplinary approach to a historical topic yields better results because it encourages a deep analysis. In this way, social historical approaches benefit from "bringing the state back in,"[21] and, conversely, political historical approaches benefit from an under-standing of emerging or widely held cultural beliefs and ideas and their effect on actions. This inclusivity, in turn, provides a comprehensive understanding of the history of the movement to support war resisters from the ground up.

I draw from Antonio Gramsci's theory of hegemony and Marxist ap-proaches to consciousness and the state to conceptualize the physical and cultural interactions, intersections, and overlap between state and society. "Civil society" groups are as much shaped by those around them and by state regulations as the state is pushed and moulded by civil society. Regulatory regimes in the form of, and enforced by, government institu-tions are powerful forces, but when lived experiences cannot be forced into predetermined moulds the result is often regulatory and legislative change. Ideas about how society should work, promoted by government actors, produce expectations in that society that those ideas will be imple-mented, which in turn pressures the government to accommodate these ideas (for example, the "Just Society," "Canada the good") in a kind of self-fulfilling prophecy. A rich analysis of these forces and their interaction yields a rich history with much to offer both historians of the social move-ments of the 1960s and theorists of subsequent movements against war and to protect conscientious objectors. To historians, this history is an example of the new political history – an illustration of how an approach using several perspectives can result both in a history to which ordinary people can relate and a history that takes account of the role of government actors without privileging their role in events. To those active in social movements, this book offers lessons about the successes and failures of movements past, in which a better understanding of similar issues arising in contemporary struggles may be grounded.

War Resisters in Context: International Relations, Immigration, and Bureaucracy

> *draft resister*
> *watching the ducks*
> *fly south*
>
> – *Chris Faiers, "draft resister"*[22]

Historians have mostly considered the topic of war resisters as a bit of an afterthought.[23] Even more recent works such as Robert Bothwell's *Alliance and Illusion, The Big Chill,* and *Canada and the United States: The Politics of Partnership* treat the phenomenon as incidental to international relations at the state level between Canada and the United States.[24] This perspective neither tells the whole story of the resisters nor attends to the possibility that the resisters and their supporters may have had some impact on those relations or on larger cultural shifts. For Bothwell and others, the war resisters are, at most, symptoms of public sentiments on both sides of the border.[25] Even Victor Levant, whose book *Quiet Complicity* is one of only a handful of books critical of Canadian involvement in the Vietnam War, examines the war resisters phenomenon and the government's attitude towards them as merely an illustration of that complicity.[26]

It is tempting to treat war resisters as a curiosity, which may explain the strong tendency for books on the war resister story to take a journalistic approach through compiling a group of twenty or thirty interviews. False polarities between voluntary expatriates and political exiles, the politically motivated and those who were not, and so on, are common.[27] Deeper examinations of the role played by Canadians in the movement, and the importance of the connections between the Canadian and American anti-draft movements, have been rare. In fact, Canadians are seldom even a part of the picture painted in this literature, whether the author is Canadian or American.

There are important exceptions. Law professor and sociologist John Hagan's *Northern Passage: American Vietnam War Resisters in Canada,* which is in large part devoted to the political history of changing immigration regulations, the sociology of the American exile ghetto in Toronto in the 1960s and early 1970s, and the socio-psychological impacts of war resistance on the future activities of war resisters, also examines the role of the Toronto Anti-Draft Programme in welcoming American immigrants and finding them housing and other services.[28] Hagan's treatment of the anti-draft movement is general and overwhelmingly positive. Historian David Churchill's study of state motivations for changes in immigration regulations regarding draft dodgers and deserters also focuses on the war resisters.[29] Churchill's work addresses the complexity of the discussion at the level of the Department of Immigration, while Hagan tends to place power more centrally in the hands of Cabinet ministers.

Churchill's and Hagan's works are important starting points for this research. However, while both leave a place for anti-draft movement pressure on officials, and both afford a place for the influence of ideas on events, neither author centres his attention on the movement's impact on government and policy. The otherwise considerable silence on the topic of draft dodgers by most authors is curious considering the extent to which the draft dodgers' era in Canadian history has taken on a mythical aspect.

On the topic of draft dodgers in Canada, then, there is, first and foremost, a lack of any broad historical work on the Canadian groups and individuals who worked to support and encourage American war resisters, deserters, and draft dodgers in their quest to come to Canada and settle here.[30] There is also a paucity of research on the interplay between Canadian political culture, Canadian anti-draft activists, Canadian government officials and state apparatuses, and American war resisters.

As draft dodgers and deserters were also immigrants, the field of immigration history is an obvious point of reference. But in most historical work, cross-border relations "below" the interaction of states are rarely considered and, if considered at all, are often seen as a mere reflection of diplomatic history.[31] A bottom-up approach can emphasize the processes unfolding "on the ground," as it were, and account for the influence of movements and individuals on political processes. The bottom-up approach also opens up space within which to consider whether American immigrants ought to be studied as a group of immigrants like any other, or whether enough substantial differences exist to merit a different treatment. The central questions here are: How is the immigrant seen, perceived, and defined in Canadian political culture? Does racialization – the categorization and differentiation of people on the basis of race – play a role? If so, how does the American immigrant – whose nation of origin, the United States, arguably has a very similar dominant idea of national identity to that of Canada – fit in?

In most interpretations, the points system introduced by the Canadian government in 1967 was a refinement of policy moves that had been taken by politicians in the early 1960s towards a goal of eliminating racism from selection criteria. The points system allocated points for certain characteristics of potential immigrants, such as training and education. Potential immigrants had to be allocated a minimum number of points to be granted permission to immigrate. The system replaced an earlier regime that emphasized quotas of immigrants from particular countries.[32] Theorists who question both the motive and impact of immigration reform debate the idea that the new points system addressed concerns of racism. As Anna Triandafyllidou writes, "Othering the immigrant is functional ... to achieving or enhancing national cohesion ... The immigrant poses a challenge to the in-group's unity and authenticity, which it threatens to 'contaminate.'"[33] The racialization of immigrants is linked to a cultural notion – contested, but dominant – of Canadian identity as white.

In Canada, cultural perceptions of immigrants as people of colour with different languages, cultural practices, and behaviours continued to dominate long after 1967. A "'national' life and culture ... commonsensically acknowledged as 'English'" and white becomes hegemonic enough to be shared even by progressive Canadians or the Left.[34] The result was a system whereby "all white people ... become invisible and hold a dual membership in Canada, while others remain immigrants generations later."[35] As sociologist Rose Baaba Folson also points out in her study of immigration in Canada, "White immigrants are often constructed as citizens, while non-white citizens are constructed as immigrants."[36]

For Americans, Himani Bannerji observes that, historically, "decisions about who should come into Canada to do what work, definitions of skill and accreditation, licensing and certification, have been influenced by 'race' and ethnicity."[37] This observation is important for its recognition of the political economy of immigration in the 1960s and early 1970s. The vast majority of American war resisters were white. Their country of origin has a similar paradigm of "whiteness"; those immigrants who had been racialized as non-white in the United States were also racialized as non-white in Canada, and not because they were American.[38] Immigrants of colour continued to be racialized in Canada, sometimes despite expectations that race would not be as central to their lives as it was in the United States. However, the majority of war resisters fit well into the dominant norm; only an audible accent, in some cases, marked them as different.

While American immigrants could most closely "pass" in the context of dominant, white, anglophone Canada, they still experienced the "othering" process, although not as racial others. They shared some experiences with immigrants in general in that they were sometimes suspected of stealing jobs from Canadians, importing radicalism, and misbehaving. But, unlike many other immigrant groups, the most important factor for Americans' experience as immigrants was their socioeconomic background.

Therefore, the analytical emphasis here is on those aspects of policy that more directly affected them – class bias in immigration policy, for instance. But most discrimination against Americans was associated primarily with their country's foreign policy and not with their individual character. The character-based discrimination that did exist was more about their military status and less about their American-ness.[39] In the anti-draft movement, the actors were generally not government officials, but Americans and Canadians interacting "on the ground" in ways affected by both nationalism and internationalism. While American immigrants were, by definition and in the eyes of government, immigrants like any others inasmuch as they crossed the border in order to live in Canada, in practice, their experiences were quite different. They were not racialized, and although they were targeted, they were not targeted for characteristics normally ascribed to more visibly different immigrant groups.

Because Canadians and Americans share some history, as well as a dominant language and many cultural norms, social movements in the two countries have often had similar trajectories. Questions about both migration and Canadian national identity tend to intersect with analysis of borders and nations, and many theorists have considered the cross-border and transnational relations between unions, social movements, and individuals in Canadian history.[40] The Canadian anti-draft movement is one such movement, strongly influenced by, and sharing a history with, the American pacifist movement and the involvement of the "peace churches."[41] These transnational linkages intersected with questions of national identity and nationalism in Canada.

International relations at the level of governments and elites are also influenced by transnational tendencies. Indeed, these ideas have been elaborated by international relations theorists such as Cox, who emphasizes the role of social movements in exerting pressure on relations between governments.[42] Similarly, in her *States and Social Revolutions,* Theda Skocpol focuses upon the "Janus-faced" nature of the state – its inherent connection to international networks of states and its dependence on social legitimacy – and incorporates the notion of states as organizations into her analysis.[43] These formulations, tempered with respect for the impact of ideas on events, have fruitful uses in a history of international relations from the bottom up because they can account for the role of institutions in historical events without reducing them to monoliths outside the agency of human beings.

Telling a story based on an analysis that takes into consideration the government-society axis must consider the specific roles of government and institutions, social movements and groups, as well as intellectuals, and how they all interacted and influenced each other. This book sees the state as non-monolithic and sees government as a contingent set of outcomes of negotiations between groups of various size and influence. I employ ideas from the theory of social movements, especially that which recognize movements themselves as actors.[44] As Dominique Marshall explains, the new political history "includes all relations of power within a society ... These relations contribute to the creation (and perpetuation) of the large categories of social relations, studied in the new history, among classes, genres, generations, regions, nations, and ethnicities."[45]

Skocpol's defence of what she and others call "historical institutional-ism" effectively sets out an integrated approach to any study of society – historical or otherwise – that can account for all of the nuances and factors inherent in any particular event:

> Institutions for me are sets of relationships that persist, although in an inherently conflictual and tension filled way. Institutions may be formal organizations or informal networks. They have shared meetings and relatively stable bundles of resources attached to them. I take an organizationalist approach to institutions, viewing them as actual patterns of communication and activity, rather than seeing them primarily as values, norms, ideas, or official rules. I am primarily interested in studying political processes and outcomes, and I see these as brought about, usually without intentional foresight and control, by actors whose goals and capacities and conflicts with one another are grounded in institutions ... It is not enough just to explore how people talk or think. We must also find patterns in what they do. I do not think that institutions are simply or primarily systems of meaning or normative frameworks. Group identities for me are grounded in organizational linkages, access to resources, and some sense of "success" over time in political undertakings.[46]

Skocpol sees individuals, groups, and government as historical actors. This perception is valuable because it offers an array of explanatory mechanisms for describing historical events. The choice of either state or society is refracted into many different potential agents of change.

Ideas also influence events. In this book, Gramsci's ideas are used to incorporate the role of intellectuals into the state-society relationship, without letting go of the importance of "grounded" group actors. In Gramsci's theory of hegemony, ideas, as part of relatively cohesive sets of ideas or ideologies that inhabit the political landscape, exist in relations to each other and to events that are historically established and recognized as part of a philosophically coherent whole.[47] In Gramsci's conception of cultural and state formation, the buildup of accepted and often dominant practices provides a backdrop of ideas, politics, and relations between people that must be involved in any strategy to make fundamental changes in that culture.[48] Further, Gramsci suggests that intellectuals aligned with either the historic bloc most clearly dominating the state, or with emerging groups and ideas, are important agents of ideological formation. "Historic blocs" – groups of people with similar ideas and objective interests, positioned to act in such a way as to have a concrete effect on the common sense of the day – can sometimes bring together unlikely allies.[49] This hegemonic process is constantly changing, and the outcome is neither guaranteed nor permanent, partly because old ideas commingle with emergent ones.[50] As Ian McKay asserts, hegemony is "not a once-and-for-all achievement of total domination."[51]

In his *Prison Notebooks,* in the section called "The Modern Prince," Gramsci discusses the often complex interface in modern democracies between the executive and legislative branches of government, that is, parliamentary bodies and the institutions of rule. For Gramsci, intellectuals are a specifically "professional category" that could be associated with classes ("fundamental social groups"). The specific functions of intellectuals, for Gramsci, were the creation of social hegemony and political government. These functions accrued to intellectuals who played the role of "deputies" to the "dominant group," or ruling class. Gramsci points out that organizing social hegemony requires an extensive division of labour, which accounts for the huge expansion of intellectuals as a social group in early 1930s Europe. According to Gramsci, "mass" training standardized individuals both psychologically and in terms of individual qualification; thus, competition between potential functionaries was induced.[52] Gramsci further suggested that the division of labour brought about the formation of a "caste" of bureaucrats, a group to which specific power accrued.[53] Gramsci's interpretation offers a way to discuss the interaction between individuals and structures without collapsing into conspiracy theory or rigid structuralism. It also points to the importance of interest groups in society and has implications for both the formation and the enforcement of laws and public policy.[54]

The historical institutionalism of Skocpol and others, and Gramscian ideas, are complemented by Max Weber's theory of bureaucracy. For Weber, bureaucracies are characterized by rules, regulations, and specialization that together promote objectivity, personified in expertise. Thus, the bureaucratic mechanism exists independently of personnel.[55] This Weberian formulation is the basis for the idea of bureaucracy as actor, as opposed to government, group, or individual. But it must be tempered with Gramsci's observations about intellectuals and hegemony to be a comprehensive approach.

By attending to the interface between government institutions and individuals and the techniques of administration, approaches such as that taken by Bruce Curtis in his Foucauldian *The Politics of Population* account for the ways in which these different historical actors – bureaucracies, institutions, groups, and individuals – interact. If government is, as Curtis argues, a "circular process," whose "subjects ... are not passive" and in which "official classifications and categorizations may be opposed or subverted as well as embraced," then not only do administrative forms such as censuses and other measurements affect what they measure, encouraging people to fit the categories, but those categories are also themselves shaped by interactions with the objects of measurement.[56] Analyzing government and the mutual influence, "in both an upwards and a downwards direction," of multiple actors, helps to explain the ability of individual Canadians and small groups to effect policy change.[57]

Steve Hewitt and others make central a contention that institutional change reflects something in society. They maintain that to judge the justice system and greater society only by its written laws ignores change, the human element in legal institutions, and the particulars of a situation. Law and order is more than just its institutions; it reflects a set of values. The behaviour of police and the policing of behaviour in the story of Canadian support for American war resisters show how broader society perceived the question, and how at least some branches of government sought to control it. As Allan Greer has argued, police are a "visible human embodiment" of the "state."[58] The war resisters and their supporters were the focus of both overt and covert attention by police. Police are relatively minor actors in this study, but to omit them would gloss over important aspects of the history.[59] Police institution "behaviour," such as surveillance, is not merely a result of a combination of a paranoid mindset and an individual desire to conform, as Irving Janis and disciples argue.[60] Instead, police behaviour says something about society, because individual police are themselves part of society.[61]

Bureaucrats are often seen as being allergic to change, seeking only to perpetuate the status quo. However, bearing in mind that bureaucracies are made up of individuals, and that there is a flow of influence between bureaucrats and bureaucracy as well as between bureaucracy and society, will help to avoid the pitfalls of stereotypical treatment of state and government activity as the result merely of a technocratic strategy. The influence of populations, or sections of populations, on state departments and officials and their behaviour and decisions, and vice versa, is an important part of the story of support for war resisters in Canada.[62] The actions of police and Department of Immigration officials and bureaucrats reflected the battle for hegemony in the realm of attitudes towards war resisters. The eventual involvement of anti-draft groups in promoting the government's programs was a characteristic example of the zone of interpenetration between the state (government and its institutions) and society, and their mutual reinforcement.

The Canadian government, like other governments, was, in the sixties, enduring a broader hegemonic crisis linked to widespread and global critiques of imperialism, colonialism, and capitalism.[63] In Canada, this critique in part took the form of tensions around the concept of Canadian identity. The critiques were also fuelled by an antiwar movement that was generally similar to that of the United States, and, later, by movements against racism, sexism, and various forms of discrimination. At the same time, Canadian social movements differed from other North American movements by the development of two distinct strands of resistance to colonialism: a distinct movement for Quebec independence, fuelled by Quebec nationalism; and Canadian indigenous resistance movements.

Further, specificities of Canadian history and the country's relatively small population meant that there were other differences in how these movements manifested. Also, while the Left and social movements in Canada shared with their American counterparts a relationship with ancestral movements – sometimes referred to as an "Old Left," a term also taken up in this work, with a few caveats – that relationship was complicated by the influence of organizations such as the New Democratic Party (NDP) and other proponents of what may be termed the mainstream Canadian Left.

That said, hegemonic struggle does not only take place at the level of the state and is not always determined by its needs. It may not take a form that centralizes one or several large questions affecting entire classes or governments, but rather take the form of multiple skirmishes in the hegemonic struggle. Hegemonic struggle here does not mean anything so reduced as a relatively unadorned struggle for power, through electoral politics or by force; rather, hegemonic struggle refers to that constant effort between social forces with varying interests in the unfolding of events, to secure support from others and, eventually, to win a kind of dominance in the cultural domain (that of ideas), which can have an impact in the economic. Thus, the concentration is on a very specific skirmish in the broader hegemonic struggle over Vietnam, postwar capitalism, and Canada's role in the world.

Skocpol's historical institutionalist approach, applied to both movements and groups including government, and combined with this Gramscian analysis of history, provides the theoretical framework for this study. In the war resisters' story, public perceptions of the resisters and their supporters changed along with the anti-draft movement's relationship to government institutions; and government attitudes shifted in a dialectical reflection of public opinions.

The first sections of this book present ideas that have influenced its approach and direction. The story of war resisters is also a story of the interaction between government and civil society groups, which, in Gramscian terms, was a hegemonic struggle for domination of both the public discourse and the concrete actions taken by various actors related to this discourse. It is also about the capacity of different institutional actors, both in and outside of government, to form independent opinions and act upon them. I outline the basic shape of the Canadian anti-draft movement, focusing on the network of anti-draft groups that existed in Canada from 1965 until the late 1970s and taking into consideration the interaction between war resisters and Canadians both inside and outside the main movement, including their respective perceptions of motivation and effectiveness.

The central section of the book deals with the treatment and perception of deserters and addresses the role played, or not played, by anti-Americanism. Anti-Americanism does not mean views held against the presence or behaviour of American individuals but views held against American policy. This distinction was slippery at the time, and, although a separate phenomenon, it was also linked to emerging Canadian nationalism in complicated ways. I give an account of the events during the months leading up to the May 1969 official decision to open the border to deserters and the campaign surrounding it. The campaign reflected debates about Canadian nationalism, which had an important impact on its effectiveness and provoked a sometimes acerbic dialogue between activists about politics, the anti-draft movement, and what could validly be called "real" political work. Taken together, these chapters constitute an analysis of a battle for hegemony in the perception and treatment of war resisters in general and deserters in particular.

The final chapter considers more generally the relationship between the anti-draft movement and government institutions as the movement matured. On one hand, anti-draft groups were under constant surveillance, and the Royal Canadian Mounted Police (RCMP) pressured the Department of Immigration to find reasons to deport young American immigrants. On the other hand, the lobbying activities in early 1969 were an example of a more regular, although adversarial, relationship with government. These elements illustrate the blurred line between government actors and social movements in the realm of social policy and practice.

1

"We Help Them
Because Their Need Is Great"
The Canadian Anti-Draft Movement

I wish that I were able to incite
Young men in every land to disobey
For wars will cease when men refuse to fight.

To kill our brothers for a nation's right
Is not a method we can use today.
I wish that I were able to incite.

When leaders threaten to resort to might,
I know that idols all have feet of clay.
For wars will cease when men refuse to fight.

The cause of peace is shared by black and white
And freedom fighters show a better way.
I wish that I were able to incite.

Non-violent resistance has no bite
While undecided pacifists delay.
For wars will cease when men refuse to fight.

With power to reinforce in what I write
The things that protest-singers try to say,
I wish that I were able to incite
For wars will cease when men refuse to fight.

– Tom Earley, "Incitement to Disobedience"[1]

If the late 1960s were a period of readjustment of the hegemonic order, the anti-draft movement in Canada was in the thick of it. The year 1965 marked a major turning point in US strategy. As the US government engaged in higher-profile engagements such as major B-52 bombing raids, raised its troop ceilings to over two hundred thousand, and watched as its people endured images of Vietnamese refugees in Vietnam and American corpses in body bags, the slow trickle of resisters into Canadian urban centres steadily grew to a stream.[2] This increase coincided with both a tactical focus on the use of US ground troops and an increase in desertions from the US military.[3]

In the midst of this global political landscape, Canadian discussions about nationalism, culture, Quebec, and the American war on Vietnam percolated in complex ways among the general public and in the halls of government. Canadian support for American war resisters in the Vietnam War era was similarly complex. The movement manifested itself in different ways. A network of anti-draft groups emerged across the country to provide various services to the American immigrants before and upon their arrival. Among other issues, anti-draft groups dealt with a quickly changing employment situation, which went from a labour shortage and 3 to 4 percent unemployment in 1966 to 5 to 6 percent unemployment in late 1969 and early 1970, with spikes especially among youth and in regions outside Ontario.[4]

The Canadian anti-draft movement, including its network of groups with varied roots and origins and different experiences in interacting with American "visitors" and immigrants, eventually helped to shape the public and personal perceptions of anti-draft activists and groups in Canada. Individuals who shared the anti-draft sentiment also played a role; many helped these immigrants without ever coming into contact, directly or indirectly, with the anti-draft network. As well, there was broad sentiment against the draft not only among activists but also among student organizations and others who were not directly involved in the anti-draft movement, but only some of these groups were actively involved in supporting war resister immigration, either working with the anti-draft groups or independently.

The term "anti-draft group" refers to all types of groups specifically organized around the issue of American war resisters in Canada. Within that broad type existed "aid groups," groups usually containing both Canadian and American activists whose purpose was to aid war resisters no matter what their motivations, and "exile groups," groups defined by a membership composed solely of American immigrants. War resisters who received help from both types of groups formed mostly positive impressions of the anti-draft groups and had mostly positive experiences of Canadian support. The groups were fairly effective, although not always entirely reliable.

The anti-draft group activists and the resisters who interacted with them had their disagreements. Debates about the relative value of draft dodging and deserting as antiwar actions, about assimilation and nationalism, and about the right way for Americans to be "political" surfaced both in public disagreements and in private moral and tactical dilemmas. Nonetheless, what emerges most strongly from the existing documents and from interviews with antiwar immigrants and supporters is the sense of a cohesive movement engaged in a dual role: direct support for immigrants and political advocacy.

The anti-draft movement emerged in a political landscape in which strong feelings about the American draft and the war in Vietnam were abundant. Indeed, anti-draft sentiments were mainly formed in the broader Canadian peace movement. Draft resistance was part of the antiwar movement's demands, and war resisters were often directly involved as participants. Groups like Students Against the War in Vietnam (Toronto) made demands to bring the GIs home now and to end the US draft.[5] Students in general played a key role in the burgeoning anti-draft sentiment. As early as 1967, student unions such as the University of Toronto Students' Administrative Council gave money to the "Toronto Anti-Draft Movement."[6] In 1968, the nationwide student organization, the Canadian Union of Students (CUS), began to take an interest in the anti-draft movement. The first time CUS discussed the war was at its thirty-second congress in the early fall of 1968. In October of 1968, the organization considered becoming a "bureau of inquiry" for draft dodgers and setting up a "cross-Canada link-up"; one subsequent conference included a war resister.[7] Off campus, antiwar organizations drew strong links between opposition to the war and draft resistance, featuring draft dodgers and deserters as speakers at public events and demanding an end to the draft south of the border.[8]

On this activist base, a movement to support the American war resisters was built. The movement enjoyed fairly consistent, albeit passive, support from the Canadian public. The young movement maintained its connections to the antiwar and student groups but also drew from other sources, and, almost from the start, it existed independently from broader movements and groups.

Groups and individuals got involved for various reasons, rooted in traditions and in current political dialogues. The groups that formed to support the war resisters reflected this complexity of beginnings. We can trace the beginnings of this movement through to its establishment as a decentralized, yet fairly unified, network of groups and individuals well-placed to advocate on behalf of war resisters throughout the period.

Emergence of the Anti-Draft Movement in Canada

While the problem of the draft was a part of a larger concern about the legitimacy of the Vietnam War for Canadian antiwar activists, eventually a specific movement arose to support those Americans who came to Canada to avoid the draft or to desert from military service. The groups through which Canadians worked to support them were numerous and geographically dispersed.[9] Part of a self-aware activist community with the capacity to use the mainstream media to its benefit, they created highly effective networks for information sharing and communication both between groups and to potential immigrants, for mounting joint campaigns, and for reinforcing each other's actions to create momentum to win gains on behalf of the war resisters. A transnational movement, they enjoyed support from American groups while also forging their own approaches towards politics and strategy and developing their own internal sense of history. Ultimately, they formed the nucleus of a broad and vibrant, though comparatively small, social movement in support of war resisters that succeeded in shaping public perceptions, bettering border conditions, and affecting public policy.

Aid groups were listed in the various editions of the *Manual for Draft-Age Immigrants to Canada*, a publication of the Toronto Anti-Draft Programme (TADP); twenty-three groups, located in Calgary, Edmonton, Vancouver, Victoria, Winnipeg, Fredericton, Moncton, Sackville, Newfoundland, Guelph, Hamilton, Kingston, Kitchener-Waterloo, London, Oshawa, Ottawa, Peterborough, Port Arthur–Fort William, Toronto,

Windsor, Charlottetown, Montreal, Regina, and Saskatoon, at some point listed contact people.[10] The history, ideological positions, and effectiveness of the groups also varied. Only a few Americans got involved in these groups, but they were very influential; some groups were run at various times by antiwar activists. Figures such as Bill Spira, a prominent activist in the Toronto Anti-Draft Programme, and Joan and Jim Wilcox, American immigrants who played key roles in the initiation and operation of Ottawa Assistance with Immigration and the Draft (Ottawa AID), and many others shared the leadership of the anti-draft movement in Canada.[11]

The anti-draft groups counselled anyone and everyone who requested it, regardless of their motivation for immigrating. This lack of bias was likely the result of the connections this new movement had with the draft counselling movement south of the border. The groups were not typically very structured, although some did have a board.[12] Groups provided headquarters and message boards, as well as drop-in centres, and developed expertise in correspondence, dealing with the media, and conducting research for publications.[13]

It is generally thought that the first committee to be formed was the Vancouver Committee to Aid American War Objectors (VCAAWO).[14] While the size and weight of that committee make such an impression understandable, the files of then co-editor of Montreal-based *Sanity* magazine Hans Sinn call the claim into question.[15] It appears that the VCAAWO was founded in October 1966; therefore, the Montreal Council was likely the first active Canadian anti-draft group, since activity in Montreal began in February of that year.[16] The truth is probably that committees formed in Vancouver, Toronto, and Montreal at roughly the same time, taking different routes for their development.

From the start, the transnational nature of the anti-draft movement and its shared roots in pacifist traditions of conscientious objection were evident.[17] Early correspondence and documents of the nascent committee in Montreal establish a picture of a group with international and pan-Canadian links, a movement that took its role very seriously and that placed a premium on the sharing of information.

In February 1966, Hans Sinn, responding to multiple requests for information from draft resisters, began compiling information for the publication of a fact sheet for potential American immigrants. The inquiries may have come as a result of the feature article on war resistance in the

February 1966 issue of *Sanity*. Sinn wrote to the Central Committee for Conscientious Objectors (CCCO) and the War Resisters League (WRL), two well-established American pacifist organizations, asking for information on an American's status regarding citizenship, draft board requirements, and legalities should he decide to immigrate while in various stages of the draft, including desertion. Sinn followed up with telegrams in late February and contacted a war resister couple with whom he was acquainted: Virginia and Lowell Naeve. They had been sponsored by friends to immigrate to Canada and had arrived with their son, who was as yet too young to be drafted, in 1965.[18] Lowell was a Quaker registered for alternative service in the United States, who had decided to evade even that. The Naeves were in touch with many other Americans who were interested in immigrating.[19] Virginia Naeve wrote,

> There simply needs to be more concerted effort. If I have the information at my fingertips and can pass on information and get people together then that will be good. The better the information the less bog down.
>
> I need information for people to hang onto. All they know for the most part is they can't stand the idea of their sons or themselves tolerating the situation in the USA.
>
> I have the contacts in the USA who can help once they know we can help up here. I've been on the steering comm. of WSP [Women Strike for Peace] since it was started. CNVA [Committee for Nonviolent Action] I've worked with, the Quakers, WRL [War Resisters League], WILPF [Women's International League for Peace and Freedom].[20]

On 4 March, Sinn received a reply from Arlo Tatum of the CCCO, who referred Sinn to the Student Union for Peace Action (SUPA) fact sheet, which was being drafted at the same time in Toronto, and to SUPA's Tom Hathaway, a landed immigrant who had just been ordered to report to the draft board.

Seeking more, and clearer, information, Sinn sought legal advice. The advice he received suggested that draft avoidance was not a legal obstacle to immigration. Further, no sponsorship was required, although a job or student status would help. Potential immigrants were advised to apply from outside Canada; however, such application could be made at a border point or from inside the country after entering as a visitor.

Using the advice and additional information provided by Tatum, Sinn drafted a four-page "Fact Sheet on Immigration to Canada." Perhaps not surprisingly given Sinn's journalist status, the original fact sheet was treated as a media release.[21] It appears that upon receiving the Vancouver pamphlet, "Immigration to Canada and Its Relation to the Draft," Sinn stopped producing the *Sanity* fact sheet.

Sinn's inquiries led to further requests from the United States, as US groups referred draft resisters to Sinn for information. The Naeves began receiving forwarded correspondence from Sinn, and *Sanity* subscribers were asked to help support war resisters. In April 1966, inquiries about British Columbia prodded Sinn to write to SUPA's Sandy Read, who was based in Richmond, British Columbia, to seek information on the involvement of BC residents in anti-draft work. Sinn, Virginia Naeve, and her colleague Mary considered whether to do a mass mailing of the information sheet. Eventually, several dozen copies were sent to American groups. Sinn also contacted Hathaway and sent him copies of the *Sanity* fact sheet.[22]

As the campaign in Montreal progressed and linkages with other Canadian cities and American groups strengthened, more and more Americans residing in the country illegally were approaching *Sanity* clandestinely, seeking legal advice and hoping to keep a low profile, as Sinn's 21 May 1966 letter to Hathaway indicates:

> We have had some experience with draft dodgers who are here furtively. They contacted us asking for legal advice without even giving their name. There seems to be some quite unjustified fear, that the peace movement would make a big thing of things for publicity purposes of its own. All we do is give them the name of a lawyer who has agreed to give free advice ...
>
> We send the names and addresses of people who are willing to assist US refugees to Virginia [Naeve] for now. Like yourself we are still trying to get the hang of things, to find out the best procedures and the actual potential ...
>
> A meeting of all those actively interested should certainly be arranged ...
>
> Alfred Friend of the Toronto Peace Center is interested and has some names of Toronto people who are willing to help ...
>
> We have tried to establish contact with people in Vancouver but so far no luck. SUPA has also put out a fact sheet and we were told that a Vancouver lawyer put the information together.[23]

By late spring of 1966, SUPA in Vancouver was working on establishing whether support already existed there. Read wrote to Sinn, "Rumour has it there is some group around Vancouver which will supply aid (mainly legal). I would imagine it is the civil liberties council but I don't know because it was a Mauist [sic] who told me about it and he wasn't saying too much. As for myself – I can't do much but I could probably put someone up for awhile when they first arrive."[24] Eventually, Sinn met Meg and Benson Brown of the Vancouver group. By 1967, Canadian anti-draft publications were getting wide circulation in the United States, and an Arlington, Virginia, student newspaper, the *Underground,* had published the Vancouver fact sheet. There were nascent committees in Ottawa and Winnipeg, and Students for a Democratic Society (SDS), the main student New Left group in the United States, had "overcome their initial reluctance" and were doing anti-draft work.[25] The February 1967 issue of *Sanity* reprinted the SDS resolution on draft resistance, which stated,

> Since the primary task of SDS is building a movement for social change in the United States, we do not advocate emigration as an alternative to the draft. Nevertheless we realize that this option is being considered by many young men. We will thus provide information about emigration, and will encourage those who emigrate to build international support for the draft resistance unions and to work for an end to the war.[26]

SDS was willing to assist emigration, and that assistance was framed as an extension of the antiwar movement. Their statement implied an expectation that émigrés would be engaged in antiwar and anti-draft activities.

The same issue of *Sanity* listed the VCAAWO, the Toronto SUPA office, and the Montreal committee as groups set up to "aid US draft resisters."[27] These groups had strong connections to the antiwar movement, but as a rule they did not require, or even expect, immigrants to get involved. The tension this engendered between activists, both American and Canadian, later provoked some debate in the anti-draft movement.

In 1967, individuals in various cities began corresponding with one another about setting up committees. They sought and shared information with each other on specific border points and conditions for crossing, employment conditions, and housing, and made attempts to make sure advice provided to potential resisters was consistent. Border experiences tended to change over time, which made the sharing of information even more important for this decentralized movement.[28]

Into late 1966 and early 1967, Sinn continued to reply to letters and to seek out networks with activists in other cities, and the CCCO and the WRL continued to refer inquiries to *Sanity*. *Sanity*, meanwhile, transitioned out of playing the role of an anti-draft group and became a source of information on draft dodgers, even encouraging war resisters to immigrate.[29] Activists also began to ask themselves whether deserters could go to Sweden, because deserters had begun showing up in Canada and the groups were unsure whether deserters could be deported.[30]

Montreal Council to Aid War Resisters (MCAWR)

The Montreal Council to Aid War Resisters (MCAWR) proper was formed in 1967, but it had existed in nascent form for almost two years prior. The board had a division of labour, which included public relations, treasurer, and secretarial positions. The Montreal committee's practice continued to be one of information sharing and communication. Like other groups, it became more and more formalized in its approach. All of its documents were in English.

The Montreal group used research and materials produced by the VCAAWO and the Toronto Anti-Draft Programme (TADP).[31] It also produced its own materials, including fundraising flyers and form letters containing additional advice and updates enclosed with copies of "Immigration to Canada and Its Relation to the Draft."[32] The Montreal committee solicited information from other anti-draft groups for regularly issued revised editions of their broadsheet.[33] It also published reports to the "Friends of the Council," donors solicited by form letter.[34] The Montreal Council also provided training to their counsellors.[35]

One of the most important activities of the council and other groups was advocacy on behalf of war resisters to the federal government. The Montreal Council "pressed" the federal government to clarify its policy on deserters in early 1969 and worked with Ottawa AID, the TADP, and the VCAAWO on various campaigns. The organization also continued to have less formal links with other groups, including the CCCO.[36] In May of 1971, the MCAWR merged with the American Deserters Committee to form the American Refugee Service, probably to reduce duplication of services, and perhaps as a result of agreements reached at a pan-Canadian conference in 1970.[37]

The Montreal Council existed in a Montreal that Sean Mills has characterized as host to many interrelated, though largely neighbourhood-based, activist groups and committees, with English- and French-speaking groups operating mainly, although not exclusively, in isolation from each other.[38] The MCAWR appears to be no exception.[39] On the whole, there does not appear to have been any substantial support by francophone activists for the war resisters in Montreal.[40]

Vancouver Committee to Aid American War Objectors (VCAAWO)

Perhaps the most significant of the anti-draft groups, partly due to its geographical location, the VCAAWO was formed in October of 1966 by a group of University of British Columbia professors, some of their family members, and a lawyer. The group initially performed some research and then began counselling American immigrants. Demand forced them to formalize their operations, and they eventually opened an office, conducted research, received and responded to correspondence by mail, and published information sheets aimed at educating potential draft dodgers and deserters about how to immigrate to Canada and what to expect upon arrival. The VCAAWO counselled more and more individuals and connected American immigrants with community members for housing, employment, and legal and health care services.[41] Here, again, was a group that began informally but became more formalized in its approach over the next several years.

Groups such as the Vancouver Vietnam Action Committee referred potential American immigrants to the VCAAWO as early as 1967.[42] The VCAAWO engaged in fundraising and began to forge links with other anti-draft groups in Canada.[43] The VCAAWO pamphlet "Immigration to Canada and Its Relation to the Draft" could be found on file in many of the anti-draft offices that subsequently formed. It likely informed anti-draft group counsellors as well as potential American immigrants. The Vancouver information sheet was adapted and published by the Montreal Council to Aid War Resisters (MCAWR) and was updated and re-issued until the early 1970s. For instance, the November 1966 version emphasized that "a number of Americans who have immigrated to Canada have renounced their citizenship and have thereby voided their military obligations," and referred to the anticipated changes to immigration policy, which were finally enacted in 1967.[44] Further revisions did not emphasize the renunciation of citizenship tactic; there was some disagreement among the groups regarding the efficacy of the tactic, and although the practice did continue, the points system made such a move unnecessary.[45] The pamphlet was mailed to individuals who had made inquiries and to some American draft counselling groups.[46] Contact information for other anti-draft groups was regularly updated.[47]

Other VCAAWO publications included an addendum memo to "Immigration to Canada and Its Relation to the Draft," which updated certain sections on regulations and provided suggestions for additional reading regarding whether to immigrate to Canada; "Teaching in British Columbia: An Unofficial Guide," aimed at American immigrants who had the qualifications necessary to apply for teaching jobs; and copies of "Why They Chose Canada," an article from *Weekend Magazine* (26 November 1966), distributed in response to requests for discussion of "the position of emigrating to Canada" in *WRL News*.[48] The VCAAWO used the media to good effect. Hardy Scott, a draft dodger who arrived in 1967, recalls being interviewed for articles in *Ladies' Home Journal*. He agreed to those interviews on the condition that the magazine also print the VCAAWO's address. As a result, the committee received more inquiries.[49]

Most of the work was done by volunteers, and linkages to other groups, while they did exist, were fairly informal. VCAAWO activities included counselling and providing information on immigration, jobs, and housing for an average of five or six American immigrants per day. Half of these immigrants were deserters.[50]

In late 1969, the VCAAWO consisted of an office and its volunteer and meagrely paid staff; no actual committee – that is, a more or less organized decision-making body with meetings – existed.[51] At the same time, however, the VCAAWO was using its own letterhead, which is a sign of formalization as well as an indication that the organization had access to resources. The VCAAWO's networks with other groups were yielding information for prospective American immigrants about other cities, border conditions, and employment prospects. Some letters referred to better job prospects to the East, including in the Prairie provinces. One letter gave contact information for the Calgary committee. Another stated that draft dodgers were still crossing the border more easily than other American immigrants, although, by late 1969, deserters should not have been subject to discrimination at border points; the minister of manpower and immigration had announced on 22 May that deserter status would not be used to keep immigrants from entering Canada, as a result of a campaign to change the policy.[52]

The Vancouver group also did its own research and produced briefs as part of anti-draft group attempts to influence immigration policy. The document "Note on Fugitives from Justice," published in May 1967, is one example; it was an opinion piece regarding the soon-to-be-announced points system and its potential for abuse and manipulation by immigration officials. Later documents were written in response to the unfair and uneven treatment of American immigrants at border points and in immigration offices within Canada. In late 1967, the VCAAWO wrote "A Note on the Handling of Draft-Age Immigrants to Canada," a document aimed at informing Deputy Minister of Immigration Tom Kent (who served under Minister Jean Marchand until July 1968) about discrimination at the border against draft-age Americans in general. The brief appended statements from thirty-six recent arrivals whose experience with officials had been negative. In January 1969, the VCAAWO prepared a brief, "A Further Note on the Handling of Draft-Age Americans Who Apply for Entry into Canada." The brief formed a part of the 1969 campaign to open the border and included affidavits from war resisters.[53]

Perhaps because of its reputation as a northern counterpart to California, Vancouver became a destination for a large number of war resisters, which meant that the VCAAWO was one of the most active committees in Canada. In *Desertion: In the Time of Vietnam*, Jack Todd describes the scene:

> The [Vancouver] committee [to Aid American War Objectors] draws the usual suspects from the radical fringe in the late '60s: crunchy granola hippies, Trotskyites, Maoists, wide-eyed do-gooders, zonked-out druggies, moochers, marchers, anarchists, macho types who babble endlessly about guns and bombs and revolution, deserters who have been to Vietnam and back (or claim they have) and who seem always on the verge of some subterranean explosion.[54]

One resister, who later became involved in the committee, recalls, "It was an active committee; there were many people who would provide initial housing for people to stay, help to find jobs, be drivers to take people down to the border and then bring them across again, to meet people when they did come in; the three big things were housing, jobs, and getting landed ... We seemed to never be in dire straits."[55]

Another Vancouver anti-draft group, Immigration Aid to Refugees of Conscience, also produced materials, including "On Being a Kept Person," a flyer originally published by the Unitarian Church group Canadian Assistance to War Objectors (CATWO, or sometimes, CAWO). The flyer encouraged war resisters to keep a low profile as boarders with temporary housing and exhorted, "No fraternization with teenage daughters (it's been tried) ... [N]or will parents of older children be receptive to having their offspring counselled on ways and means of subverting parental authority (it's been done)." A commensurate document, "So You're Having a War Resister," exhibited the same light tone in encouraging housing volunteers to be clear about their expectations from boarders.[56]

CATWO, the Unitarian group, had a steering committee that met regularly from at least January until August of 1968. The group kept minutes of its discussions of the job situation and set up a hostel, among other activities.[57] "The Care and Feeding of War Objectors" was the CATWO precedent to "So You're Having a War Resister," titles that compared war resisters to pets and babies.[58] The humorous tone was likely adopted in order to approach non-activists in a friendly way, to encourage their active support through the provision of housing. Depicting war resisters as dependent and in need of help was also part of the tone of these flyers.

CATWO and the VCAAWO had a friendly relationship. The January meeting of the steering committee welcomed a guest from the VCAAWO, Mrs. Riddell, who outlined the need for job offers, a hostel, drivers, money, duplication services, and volunteers.[59] The CATWO began funding the VCAAWO at one hundred dollars per month in March 1968. It sought to avoid duplicating efforts of the VCAAWO and concentrated on job counselling. Eventually, the CATWO and the VCAAWO decided to discuss amalgamation. They also sought to integrate the North Shore Housing group because "an accident of history" had resulted in three overlapping groups forming at the same time.[60] It is unclear whether the amalgamation ever occurred, but the VCAAWO certainly continued to exist until at least 1972.

Ottawa Assistance with Immigration and the Draft (AID)

Meanwhile, in Ottawa, the group Ottawa Assistance with Immigration and the Draft (AID) helped American immigrants with immigration regulation legalities. A third of its budget was dedicated to these services. By some accounts, Ottawa AID was founded by Jim Wilcox, an American who became an English professor at Carleton University, but Joan Wilcox (Jim's wife) recalls that two women started the group (the other the wife of a Carleton sociologist).[61] Ottawa AID later established the Coffeehouse as a gathering place in a francophone United church at the corner of Elgin and Lewis Streets, run in late 1970 by Mennonite Bob Janzen and his wife.[62] By that time Jim Wilcox had stepped back, but the committee was still very active. Joan Wilcox recollects,

> We started up really under the tutelage of the Toronto Anti-Draft Programme ... for two reasons: one, they had been doing a lot of work, but they were primarily getting people landed at the border, which was then possible under the Immigration Act, but sometimes the border was getting increasingly tight ... So they enlisted the Ottawa Peace in Vietnam group to work with Parliament to try and do what could be done ... and secondly, to assist with the actual immigration of those young men who would qualify with an internal application ... So those were the two initial reasons for our start up, and then it just expanded and expanded.
>
> My husband and I had just recently moved here, and he was in his first year teaching at Carleton. He was teaching all new courses, and I was looking for something to keep me busy and was ready to start getting a little more politically active, and I wound up attending a meeting of the Ottawa group for peace in Vietnam, whatever it was called, and found that their most pressing need at the time was to develop something Toronto had been asking the peace group here for help [with], and they'd had the odd draft dodger come and they didn't know what to do with him and so on. So another young woman and I, the wife of a sociologist from Carleton and I, said, well, [it] sounds like we could do that. So we got a hold of copies of the Immigration Act and it just grew from that.

My husband became interested; he was more interested in lobbying, although we both did some of everything, but that's where he focused. And gradually our group expanded.[63]

Wilcox was one of many women involved in the anti-draft groups. There was no noticeable gender division of labour in the groups themselves. Women in these groups, however, were acting in the context of growing awareness of women's rights on the one hand and observable male dominance of activism and war resistance on the other.[64]

As the Ottawa group expanded, so did its services:

> [We did] everything there was to be done *[laughs]*. Our primary focus was providing info and support to the young men and women who were here as a result of the war – mainly draft dodgers, increasingly war deserters, and their partners if they came with a partner ... The specific work entailed immediately providing for their physical needs, housing, food, that sort of thing, but in the long term providing ... [assistance with] preparing their applications ... helping them get documents, helping them understand the forms, helping them understand the ways of presenting themselves that would be truthful but the most positive.[65]

As Wilcox recalls, the Ottawa group met from time to time with the Toronto Anti-Draft Programme (TADP) and a group from Montreal: "We worked closely in the sense that Toronto would send us people that they were feeling they might have trouble with or just their overflow, and Montreal would send us people they thought we could be more of assistance with."[66] The Ottawa group also placed great importance on information and communication across the growing pan-Canadian network.

"Words from Canadians": Toronto Anti-Draft Programme (TADP)

If the VCAAWO was a significant group, and Ottawa AID was important for its proximity to Parliament Hill, the Toronto Anti-Draft Programme was perhaps the most influential, given its base in Canada's largest city. The TADP formed in late 1966 out of a committee formed by the Student Union for Peace Action (SUPA) at the University of Toronto.[67] SUPA had begun to receive queries about immigration in the winter of 1965, which had resulted in the SUPA pamphlet "Coming to Canada?"[68] After SUPA placed the VCAAWO publication "Immigration to Canada and Its Relation to the Draft" on its literature list, it received dozens of requests for further information; SUPA subsequently set up a support office on the University of Toronto campus.[69] Tony Hyde, a twenty-year-old university dropout from Ottawa, conducted research, information, and publications work, and, in 1966, he had already helped "about fifty" resisters, meeting them at the bus station and finding them temporary housing.[70]

Eventually, SUPA published its own pamphlet titled *Escape from Freedom, or, I Didn't Raise My Boy to Be a Canadian.*[71] Boasting a yellow cover with a political cartoon lampooning an American mother, which reflects the often tense familial connections of many American immigrants, its twelve pages dealt with the questions of how to oppose war and how to deal with conscription. The pamphlet also provided a basic outline of immigration laws, including prohibited classes, visitor status, student status, and landed immigrant status. It suggested that "any American deserter would not be accepted as a landed immigrant." The booklet instructed potential immigrants how to apply (in person from within Canada, by nomination, by mail from outside Canada, or in person at the border) and explained the details of the border application. Finally, it outlined questions of extradition and deportation and sketched the basics of life in Canada. While the authors' position on desertion was somewhat inaccurate, they were correct in stating that deportation was illegal, describing it as a "blatant infringement" on individual rights.[72] The pamphlet concluded with contact information for consulates, immigration offices, SUPA's 658 Spadina Avenue offices, and the Vancouver Committee to Aid American War Objectors. There was also a condensed leaflet form of "Escape from Freedom."[73] The ironic title was typical of many anti-draft publications and fact sheets and reflected a common war resisters' stance on US foreign policy. It also quoted Erich Fromm's 1941 work, *Escape from Freedom*, a Freudian and Marxist analysis of social tendencies to seek out authority. Fromm was a member of the Frankfurt School at the same time as Herbert Marcuse, whose influence on the New Left is well-documented.[74] The title thereby suggested that to leave the United States was to resist authority.

SUPA did not encourage Americans to immigrate because they did not want to offend the American peace groups who wanted them to stay home to oppose the war. Instead, as Hyde explained in a 1966 interview with *Weekend Magazine*, SUPA counselled American immigrants about work regulations and helped with filling out forms and the process for getting landed status. "It's all very informal, but we might have to get some kind of organization going," he said.[75] For various reasons, including pressure from New Left figures such as Tom Hayden, who viewed draft dodging as a weaker tactic than desertion or direct opposition to the war, SUPA eventually dissociated itself from the anti-draft movement.[76] Ultimately, SUPA dissolved, leaving the Toronto draft resisters program and its office as a legacy of its Toronto activity. The anti-draft committee reinvented itself as the Toronto Anti-Draft Programme.

The TADP, like other anti-draft groups, existed mostly because of the willingness of volunteers to act in various capacities, including immigration, housing, and employment counselling.[77] A series of individuals played a coordinating role, starting with Mark Satin, who worked for several years with the TADP from before its break from SUPA in 1967. Satin drafted the first edition of the *Manual for Draft-Age Immigrants to Canada*. In September of 1967, the TADP set up a restructured Anti-Draft Committee to provide assistance with the program, with subcommittees and regularly scheduled meetings. The subcommittees included Information Campaign, Fundraising, Legal Research and Aid, American Immigrants Employment Service, and Newsletter.[78]

Quaker Nancy Pocock and her husband, Jack, were steadily involved in the Toronto group from 1965 into the 1970s. The Pococks administered a Quaker fund to address immigrants' immediate needs upon arrival.[79] The funds came in large part from American Quakers. Pocock recalled that the work could be overwhelming: "Pretty soon they were almost swamped, and finally one of them ... took it on as a full-time thing ... everybody finds after they do it for a while, they get completely exhausted and drained."[80]

The Pococks were central figures in the TADP from its inception. In a May 1970 interview, Nancy noted that "[Jack has] been on the committee [executive board], ever since they've had it ... We were always sort of advisors for the Toronto-Anti-Draft [sic] ... They put him onto dealing with the media ... We had a steady stream in here of newsmen from all over the world."[81] With Bill Spira, the Pococks likely represented the steadiest involvement in the anti-draft movement by Canadians. By 1968, the TADP was receiving one hundred letters and an average of seventeen visitors every day; it had six staff and provided hostel accommodations, an employment service, a loan fund, and legal referrals. Its support came especially from church groups and University of Toronto faculty members, some of them perhaps recently involved in student movements. The program made use of volunteers, both Canadians and American immigrants.[82] By 1970, the TADP boasted several full-time staff, of which Spira was one.[83]

The Canadian anti-draft movement produced publications and pamphlets, the tools that the movement used to coordinate its work, which, while illustrating a level of maturity and development, now also constitute a valuable source of information about the groups, their history, and their activities.[84] Overall, the movement was fast-paced, with a high degree of mobility and turnover. The generation of large amounts of information was part of its architecture.[85] Self-conscious as a movement with a purpose, the endeavour, driven in part by intellectuals including journalists, students, clergy, and academics, contributed directly to the ideological debates playing out in the period.

Arguably, the most important publication of the Canadian anti-draft movement, the *Manual for Draft-Age Immigrants to Canada,* was a window into the activities of Canadian supporters of draft dodgers and deserters from the American military between 1967 and 1970.[86] The *Manual* promoted itself and the TADP as the authority on immigrating to Canada and discouraged the use of "amateur" or "underground" information sources.[87] It also documented the movement's achievements and played a role in the swiftly changing ideas among anti-draft activists and American immigrants.

The *Manual* was published six times between January 1968 and 1971.[88] It provided a snapshot of the diversity of the Canadian anti-draft movement, with contributors representing a cross-section of antiwar and New Left circles in Toronto, where anti-draft activity was the largest and best organized.[89] Each new edition of the manual provided updated information such as group listings and changes in immigration procedures, and, in 1971, the manual referred potential immigrants to American draft counselling services in part to reduce the number of refugees, given the high unemployment rate of the early 1970s.[90] The first edition had a limited run of five thousand copies and cost two dollars per copy. The demand for the first edition was such that the second edition of the manual, which was published in March 1968, had a run of twenty thousand copies, and the third, ten thousand.[91]

The fourth revised edition of the *Manual for Draft-Age Immigrants to Canada,* published in December 1969 but cover-stamped 1970, also in a run of ten thousand copies, contained quotations from two immigration officials. The first was from John Munro, a parliamentary secretary for the Department of Immigration, who on 12 June 1967, said, "An individual's status with regard to compulsory military service in his own country has no bearing upon his admissibility to Canada either as an immigrant or as a visitor; nor is he subject to removal from Canada because of unfulfilled military obligations in his country of citizenship." The second was an extract from Minister of Manpower and Immigration Allan MacEachen's 22 May 1969 speech in the House of Commons; MacEachen stated, "If a service-man from another country meets our immigration criteria, he will not be turned down because he is still in the active service of his country ... The selection criteria and requirements applying to him will be the same as those that apply to other applicants."[92] These quotations were probably included for political reasons, coming as they did soon after the May 1969 victory of the anti-draft groups' campaign to open the border to deserters. By including them, the anti-draft movement both asserted its victory and claimed responsibility for it.

Later editions moved away from national symbolism in cover art and content. The 1971 edition included a section titled "Of Frying Pans and Fires," by Ron Lambert, which outlined a debate between two streams of Canadian nationalism – one resistant to United States domination, and one, "colonially-minded," justifying US foreign policy and its domination of Canadian decision making – and encouraging readers to choose one or the other. The inclusion of Lambert's piece points to how Canadian nationalism and debates about tactics and identity were intertwined among American war resisters and Canadian anti-draft activists.[93]

Historians, including J.M.S. Careless, professor and chairman of the Department of History at the University of Toronto, Elliott Rose, associate professor of history also at the University of Toronto, and Kenneth McNaught, professor and editor of *Saturday Night Magazine,* helped with the general text of the manual and with the sections on war resisters' immigration history.[94] In these historical sections, the authors claimed that

Canada's history was one of providing sanctuary to various kinds of war resisters. This idea was a major part of advocacy efforts on behalf of war resisters. The introductory section, titled "Words from Canadians," contained short messages from lawyers and church officials, welcoming American immigrants.[95] These pages suggested that Canada and the United States were not much different from each other in many important ways, and that Canadians ought to welcome resisters, without judging them. In the network of anti-draft groups, activists commonly held the idea that resisters deserved support no matter their personal reasons for coming to Canada. There was a debate about tactics but it tended not to affect the decision of whether to support individual resisters.

Reflecting the continuing transnational and decentralized nature of this movement, the TADP kept copies of other groups' publications, including CCCO counselling handbooks and US military directives and regulations.[96] The TADP kept careful track of policy and legislative changes to immigration processes, including the Immigration Act and amendments.[97] Extensive and thorough counselling services were available to American war resisters at the TADP offices. By 1968, the caseload of the 2279 Yonge Street office had risen to around twenty-five per day from five or six in 1967.[98]

Correspondence with anti-draft groups in the United States and Canada kept the TADP informed about rumours and facts about border crossings and other issues that were useful in counselling prospective immigrants. For instance, a 1968 letter stated that rumours regarding plans to "close" the border had been denied by Department of Immigration officials, but the Detroit/Windsor, Toronto Airport, Buffalo/Fort Erie, and Lake Champlain (NY) border crossings were not reliable due to officials who "believe in the war"; "we are keeping the draft counsellors listed in Chapter 24 [of the *Manual*] informed of all new developments."[99]

TADP received financial support from a variety of sources. Donors included individuals, such as lawyers, professionals, rabbis, reverends, immigrants, and individual Canadians, and groups, including the Buffalo, New York, branch of the Women's International League for Peace and Freedom, Women Strike for Peace, the Queens College of the City University of New York Student Activities Financial Board, the United Methodist Church, the Friends Meeting of Washington, and the Windsor War Resisters.[100]

As the largest of the anti-draft programs, the TADP eventually developed a minimal amount of bureaucracy to keep track of its activities and communications. A TADP counsellor form tracked first and repeat visits and phone calls and categorized them, American or non-American, priority or non-priority.[101] This checklist approach may well have been introduced to deal with a high volume of queries in 1972-73, when the Department of Immigration introduced programs to fast-track visitors and illegal immigrants. A description of services from around 1971 shows that the TADP classified American immigrants to prioritize their being processed. The "middle-class draft dodger," twenty to twenty-four years old, with wife or girlfriend, often with money, a car, and familial support in the United States, was the easiest to get landed. The "working-class draft dodger," eighteen to twenty-one years old, with a high school diploma but few skills, not much money, and usually no prior counselling, often either returned south or was sent back for counselling and a more considered decision. Deserters, the "largest and most difficult group," were mostly working-class, stereotyped by a negative perception of desertion, typically alienated from family, with little if any work experience or skills, sometimes no high school, and often no hope; some deserters, typically aged seventeen to twenty-one, were deported for breaking laws in Canada.[102]

Other Toronto Anti-Draft Groups

The TADP was not the only anti-draft group in Toronto. In 1970, the Black Refugee Organization (BRO) formed to cater to the needs of black American immigrants. The BRO worked with the TADP; the TADP referred black American immigrants to the BRO.[103] After 1970, further Toronto services to black resisters were provided by Ebony Social Services.[104] Red White & Black (RWB), also formed in 1970, attempted to foster communication between Americans, Canadians, and the various anti-draft groups through its publication *EXNET*, which provided updates from anti-draft groups.[105] A flyer titled simply "Red White & Black" stated the purposes and intentions of RWB: a free school, news bureau, drop-in centre, bulletin and news; fostering a sense of community among Canadians and American immigrants; and encouraging communication between anti-draft groups.[106] Its offices, donated by the University of Toronto Students' Administrative Council, contained its services and a drop-in centre.[107] RWB successfully forged links with Toronto area groups, including churches. Around 1970,

RWB held a Vietnam War memorial service at Queen's Park; representatives from the Canadian Council of Churches, Anglicans, Mennonites, Catholics, Lutherans, the United Church, Presbyterians, Jews, Buddhists, and atheists attended. Music at the event was provided by "Munoz," a deserter.[108] In 1970, the TADP, Toronto American Deserters Committee (TADC), and RWB discussed merging into the Committee to Aid Refugees from Militarism (CARM).[109] CARM eventually established itself in a community centre in a Toronto area with many immigrants.[110]

Nova Scotia Committee to Aid American War Objectors (NSCAAWO)

Like other groups, the Nova Scotia Committee to Aid American War Objectors (NSCAAWO) was part of the pan-Canadian network, keeping regular contact with other aid groups. The Nova Scotia committee also kept copies of publications on file, and, like other groups, monitored border conditions in order to advise potential American immigrants. The Nova Scotia committee existed from 1966 until 1972, overlapping with the Halifax Committee to Aid War Resistors [sic]. Quaker and landed immigrant war resister Richard Lind was the main organizer, with assistance from Rev. Don McDougall, the Dalhousie University Chaplain.[111] In 1971, both of the main NSCAAWO counsellors were students and landed immigrants.[112]

The NSCAAWO kept in touch with other anti-draft groups, including the Winnipeg, Toronto, Vancouver, and Montreal committees and American exile organizations such as *AMEX* magazine.[113] To facilitate counselling, the committee kept copies of government publications, lists of other anti-draft groups in Canada and their contact information, as well as some directories of American counselling centres, and made use of the MCAWR broadsheet and the *Manual,* as well as TADP fact sheets.[114] The committee also played its role in keeping track of difficult border points and monitored the ongoing status of American immigrants.[115] In 1971, the committee noted that more American immigrants were finding their own way through the system, but also anticipated more referrals from Toronto.[116] The NSCAAWO maintained close ties with Nova Scotia church organizations and academics, who often offered temporary housing.[117] It received its 1971 funding from the Canadian Council of Churches, the Halifax Friends Meeting, and individual donors.[118] The NSCAAWO also maintained links with local student groups and international groups and organizations.[119]

Dozens of other groups existed in various centres, at various times from 1966 to 1974. For instance, the Lakehead Committee to Aid American War Objectors formed in late 1969 or early 1970.[120] The Winnipeg committee was likely established in 1970 and formally closed its operations on 17 April 1974.[121] The Alexander Ross Society, based in Edmonton and founded in early 1968, published its "Notes on Immigrating to Canada" in March of 1970; the publication outlined the factors considered in the points system of assessment for immigrant status and provided information on sponsorship, nomination, and student status.[122]

Black War Resisters

Some black draft dodgers came to Canada as well. One compared his situation to that of the slaves who came on the Underground Railroad.[123] However, numbers remained low in proportion to the percentage of black military personnel. American scholars have examined the economic stratification among war resisters that divided deserters from others along class and racial lines. Renée Kasinsky, Frank Kusch, and historian David Sterling Surrey all argue that war resisters with "marginal" backgrounds were more often returned to the United States by border officials and immigration officers, and that black dodgers found immigration particularly difficult and wished to return because they could "go underground" more easily. This argument stands in stark contrast to the media's explicit use of the term "underground railroad" during the 1960s and 1970s to describe the conduit for draft dodgers and deserters seeking to cross the border – a large part of the myth of Canada as a haven for war resisters. The beneficiaries of this "underground railroad" were, apparently, overwhelmingly white.[124] As one black draft dodger told Kasinsky, "From where I was the tendency for the blacks was to go into the army because that was a way out ... It represents a way out for any poor person."[125]

In 1970, black war resisters in Toronto formed their own aid group, the Black Refugee Organization. They noted the *Manual* did not even mention a black community in Canada, and they saw a need for housing with black families and for counselling for blacks by blacks to make the experience less alienating. As one black war resister commented at the time, "There's not much in the way of a concentrated black community, like in the big US cities. They're just not organized here – they're very un-together. And a lot of American kids, the whites, are here for bullshit reasons – that makes it hard on the rest of us."[126] This resister may have been referring to a perceived lack of commitment to the cause of war resistance. Black resister groups formed in response to this lack of community and support. The BRO was explicitly conceived as having "no political thing in mind. Like, there's no political objective or anything like that. Like, our main concern is the guy that is in trouble with the military. The organization itself is just to help black resistors [sic] and deserters."[127]

Bill Spira estimated that 2 percent of resisters who contacted the TADP were black, which he put down to a combination of economic deprivation as a motivation for staying in the army and the availability of close-knit black communities in which to take refuge instead of emigrating.[128] In 1970, black deserters told *Race Relations Reporter* of a "subtle anti-black bias" among Canadians and surmised that the reason for lower numbers of black war resisters was racism.[129] The Vancouver Monthly Meeting of the Religious Society of Friends suspected racial discrimination at the border. In a June 1969 letter to Minister of Manpower and Immigration Allan MacEachen, the group described the hostile demeanour of an immigration officer towards a white war resister whose wife was black, both of whom had recently tried to immigrate. The letter was a follow-up to a face-to-face meeting that had occurred in May.[130]

Women War Resisters

Although many women were active in the anti-draft movement, the extent to which aid groups considered women war resisters is unclear. At least some anti-draft activists took note of the existence of women resisters. In early 1970, *AMEX*, the magazine of the Union of American Exiles in Toronto, reported the creation of a women war resisters group made up of wives of resisters.[131] A women's caucus meeting at the May-June 1970 Pan-Canadian Conference of US War Resisters was rated a success by *AMEX;* critical of the common assumption that they were in Canada only because their husbands or boyfriends were there, the women made a "non-proposal" to respect women war resisters as equal alongside their male counterparts.[132] The October-November 1970 issue of *AMEX* contained a letter from Stephanie Durant berating the magazine for continuing to report that *ANTITHESIS,* the Montreal American Deserters Committee publication, was written by deserters, thereby excluding women from their reportage.[133] Generally, both the anti-draft movement of the period and scholarship about American war resisters have neglected women war resisters, treating them as either companions of men or ignoring them completely.

Some women war resisters became part of the women's movement in Canada. Carolyn Egan recalls,

> We came in August of '69. I think in the Spring of 1970 I was walking down Bloor Street and saw posters for a series of meetings being put on by the Toronto Women's Liberation Movement and I got involved in that, and that was my first political involvement aside from my union ... I started getting involved in meetings of the Toronto Women's Liberation Movement, which was a movement made up of women from the student movement for the most part, some working women, who came from a socialist perspective and had been active in the antiwar movement, and one of the first things I got involved with was the Indo-Chinese women's conference, which the Toronto Voice of Women got involved with, and other women's groups.
>
> It was primarily Canadian women who were involved in organizing it, and it was very political, very anti-imperialist, and it was a very good organization ... Quite a good group to get involved with. The Toronto Women's Liberation Movement saw itself as a socialist organization, and the war was seen as an important part of our work.[134]

Many of the women who came to Canada as war resisters probably found their voice through the women's movement. Only rarely did they find their voices as women within the anti-draft movement. Voice of Women (VOW), a pacifist organization that participated in anti-draft activitism, did so as only one part of their antiwar activity.[135]

Exile Groups

Another type of group was the exile group. Exile groups existed in several centres and were made up exclusively of American immigrants. They were narrowly defined as self-identified exiles – that is, participants understood themselves to be maintaining an American identity. For some of these immigrants, while the act of immigrating was itself political, exiles had a continuing political duty to continue to oppose the war.[136] For others, the importance of exile groups was less about politics and more about recognizing that Americans in Canada should help each other. In general, exile groups either worked for assimilation of Americans into Canadian society (a minority viewpoint), or advocated a militant set of exile politics. This debate played out inside the groups and in the pages of exile publications such as *AMEX*. Tangled up with these ideas were contested notions of Canadian independence and colonial status as well as competing ideas of what types of actions and ideas could in fact be considered political.

The Toronto-based Union of New Canadians was founded by Mark Satin, an activist with the TADP and editor of the *Manual for Draft-Age Immigrants to Canada,* and others in May 1967. As its name indicates, the Union of New Canadians was oriented toward assimilation. The group sought to maintain a decentralized structure, with a meeting chairman, a secretary to keep notes, and an editor for a publication, the *New Canadian.*[137] A later formation, the Toronto-based Union of American Exiles (UAE), was formed some time before February 1969. Their initial goal was also the acclimatization of Americans into Canadian society. A UAE flyer explicitly called for Canadians to offer housing to draft dodgers and Americans to help with acclimatization.[138] Another flyer invited Americans "in social exile" to drop by a table with a UAE banner to get help with "employment, housing, and social contact."[139] Eventually, the Union of American Exiles and its magazine, *AMEX,* clarified their political position to the effect that they advocated for exiles to continue to actively oppose the war. The pages of *AMEX* make the transition clear.

Another major group of this type was the Regina Committee of American Deserters (RCAD). Formed in 1969, it was likely the result of mergers of earlier, looser efforts. RCAD was founded by Dick Perrin, who worked with a variety of individuals and organizations to make the group effective.[140] RCAD was a practically oriented group, working to support deserters, proposing the establishment of a farm with support from the other Regina-based aid group, and actively helping American immigrants who were seeking assistance, sometimes by interacting with their family members. The group's appearances in the local media drew donations and other support.[141]

The Toronto American Deserters Committee (TADC), formed in December of 1969, was an example of an exile group whose orientation focused on the supposedly inherently radical nature of desertion and the need to maintain the deserter (and ergo American) identity as means of opposing imperialism. The TADC's stated goals were to house and feed deserters or draft resisters until they could become landed immigrants; to provide facilities for socializing; and to provide personal counselling, including medical and psychiatric care.[142] The TADC believed not only that deserters were a special group with special needs but also that the act of desertion, as opposed to draft dodging, was inherently radical, as this excerpt from a TADC flyer illustrates:

> Failing to understand the sequence of events involved in the act of desertion is to have failed to comprehend the act itself and the effect desertion has on the future of the individual and the society in which he will assume a role.
>
> A breakdown in the understanding of Desertion as a total life committment [sic] comes precisely at this point. This breakdown is revealed in a common misconception of people involved in aid work and those people who should be involved but are not because of a failure to understand the committment required and the application of energy and resources necessary to fulfill the needs demanded by the act of Desertion and its newfound relationship to the world community.
>
> This failure has derived from aid persons and groups recognizing their role, at this point, as being only one of:
>
> 1   finding immediate shelter, food and a means of self-support;
> 2   immigrating the individual as soon as possible;
> 3   help in finding a job, educational opportunities, etc.;
> 4   opposing discriminatory practices of the country into which the Deserter has sought safety.
>
> They are essential; but to stop here could, in fact destroy all that of value which has been accomplished thus far.[143]

Thus, for the American Deserters Committee, the traditional role of aid groups such as the TADP fell short. The committee outlined further needs that could be fulfilled, including psychological counselling and transition measures that must embrace the act of desertion, not merely treat deserters like any other immigrants. Implicit in their outlook was the assumption that deserters would maintain their identity as a deserter, and thus that they needed to be connected with deserter-oriented community work, the form of which was not specified. Of course, the other implicit identity to be maintained was American. This identity played into debates about assimilation and later about the fight to win an amnesty from the US government after 1973.

Another example of this type of exile group was the Yankee Refugee group, based in British Columbia, which established an American Deserters Committee Program in 1969. The program took partial credit for MacEachen's admission of discrimination at the border and the internal directive to bar deserters in what the group referred to as his "early June" announcement. The success had been a result of movement activity, not benevolence on the part of government, the group argued in its newsletter.[144] Melody Killian, a Yankee Refugee organizer, had been pessimistic about the possibility of success of the campaign and even went so far as to attempt to find ways to ship deserters to Sweden. While MacEachen had indeed admitted to the policy of discrimination at the border, his policy reversal took place in May, not June. The inaccuracy of the Yankee Refugee group's knowledge of the campaign timeline and the evidence of animosity between, at least, Killian and members of both the VCAAWO and the TADP, cast doubt on their active involvement in the campaign.[145]

The group asserted that summer 1969 did not mark the end of the "deserter crisis," a reference to the border difficulties addressed by MacEachen's 22 May policy announcement, and urged readers to apply class analysis to the issue. They were drawing attention to the ongoing issues deserters in particular were having with amassing the necessary employment and education points to get landed status. In the meantime, the Vancouver American Deserters Committee (ADC) Program was committed to several ongoing tasks, with a particular radical twist to each: aiding all deserters, including providing underground sanctuary; fighting repression, including RCMP harassment; making propaganda, armed with which draftees could enter the military and disrupt from within; organizing American immigrants within Canada because "deserters are the most radically conscious"; supporting Canadian and Quebec struggles for "self-determination and socialism"; fighting "American chauvinism in ourselves";

and being active as revolutionaries. The group expected that getting Canadians involved in these activities would "radicalize" them as well.[146]

The exile groups did, of course, undertake helpful concrete and substantial actions to support American immigrants. The Vancouver ADC, for instance, ran two hostels.[147] The Vancouver and Montreal deserter groups published newsletters. The Montreal group had an informal division of labour with the MCAWR, whereby the ADC helped deserters and the MCAWR helped draft dodgers. Over six months in 1969 and 1970, the Montreal ADC claimed to have helped around five hundred deserters and estimated a further 1,200 would be helped by the end of 1970. The Montreal ADC also operated a hostel and participated in public meetings and demonstrations.[148] A deserter committee also existed in Ottawa.[149]

The Anti-Draft Movement: Transnational, Pan-Canadian

Throughout the period during which Americans required their assistance, the Canadian anti-draft groups forged and maintained a domestic network of communication among themselves and with the resisters. These connections included communication and interaction between the Canadian anti-draft movement and similar groups and activists in the United States, and with disparate Canadian groups and individuals including lawyers, churches, and the Voice of Women.

Groups in the United States provided assistance in distributing materials and information. In Canada, lawyers and intellectuals, MPs, and especially church groups were instrumental in helping the war resister network pave the way for immigration. Until the churches got really invested in the cause, funding was a significant obstacle for the network. The actions of these external groups and individuals shaped, in turn, the perceptions held by war resisters of Canadian society and the Canadian anti-draft movement.

2

Transnational Connections

US Groups and Other Canadian Groups

The *Manual's* full title – *Manual for Draft-Age Immigrants to Canada* – highlights the reality that draft dodgers and deserters were also technically immigrants, which is the source of the transnational nature of this movement.[1] Anti-draft groups maintained links with dozens of American groups, including Quakers, Students for a Democratic Society, and the War Resisters League.[2] American New Left politics had a great deal of influence on the anti-draft movement. Heather Dean, author of a section in the *Manual* about Canada's political system, was a figure in the Canadian New Left.[3] And Mark Satin, the *Manual's* editor for its first editions, was himself a former American New Left activist.[4] A Pan-Canadian Conference of US War Resisters was held in Montreal in 1970; Carl Oglesby and Tom Hayden of the American New Left attended the conference.[5] These links helped Canadians reach out to potential American immigrants by providing access to American groups, such as Students for a Democratic Society, the American Society of Friends, and the War Resisters League, which could distribute the *Manual* south of the border.[6] This cooperation was the continuation of earlier connections between the Canadian and American movements. For instance, in the summer of 1963, the *War Resisters League News* had carried an article covering a joint conference of the US and Canadian peace movements in Nyack, New York. The conference was weighted towards New Left politics, with participation from Tom Hayden of the American New Left and Dimitrios Roussopoulos of the nascent Canadian New Left.[7]

In addition to these relations with American activists, the anti-draft movement also enjoyed the participation of a wide array of groups at home.

On 1 December 1967, the Faculty Committee on Vietnam at the University of Toronto released a "Statement on Draft Resisters," inviting Canadians to welcome them out of respect for their decision, a desire to avoid discrimination, and recognition that they would be valuable additions to Canadian society.[8] The committee included more than forty faculty members. Coffee houses, clinics, hostels, and community centres also lent support.[9]

Lawyers played a key role in supporting immigration and providing accurate information to American immigrants. For instance, Ottawa movement lawyer Vincent Kelly wrote the first section of the introduction to the *Manual for Draft-Age Immigrants to Canada*, a piece titled "We Are Happy to Welcome You." In it, he noted the legal similarities and differences between the two countries, encouraging potential immigrants to seek advice from "an anti-draft programme" that might, in turn, put them in touch with legal counsel.[10] Besides their contributions to the *Manual,* lawyers also provided direct legal counsel to the movement and to the resisters it helped. Paul Copeland, a Toronto-based lawyer, and his partner Clayton Ruby, were probably the most highly involved, but there were many others. Copeland recollects,

Clay Ruby and I were the movement office in Toronto. We did all the American exile work in central Canada. There were a couple of other people who did it, but we were mainly the people who did it. There was a guy named Rosenbloom out in Vancouver who did some of it. Bernard Mergler, whose greater claim to fame was he negotiated the FLQ [Front de libération du Québec] people going to Cuba in exchange for Mr. Cross, he did most of the Montreal work. There was a link across Canada. There were links to the United States. We were just all very hooked up. It was harder than it is now, no Internet, but long distance phone calls worked pretty well.

Lawyers and activists [were hooked up]. We were counsel to the [Toronto] Anti-Draft Programme [TADP] and worked really closely with the TADP. There were Quaker groups in the United States. There was something called the New York Law Commune in New York City that did a lot of the work, and they were counsel for Jerry Rubin and Abbie Hoffman.[11] I mean, you name it, we represented them.

There was also a guy named Dee Knight ... After the war was over or around when it was ending, he actually worked for me as a secretary.

Clay and I practised together from '69 to '72, and we were doing activist stuff before that. I was called to bar in '67 and he was called in '69.[12]

As Copeland states, besides the expected professional connections, the lawyers also had some US connections, which were put to good use during the Heintzelman affair – a coordinated action in which five students posed as deserters, tried to cross the border, and documented the results. Thus, lawyers were both directly and indirectly involved in the movement to support the war resisters.

Church groups and clergy played an important role throughout the period, both as activists and as a source of funds for the anti-draft groups.[13] Historian Donald Maxwell contextualizes the official church support – that coming from the national and international structures of the churches and from clergy – in relation to the anti-draft groups, noting both individual church support and donations, and the extensive support program offered by the Canadian Council of Churches beginning in 1970. Church support also came directly from church members. Churches and their members provided funding, of course, but also lent direct help in the form of housing; and activists often had church backgrounds. Maxwell notes that assistance in the form of donations and individual aid came from Catholics, Unitarians, the United Church and its members, the Canadian Jewish Congress, and the Quakers.[14] Assistance was also forthcoming from Mennonites, Unitarians, and Anglicans. In fact, it is difficult to think of a major church that is not mentioned in the literature or in the documents as having helped, in some way, the resisters and the groups that supported them.

Many examples of church and church member support can be found in both activist recollections and in the movement documents and literature. Copeland recollects that "the Quakers did a ton of that underground railroad stuff," and Quaker involvement is evident in the early history of the committees.[15] Perhaps the Quakers were a source of the idea that Canada as a whole had a pacifist tradition. As Quaker activist Nancy Pocock stated in a 1970 interview:

This sort of thing's been going on for a long time, you know. In the Revolutionary War, what we call United Empire Loyalists were coming because they didn't agree with the war. And then there's a place in New Brunswick, called Skedattle [sic] Ridge, and it was called that because men from Maine who didn't want to be drafted into the army during the war, the Civil War, came over to New Brunswick and settled there. I have a [recipe] for Skedattle Ridge cookies, which I often make for the boys, and they get quite a kick out of it. So it's not a new thing to Canada. And remember, too, many Dutch boys came here during the Indonesian War, to escape going into that war. And of course many young Greeks and Italians have escaped conscription, so nowadays it's not a new thing for Americans to be doing it, but they get more publicity.[16]

Multi-faith organizations also played a role. For example, in December of 1969, the American group Clergy and Laymen Concerned about Vietnam (CALCAV) raised money and donated goods to support Canadian aid groups.[17] In a 1969 media interview, Peter Mally of the Vancouver Committee to Aid American War Objectors (VCAAWO) stated that the funds would primarily be used to help deserters in need, in the tough employment climate of that period. Canadian church supporters were also organizing Christmas dinners for five to ten war resisters at a time.[18] Around 1970, the Toronto-based Inter-Faith Committee on US Exiles formed,[19] with members from the Jewish Temple Emanu-El, Metro Toronto Urban Church Board, and Anglican, Wesley United, Mennonite United, Unitarian, Dutch Reformed, United, and Presbyterian churches. The group held executive committee meetings and provided some funds to the TADP.[20]

For some church leaders, the level of assistance coming from the churches was not adequate, and steps were required to encourage further commitments. In 1970, Frank Epp, of the Canadian Council of Churches, published *I Would Like to Dodge the Draft-Dodgers, But ...* The book was intended to allay the fears of the rest of the church community in Canada and to encourage them to support both the draft dodgers and deserters and those Canadian groups who helped them.[21] The book featured people involved in anti-draft work, including some from the Ottawa Mennonite Church and the Canadian Council of Churches.[22] The council's Jim Wert and Leonard Epp contributed a chapter titled "Some Churches and Their Leaders Are Calling for Help," in which they pointed out that most of the money for war resister support in Canada came from Americans. In 1969, they explained, Toronto, Montreal, and Vancouver combined had spent around $35,000, an indication of how much the assistance was needed.[23]

The book not only exhorted the churches to donate money; Wert was also concerned by the fact that the Canadian Council of Churches had not yet taken a stand on the fact (for them) that draft dodgers and deserters were taking fundamentally moral action in refusing to fight.[24] Frank Epp donated an office to the Ottawa Assistance with Immigration and the Draft (AID), and Mennonite farmers hired draft dodgers and deserters to work on their farms, which provided valuable employment to help in the immigration process.[25] Epp, Wert, and others were motivated by a concern that all war was immoral, and they hoped to convince church members and clergy that war resisters ought to be supported in as many ways as possible.[26]

Pressure on the churches to make tangible commitments to the cause came from both church members like Epp and from the anti-draft groups themselves. In early December 1969, Bill Spira of the Toronto committee notified Betty Tillotson of the VCAAWO that he also was working on securing funding from the Canadian Council of Churches (CCC).[27] His efforts appeared to bear fruit. Indeed, a CCC document titled "A History of the Involvement of Canadian Churches in Programmes of Assistance to US Draft Age Immigrants in Canada," sent to members of the Halifax clergy in 1971 by the Nova Scotia Committee, stated that the "Windsor Consultation" of December 1969 was the inception of the CCC's program called the Ministry to Draft-Age Immigrants.[28]

The "Windsor Consultation" was a meeting of clergy from the United States and Canada. It followed a similar consultation that had taken place between the CCC and the National Council of Churches earlier in the year.[29] The participants discussed how to receive and distribute funds, whether to hire staff, and how to prepare a "project request" to the Division of Inter-Church Aid, Refugee and World Service of the World Council of Churches to propose a matching of funds.[30] At the meeting, CALCAV reported it had raised five thousand dollars already, five hundred dollars of which it gave to each of four groups in Toronto, Montreal, Vancouver, and Ottawa; the rest would be transferred to the CCC's ministry. The CCC should expect up to $100,000 to come from CALCAV's efforts. Meanwhile, the US-based National Council of Churches reported it had hired a staff member dedicated to the issue of war resisters in Canada, whose concerns would include, for instance, ministering to the parents of resisters.[31]

The CCC reported that the ministry's mandate was to raise funds in Canada; to locate resources for jobs, housing, and the like; to act as a repository for donations; to motivate churches to help; to evaluate and strengthen the aid groups; to help with information and interpretation; and to establish a network of resources for war resisters. The CCC was considering sending Bill Spira of the Toronto group on a tour to outlying regions to help them and to outreach to other churches. Gordon K. Stewart of the United Church of Canada announced plans to contact the Montreal and Ottawa groups in January. He intended to gather information on the groups' activities and aspirations, knowledge about other groups, caseload, and most urgent needs.[32]

In early 1970, the CCC formally initiated its Ministry to Draft-Age Immigrants.[33] While individual churches, officials, and members certainly did their part, Maxwell argues, and the evidence supports, the view that the Canadian Council of Churches' Ministry to Draft-Age Immigrants was by far the most important form of support received by the movement and the support groups. The anti-draft groups received a big financial boost when the council established its ministry.[34] Until that point, funding had been a significant challenge.

After the ministry's inception, individual churches appeared to take notice. In February 1970, the Draft Dodger Project of the First Unitarian Congregation of Toronto sent an appeal to 1,300 Unitarian churches; in response, they received twenty negative letters and 240 cheques totalling $6,400.[35] The Draft Dodger Project's appeal, addressed to "fellow Unitarians," mentioned the great number of American immigrants arriving at the TADP offices. It reported on the December consultations. Finally, a general appeal to North American Unitarian churches was attached to the letter.[36] The Vancouver Unitarian Committee, called Immigration Aid to Refugees of Conscience, also raised funds for the VCAAWO.[37] By mid-1970, church support was consistent.

The CCC received financial support from American churches including the United, Methodist, Presbyterian, and Protestant Episcopal churches, as well as the Church of the Brethren, the Disciples of Christ, the United Church of Christ, the National Council of Churches, and Clergy and Laymen Concerned about Vietnam. Internationally, they received funding from churches and church organizations in Denmark, Germany, France, and the Netherlands. Canadian official support came from the United, Lutheran, Presbyterian, and Anglican churches, as well as the Mennonite Central Committee.[38]

Canadian church involvement was remarkable, not just for fundraising but also for church members' involvement in the movement directly.[39] The CCC ministry staff was Wert, who volunteered and worked a three-day week for six months. The ministry also sent Spira on a speaking tour to visit "all aid centres from Thunder Bay to Victoria," and sent Canon Maurice P. Wilkinson to visit the councils of churches and the aid centres. Based on the information gathered from Spira's tour, the ministry began grants to Winnipeg, Regina, and Vancouver anti-draft groups. The result of the World Council of Churches appeal was that Robert Gardner was added to the staff.[40]

The CCC operation, like other CCC undertakings and like other sections of the anti-draft movement, was very professional in its organization and methods. Groups were required to provide receipts and staff reports for the ministry's accountability committee. The ministry and its committees met regularly, kept records, and published a newsletter to aid groups. Groups did not always receive funding. For instance, the Nova Scotia Committee to Aid American War Objectors (NSCAAWO) submitted a report in late 1971, but made no funding request. In the third quarter of 1971, aid groups received a total of $8,640. The Calgary Committee on War Immigrants received three hundred dollars for hostel expenses; the TADP received $2,250, mostly for staff expenses. Edmonton, Halifax, Ottawa, Regina, Vancouver, Victoria, and Winnipeg all also received funding.[41]

Churches were involved in the war resisters movement for many reasons. Some churches took the official stance that war is immoral. Others may have seen supporting the war resisters as part of a Christian duty to help those in need; John May of the Canadian Unitarian Council remarked to journalists that "The [CCC Ministry to Draft-Age Immigrants] ... is not a matter of being for or against US policy in Vietnam," but rather a matter of supporting men who had made a decision in good conscience that had subsequently placed them in a position of needing "urgent" assistance.[42] One other possible thesis might be that churches' involvement lent legitimacy to the movement. Certainly, this involvement did encourage the participation of some groups – Voice of Women, for instance, as evidenced by their papers at Library and Archives Canada. However, the reverse – that churches lost some supporters as a result of their support for war resisters – is also possible, and even likely, considering the evidence provided by Maxwell that church members did not support the war resisters to the same extent as clergy.[43] What the churches lent in terms of legitimacy to the entire anti-draft movement they sacrificed in terms of their own members' support. The evidence examined here neither supports nor undermines Maxwell's contention that the churches – or at least the United Church – knew they could benefit from their association with the resisters by demonstrating their relevance in a changing world.[44] They may have sought simply to adhere to their own morals despite the opinions of their members.

Another significant and steady source of support for war resisters was the Voice of Women (VOW). Although VOW began as a predominantly maternalist women's organization with roots in first-wave feminism, by the mid to late 1960s, its membership had taken a turn towards a more egalitarian emphasis, situating the group as a bridge between first- and second-wave feminism.[45] VOW's activities were varied and included a great deal of attention on the Vietnam War.

VOW's central office kept files on the issue of American war resisters from 1966 to 1973.[46] A Canadian peace organization formed in 1960, VOW had branches, or chapters, in several provinces, as well as significant international links.[47] VOW support for the war resisters was fairly steady. Chapters in British Columbia spearheaded a petition campaign that probably played a role in opening the border to deserters in May of 1969. VOW chapters also sometimes referred inquiries to the anti-draft groups. For instance, in January 1970, Mrs. Matthew T. Corso wrote to VOW Toronto announcing her imminent arrival with her son and wondering if she should bring bedding with her. Mrs. Corso had already contacted the TADP and the Toronto ADC.[48] Accounts such as these helped to dispel the myth that war resisters were overwhelmingly single men with no support.

The National Executive adopted a policy statement in January 1970, which stated,

At a time when the number of deserters and draft resisters coming to Canada is increasing daily, it seems appropriate to clarify Voice of

Women's position. We have avoided making public statements and resolutions because until May 1969 Canadian Immigration policy regarding
deserters and draft resisters was unclear. Publicity might have jeopardized
the chances of some men to complete the requirements for immigration.

The statement outlined the May 22 announcement of an open border by
Allan MacEachen and went on to encourage their members to provide
homes and a welcome to incoming war resisters.[49] It showed a concern for
those resisters who had remained underground and echoed some of the
anti-draft movement's fears about publicity. VOW's records suggest that
VOW supported war resistance as an act that concurred with their advocacy of peace. But VOW's positioning on the issue was not without tension,
and at least some chapters were late in adopting policy in favour of war
resisters.

In early 1970, president Muriel Duckworth corresponded with several
members about how to approach the question of draft dodgers and deserters.[50] In a January letter to Mrs. Freda Pryce of Vancouver, Duckworth
thanked Pryce for her letter outlining the Vancouver chapter's programs
and congratulated her on their work with draft dodgers and deserters,
which was "going ahead marvellously in several aspects of VOW work."[51]
However, a letter to "Betty" from Duckworth in February defended the
National Executive decision, addressing the correspondent's concerns
about the rule of law:

> This is the way I feel about giving asylum to draft resisters and deserters.
> It seems to me that this is what we are called upon to do *now*. As I said
> in a previous letter, these young men have made a decision to do what
> men were severely punished for not doing in World War II – by the
> Nuremburg trials ... it is by actions of this sort that laws are changed to
> respond to the needs of the times.

In this statement, Duckworth illustrates her personal commitment to civil
disobedience. Civil disobedience was a common tactic of the civil rights
movement, whose connections to the anti-draft movement have been
established. Duckworth also replied to concerns about VOW participation
in questionable events; she stated, "The notion that the actions in which

the VOW of Vancouver wish to take part [are inappropriate] I find hard to understand. Is it not correct that the United Church is officially supporting this project?"[52] The last sentence indicates an awareness of church activities, and, indeed, the VOW files contained correspondence from churches on the topic – the First Unitarian Congregation of Toronto appeal for funds referred to above, for instance.

An interim report to the British Columbia membership in February 1970 reflected the apparent divisions in the BC organization, suggesting that more research was needed, but that action ought to be taken as well on the issue of supporting the war resisters.[53] In February 1970, a decision was made to send observers to a meeting of Canadian Aid to American War Objectors (a coalition of Vancouver groups).[54] In March, a document by Nancy Pocock, "Opinion on Draft Dodgers and Deserters," likely solicited by Duckworth, stated emphatically that there was no reason not to help the war resisters and that individuals make individual decisions about how to oppose the war. Pocock suggested that "Betty" had received erroneous information, which, it was implied, was swaying her opinion against supporting war resisters.[55]

The Impact and Effectiveness of the Anti-Draft Movement

By virtue of the support it received from various quarters, and having developed networks of communication and counselling skills, the anti-draft movement began more and more to act in a unified manner. By all accounts, the anti-draft group offices and gathering places were social in atmosphere, with political posters, message boards, reading materials, socialist publications, and immigration counselling guides all occupying the same space. By 1969, the committees in various cities had become a network, in regular correspondence and occasionally meeting face to face. They shared funding, provided by the Canadian Council of Churches, as well as information, albeit of varying accuracy, with each other about border conditions, employment issues, and immigration regulation interpretation and changes. The groups relied on volunteers, and, although Canadian involvement remained strong throughout the period, American involvement was also steady. The anti-draft groups ebbed and flowed with the political tide. They experienced a spurt of activity after such incidents as the announcement of the invasion of Laos and the elimination of student deferments in the Selective Service System.[56] They occasionally attended delegated meetings with each other and with groups from the United States and Canada. They worked together on some campaigns and priorities and debated with each other about strategy and tactics. This vibrant dynamism allowed the movement to respond quickly to events as they developed. Through sharing information and resources the movement became more and more skilled at supporting the resisters whose existence was their raison d'être.

Although most groups were founded by Canadians, by early 1968 American immigrants were also involved and, in several cases, were the key activists. In 1967, correspondence between the Montreal group and others noted, "It is our experience that the US draft resisters are interested, once they are settled, to help their friends in the US. That means our group as well as those in Vancouver and Toronto are comprised of Canadians as well as recent US immigrants."[57] Joseph Jones, a draft dodger, recalls, "I never had any sense that the Canada-based groups were composed of much besides Americans. I suspect that was generally true by the time of my arrival in 1970. From my research, I think Americans had a lot of involvement even at the outset. The Canadians who spring to mind are Tony Hyde at Student Union for Peace Action (SUPA), the Pococks at the TADP, Frank Epp in Ottawa, and Walter Klaasen in Waterloo."[58] To this list can be added Sinn, Virginia Naeve, several lawyers, and dozens of others. According to Spira in a 1970 interview with Renée Kasinsky, only one of the five TADP board members was American, the rest Canadian. Spira asserted that the involvement of Canadians led to broader community support for the committee's work.[59]

Of course the very existence of the anti-draft movement in Canada was a result of American policy. Without the war, and without American actions, there would have been no movement. As Marvin Work, a draft dodger who arrived in 1970, observed, "American foreign policy and American attitudes influenced Canadian anti-draft groups by encouraging them to offer refuge and support to American war resisters."[60] Americans also directly influenced the groups in two other ways: by becoming involved as volunteers or staff; and through the debate about politics.

Americans often went on to provide housing or other assistance to newer arrivals. They also used their new connections to help war resisters secure employment. Michael Goldberg recollects, "A number provided services once they landed themselves. People who became landed provided short-term housing for new draft dodgers or deserters; if people were in employment situations where a job opened, they would try [to find employment for newcomers] through a number of employers, who were incredibly helpful. Whenever they had job openings, they would try to get them filled by people from the US. They were part of the movement."[61]

About the media, anti-draft activists were pragmatic. Bob Lanning of Ottawa AID told Kenneth Fred Emerick that "radio and television usually give us a fair shake and are usually more objective. The newspapers in Ottawa are very bad, although the *[Sun]* is far worse than *The Citizen*."[62] Bruce Garside in Montreal commented that the CBC and the *Montreal Star* were "very favourable." However, Emerick himself suggested the American media gave poor coverage to the anti-draft movement.[63] This pragmatic approach to the media stood the activists in good stead when it came time to use them in a concerted effort to open the border to deserters in 1969, as well as in other efforts.

These groups, taken together with their transnational and pan-Canadian links to other groups and individuals, formed a movement that acted together with a common set of goals. Intellectuals played an important role by developing knowledge that intervened in public opinion, which, in turn, had an impact on government actions. The anti-draft movement was decentralized and often divided on questions of priorities and structure. The anti-draft activists also occasionally intentionally and unintentionally undermined each other in movement publications. Furthermore, there were debates about the appropriate use of resources, especially after the inception of the Canadian Council of Churches' funding mechanism. But, overall, the movement was unified in its support of war resisters and sought to better their situation in various ways.

Personal conflicts did flare up, sometimes connected to political debates among the anti-draft movement activists. Despite the divisions that existed, the anti-draft movement was in constant communication. Examples of this communication pepper the group histories outlined above. Additional examples include an October 1968 communication between Stephen Strauss of the VCAAWO and Allen Mace at the TADP. Strauss sought information on jobs in Toronto and border information. He indicated to Mace that no jobs were to be had in British Columbia. In August 1967, Meg Brown of the VCAAWO corresponded with Ed Miller of the Montreal Council (who had recently taken up a central role in the group) on the topic of the council's broadsheet. The letter was a list of questions and concerns about the Montreal publication, and it suggested pooling efforts into a pamphlet for bulk distribution and a longer booklet with detailed information. Miller responded in September, addressing his reply to "Myra" [Riddell]. Further correspondence between the two included securing immigration documents and conversing with Mark Satin of the TADP in the effort to streamline the publications.[64]

Groups also shared lists of American immigrants, resisters, or people posing as such, who had stolen from groups or supporters, or who were perceived as dangerous. For example, a comradely letter from the Nova Scotia New Democratic Youth in February 1969 informed AID about a suspected poser. A December 1969 letter from the VCAAWO to the TADP shared similar information about one individual.[65] Wilcox recollects, "As time went on and we found ourselves getting burned more and more we would let [other] groups know who had come and ripped us off or whatever, because there would be some who would just hop from one group to the next looking for free housing, free room and board, who might not have had any military record; there are always a few of those."[66] The anti-draft groups saw themselves as part of a pan-Canadian network, a movement that was, more or less, united.

Developing the Network

Overall, the anti-draft movement provided a valuable service to American war resisters. Resisters often knew about the Canadian movement publications and were inspired by articles derived from them in American magazines. Although it will likely never be known for certain, it appears that many – perhaps most – American immigrants had little or no contact with anti-draft groups before immigrating. However, some did acquire information they needed to make the trip, in ways that suggest that the North American network of anti-draft groups was at least somewhat effective in reaching potential immigrants as early as 1967. On the other hand, immigrant experience was varied and showed that the anti-draft groups were not always reliable sources of accurate information or assistance. As *Weekend Magazine* reported in 1966, the experience was mixed; one resister recounted, "It was very comforting, when we had this feeling of fleeing, that there was somebody who could give us advice and help us. We had no one really to talk to in the United States. There has been a real loss of freedom, I think." Another resister, settled in Toronto, did not require assistance apart from advice.[67]

Letters to the VCAAWO show that potential American immigrants communicated, directly or indirectly, with other groups as well. One letter referred to having read the Montreal committee's broadsheet, and others referred to the *Manual.* The letters show that often potential immigrants wrote on behalf of their spouses. Approximately half of these letters were from women in heterosexual couples. Immigrants also sought information on employment availability.[68] Letters to the NSCAAWO expressed gratitude and optimism. A letter from a resister immigrating to Canada via Sweden said his appeal was "coming from the utmost depths of my heart. The one which doesn't have a bullet in it yet." Another stated, "This is just to say that it feels very good to have people to rely on just being there." Other letters sought advice on employment and reflected impressions about the employment situation elsewhere in Canada. One letter sought employment for a man with a "multi-engine commercial pilot's license" and went on to say the writer was "contemplating the purchase of an expensive FM stereo receiver. Are there any hip progressive FM stereo stations in your area such as the ones in the San Francisco area?" Letters in this period reflected a general (and erroneous) perception that teaching jobs were fairly easy to come by in Nova Scotia.[69] Letters from parents sought information on their sons. Letters from resisters mentioned having been referred by American groups.[70]

Not all American immigrants communicated with groups before immigrating. The vast majority (93 percent of both draft dodgers and deserters) of the more than four hundred immigrants interviewed by Kasinsky, for instance, did not communicate with an anti-draft group before immigrating, although the records do not clarify how many nonetheless had access to Canadian anti-draft publications.[71]

The groups fostered communication with individual Americans through American anti-draft groups. Contact information was also printed in left publications in the United States. One of Kasinsky's interviewees mentioned finding Montreal contacts in the *Movement* out of San Francisco, a copy of which he found in Kentucky.[72] A full-page ad in *AMEX* for a magazine called *Contact* asked for assistance in facilitating communication between war resisters and Americans who might be supportive.[73] Canadian contacts were also printed in American publications such as "It's Your

Choice: Guide to Opportunities Open to Volunteers for Military Service," a pamphlet distributed to GIs and military personnel encouraging them to desert and explaining how.[74] There were also examples of less direct experiences. As "James" explains,

> I might have been in [the Spadina TADP offices] once ... I ... found the office, and I don't think I was in there more than once or twice, but I never used any of their services ... They were there had I needed anything, but I prepared very carefully for the whole adventure.
>
> I got in the country on a student visa at the U of T ... and then I proceeded to get a job at the U of T. And at that point, I went down to the border with a job offer in hand, and everything else it took, item by item on what you were supposed to do when you got to the border ... [I'm] not sure [how I knew what I needed]. I had been in contact with the Canadian consulate. I actually made a trip from [my hometown] to Chicago with a friend of mine, trying to find out about moving to Canada. The guy there was very uncooperative.
>
> I went across Niagara Falls, walked around a bit, walked right up to the pedestrian crossing, I was wearing a white shirt, clean-shaven, short haircut, pressed pants, and all the documents required ...
>
> Where I got the idea, it would have been early 1966, or maybe 1967, when I read a copy of *Ramparts* magazine, one of the articles, I think the title was "Sanctuary." They had a picture, and arch-like entrance to Canada, and they gave a description of what people were doing, taking off to Canada and everything was cool ... Then I found out on my own the rest of the things. I may have gotten the [Spadina address] from *Ramparts,* but I don't remember.
>
> The first guy I met was ... anything but antiwar; he befriended a number of draft dodgers, and he let a deserter from the American army stay with him, so he was very sympathetic on a personal level ... He was in favour of American involvement in a certain way, but his friends were all draft dodgers. As far as any organized Canadian groups, I never was involved.[75]

James's experience indicates that the anti-draft movement was effective, but at least some of the time the effect was indirect. James asserts he did not get the information he had about what to do at the border from any specific source; but he was exposed to at least one movement source. The *Ramparts* article in question, titled, as James recalled, "Sanctuary," did not detail how to go about contacting Canadian supporters, but it did mention the existence of anti-draft offices and gave the Spadina address he mentions. It also combatted the idea that emigrating was not a responsible way to oppose the war.[76] This information likely gave James a sense of security in attempting the crossing.

The information sent to American groups was received and redistributed to potential immigrants. "Ben," a draft counsellor based in New Mexico who arrived in Canada in 1978, recollects,

> My main involvement was with New Mexico Resistance, a group which mostly provided draft counselling, but occasionally participated in public education and consciousness-raising. I first contacted them to get advice about my own draft liability, then took training sessions from them so I could help others as I had been helped. Promotion was fast in that organization, as all the senior people went underground, off to jail, or off to Canada, and within a year or so I was heading up the counselling for most of the state. There were never more than ten or twelve people working with our group.
>
> The immigration manual put out by the Toronto Anti-Draft Programme was our main connection to Canada. We routinely encouraged people to fight within the system as long as possible and clog up the Selective Service appeals process, with emigration to be considered only as a last resort. When people were getting close to induction, I sometimes put them in contact with the Toronto group, but after contact was made I had no further involvement with Toronto except to buy their booklets.[77]

Carolyn Egan recalls having consulted with a Buffalo group for advice about immigration:

> We didn't [get advice directly from anti-draft support groups in Canada], although we were aware of [them], simply because we had our own connections, so we didn't need it. We had spoken to people in Buffalo in the anti-draft movement, and they filled us in on things that were important to know, but I think we were lucky in that we knew people here, so we could connect with them and had the support of living with them, and

we applied at the border and they gave work permits when you applied. At the end of December, the landed immigrant status came through.[78]

It is likely that a significant number of war resisters followed this type of chain migration approach – making use of existing networks of immigrants and connections in the United States to emigrate.[79] It also likely accounts for the tendency of war resisters to settle in the same cities, and the same neighbourhoods, as other resisters, creating "ghettos" of the type examined by John Hagan.

For some American immigrants, group connections were direct but tenuous. Marvin Work came into contact with anti-draft groups only once, and very late:

> Essentially, I had no contact with Canadian anti-draft groups until 1977, when I was contacted by a group in Winnipeg and told that I was about to be granted amnesty for my refusal to submit to induction. They suggested that I contact the attorney general for the San Francisco area. I called him, and when I spoke to him, he confirmed that he had just signed the paperwork granting my amnesty.[80]

Similarly, David Brown, a resister who arrived in 1968, was only "aware in a vague way that they existed and could offer support, but ... did not personally try to contact a Canadian anti-draft group."[81] Most immigrants probably arrived with some information, provided by some groups, whether American or Canadian, and got most of what they needed after their arrival. However, despite all the efforts described above, the information received was often of a low quality. As Mark Phillips, a draft dodger who arrived in 1968, recounts,

> Ruth [Phillips's wife] and I came in June of '68, and prior to leaving, we were coming directly from Berkeley, and prior to leaving we phoned the group in Vancouver. I don't think I contacted the people in Toronto. The amazing thing was that they warned me that the border was unfriendly and that we would be stopped and that if Toronto was my destination I should in fact not come across there, but instead head east ...
>
> We came through there, went through the immigration process. We had to go and get an x-ray and do something about the brakes in our

car. And then we got in the car and headed across the continent. I just wanted to get across the border as quickly as possible. So I ignored what they told me, and it turned out to be a sensible thing to do.

In Toronto, my concern was mostly what I was going to do, whether I'd be able to go to university. I had been told – second piece of misinformation – that I should not apply to U of T before coming because I would end up with a student visa. So I expected to be out of school for a year or so.[82]

Anti-draft group correspondence shows that the border situation changed constantly, so the misleading information was understandable there – or, perhaps, Phillips was lucky. Similarly, Joseph Jones, a draft dodger who arrived in 1970, received uneven information. He describes his trajectory:

After I decided to pursue the possibility of emigrating to Canada, my initial information came from a young faculty member and nearby Quakers. A low number in the December 1969 draft lottery left me with the apparent choices of military service, jail, or Canada[83] ... My transition to Canada was made easier by knowing a Canadian student in Toronto, through whom I connected with another student in Montreal, where I spent my first year. Both of their ordinary middle-class families provided welcome and hospitality and things like holiday dinner invitations.

In the summer of 1970, before emigrating, I visited the Toronto Anti-Draft Programme and the Montreal Council to Aid War Resisters. TADP counsellor Dick Burroughs just said go back to the US, we won't help you. Montreal counsellor Bill Mullen went over my case and gave me effective information on when, where, and how to enter Canada. In the fall of 1970, I attended one University Settlement House meeting of what I now realize must have been the Montreal American Deserters Committee, and found it tendentious ... While associated with *AMEX* I had occasional contact with TADP people, and with representatives from other groups when meetings were held in Toronto ... In Vancouver, I had some contact with the Vancouver American Exiles Association, mainly in the period before the 1977 international conference.[84]

Jones's negative experience with the TADP was both during a period of high volume when the TADP had a triage approach to cases, and after the

decision of anti-draft groups at the 1970 Montreal pan-Canadian conference to recommend to American immigrants that they consider all other
options before deciding to come to Canada. Whatever the reason, Jones's
experience was not unique. It shows that the information anti-draft groups
provided was not necessarily reliable. His multiple contacts with anti-draft
groups show the extent of potential incidental encounters by some
immigrants.

Similarly, "Daniel," a deserter who arrived sometime after January 1968,
had multiple incidental contacts with the anti-draft movement. Daniel also
became peripherally involved himself:

> I don't remember the groups, but in Canada I received help from the
> Winnipeg office for deserter/resister support that was funded by an
> alliance of church groups in the US. I was featured in one of their
> magazine articles. I also represented Manitoba deserters/resisters at a
> national (international?) conference in Toronto in the winter of 1973
> ... Following graduation, I was employed as a civilian analyst with the
> Defense Intelligence Agency – the intelligence arm for the Joint Chiefs of
> Staff – and joined the Air National Guard in the fall of 1965 to avoid being
> drafted. Becoming disillusioned with the Vietnam War and contributing
> to it through this job, I resigned and returned to graduate studies, only
> to have my unit activated in January 1968 following the Pueblo Incident,
> and, following the receipt of orders to go to Vietnam, I took an extended
> leave without pay from the US Air Force to immigrate to Sweden, where
> I obtained "humanitarian asylum" ... In Sweden, I knew the group that
> tried to help similar Americans, but I don't remember their name. They
> were funded by American religious organizations.[85]

Another type of American immigrant experience was that of Michael
Goldberg, a draft dodger who came up without Canadian assistance but
subsequently got deeply involved:

> I had been very involved in opposing the war, and the civil rights stuff,
> and the grape boycott, back in the early sixties, and it became pretty clear
> to me working in SDS [Students for a Democratic Society] and other
> things that there was no chance that I was going to go to Vietnam ...
> So when I left the peace corps I had been back in the US for three days

when I received my notice to report for induction. So I came to Canada. That would have been in '67 ...

I had been in touch with the [American Friends Service Committee] in Chicago, and knew that the immigration law was changing. It changed in October '67, and I came up on 8 October '67. So I knew that if I was going to emigrate to Canada having a job offer would be a really helpful set of points.

[I had no contact with Canadian anti-draft groups] until I arrived here. I became involved the second day I arrived here with the Committee to Aid American War Objectors in Vancouver ... I got in touch with the committee to find other war resisters, and maybe to share an apartment, which I ended up doing. And that was '67.

And then [I] was able to offer jobs and help other Americans become landed ... We would drive people down across the border and that kind of stuff ... I then went back to school to do a master's degree at the school of social work, and for my practicum I was assigned to an entity called the inner city service project, and my work for the entire summer with them was to help American war objectors. I did most of the counselling in the summer of '69.[86]

In contrast, some immigrants relied quite happily, and to good effect, on the anti-draft groups. Lee Zaslofsky, a deserter who arrived in 1970, was one immigrant who received helpful support and information in Toronto:

I received help from the Toronto Anti-Draft Programme (TADP), especially when I crossed the border several months after arriving in Canada, as part of applying for Landed Immigrant status. The help included arranging travel to a "safe house" in Welland; arranging for travel to a Catholic college adjacent to the border; arranging for me to be picked up by an American supporter and driven into the US (she waited in her car while I applied); and then being driven back to the college and back to Toronto. I did not volunteer at the program as I was preoccupied with finding work, etc.

I believe they offered assistance in finding housing. They also connected war resisters with employers who were willing to sign Offers of Employment for use in applying for Landed status.[87]

Similarly, Hardy Scott recalls the Vancouver committee and his subsequent involvement with its work. Scott, a draft dodger who arrived in Canada in January 1967, came to Canada after seeing an article in the *New York Times* that gave the address of the VCAAWO. Scott's experience with the Vancouver group was positive, partly because he knew the woman he had contacted – it turned out they had met previously while both living in Philadelphia. Scott recalls that the VCAAWO gave advice about immigration, where to secure housing at cheap rent rates, finding work, and accommodation sharing. Scott worked with the VCAAWO, answering letters from potential immigrants. He used a pseudonym for this work.[88]

Some Americans got involved, at least temporarily, with the anti-draft groups. Dick Perrin, a deserter, started a group himself:

I started an organization called the Regina Committee of American Deserters. My wife of that time and I rented a house, then two, then three houses, and we provided shelter and immigration help to resisters arriving in Regina. I was a resister myself and wanted to remain involved in the effort to stop the war, and in Regina establishing the RCAD seemed a good fit.

When I arrived in Regina, there were a few people loosely organized to help resisters, mostly professors. [They provided] immigration counselling, shelter, sometimes counsel for emotional difficulties, especially for veterans of the war. They were mostly leftist professors, mostly Canadian, but a couple of Americans too. At least two labour leaders were involved. [They had] a wide variety of views, from Mennonite to Maoist, and I worked comfortably with all.[89]

Perrin, a co-founder of the Resistance Inside the Army (RITA) group inside the US military, was no stranger to political organizing.[90] The varying interactions American immigrants had with the anti-draft groups show that, although the anti-draft groups may not always have been reliable sources of support or information, the anti-draft network as a whole, through its exchange of information with other groups both in the United States and in Canada, had a positive impact on many individual lives. Further beneficial effects derived from the successful political campaigns waged by the anti-draft movement.[91]

In its seven years of existence, the Canadian anti-draft movement overcame obstacles with a great deal of success. Had it lasted, it might have been able to find new ways to build international solidarity. The Canadian anti-draft movement had disparate beginnings, and it ended as a network of support groups that, despite disagreements about some questions of tactics, maintained a constant line of communication. It enjoyed a neutral-to-favourable public opinion, and it was strengthened by horizontal linkages both to other groups in Canada and the United States. With roots and methods that were partly pacifist tradition, partly New Left, it reached out to potential immigrants and, in many cases, lent a solid hand. In the end, by June 1973, as the war was winding down and after the Canadian government had tightened its immigration policies, only the Montreal, Toronto, and Vancouver committees were still active.[92]

As Theda Skocpol has posited, the shape and activity of social movements are historically determined.[93] The network of anti-draft groups reflected the times. Its very decentralization also lent itself to the needs of a movement aimed at supporting American immigrants who could cross the border at any one of dozens of different points. Through its unification by communication and information sharing, it was able to overcome its geographical characteristics to mount effective campaigns to change immigration policy.

During its tenure, its social work methods, combined with political advocacy, increased its effectiveness and contributed to tensions. Although there were disagreements about how to go about it, the movement also undertook political advocacy on behalf of American war resisters. In this work, the anti-draft groups received support from dozens of other groups and individuals, such as church groups, student groups, members of Parliament (MPs), and lawyers, without which many of their achievements would have been impossible. But at the height of its work, discussions about identity, nationalism, and tactics, originating both inside and outside the movement, demanded responses that could enable the network of groups to continue to be effective.

3

Deserters

Treatment, Tactics, Identity

This I believe: to oppose
Is the only fine thing in life.
To oppose is to live.
To oppose is to get a grip on the very self.

– Kaneko Mitsuharu, Opposition[1]

In a way, draft dodgers and deserters were not much different from each other. Both groups were resisting the same war. However, real differences existed between the groups in general terms. The draft dodgers came to Canada in larger numbers at the beginning of the period, while deserters arrived in larger numbers later. Deserters and draft dodgers were also different from each other to the extent that they had done different things prior to arriving in Canada. Deserters had usually served a tour of duty in combat and arrived with that experience and little else in terms of formal training or education. Draft dodgers tended to be from higher income brackets and were much more likely to have some post-secondary education. Deserters were further differentiated from draft dodgers by the Canadian government and by anti-draft group activists. Initially, anti-draft groups attempted to protect deserters from exposure, by helping them live "underground," until government policy forced a different strategy. Government policy at first seemed not to differentiate between draft dodgers and deserters, but later the Department of Immigration took action to exclude deserters from Canada, which provoked a campaign to reverse this measure. This differential treatment of deserters was one of the reasons for some deserters' tendency, and later the tendency of other war resisters, to organize into exclusively American groups. In turn, the trend provoked some controversy among anti-draft activists.

The question of differential treatment and consideration of deserters and draft dodgers must be understood as part of the broader interaction between war resisters and anti-draft activists in Canada. This interaction was taking place in a context of developing ideas, prevalent especially among youth, about how to effect social change and about how Canada might shape itself as an opposition to the United States' bad behaviour. The experiences of anti-draft activists, both those centrally and those peripherally involved in the network of anti-draft groups, were shaped by this context. These experiences began to affect the interaction they had with Americans, and to affect some of the resisters' perceptions of the anti-draft movement. The anti-draft movement became more conscious of its own ideals of universal assistance to resisters, and this maturation of the anti-draft movement exposed debates that had initially been of lesser importance. Some of these debates, around tactics, identity, radicalism, and assimilation, developed into serious divisions. Initially, these developing debates affected the movement's ability to act on behalf of war resisters. In part, these debates also brought about discussions of the differences between deserters and draft dodgers.

Opinions about the effectiveness of desertion as an antiwar tactic shaped how anti-draft groups and activists treated deserters. On this question, there were differences on both sides of the border between the orientation of groups and the opinions of the activists in those groups. The judgment of difference, where it existed, was largely on the part of American immigrant groups. The motives of the resisters, real and perceived, both encouraged the differentiation between deserters and draft dodgers and contributed to the romantic image of the act of emigration. However, the American immigrants interviewed for this study largely regarded immigrating as a matter of individual conscience.

The various perceptions of the tactical differences between emigration and staying in the United States, desertion or otherwise avoiding the war, had an impact on Canadian groups' choice between encouraging Americans to assimilate or to retain their American identity. Some argued that, in order to effectively oppose the war, Americans needed to be separately organized into exile groups or deserter committees. Partly, this assertion belonged to a developing debate about what constituted effective, or even "real," political or antiwar work. Although the debates – influenced to some degree by an anti-Americanism that did not distinguish between individual Americans and the US government – from some in the Canadian Left at first impacted the resisters little, if at all, the latent instability in the anti-draft movement eventually became evident.

Expectations and First Impressions

Individual Americans had an appreciation for the commitment of Canadian activists and for Canadian society, finding it generally open and welcoming, and connecting the anti-draft movement to the mostly friendly reception they received. However, they did not, at least at first, need or want a very deep understanding of the motivations of the Canadian activists; nor did they expect them to feel one way or the other. In turn, the Canadian anti-draft activists, by and large, did not expect war resisters to actively oppose the war. Of course, not all Canadians supported the war resisters; but, for the most part, the non-supportive Canadians had no impact on resisters and made their presence felt in the Department of Immigration mostly when public debates were taking place about immigration policy, such as the early 1969 discussion about border policy and deserters. These mutual perceptions were important because they affected the emerging discussion about war resistance tactics and how that discussion interacted with discussions about what it meant to be a deserter, a draft dodger, or an American.

War resisters generally had good experiences with both the movement and individual Canadians. The motivations of those involved in supporting the resisters were clarified through these interactions. Church groups and members, antiwar activists, American immigrants, professors, students, and far left activists all worked together to support the waves of Americans arriving on a daily basis. Some anti-draft activists certainly viewed draft dodging as an antiwar act.[2] Others, like Voice of Women, saw it as part of a tradition of civil disobedience. The Vancouver Committee to Aid American War Objectors (VCAAWO) viewed draft dodging as "at least a minor obstruction" of the Vietnam War: "We help them because their need is great and because they come to have this need through a belief that 'wars will cease when men refuse to fight,' which we share."[3]

The recollections of Canadian activists and American immigrants confirm that the reception for resisters in Canada was generally supportive. Lee Zaslovsky, a deserter who arrived in Toronto in 1970, observed,

> Although there were some Canadians who regarded us as cowards, etc., I found that most Canadians were very welcoming. When I would be asked about my background ... I would say I had deserted, and the response would often be, "That's what I would have done." Canadians based their welcome in part on their opposition to conscription, as well as, in many cases, to their opposition to the Vietnam War. But conscription was seen as wrong in itself ... I became a cab driver soon after arriving in Canada, and I met draft dodgers and deserters from a number of countries, including Israel, Yugoslavia, and even Norway. They, like me, benefited from the Canadian attitude to [US Selective Service] conscription.[4]

"James," a draft dodger who arrived in 1967, shared the view that Canadians in general supported war resisters, or at least that negative opinions were not in evidence, in a country where, it seemed to him, political opinions were not sharply expressed: "I had the sense that they thought that what the US was doing in Vietnam was basically wrong, and at that time public opinion was against it. Of course, then, as now, there were Canadians who thought everything the US did was right as rain ... But Canadians don't get in your face so much."[5] Still, for some, the extent of Canadian support came as a surprise. "Ben," an anti-draft activist who immigrated to Canada in 1978, "pretty much assumed that Canadians were just like Americans except for a couple accidents of history. I remember being quite surprised to hear from a couple resisters who had come to Canada that they were treated with respect here, that many people were actually friendly toward them."[6] Ben expected Canadians to be suspicious of war resisters, perhaps because of negative experiences in the United States. These general perceptions helped shape these potential immigrants' opinions of Canada.

Their general perceptions about Canada augmented war resisters' direct interactions with individual Canadians. These interactions solidified the resisters' idea of a welcoming Canada. Their experiences also demonstrate connections between general political culture and the positioning of government. The motivations of individual Canadians who supported war resisters were linked, at least for some resisters, to official policy on the war and on the draft dodgers.

Perhaps not surprisingly, some war resisters had experiences with individual Canadians that pointed to pacifist motivations. Marvin Work, a draft dodger from California who arrived in the Kootenays in British Columbia in June 1970, remembers the following:

> During my first months in Canada, we rented a small house from Doukhobor landlords who knew that I was a draft dodger, but were extremely supportive. Being pacifists, they were happy to receive us and to provide support. Once a week they made borscht for us, let us have their buttermilk gratis, and taught my wife to bake bread. We established a very close relationship with them. We were similarly supported by other friends we made in the community.[7]

However, the motivations of Canadian activists probably varied a great deal. Hardy Scott, a draft dodger from New York City who arrived in Vancouver in 1967, recalls that

> the views of the Canadian antiwar folks, like their counterparts in the United States, varied considerably. There were pacifists. There were Canadian veterans who saw this particular war as being unjust. There were Canadians who were angry at the United States for threatening economic sanctions against Canada for Canada's selling buses to Cuba ... The common element is, "this war is unjust and refusal to cooperate is only one of the means to show opposition and give others the courage to show opposition in their own ways."[8]

Some resisters made assumptions about the individual opinions of Canadians based on the positioning of political parties at various levels of government. For them, the mostly favourable immigration regime meant that Canadians felt generally well-disposed towards war resisters. Michael Goldberg, a draft dodger who arrived in 1967, observed the positive immigration environment for draft dodgers created by the points system, which was adopted in 1967. The points system awarded points to potential immigrants on the basis of factors such as age, job offer, education, and training.[9] While the system was crafted to facilitate the immigration of individuals with education, training, or job experience that the government felt was needed in Canada at the time, the result was that American immigrants, in comparison to other immigrant groups, had an easy time immigrating, at least in Goldberg's estimation:

> [The] federal government was incredibly supportive, both with the way they set up the immigration rules in the Trudeau era and everything else at the federal level. The barriers were made as simple as possible for people to get landed, is the feeling that I had. The points system – at. that point you only needed fifty points to get in.
>
> And at the [BC] provincial level the opposition party, the NDP [New Democratic Party], was clearly supportive, and the federal NDP was clearly opposed to the war in Vietnam.
>
> The vast majority of Canadians, I felt, had serious reservations about the efficacy of the war. At the city level, one of the things I found was that politics in Canada was much more entertaining. Things didn't always converge in the middle because you had multiple parties here, so people would try to stake out their territory. So even when the Right was in power, you still had left-wingers who were supportive and made public pronouncements, so the right-wingers were often upset with the "hippies."[10]

Through connections with Americans still in the United States, activists in Canada became aware that the idea of a welcoming Canada was a fairly common one south of the border as well. However, American activists were divided on whether that welcome was appropriate. Joan Wilcox, an American immigrant who arrived before most American war resisters and was a founding member of Ottawa Assistance with Immigration and the Draft (AID), interacted with friends who remained in the United States, from whom she and her husband gathered impressions of opinion south of the border:

> [Some] thought we were terrible communists ... [and others] were laudatory. We had come from the States, and many of our good friends there were politically active; the majority of them tended to feel that, from their point of view, they would rather see them continue the fight there

in the States. But there were others that were very supportive and very interested in what was happening here.[11]

The anti-draft movement on both sides of the border debated the idea that Americans should stay in the United States and try to end the war from there. This notion also constituted the principal objection to emigrating raised among some elements of the American New Left. However, Wilcox was philosophical: "By and large Americans felt strongly about it one way or another; a lot of Canadians couldn't have cared less."[12] Canadians, for the most part, did not consider either immigration to Canada or going to a US jail a preferred mode of draft resistance.

Starting from a deep commitment to sets of ideas like pacifism, or acting out of professional interest, or through incidental involvement in the anti-draft movement, Canadians' perceptions of the resisters were shaped and changed by real experiences with war resisters. Many activists held the romantic notion that all resisters were acting out of basic courage and from the principle of resistance to the war. Others never harboured such illusions. Just as some immigrant experiences were peripheral to the anti-draft movement, so some Canadian involvement with the anti-draft movement was peripheral to the main network of anti-draft groups. The evidence shows that, the closer to the organized networks an individual supporter was, the less likely they were to either romanticize the cause or to expect war resisters to adopt an explicitly "political" outlook upon their arrival.

Ken Fisher, then a student at Queen's University and a Canadian peace and civil rights activist, was one individual whose lack of proximity to the organized networks meant that he injected his own predisposition to be antiwar into his expectations for war resisters. Below, he describes his experience as a border courier for deserters as a young man hoping to make a difference through involvement in antiwar work and by helping these resisters specifically. While his involvement was brief and limited, his experience was so far from his idealistic expectations, based on an idea that war resisters were themselves idealists, that it had a profound effect on him:

> Growing up in Ottawa I was ... involved in student politics, and as the war in Vietnam progressed, I was peripherally or directly involved. I would go to the antiwar demos and all that. I was [the Queen's University] SUPA

[rep], and at SUPA I was with the [Combined Universities Campaign for Nuclear Disarmament] ... and I was enamoured with SNCC [Student Nonviolent Coordinating Committee, an American civil rights group]. I don't remember how it happened, but I was approached to see if I would be a courier, so to speak, and go to the United States somewhere over the ... bridge and pick up three deserters. And I agreed to do that ... [The initial contact] could have been in conjunction with the SUPA. There was a group that was concerned about draft dodgers; it could have been a draft dodger connection. Being a deserter was another step along the way.

Part of the period was a deep romanticism about social change and the future, and this was before Kent State, before it became apparent to what extent the state would go to repress social change. Romanticism was unbridled. There was free love, free imagination; you would engage. So considering the risk I took at that time – in terms of my record, my ability to travel, anything – I gave it no consideration whatsoever.

In his description of his involvement, we can hear Fisher's perception of himself as a young man, involved for romantic reasons in helping men he expected to behave as heroes behaved:

So I borrowed a friend's '58 Studebaker, my roommate at Queen's ... As we were heading back to Kingston, I started to talk to these guys. Their general impression of Canada was that we skied all year, [that] there were no high-rise buildings; it was just some rural fantasyland north of the United States. In other words, what I got was that they had no politics other than saving their own ass; they did not want to die in Vietnam, and they were scared shitless, and they knew nothing about the real world other than that. Perhaps I'm exaggerating slightly. So the romance of, in my little narcissistic mind, of doing something extraordinary, of having new colleagues in the great campaign to make a new Earth, or however you want to talk about it, was reduced to rubble on this trip because these guys knew nothing about the world whatsoever, and I started saying to myself, "I'm risking life and limb. For what?" That was part of the experience for me.

And I was truly scared myself. It was all theoretical until you got to the American checkpoint. There's these guys with guns, and you really are breaking the law, and you really could get caught. I mean, there were lots of people who did far more than I did. I mean, that was my contribution, and that's the way it looked to me at that moment. My feeling was that if I was stopped in the United States assisting deserters to leave the country, and they were already known to be deserters, that I would be aiding and abetting.

His young self, whom he forgives for this naïveté at a time when protest was romanticized, had a rude awakening about the deserters he was helping: they sought to avoid being killed, and their motives were no more protest-oriented than that. His conclusion, in retrospect, was that he was not aware of the reality of the situation such young men faced:

I wouldn't have traded that moment of disillusionment for anything. Disillusionment is one of my best friends in terms of having another chance to create a world, see how that world works. I was even more frightened for myself. I realized how stupid I had been. I was as confused as they were, as naive as they were. In terms of what was going on, how to deal with it ... there was a naïveté within myself that I had to deal with ... It altered [my convictions] in the sense that things weren't black and white.

I realized the coefficient of adversity was a whole lot greater than I could possibly imagine, because these guys were coming to be citizens of Canada and knew nothing. The way the draft was working it was ... sucking up young men who had no skills and no options. Guys with re-sources and good families were somewhere else. That was the way their society was circulating their youth.[13]

Thus, Fisher was acting out of an idealistic expectation about war resisters, which he shared with many people his age in the 1960s. His experience changed his outlook and shook his assumptions that resisters were uni-formly acting out of idealistic antiwar sentiment, like he was. Who knows how different his experience would have been had the young Americans he was helping been among those with political convictions.

Fisher's experience and that of others can be seen as part of a general culture of fashionable radicalism and political activism. As historian Doug Owram has observed, "The idealism of the era meant that individual causes or concerns – Vietnam, Native poverty, campus politics, women's liberation – could gain the support of many who were far from being political activists." The "media and the peer group" reinforced the message that "to be youthful was to be politically aware, politically critical": "Only a small percentage of young people in the 1960s were political radicals, but a much greater number, especially in the universities, grew up in an age in which youth and radicalism were connected. New ideas swarmed over the generation."[14] Of course, not all of the activists considered in this study fall into the category of youth; but this movement, like others of the time, was nonetheless part of the tapestry of youth-identified protest causes. Historian Cynthia Comacchio emphasizes the cultural aspect of the category of youth and the mutually determining categories of young and old.[15] The constellation of concepts wrapped up in the term "youth" include its cultural and social dimensions, as well as its relationships to other concepts. This layered complexity, groundwork laid in the period between the world wars, is the context within which youth movements existed in the 1960s.[16]

Fisher's experience was probably not unique, but it appears to be unusual in light of the beliefs of other activists. Most activists involved in the anti-draft movement knew exactly how much work there was to be done, and they harboured no illusions about who the draft dodgers and deserters were. For them, the resisters were just individuals who needed help, and the act of helping them might indirectly affect the outcome of the movement against the war in Vietnam. The resisters' political views were, by and large, not relevant to the anti-draft activists.

Most of the key activists in the anti-draft groups did not consider resisters' reasons for immigrating to be a factor in whether they should receive assistance. Nancy Pocock and her husband, Jack, were Quakers and long-time peace activists. In a 1970 interview with Renée Kasinsky, Pocock describes working with the young Americans and their supporters as refreshing. From 1965 to 1970, a steady stream of American immigrants stayed with the Pococks.[17] Pocock believed that Canada had a pacifist tradition. Pacifism also led Quakers to an unconditional support for war resisters, no matter their personal reasons for leaving the United States. On deserters, Pocock was candid but sympathetic:

[F]or the deserters, most of them have just cut and run, and they're bewildered, many of them younger than the other boys. Less educated, less thoughtful, and they just know they don't like what they saw down there. And they don't like what they're being forced to do in the army. But I think that they're a positive thing for peace ... and the fact they just said, "No, I'm not going to!" Whatever their motives, it's a good thing.[18]

Bill Spira's reasons for involvement were similarly characterized by a concern for the larger impact of the anti-draft movement, and not for the individual beliefs or principles behind resisters' decisions to come to Canada. He saw helping war resisters as far more effective than antiwar demonstrations. As he recounted to Kasinsky, "A lot of people have asked me, why are you doing it for Americans? My answer always is I'm not doing it for Americans. I'm doing it for the Vietnamese."[19] Joan Wilcox shared Spira's commitment to opposing the war:

> Were my expectations [of having an impact on the war] met? Yes, but maybe I'm kidding myself. But I'd like to think we were one cog on a very major wheel that helped grind the war down, maybe not as soon as we would have liked, but sooner than it would have otherwise ... We saw a lot of young men, [men] who would have had wasted lives ... had they gone to war, become very fulfilled and fulfilling citizens of this country and some who went back to the States but also did lead productive lives, and that's always fulfilling.[20]

For Wilcox, Spira, and others, opposing the war was one of the primary reasons people got involved; their work was aimed at resisting the war just as surely as street demonstrations.

Lawyer Paul Copeland's interest might be expected to have been purely professional. But he, like the others involved, was a product of the times. It is interesting to compare his story to Fisher's. Both were typical of youth culture in the sixties, but Copeland's path led him to a deep commitment to the needs of "exiles":

> This is a story I tell fairly regularly. I come from sort of a leftist family ... and what I regard as the seminal point of my life was: I'm thirteen years old. I'm in high school in Toronto. I'm a member of the ham radio club in high school, and I have in my bedroom a converted tank set that allowed me to listen to short wave radio. And ... I'm reading the media some about

what's happening at Dien Bien Phu. And the Western media is saying the French are fighting the communists for control of Vietnam. And one night, I'm listening to Radio Moscow. They had an English-language news program on late at night, and Radio Moscow, they say, "The Vietnamese are fighting the French for freedom," and I said, "Holy shit, that sounds really a lot more accurate ..." And it was the first time I sort of woke up and said, "Gee, there are biases in the media ..." It was really for me a ... pivotal point in my life for how I approached things.

So there I am, however many years later ... When I'm in law school, I was getting more radical. I had been a little bit radical, but there was nothing going on in university [as an undergraduate]. I started university in 1957 ... There just wasn't very much going on, a bit of "ban the bomb" stuff. And then, when I was in third year of university ... there was a lot of stuff going on in the United States with the civil rights movement ... And I thought (I was in geophysics) I could finish geophysics and go off and be a geophysicist. I could do political work maybe two days a year if I happened to be in the city.

Copeland was a fairly typical university-age person in the early sixties, influenced by news of civil-rights activism in the United States. His experiences made possible his perception of the connection between antiwar work and protecting the rights of all sorts of resisters:

I was certainly supportive, generally speaking, of the North Vietnamese during the war. I was an admirer of Ho Chi Minh. I mean, he was quite a remarkable man ... and a Vietnamese nationalist, and he happened to be a communist, but who gives a shit? It's a pretty rotten system in Vietnam, but, between the American puppet regimes in Vietnam and the Viet Cong, the Viet Minh before, there was no question in my mind whose side I was on. And then working with the exile community, and just the people who didn't want to go and fight that war, was obvious ... We certainly hoped [to weaken the American war effort]. It wasn't the overarching theme. We were representing every demonstrator almost that existed, so, there was a lot of antiwar stuff going on in Toronto. It got bigger as it went on. Probably the largest demonstrations with the largest number of arrests [were] in May of 1970, just after the invasion of Cambodia.[21]

Copeland, like Fisher, places his experience in the context of the sixties counterculture and protest movements. Both were idealists; but perhaps because of Copeland's family connections to the Left, where contact with people of a range of political beliefs was part of organizing, Copeland's idealism did not lead him to expect all war resisters to be committed to opposing the war, and he did not have the rude awakening that Fisher experienced.

In general, American immigrants and war resisters also did not particularly care what beliefs or political orientation Canadian activists held, at least in the first few years of the period. Resisters who came into contact with the anti-draft groups generally felt positive about them, at worst finding them somewhat irrelevant. The resisters that Kenneth Fred Emerick interviewed thought Canadian groups could use more money; that they took in more people than they could handle; and that they needed better publicity in the United States. Some felt that exile groups were oriented towards deserters to the exclusion of draft dodgers. Others felt that the exile groups needed to interact more with Canadians. One or two felt that the Ottawa group was better organized than other anti-draft committees.[22] Many immigrant memories of Canadian activists and Canadian attitudes were either shaped by electoral political choices or by chance encounters with Canadians. Wilcox, who was an American immigrant herself but who had immigrated in the early 1960s, remembers the political orientation of those she worked with as

primarily NDP. However, the Liberals were in power at the time, and we got very good support from the Liberal bureaucracy, and we didn't much ask each other how we voted. One of our counsellors was a very strong feminist. But we all generally took the point of view that, first of all, we disagreed with the war in Vietnam and basically anything we could do, well anything legal that we could do, to throw a spanner into the works was a good thing.[23]

Regardless of how non-partisan the atmosphere inside the groups might have been, as Wilcox suggested, there is no question that the anti-draft activists were seen to be on the Left of the political spectrum. Lee Zaslovsky, a deserter who arrived in 1970, remembers the following anecdotes about Toronto Anti-Draft Programme (TADP) activists and Toronto politicians:

I remember two of the people at TADP: Joe [sic] Spira, an older man, and a woman about my age, Naomi Wall. They were helpful in making the arrangements mentioned above. Naomi, I remember, also commented on my enthusiasm for the NDP ("Wow! A socialist party!"), saying many people found the NDP "wishy washy." She was right! ...

I remember attending a public meeting of the "Waffle" [an internal caucus of the NDP that had sought to reform it into a socialist party], at which I asked Walter Gordon during the question time about his attitude towards people like me, and he was very welcoming, saying, "Welcome aboard." I don't think he was an MP at that time, though. Mel Watkins was also on stage with him.[24] I was aware of the NDP being supportive and became active in the NDP in 1971, during a provincial election in which Dan Heap was a candidate. He and his supporters were very antiwar and pro-war resister.[25]

This general left positioning combined with a dedication to assisting war resisters had an effect on the anti-draft movement's interaction with the broader antiwar movement. One resister recalls that "[Canadian activists] seemed like reasonable people, caring and humane ... [They were] generally supportive [of the broader movement] but not always willing to be co-opted to the extent that it diverted them from their primary goal of being supportive of deserters and resisters."[26] By this he meant that the anti-draft groups were focused on support for war resisters and did not want their energy and resources to be drawn into broader antiwar efforts. They also resisted efforts to promote war resisters as symbols of the antiwar movement.

Overall, contact with the anti-draft groups reinforced war resisters' views of Canada as a welcoming country. Draft dodger Michael Goldberg's view of the VCAAWO linked the individual political views of activists to broader strategic debates within the movement and to the electoral political scene in Vancouver:

There were clearly differences just like there were in the US about which direction the antiwar movement should take. There were lots of arguments about how many Marxists there were on the head of a pin, and all the usual kind of stuff that was going on, but the big thing that impressed me was just how open the country was compared to the US. In part, that may have been a bit of luck on my part, because at the Jewish community centre where I worked, the exec director of Jewish family services, which was a very small family counselling group, was a person who later became the premier of the province a couple of years after that, and we became very good friends. So I had this extraordinary introduction to Canadian politics ... [American politics] were just closed to people like myself in the US, folks who didn't have money or connections ... So I walked in as a refugee, I got a job, and make friends with a person who three years later was the premier of the province.[27]

For Goldberg and others like him, the important thing was the support received, not the reason it was given.

As more and more resisters arrived, and many got involved in the anti-draft movement, that support shifted. As the movement progressed and events unfolded, the actions and interactions that took place began to have an impact on the views of those involved. The resisters who were in touch with the anti-draft network discussed how to be an effective part of the antiwar movement; but, in order to address that issue, they had to answer the question of whether, or to what extent, they were still American. For the anti-draft activists' part, various considerations, both external and internal, had from the start exerted pressure to treat deserters and draft dodgers differently. This pressure provoked discussion and debate about the relative merits of various types of war resistance.

Differential Treatment and Perception of Deserters

One source of the differentiation was the American immigrants themselves. Kasinsky observed that deserters, compared to draft dodgers, experienced discrimination from both the Canadian aid groups and the Canadian government. While government policy changed several times between 1966 and 1973, no matter the policy, war resisters often experienced discrimination from immigration officials. In 1968 and 1969, immigration officials were explicitly directed to prevent the entry of deserters, while draft dodgers were still ostensibly allowed to enter under the same rules as other immigrants. This situation continued until May 1969. Aid groups, for their part, differentiated between the two categories of resisters, due to their differing legal status both inside the United States and in Canada. Later, the groups also recognized that deserters were typically less educated and experienced, and therefore faced specific obstacles to being landed.

Canadian anti-draft groups did treat deserters differently from draft dodgers, at least at first. Spira told Kasinsky that eventually TADP research and experience showed that draft dodgers and deserters were not different legally. They observed, however, that, despite this equivalence, government authorities still treated the two groups differently, which eventually necessitated some differential treatment by anti-draft groups. It is not clear that this differential treatment on the part of the government was actually illegal, but that was certainly the perception of those who supported opening the border. Unknown to activists, a secret memorandum from the Department of Immigration was sent to immigration officers instructing them to take unfulfilled military obligations into account with border applications. The memo was circulated to exclude deserters without necessitating a public debate. Spira asserted that the anti-draft groups did not treat deserters differently as a direct imitation of differential treatment by government, but because of the anti-draft movement's ignorance about the fact that the resisters were legally equivalent. He also suggested that the differential views of deserters and draft dodgers were also partly a reflection of American attitudes towards resisters, which saw deserters as breaking the law more blatantly than draft dodgers.[28]

Anti-draft groups also dealt with deserters differently because deserters tended to require different counselling. While no clear statistical proof exists because no scientific study was ever conducted, the evidence is overwhelming that deserters tended to be less educated than draft dodgers. The "meagre" evidence Vietnam veteran David Cortwright, now a peace studies scholar, was able to amass in 1975, such as United States Department of Defense statistics presented to the Senate Armed Services Committee hearings on desertion in 1968, supports this notion.[29] As one resister told *Weekend Magazine* in 1966, "Guys who don't go to college don't even know you *can* come to Canada."[30] The recollections of resisters also bolster this theory. War resister Joseph Jones remembers that deserters were different "in terms of socioeconomic class, personal adaptability, needs for counselling and support, ease of immigration, et cetera."[31] Immigration was more difficult for deserters because they could amass fewer points – based on education, skills, and work experience – towards landed immigrant status. Since many deserters had also seen combat, it is worth pointing out that Vietnam veterans are well known to have suffered in great numbers from posttraumatic stress and other problems perhaps not yet fully understood, even by sympathizers. This, combined with the stress of leaving the United States to come to another country full of strangers, would have made immigration more difficult as well.[32] Also, the US Selective Service program had a way of streaming men from the lower-income strata of American society into the military, as Joan Wilcox describes:

> [It's] probably true [that deserters had lower levels of education]. For one thing, if you were going to university, that generally equalled a deferment until after university, and so a lot of people who otherwise qualified [for the draft] would go to university who might not have done, in order to get another four years of deferment, hoping the war would be over; so that automatically added to their eligibility [for further deferments] ...
>
> Secondly, the better educated, and I use that term loosely, generally had a better understanding of the political situation, an awareness of what was happening in the Far East, and an awareness of what going to war meant and were in a little better position to assess their options. And also ... an awful lot of the deserters came from very poor, very ill-educated backgrounds who hadn't a hope in hell of getting a decent job as it was then, and to go into the military, they could be promised the moon on a string ... and it wasn't until they got into the military that they realized what they had signed into.[33]

These political and cultural factors combined to make the deserter experience qualitatively different from that of other war resisters.

In response to my questions about the difference between deserters and draft dodgers, those I interviewed corroborated the sense of differential receptions. Their responses are augmented by the views of those interviewed by Kasinsky in 1970. War resister Marvin Work suggested that "the public perception of deserters was more negative than that of draft dodgers."[34] Goldberg remembers similar trends from his work with the VCAAWO:

> I think from my experience, when I was working at the committee and seeing a lot of both draft dodgers and deserters, that generally draft dodgers tended to have higher levels of education. That made it easier

for them to get landed, [for] the vast majority of draft dodgers who came up. Among the guys there were also women who came up, but they were either with males or just were really pissed off at what was going on in the US – but among the draft dodgers, almost all of them had some university or were in university. Among the deserters, it was rare that you had that. I did have one deserter who had a master's degree, but that was an exception rather than the norm.[35]

Fisher, who was a movement activist on the periphery of the anti-draft groups, also believes the trend existed, although his experiences with war resisters were comparatively limited. He goes further, suggesting that draft dodgers were more committed to being Canadian than many who were born here:

> [Draft dodgers] had a much clearer vision of where they were going and why, and for me, my major awareness-learning souvenir of talking to men who were draft dodgers is that without exception they became more Canadian than Canadians ... Their process of becoming Canadians was to become [today's] devoted Canadians. In contrast to the deserter who knew nothing, they became extraordinary contributors to Canadian society. That's my – without exception – experience.[36]

The differences were lost on many Canadians, who conflated all resisters into the category of "draft dodger." Zaslovsky notes,

> There was (and is) a lack of clarity among many Canadians as to the difference between "draft dodgers" and "deserters" – the common term was "draft dodger," and Canadians based their welcome in part on their opposition to conscription, as well as, in many cases, to their opposition to the Vietnam War. But [US] conscription was seen as wrong in itself.[37]

Dick Perrin, who deserted in Germany in 1967 and arrived in Canada several years later, noted that deserters tended to be poor and uneducated, which made it harder to get immigration papers.[38]

One reason for the different treatment of deserters by anti-draft groups was a desire to protect deserters from exposure. This desire was the reason why the TADP ran a separate – and, at first, secret – program for deserters. As Nancy Pocock explained in a 1970 interview with Kasinsky,

> [TADP activist Bill Spira ran] what we called the sub-program. We weren't sure at that time just how deserters stood, with the government ... [in] '67-68, when we started getting deserters ... And the press was very anxious to get this story about deserters. They knew they were coming, and they were poking and prying all the time. They haunted the office. So we decided the best thing to do was to handle deserters separately. So Bill took over that, and we called it the sub-program. He had a group of advisors who advised in their own homes ... and kept the boys in their own homes.[39]

Spira claimed to be the first person to start counselling deserters, as part of the TADP sub-program.[40] He thought that deserters had begun to outnumber draft dodgers for a number of reasons: first, because of the decision by Allan MacEachen to open the border to them; second, because draft dodging in the United States had become "a sophisticated art where guys can dodge for two or three years"; and, finally, because increased opposition to the war in public opinion both in the United States and in Canada made desertion more "socially acceptable." As more men deserted, others saw it as a better option than they had before.[41] By around 1970, the number of deserters coming through the TADP was high enough to require a triage approach to the counselling.[42] The differential treatment of draft dodgers and deserters at the border continued to be reflected in the application of the Canadian immigration points system, even once the border situation was changed to allow deserters to enter more easily.

Despite their desire to tailor counselling to the needs of different kinds of war resisters, anti-draft activists outside of the exile groups did not assign a value to one tactic over another. This approach may have been handed down to them from American draft counselling materials and training. Whatever the reason, most activists maintained a neutrality that was not contrived. Joan Wilcox recalls,

> I personally didn't care, and I think most of us here didn't care if they were dodging or deserting ... My position – I think it was fairly representative of our group – is, if you knew the situation in the States, you'd realize .

how poverty-stricken some of these young men were. All of the forces
that would cause them to, and the political hype and so on, and they had
no idea what they were getting into.[43]

Goldberg also recalls the debate among antiwar activists but affirms that
the groups he worked with approached the question neutrally:

> The debate I remember is that there seemed to be three choices. Go and
> gum up the works by joining the military. Go to Leavenworth [military
> prison]; refuse the draft and go to prison but stay in the country. Or leave
> the country. I think for different people, different things worked for them.
> While there was a debate about what was better, it became very clear that
> it was a debate about nothing, that all of them were important ways in
> which to get across the point. It was time to move away from "the most
> important strategy" to "strategies." The strongest debate was probably
> whether to stay in the US and fight through the antiwar movement (either
> underground, in the prison system, or directly in Vietnam) or leave the
> country, and I always felt, and I think it's where many people got to, that
> it wasn't an either/or issue. It depended on the circle of people and what
> they felt would work for them.[44]

This neutrality was challenged by elements among the resisters themselves after 1969, but initially at least, it was important for the aid groups
themselves not to differentiate between the two groups in order to provide
counselling to resisters regardless of background or experience.

It appears that these debates had their origins in discussions about the
relative effectiveness of draft dodging, deserting, or disruption as antiwar
tactics. Since a significant number, if not the majority, of war resisters did
not undertake their journey solely, or even partly, as an antiwar tactic, it
is not surprising that the question was contested. The most radical argument, expressed early in the period by American New Left figures and
some antiwar activists, was that rather than run to Canada, men should
remain in the United States and resist the war directly, by going to jail,
going underground, or by other means. To emigrate merely meant that
some other man would take the place of the dodger or deserter on the
front lines. This view saw war resistance in terms of its immediate effect
on the war, and not as part of a set of tactics that, taken together, had

an increasing impact on public opinion and could be seen as just one part of a broad antiwar movement. In contrast, war resisters interviewed for this project were nearly unanimous in their opinion that the question of whether to dodge or desert, or to stay in the United States to oppose the war from there, was a matter of individual conscience. Draft dodger Joseph Jones remembers,

> Early on, there was a notion that "real resisters" go to jail, or maybe into the army to organize – but not to Canada ... There were a lot of players, a lot of jostling, and a lot of events cobbled together ... I did not like the thought that some other body would take the place I left vacant, but the bottom line was that I could only choose for myself and not for anyone else. If everyone had chosen something besides military service, the army would not have existed. Anyone who presumed to judge how someone else should resist was just plain arrogant.[45]

Similarly, Marvin Work thought that both draft dodging and deserting "were effective antiwar tactics":

> Although draft dodgers refused induction [the call to report for duty] into the US military and deserters had joined and then made a decision to desert the military, in my mind I have lumped these two categories together because both were critical of the war in Vietnam and both made the choice to leave the US.[46]

Finally, "Daniel" also thought the decision was up to the individual:

> I think it is a very personal decision, depending on individual circumstances, and it is more important that both groups maintain a united front and acceptance of each other's different life experiences ... I knew the difference [between draft dodgers and deserters], but it never mattered to me ... There was much variation in backgrounds, education, and motivation. Most were principled people as opposed to being opportunists.[47]

Although Canadian activists generally did not question the tactics or commitment of resisters, American exile groups largely viewed all kinds of immigration as only a beginning, a first step, in political activity and antiwar action. The earlier American New Left position that emigration was a cop-out was in stark contrast to the views of at least some of the anti-draft groups that were not identified as exile groups. However, in Canada, aid groups and exile groups alike varied as to whether their outlook would be one of outright political advocacy in the form of pressure on government, or one of mainly aiding immigrants with concrete problems such as housing and immigration status. Moreover, among groups, personnel varied in their personal views about the tactical debate about draft dodging; some believed resisters should stay in the United States, while others thought the method of war resistance was an individual decision.[48]

Another, and starker, debate concerned whether desertion was more effective than dodging the draft. Related to this question was the further problem of the meaning of desertion itself: some deserters groups asserted that desertion was only a radical act when motivated by opposition to the war, and that desertion for other reasons was not real desertion. This particular position led to public disputes and alienated some war resisters from anti-draft groups. For example, according to Emerick, the American academic who visited the war resisters and wrote a book about it, the Montreal "scene" was seen by some resisters in the early 1970s as "extremely political ... it discouraged immigration so long as an alternative possibly existed, and advocated obstruction of Selective Service or the military establishment [over desertion or draft dodging] ... The political emphasis invariably led to less effective aid and obviously turned many resisters off completely"; resisters "described the scene in Montreal as unfortunate."[49] The impression Emerick describes was formed at a time when the Montreal Council to Aid War Resisters (MCAWR) was trying to work constructively with the Montreal American Deserters Committee (ADC); at one point, they even moved into the same office. However, the move was short-lived because MCAWR came to understand that the ADC wanted to select deserters to help on the basis of their political orientation, a position they could not share.[50] Thus, the debate had a real impact on groups' ability to help American immigrants.

This debate simmered in Montreal throughout the period. In early 1970, Bill Mullen of the Montreal Council described the group's role as providing immigration counselling and assistance with integration, a role he saw as explicitly different from, and broader than, forming a Union of American

Exiles, an option some advocated.[51] In contrast, the American Exile Coun-selling Center sought to deliver political education to "undermine the in-dividualistic motivation of a possible resister," and to "destroy the myth of Canadian neutrality." Its overall purpose was to help non-political Amer-ican immigrants to radicalize. In November 1970, a letter of information concerning the American Exile Counselling Center found its way into the Voice of Women files; the AECC's self-description in the letter made its political divisions with MCAWR clear. The centre was conceived as an alternative to both the "apolitical" Montreal Council to Aid War Resisters and the Montreal ADC, beleaguered by a lack of resources and by the political orientation of "liberals."[52] In other words, the centre sought to position itself as the most radical option for war resisters in Montreal. Such efforts were not always well-received by Canadian activists and Left figures. Later, such purposes were seen as a threat to Canadian autonomy.

Another example of how this division of approaches played out in a way that could affect the groups' ability to help war resisters is laid out in documents regarding the life of the Vancouver American Exiles Association (VAEA). In an essay dated 12 August 1975, to accompany a submission to the archives, Ed Starkins, a co-founder of the association (sometimes known as VEA and VEU), explained that the group was formed in 1971 by a group of Americans looking for support beyond what was offered by the VCAAWO. Retrospectively, Starkins viewed the importance of the group as "somewhat minor" in terms of its impact compared to the VCAAWO.[53] The VAEA held social events and had a public face in the media. Its most public period was during the debates about Ford's amnesty of 1974.[54] The VAEA was most active in 1973-74, with a "largely political, and somewhat social, program." Starkins suggested in his document that many exiles were not interested in the group because they wanted to move on and assimilate as Canadians, while the VAEA was more concerned with securing an unconditional amnesty from the United States for war resisters to return there. Also, its self-image as "political" was a problem: "The VAEA's inter-nal problems were monumental, taking a minor root in the radical-liberal divisions of the displaced American Movement."[55] The commitment of members of the group to conflicting ideological outlooks led to the organ-ization's disarray. Starkins's undated resignation letter states that he resigned as chair of the VAEA because of conflict with the program director: "My participation in the group has become a kind of holding action designed to keep certain parties from ripping off the organization financially and otherwise representing their *Georgia Straight*-Abby Hoffmanesque delirium as the 'line' of Canadian resistors [sic]."[56] Starkins was referring to his perception of those "parties" involved as being associated with the newspaper *Georgia Straight*, which he perceived to have New Left leanings. A further letter urges a potential funder to support the VCAAWO instead, stating that the VAEA had been

> taken over by a small group of personal friends who apparently share an obscure leftist political orientation ... we have been systematically alienated from the [VAEA] through a number of tactics ranging from the calling of illegal [that is, unconstitutional] ... meetings to the use of epithets like "bourgeois" and "class enemy." These tactics, in our opinion, have served to discredit the VAEA ... In short, we feel that the VAEA is no longer representative of the local exile community.[57]

However, it would not be accurate to conclude from this letter that the divide being expressed was a left-right one; Starkins and his colleague Lawrence Warren signed the letter, "Yours for Peace and a Universal, Unconditional Amnesty," which was not a moderate position at the time.[58] They were aligned with left-leaning opinion on at least some issues. Their frustration was due to their inability to maintain the group as one that did not try to represent itself as the voice of all war resisters, and that therefore was more able to help resisters regardless of their ideological beliefs, motivations for immigrating, or future plans.

Thus, resisters tended not to place a value on various forms of draft resistance, including immigration to Canada. On the other hand, a distinction could be made between the attitudes of an individual and the approach of a particular group. There could be a disjunction between members' ideas about the difference in tactics and their group's policy. "Ben," the draft counsellor (an individual who advised young men on their options for avoiding the draft), remembers that anti-draft and antiwar were generally synonymous. While he himself made a distinction between draft dodgers and deserters, the New Mexico Resistance – the anti-draft group he had worked with in the United States in the 1960s and 1970s – was careful not to make the distinction, leaving the choice to the individual:

At the time, I don't think I made much distinction between anti-draft and antiwar. My own concern was with the draft, and interest in the broader peace movement didn't develop until several years later ... In our counselling, we were very emphatic that resisters should *never* accept [being drafted]; that they were much better off to face whatever sanctions awaited them as civilians. I didn't see it as an issue of effective protest ...

[But] I think I made a very sharp distinction in my own mind. Which puzzles me. Even as I worked through the moral issues around resistance, I never applied them to desertion, as it somehow seemed a very different circumstance ...

In the prevailing ethic of the resistance movement, emigrating to Canada was considered less heroic than going to jail – better than serving, even as a non-combatant, but still a bit of a cop-out. I wrestled with the decision when it looked like I would be facing jail myself, and at first resolved that I would go to jail instead, but as the moment of truth got closer, Canada was looking more and more like the better option. (I ended up getting a classification as a conscientious objector, so I never had to make the choice.)[59]

The counselling group "Ben" worked with received training from similar groups in California. Similarly, Mark Phillips, himself a draft counsellor before his arrival in Canada, recalled that the counsellors in Boston were careful not to differentiate between resistance tactics; but individuals nonetheless found resisters particularly intriguing:

In the Boston anti-draft group which I was part of, we used to [try to] persuade people who were about to be inducted that they had one last chance, that sort of thing. We were a bunch of scared college kids really, showing some bravado. But I don't think it was ever debated in those terms. We were instructed to take as even a hand as possible, to give them information rather than to push them in any way. But there was a kind of awe around draft dodgers, let alone actual deserters or resisters who had been in the army, because we knew that their lives were tough.[60]

Thus, deserters might be seen as more awe-inspiring than draft dodgers by the young men counselling them; but the policy of the groups was not to discriminate. However, the element of risk did lend a certain romantic air to deserters and resisters who did not dodge the draft.

Lee Zaslovsky draws a distinction between the tactical issue and differences of how the two groups were perceived:

> I wasn't aware of such a debate [about tactics]. I thought they were both effective [tactics], in that they denied cannon fodder to the US military ... I have always insisted on being known as a deserter rather than a draft dodger, in part because that is an accurate description of me, in part to resist stigmatization of myself or others [through the act of reclaiming the word], since "deserter" is thought by some to be a demeaning term. But I don't think what I did was "better" or more effective than what draft dodgers did.[61]

Regardless of this equivalence in Zaslovsky's eyes, according to Kasinsky, American immigrants reversed the status of the two groups, giving desertion a higher standing since it carried a greater risk. Additionally, as resister David Brown, who arrived in Canada in 1968, points out, there were very good reasons to be afraid for one's personal safety if one decided to go to jail for the cause:

> The floors in the military prisons had a lot of wax on them, and prisoners had a tendency to slip on this wax and break ribs and jaws or sustain damage to their testicles. For this reason many people felt that if you were going to refuse military service and allow yourself to be captured by the pigs (US Department of Justice, or the military, depending on circumstances), it was better to get sent up on civilian charges before induction and go to a US federal prison, rather than get sent up by court martial under UCMJ [the Uniform Code of Military Justice] and go to a military prison ...
>
> No one really knew what was effective and what was not, except that the individual personally could deny his body to the war machine. Then the pigs (Selective Service) would call up someone else, and it would fall to that person to decide whether to allow himself to be inducted or not. But what would happen if they gave a war and nobody came? ... [But] neither [the draft dodger or deserter nor the resister who went to jail] is a tool of American imperialism.[62]

In a similar vein, Hardy Scott recalls that a certain differentiation was imposed by a combination of somewhat romantic notions about desertion and the need to be more careful with deserters at the border:

> The Americans who came to Canada included a wide array of folks. Many were here for what I perceived to be personal and selfish reasons. Some were here because they opposed all war and violence. Others saw that particular war as immoral.
>
> I always considered the deserters to be more daring and greater personal risk-takers. In helping people, deserters and draft dodgers, go into the US from Canada and make the U-turn to come back and apply at the border for immigrant status, I always felt a greater degree of fear when I had deserters in the car.[63] In casual conversation, we would commonly refer to each other as deserters and draft dodgers to identify one's status towards the US authorities.[64]

So, the aid groups, and at least some, if not most, individual American war resisters, did not tend to privilege one tactic over another, or to differentiate between draft dodgers and deserters, apart from their differing material needs.[65]

The question of tactics is linked to the question of whether all, most, some, few, or none of the war resisters made their decision to immigrate solely, or even largely, to oppose the war. There has been a tendency on the part of historians and academics to conclude that most war resisters were ideologically opposed to the war and were likely to go on to become activists of one sort or another.[66] It is likely that at least some of the conclusions of these authors have been based on the biases associated with self-selecting samples.[67] As Phillips states,

> It's an optical illusion [that war resisters were activism-oriented] ... If you follow the people for whom [being activists] was their identity, that distorts the results of a study. You can't just look at the people who were cured of cancer; you have to look at all the smokers. And it's much easier to contact the people who retained that identity ... My own sense is that, if you want to understand the phenomenon, you need a much, much broader lens than that.

I don't think I exaggerate much to say that every little autobiography that you read – certainly a very, very large number of them – carried a kind of secret handshake of that time ... [T]his person's whole life was somehow deflected, changed, reworked, by selective service. They [may] never [have] showed up on the record as draft dodgers, but that was the central preoccupation of two years, four years, six years of his life, and that was true for every single [one.][68]

"James" is an excellent example of a war resister whose motives were antiwar only in the most general sense:

I arrived on the 1st of September, 1967. I have very clear memories of the day and the preparation – why I did it, et cetera. I had been called up [to begin service], and that's why I did it. I had gone through my physical, and I became A-1. In other words, I could be drafted at any time. I wasn't willing to be drafted. I got into Canada before I was actually drafted or was drafted, and then I informed my draft board where I was living and why, and nyah nyah, you can't get me almost. I don't know why I did that, exactly. I was playing everything for number one, me, to stay out of the clutches of the military. That was it; that was pretty well it. I mean, I was against the policies, et cetera, but I really didn't want to get involved with the military, even if there wasn't a war going on, but especially because there was a very dangerous sort of thing going on.[69]

Even if most resisters did not, there is no question that some American war resisters, in particular deserters, did differentiate between the tactics, and so did at least some individual activists within the aid groups. A letter from Francis Marion of the VCAAWO to the Yugoslavian embassy (seeking alternative havens for deserters in the months before the border was opened to them in 1969) stated that the committee saw desertion as "a politically and tactically effective act, and as such we encourage it. We also feel that aiding desertion is a means of lending more than just tacit support to liberation struggles throughout the world and most especially that of the Vietnamese people."[70]

Debate also arose around the question of whether to assimilate into Canadian society or retain American identity. In general, opposition to American policy did not translate into opposition to the presence or behaviour of American individuals. This is an important distinction for a discussion of anti-Americanism among both Americans and Canadians. At the time, a common tendency was nonetheless to conflate individuals with their country of origin, and there existed expectations among some, both Americans and Canadians, of assimilation to various degrees, ranging from behaviour in the movement to citizenship.

The aid groups were in favour of assimilation (or at least were perceived as such), while exile groups pressed Americans to retain their American-ness. Joseph Jones recalls, "The aid groups tended to focus on social work and wanted their clients to assimilate quickly and quietly ... *[AMEX Magazine]* went through several phases, and my direct experience was limited to the final phase, the campaign for amnesty. At the time, I was scarcely aware of the [American Deserter Committees]."[71] In contrast, Phillips's experience illustrates the pressure exile groups brought to bear on war resisters. Phillips remembers the TADP as being among the groups pressuring him to keep his American status, but it was more likely the American exiles he also mentions:

> We had some connection with friends who were involved with the Toronto group ... I think it was the Toronto Anti-Draft Programme, and they seemed to be wanting to keep Americans together as a group, which wasn't my intention ...
>
> I had been active in antiwar activities from a very early age. So, well before Vietnam, my parents were politically very aware ... So I had been involved in [the Committee for a SANE Nuclear Policy] stuff. I had been in big marches. I had been a draft counsellor in Cambridge Mass. I had organized the Vietnam summer group in my home town outside Boston. So, in terms of information, I had as much information as others. But also, I knew in coming to Canada I had made a decision to leave the United States, so I wasn't interested in retaining American-ness, I wasn't interested in the condition of exile.

The exile groups specifically sought to maintain a unity among American resisters, a perspective Phillips did not share:

> When I received my draft notice, I wrote back and said I had left and I wasn't American anymore. And, essentially, they said prove it, and so

I went to the American consulate and renounced my American citizen-ship, which was something the draft groups didn't like, didn't want you to do.[72] Their interest was maintaining a kind of cohesiveness of the Americans in Canada, where I had certainly gone through a struggle about leaving, but it wasn't a struggle about whether I was going to spend the rest of my life as an American. It was a struggle about what was the appropriate action. And having once left, my idea, and I think it was Ruth's [Phillips's wife's] as well, was to make a new life as quickly as possible in my new country.

Phillips specifically remembers being pressured, and he puts the pressure down to anti-US policy sentiment among Americans:

I know I raised the issue around Canadian citizenship and was discour-aged from that ... I can't remember in any specific way that there was anything in the literature ... I don't remember where along the line I came across it, but I remember there was a strong group at U of T whose sense of cohesion was about that, and I really strongly felt the other way around ...

There was obviously a huge amount of anti-Americanism amongst these Americans ... And I may have been responding to the Union of American Exiles as much as anything, which had a presence in Toronto.

I think there was strong assumption, which people shed over time, that, of course in the end you were going to go back. And I just didn't have that assumption from the first moment. The first year in Toronto was the best year of my life. I just loved it.[73]

Generally speaking, the expectation groups had of Americans was driven by their own self-identification – whether as exiles, as immigrants seeking to assimilate, or as Canadians hoping to help Americans choose their own path. Despite some perceptions that they were in favour of Americans' assimilation into Canada, anti-draft activists recall the same neutrality as they held on draft dodgers and deserters when it came to questions of citizenship.

Joan Wilcox of Ottawa AID, herself an American at the time of her involvement, remembers that the group "felt that [citizenship] was an individual choice."[74] Like her, Michael Goldberg recalls, "No one said you ought to [assimilate]. I was probably the strongest anti-American in my group ... I renounced my American citizenship and became a citizen the day it was legal for me to do so."[75] Similarly, Hardy Scott recalls that he "was happy to become a Canadian citizen [as soon as possible] after five years as an immigrant. When the [United States] Justice Department sent me the forms to formally renounce my US citizenship I just threw them away with little thought to the consequences. I was thankful just finally to be a citizen of the country of my choosing."[76] Both Phillips and Goldberg considered the attitudes of some Americans to have been anti-American. Both were talking about opposition to American policy, and not opposition to American people. However, in the case of individual resisters, opposition to American policy meant a need to embody that opposition in their identity – and thus to denounce, renounce, or otherwise oppose their own self-perceived American-ness.

Many war resisters and anti-draft activists believed that separate American exile groups were not a positive development. Different groups and individual activists took different positions on the question. Nancy Pocock, in an interview with Kasinsky in 1970, expressed a belief that Americans should not keep to themselves:

> We found out more about our own country at this time, the differences between Canada and the US ... That it's a less violent society, that they should not bring their Americanism up here. They should just listen for a while and do a lot of reading, try to get to know Canadians. Always pushing them out into knowing Canadians, rather than staying together. We felt it was better for them, and better for their adjustment and better for everybody, if they made contact with Canadians.[77]

Pocock went on to state that most American immigrants were interested in settling in and adjusting well. She agreed with the interviewer that they were "pretty well assimilated." She pointed out that most of the war resisters were not interested in amnesty because they wanted to stay in Canada and become Canadian citizens.[78]

Similarly, one deserter stated, "I think [American exile groups are] a bad idea. Because the Canadian people feel that you're an American exile just waiting for your chance to return. And recently they thought of changing their name to the Union of American Expatriates, which to me has exactly the same meaning. I would be in favour of a name like 'The

New Canadians' because this is my idea, to become a Canadian."[79] On the same question, TADP activist Bill Spira said to Kasinsky,

> Politicization yes, American organizations no. There's absolutely no need for them and I think we're really only talking about a minority of people that come in. For those who are politically aware and have been politically aware in the States, their awareness usually does not go so far as to realize that they are in a different country; all our Coca Cola signs look the same, Americans are not generally known for their understanding of the national aspirations of other people and even the American radicals that come, especially the American radicals, are very insensitive about it. While many of them bring their body here, it takes a good two to three years till their head catches up with them. For the first two years they're still fighting the battle of the imperialists, they'll fight American Imperialism around the Pentagon and this is the thought I'm afraid of in the polls. This is why I'm opposed to organizing Americans as Americans. We have the same spectra of ways of political persuasion that you have in the States and there's absolutely no reason to organize SDS [Students for a Democratic Society] in exile or any of the other groups. We have our Trotskyists and our Maoists and if someone wants to get into that let them organize politically in the Canadian groups, instead of trying to organize Americans as such ... If Canadians and those Americans who are serious really want a way of ending the imperialist role, their role is very clear, try for Canadian independence. In effect we're like an American colony and we have to wage an anti-colonial struggle.

Spira considered real radicals to be the ones who had joined in with Canadian political organizations and antiwar efforts. For him, Americans should support the Canadian movements, not merely import American forms and targets of protest. Later in the interview he added, "I probably misled you when I said they were not political – what I meant was that they were not political activists. I can't think of a single one who hasn't been radicalized in the process at least in their attitudes to the United States. So that will certainly have an impact on Canadian politics." Spira also asserted that the involvement of Canadians in the TADP had led to broader community support for the committee's work, whereas in Vancouver a small group of self-defined exiles alienated the community's support by putting out a newsletter called *The Yankee Refugee,* which was implicitly against assimilation of American immigrants, and which often contained articles denouncing Canadian complicity in the war. He anticipated that the broad appeal of the committee in 1970 would overcome the problems created.[80] This position was no doubt informed by the *realpolitik* of advocating in Canada, with its own specific political and social context; but in its immediate terms, for Spira, it was a question of how and whether to involve Americans in the work.

The opposite viewpoint, that Americans should remain American, was predicated on the assumption that Americans could more effectively oppose the war by opposing the American government as exiles. Americans who organized separately also did so in order to continue to oppose the war. As deserter Fred Gardner wrote in *AMEX,* "[The ADCs do not] put down the other committees as do-gooders; they understand [their] worth ... But the ADC people want – for themselves and their constituents – to retain their political identity as Americans. The objective of their counselling is not a smooth adjustment to Canada, but continued opposition to the war and confrontation with the Mother Country."[81] Similarly, Joseph Jones gravitated towards the exile groups once he had become settled because he sought an outlet as an American immigrant to oppose the policies of the American government:

When I came to Canada, I believed that I could never return to the United States and that I needed to establish myself. This was a primary reason for avoiding connections with any American groups, although I did attend scattered events, meetings, and demonstrations ... After I had been in Canada for three years, I was a graduate student with a good fellowship and felt established. In the summer of 1973, I connected with the people at *[AMEX],* liked the group, and agreed with the politics. Part of my motivation was to put my exile in the face of the United States. The two fundamental issues were the ongoing injustices of the Vietnam War and the wide range of people whose lives might be improved by a universal unconditional amnesty (not least the deserters who could not get established in Canada) ... For two years, I regularly participated in meetings, demonstrations, magazine production, and media work ... For a while we had a separate group oriented toward this called the Toronto American Exiles Association.[82]

The use of the word "exile," likely popularized by the magazine *AMEX* (short for "American Exile"), carries with it connotations of affiliation with the country of origin. Mark Phillips's surmise that self-identified exiles expected to return to the United States was therefore not surprising, and probably accurate.

There was a connection between these tensions and the emerging notions of left nationalists that Canada was in a colonial position vis-à-vis the United States. Often, the assumption made by American exile groups was that Canada was an actual colony of the United States – a view they shared with activists like Spira who were opposed to American-only organizations. As Tom, a deserter Kasinsky interviewed, put it succinctly,

> I think that Americans in Canada have a lot to contribute. It's the old melting pot thing. Canada doesn't quite melt, though – everything just kind of sits there. There's not this pressure to conform to some Anglo Saxon way of life. But, the Americans as such can offer a lot. Especially to Canadian politics, Canadian groups, and things like that. Also because we have to stick together to assist people coming up.

Although these comments do not suggest a clear idea of what exactly Americans could actually contribute to the Canadian groups, they also indicate a perception of Canada as a mosaic, a notion connected to the idea of Canada as welcoming. These comments also suggest an underlying assumption that Americans were better off preserving their American-ness. Tom did not believe it was possible to assimilate so much that one could ignore the United States completely, partly because of the similarity between the two countries and their people:

> It's possible to assimilate and become a Canadian, but I think it's kind of foolish to imagine there's nothing there beyond the border, whereas actually it affects your whole life as a Canadian ... Little things from the US influence everything. The bad things of the US seep in, and of course the US corporations own so much of Canada. You're fooling yourself ... a lot of people ... say they've dropped out and this is it. Canada. Start off anew. And you know, you can't do it. Canada's the 51st state, for all intents and purposes ... I'll always be an American. I can't help it.[83]

The pages of *AMEX* captured some of the discussion – and displayed the connections to the burgeoning left nationalist movement. As one writer explained, "We can help by joining in and helping a young but growing movement for Canadian Independence. By studying things like the Watkins report on Foreign Ownership of Industry ... By informing our many contacts Stateside of the concrete situation with regard to US domination and the growing resistance to it."[84] The article suggested that real Canadian nationalists should see draft dodgers and deserters as allies in their cause, and not react "chauvinistically" – that is, in a biased and prejudiced way – to average working-class Americans. The article encouraged the formation of autonomous Unions of American Exiles, as long as they did not "adopt weird ideas of Canadian nationalism" such as those asserting the importance of assimilation.[85]

Some historical accounts have asserted that Canadians in general, and not only anti-draft activists, wanted Americans to assimilate, and certainly there is some evidence of such a viewpoint.[86] Sometimes, left nationalism manifested itself as anti-American sentiment.[87] For instance, influential leftist Robin Mathews, an academic and promoter of the so-called Canadianization movement, wrote a letter to the Department of Immigration in 1969 stating,

> If the reasons for difficulty at the present time are that the Canadian government fears to offend the US govt., then the Canadian government deserves the criticism it is receiving. If the Canadian govt. fears the results of influx, then it had better set up citizenship courses that make possible for immigrants some idea of Canada other than that it is a cow to be milked by whatever hand reaches for the udder.[88]

The letter was, paradoxically, one among many exhorting the government to open the border to deserters. However, its decidedly ambivalent tone reflected a tendency among at least some Canadians who saw themselves as progressive to see American immigrants' resistance to assimilation, and their influence on Canadian activism, as a problem.

However, most individual American war resisters apparently encountered very little of this sort of thing. For instance, Lee Zaslovsky recalls, "I never encountered anti-Americanism among Canadians until the past decade. I was sort of anti-American myself in a way – I had seen some of the 'ugly American' side of things in the years before I came to Canada, both personally and as a member of the American public ... I regarded myself from very early on as a 'New Canadian.'"[89] He continues,

> My own view was that I had come to a new country, and I had little prospect of ever returning to the US, so I should adapt as quickly as I could, become involved in Canadian life, and take up Canadian citizenship when I could. (I applied the day I was eligible.) I know others saw themselves as "exiles" and tried to influence American events, et cetera. I didn't.[90]

On the other hand, while Joseph Jones does not recall personal negative experiences, his recollections reflect the increased Canadian nationalism of the early 1970s:

> For the first seven years, I mainly lived in student ghettos in large cities and went to university. I had no negative experiences and encountered occasional personal sympathy from people – like the mother in Montreal who sold me her son's used bicycle through a newspaper ad. Generally, I felt invisible, which is what I was aiming to be ...
>
> Some UBC administrator involved with student housing wanted to see Americans who came to Canada "burning their bridges." If I had been more sensitive I might have noticed more.[91]

Similarly, Marvin Work recalls a possible effect of Mathews's movement:

> In the early 1970s, there was a wave of Canadian nationalism that was heavily anti-American. It suddenly became much more difficult for an American professor to come to a Canadian university or for a school teacher to teach in a Canadian school. Documentation was required showing that there were no qualified Canadian citizens available who could do that particular job. I was glad that I no longer had a strong American accent![92]

Of course, we need to take into account that these recollections were quite subjective and that other factors were at play in the shift to hiring Canadians on Canadian campuses. Meanwhile, others had no recollection of such sentiments, at least when it came to the anti-draft movement.[93] Mark Phillips describes that his and his partner's "experience was of overwhelming welcome":

> We were amazed by how supportive, how open, how liberal the country was towards us. The symbol of that for me was that we ended up going to London for Ruth to pursue her doctorate ... the two of us on Canada Council fellowships. We thought, what kind of amazing utopian country is this? ... And that support seemed to be there in daily life.
>
> There were occasional remarks; the doctor who examined me in ... Vancouver said to me inappropriately, "Well I guess they would have taken you!" So there were a few signs of negativeness, but not much.[94]

Carolyn Egan, war resister in Toronto, recalls a generally welcoming atmosphere in the women's movement:

> I was aware that I was American, and you got the odd barb about [being American], because there was a certain Canadian nationalism around, and you did get that on occasion. I think, and I don't know how broad this was or widespread, but I think Americans coming here were very conscious of being American in a different country and therefore being respectful or sensitive to that, and I think even the use of "I'm an American," well, this is North America, how do Canadians even view the word ... You were never sure how people would take things. But on the whole, because there were a fair number of Americans in the progressive movements here at the time, I don't think it was a stumbling block at all. I think people were aware of where we were coming from ... I think that the acceptance and the ability to function politically as an American in Canada was not a stumbling block.[95]

Overall, it seems that Canadians made a distinction between the actions of the American government and the individual Americans they encountered. However, occasionally, as in the case of Robin Mathews and others, the distinction was not so clear, likely because of the rise of Canadian nationalism as a form of resistance to American influence on several aspects of Canadian society.

Policing the Anti-Draft Movement: The RCMP and the FBI

The debates over the place and role of Americans in Canada were reflected in other aspects of anti-draft movement interactions with state apparatuses, including both police forces and immigration officials. The police contributing to this interaction often took the form of harassment and surveillance of anti-draft groups and war resisters.

Debates about politics in the anti-draft movement only sometimes focused on the issue of the effect of American immigrants on Canadian antiwar efforts. For government and the police, however, how to address what they perceived as a problem of an increasing presence of American immigrants was the central question. This presence and their support network were often seen as disruptive by government officials in the Department of Immigration. In Gramscian terms, this was a skirmish, in the battle for hegemony, over the population's attitudes towards war resisters. The actions of police and Department of Immigration officials illustrate that some sections of Canadian society and some government officials did not support the war resisters. Immigration Department officials discussed the potentially bad influence of US immigrants on Canadian society. Meanwhile, federal police conducted raids on war resisters and their supporters, and the RCMP kept dozens of groups under constant surveillance throughout the period.[96]

Police behaviour was a reflection of opposition to the war resisters among Canadians. At the same time, government actions such as the decision to open the border reflected the opposing view in what can be understood as a hegemonic struggle over the treatment and perception of war resisters. Anti-resister and pro-resister sentiment, anti-draft group priorities, police behaviour, bureaucrats' opinions, and government actions were in a state of constant change and conflict that was never completely resolved, although the balance shifted in favour of the war resisters in late 1969 and stayed there until well into the 1970s.

Many anti-draft groups attracted the attention of the RCMP. For many war resisters, it was a matter of fact that RCMP officials were sharing information with the FBI. As Michael Goldberg recalls,

> When I came up here, I had my job [in Vancouver], and I obviously didn't report [to the draft board], but I sent a letter – one of the tactics

that was standard was to send as much paper as possible and delay as long as you could, so the file just got bigger and bigger and bigger. You know, like, send them a phone book and say, "Here, my number's in the phone book" ... Eventually, they got fed up and just said, "If you don't show up on X day, you will be declared absent, and your information will be sent to the FBI" ...

And about two months later, I was visited by the RCMP at my workplace in Vancouver, so clearly the stuff went to the FBI, and the FBI asked the RCMP. And what they were interested in was, "Are you planning to stay in Canada?" And I said, "Wait a minute. What are you doing their work for?" But they were simply saying, "Is this going to be an active case, or should we shut this thing down?" They were clear that I was going to stay [in Canada]. But the fact that they had no authority but that they would do the work [of the FBI] just appalled me. I was just astounded.[97]

Goldberg's assumption that RCMP officers were working directly with the FBI was widespread. And as early as 1966, the RCMP appeared to acknowledge it, suggesting that FBI agents operated directly in Canada, accompanied by RCMP.[98]

If an official policy to this effect existed, it was negotiated in or after 1966.[99] It is probable that the question was considered as part of a government response to scrutiny around the case of Glen Briscoe of Clark Road, Port Moody, British Columbia, a Canadian who had turned eighteen in Canada and whose mother had been interviewed by FBI agent Alfie Gunn about his failure to register for the draft.[100] Opposition MPs in the House of Commons took the government to task over the event, and soon Prime Minister Lester Pearson agreed that it was improper.[101] Internal discussion in the Department of External Affairs during that week shows that a flurry of correspondence followed to determine what arrangements, if any, existed between the two countries in the area of police jurisdiction. After polling the RCMP and Privy Council, the Department of Immigration determined that the arrangements were informal and implied rather than written or negotiated. The RCMP's stance was that any FBI interrogations were in fact conducted with the aim of referring individuals to the RCMP. The Privy Council office communicated that they

[had] been unable to find on our files any general record of instruction to either the Department of Justice or the RCMP regarding RCMP – FBI co-operation. There may be such instructions, and there may be instructions giving explicit guidance on how police, Federal or other, are to perform any duties which might bring them into Canada but we are unable to locate them. Nor have we found any record of a communication from the RCMP or the Dept of Justice giving direct or explicit information about any such arrangements between Canadian and US police authorities.[102]

The Privy Council Office said there were implied arrangements, due to previous cases of confusion about police jurisdiction that had resulted in protests to the US government being made by the Canadian government.[103] Thereby, the executive branch refused any responsibility in the matter. But in April 1966, the government sent instructions to Washington to "make representations" on the question, calling for "no departure from the established procedures."[104] In the eyes of the government, the Briscoe incident had been a departure from normal practice.[105]

While insisting that the arrangements with the US government were long-standing and consistent, Cabinet decided to establish an interdepartmental committee of officials to consider more formal procedures for cooperation, so that the "present informal arrangements [would] be modified ... so that in these matters contact by mail only, and not personal contract as heretofore, [would] be provided between special agents of the FBI and persons located in Canada."[106] Thus, the call for accountability in the House led to a call for more accountability in the administration, if not an admission of impropriety.

Indeed, it may have been this police activity that initiated public interest in the question of war resisters in Canada in the first place, as media picked up and highlighted the issue. In May, External Affairs senior staff prepared briefings on possible questions in the House of Commons on the issue of the FBI in Canada following a CBC television news program that had claimed that young American draft dodgers were arriving in the country.[107] Undersecretary Marcel Cadieux explained that no government position, nor any treaty allowing for expulsion or even the prevention of entry of draft dodgers, existed, and no representations had been made by the US government. "Probably most of the young men involved purport to enter as visitors and maybe in some cases they will try later on to obtain landed immigrant status in Canada," Cadieux stated prophetically, suggesting that Canada should avoid the impression of becoming an "asylum for such US citizens."[108] By October, still no representations had been received from the US government, and the positioning of External Affairs and that of the Department of Immigration had been synchronized.[109]

Controversy surrounding FBI-RCMP cooperation continued throughout 1966 with journalist allegations that plainclothes FBI agents had conducted searches for deserters in Vancouver, apparently unaccompanied by the RCMP. These incidents became more frequent, increasing public concern and scrutiny of police behaviour. The RCMP spied on anti-draft groups' everyday activities and their events, and on groups with informal links to them and to war resisters. The Regina Committee of American Deserters, for instance, experienced surveillance and questioning by RCMP and local police.[110]

Public concerns about police behaviour often played out most effectively in the debates over war resisters through scrutiny in the media. Police behaviour was both a reflection of and an influence on public concerns about both war resisters and the official response to their presence in Canada. Police raids and surveillance activities reflected divisions among ruling elites and the general public. This tension also expressed itself in internal discussions among government officials.

Police surveillance reflected official paranoia about Americans and their influence on Canadian society. Police attitudes reflected debates occurring among government bureaucrats, especially in the Department of Immigration. The Department of Immigration and the RCMP exchanged correspondence during the year following the government's 1966 White Paper on Immigration and the initial trickle of war resisters arriving in Canada. The RCMP raised concerns about how immigration policy was being enforced by the regional offices of the Department of Immigration. In one exchange in October 1967, the RCMP's M.J. Nadon, the superintendent and officer in charge of the Criminal Investigation Branch, wrote to the director of immigration, Home Branch, suggesting that immigration officials were withholding information necessary for a criminal investigation from the RCMP because they were considered an "outside agency."

Nadon was inquiring if the action taken by regional officials reflected a change in policy or a mistake by Winnipeg staff.[111] The interdepartmental tension rose following a new arrangement of powers over immigrants, coinciding with the 1966-67 regulatory shifts in immigration policy in which the RCMP's powers to deport were curtailed.

From the perspective of the anti-draft groups, police behaviour constituted harassment. The scale of the surveillance is remarkable. The police surveillance and internal discussions between and among departmental officials show that there were divisions both at the top and at the bottom of society – part of the hegemonic process.

Deserters and draft dodgers were treated and perceived differently, by activists, groups, and government. American immigrant groups, in part responding to this treatment, decided to organize separately as "exiles" or "refugees." Although most activists did not place a value on different draft resistance tactics, the debate that did exist, and the very formation of the American groups, impacted groups' policy on assimilation. While opposition to American policy and the influence of American institutions in Canada among the Canadian Left was connected to this push for assimilation, for the most part the anti-Americanism that did exist did not have a great effect on individual resisters.

To the antiwar activists of the early twenty-first century, some of these debates may ring familiar. The debates were quite acrimonious at times. These discussions interacted and combined in ways that produced a minefield of obstacles to effective coordinated action on the part of the movement. Its capacity to continue to be effective as a movement is a testimony to its rapid maturation. These debates continued to develop with consequences that made themselves felt in ongoing efforts to improve the situation for war resisters. Debates about the role of Americans in the antiwar movement were connected to broader concepts and ideas held by Canadians about their country and its relationship to the United States.

Although activists were debating politics, the anti-draft groups, whether exile groups or not, along with individual Canadians and American immigrants, still engaged in coordinated campaigns that were clearly aimed at affecting Canadian politics. The most important of these was the 1969 campaign to remove barriers to deserters attempting to enter Canada and gain landed immigrant status. The debates outlined above were reflected to some degree in various aspects of the campaign. Further, and more importantly, ideas that may be termed "left nationalist" were present in almost every debate on the Canadian Left in the late 1960s and early 1970s, and the war resister support movement was no exception. These ideas were a driving force in the campaign to open the Canadian border to deserters in 1969.

4

Opening the Border

1969

One of the first things I noticed
when I arrived in Canada
was that men seem to
write on bathroom walls
less than they do in the US

Yes, I thought, the people are sane
here; they do not have to
relieve their aggressions
by writing on bathroom walls.

Since then I've been thinking
maybe they wash the walls in
the bathrooms every night
or maybe it's because there's
less people or maybe it's
because they are not as violent
or maybe they are just lost
for words.

– Wayne Padgett, "Do People in Canada
Write on Bathroom Walls Less?" [1]

For the Canadian government, the immediate need in 1968 was to be a full partner with other strong postwar nations such as the United States and France. Economic interests heavily invested in the war in Vietnam and allies to the south might reasonably be expected to react negatively to the presence of war resisters in Canada, and, indeed, many internal communications at the Department of Manpower and Immigration reflected exactly that anxiety. However, as time wore on and the negative reaction was not, to all appearances, forthcoming, the historic bloc came to see the advantages of opening the border as outweighing the more nebulous disadvantages. The movement to support war resisters took full advantage of this underlying ambivalence, and in the end, they tipped the scales.

In mid-1968, the Department of Immigration's immigration manual, which guided the actions of officers at the border, was amended by a directive to allow the use of discretion to assess whether an applicant had an unfulfilled legal, contractual, or moral obligation in their country of origin. Instead of requiring proof of discharge from the military, immigration officers now had the "discretion" to refuse an applicant, even if they met all other criteria, if they suspected that there were obligations that might make it difficult for the applicant to settle in Canada. A list of examples of such obligations was provided to the officers, and one was military status.[2] This measure encouraged immigration officers to question the military status of young American men, both draft dodgers and deserters; and while previously, if they had not volunteered the information, they had a fairly good chance of being able to enter the country, now all resisters began to feel the effects of the new directive.

Thus, although, strictly speaking, military status remained irrelevant under Canadian immigration law, though regulations applied in practice, immigration officers were prejudiced against deserters and prevented them from entering, going so far as to report them to American authorities as they returned to the American side. As opponents claimed, this prejudice was encouraged by the regulatory regime. At first, the minister and his staff denied the existence of the new instructions. In the end, the discretionary power was removed, partly because of a pan-Canadian and coordinated campaign undertaken by Canadian anti-draft groups and war-resister supporters.

Anti-draft groups took various types of action to pressure the government against refusing entry to deserters. In addition, likely at the encouragement of the anti-draft groups, hundreds of individual Canadians wrote letters to the minister of manpower and immigration, Allan MacEachen, for the same reason. At the same time, lobbying efforts took place. The movement also made a special use of the mass media. In this skirmish in the broader battle for hegemony, the movement made significant steps in the "war of position."[3] However limited, the result was an unprecedented opening for Vietnam War resisters to make their way to Canada.

Regulatory Changes and Departmental Exchanges, 1966-69

Early 1960s discussions in the Department of Immigration suggested that attracting American immigrants would be a good policy for the Canadian job market, which then lacked skilled labourers.[4] In 1962, for instance, internal discussion indicated that, despite ongoing changes to the Canadian immigration regulations, the preferential treatment of American immigrants would not be affected; they would still only be required to be "of good health, of good character, and have sufficient funds to maintain themselves until they have obtained employment."[5] Moreover, a mid-1965 memo from the deputy minister, J.L.E. Couillard, to R.B. Curry, assistant deputy minister (immigration), outlined Cabinet approval of a plan to initiate an "active program ... to attract suitable immigrants to Canada from the United States.[6] In 1966, Department of Immigration correspondence continued to show a desire by immigration officials to see increased immigration from the United States.[7] By then, however, the draft dodger issue was beginning to complicate things. For instance, the United States was still seen as a potential source of skilled workers, being conveniently located and highly educated; most American immigrants had pre-arranged job prospects, although they did not know much about Canada.[8] Although the war in Vietnam was identified as a factor that encouraged immigration to the benefit of Canadian employers, the "draft dodger issue" caused some concerns about appearing to encourage war resisters. In a 1966 branch-wide memo, R.B. Curry, assistant deputy minister (immigration), listed uncritically some "social factors" in the United States at the moment that were encouraging immigration: "the coloured problem ... the war in Vietnam ... the economic situation and loss of gold reserves." He insisted, however, that the department "should take into account the potential sensitivity of the draft dodger issue."[9]

In August 1967, Canada introduced, through an Order-in-Council and a set of regulations, a new protocol for establishing the eligibility of potential immigrants to come to Canada. Called the points system, it was supposed to remove any bias from the immigration process, in contrast to the previous system, which had relied on quotas of immigrants from specific countries – a practice seen as racist because it excluded people based on their country of origin. Some historians have agreed with the official story and understood this shift to be motivated by a desire to eliminate racism in immigration policy; others have seen it as purely an economic measure to address changes in the postwar labour market.[10] In any event, the changes were significant. Under the points system, potential immigrants answered a questionnaire about their education and skills and were awarded points on that basis; some points were still awarded at the discretion of immigration officers. Fifty points were required to be successful. The general outline of the system was the following: up to twenty points could be awarded for education; ten for vocational training; fifteen for occupational demand; ten for age; ten for a job offer (at the border only); ten for language; fifteen for personal suitability; five for a relative living in Canada; and five for destination.[11] Accompanying the new system's implementation was section 34 of the regulations, which allowed entry to the country as a visitor and subsequent application for "landed immigrant" status from inside Canada.[12] In 1967, legislation also introduced the Immigration Appeal Board, which would experience a significant backlog by the late sixties.[13]

The changes in the system were announced, at first, as part of Pierre Trudeau's 1966 White Paper on Immigration. The White Paper called for increased immigration, but also for the creation of categories of barred immigrants. The policy incorporated categories of people to be automatically barred from entry to Canada, membership in which could be only subjectively judged by immigration officers. It also endorsed earlier moves away from quota systems. In general, it laid the groundwork for the points system. From the outset, anti-draft activists saw the potential legal pitfalls of the new immigration proposals. In May 1967, the Vancouver Committee to Aid American War Objectors (VCAAWO) wrote a letter to Minister of Immigration Jean Marchand, Deputy Minister Tom Kent, Minister of Justice Pierre Trudeau, and MPs Andrew Brewin and Gérard Pelletier. The letter objected to the White Paper on Immigration's "stress on the need to re-evaluate those classes of people who should be barred from Canada because they represent a danger to public health and safety

... The White Paper proposes a new prohibited class, 'fugitives from justice.' We feel that this proposal ... might restrict the immigration into Canada of Americans who refuse to participate in the war in Vietnam."[14]

The VCAAWO included with their letter a submission, "A Note on Fugitives from Justice," in the form of a brief – a method whose choice probably stemmed from the involvement of intellectuals in the anti-draft movement. The brief suggested that such a category could conflict with existing treaties, that the term was difficult to define, that administration would prove difficult, that the category would invite biased manipulation, and that the measure would contravene "one of Canada's oldest traditions" in its restriction of entry of war resisters – an idea that was taking hold in Canada, and that would be used to good effect in the campaign to open the border in 1969. The brief also made a prophetic statement regarding the future pressures on the department. The VCAAWO was arguing that by including the "fugitives from justice" category as not admissible to Canada, the Canadian government would, in effect, be taking a position on the American draft – a position they might not be able to defend:

> Should this [category] be written into law, then the Immigration Department will have to take a definite stance on offences against American draft laws ... The Immigration Department will no longer be able to rely on the argument it has used up to now that "there is no basis in law for barring their entry" [a quote from a letter from then Deputy Minister Tom Kent to *Ramparts Magazine* in September of 1966]. In order to maintain the present policy the ... Department will have to defend that policy by a political argument about the nature of obligations laid upon American citizens by their government, and about Canada's ... recognition or non-recognition of the "justice" of these obligations.[15]

The brief also asserted that immigration officials would adopt a policy of rejecting all war resisters if only some draft-related offences were considered part of a "fugitive from justice category" of immigrant: "It could well become the practice of most immigration officials to deny entry to any American eligible for the draft." The brief concluded by suggesting that, if the clause were to remain in the law, then it should be defined as applying to non-military and non-political offences and should apply only to cases in which the law being broken is also a Canadian law.[16] Thus, they suggested that, for immigrants to be excluded, they needed to have committed an offence that broke a Canadian law – to which their military status bore no relevance.[17] War resisters were breaking American laws by coming to Canada, but, the VCAWWO argued, they should not be considered law-breakers in the eyes of Canada. It should be noted here that no extradition agreements existed for military personnel unless they had deserted while on duty in Canada, and these agreements had not existed for some time.[18] Be that as it may, these words fell on deaf ears, and the fugitives from justice exclusion category proposed in the White Paper survived into the new system in 1967. Perhaps concerns about the draft dodger question as expressed by Curry in 1966 had even encouraged the government's eventual decision to create the category.

The public story of regulatory changes in the Department of Immigration between 1967 and 1968 is very different from the discussions and actions by department officials that were occurring behind the scenes. In other words, the government said one thing while doing quite another. The backstory also shows the strength of the bureaucracy in proposing its own solutions to various problems, even against the opinions of the minister. This tale diverges significantly from the common notion of civil service mandarins hand-picked for their political loyalties – with autonomy, to be sure, but operating within a specific framework.[19] It also shows that, during a short period of time, changes took place at such a rapid pace that the minister of immigration seemed to be forced to react immediately to public pressure and public opinion, rather than proactively initiating policy with some measure of autonomy. Governments always respond to some extent to public pressure; but departmental analysis that might normally have allowed MacEachen to anticipate public reaction and weather various storms in this case failed him, and he was in a reactive mode for several months.

Almost immediately after the implementation of the points system in August 1967, resisters began encountering problems at the border that had not existed before. In fact, the increased occurrences began before its implementation, indicating that public discussions around the White Paper had an impact on immigration officer behaviour well before 1967. In response to these occurrences, in late 1967, the VCAAWO wrote a second brief, "A Note on the Handling of Draft-Age Immigrants to Canada," a document aimed at informing then Deputy Minister of Immigration Tom

Kent (who served under Minister Jean Marchand until July 1968) about the discrimination against draft-age Americans at the border during the preceding several months. The brief appended statements from thirty-six recent arrivals whose experience with officials had been negative. The brief argued that false information was being provided to applicants by immigration officials at consulates in the United States, border crossings, airports, and immigration offices inside Canada. Many of the examples cited were cases of conscious and explicit obstruction by immigration officers.[20] Immigration officers, the brief argued, had been using various methods to obstruct entry, including withholding of readily available forms; refusal to process border applications; refusal to recognize qualifications; refusal to grant medical examinations; and random application of rules whose existence was dubious, such as parental consent or marital status, or amount of cash on hand. These practices, the group asserted, stood in stark contrast to a new system that was supposed to be free of bias. Generally, the cases cited described "derogatory, sarcastic, offensive, and generally discouraging" attitudes on the part of immigration officials. The brief asserted that personal views were motivating these officers, and that such personal "biases" ought not to play a part in the decision of whether to accept immigration applicants. Indeed, the authors suspected a too-great degree of autonomy was being granted the officers, which was significant because the regulation encouraging the use of discretion would not be introduced until the following summer. In one border station, the officers falsely cited a new "policy" of requiring applicants to apply by mail, which apparently came into force "around the end of July." Another indicated that "the laws are going to be changed 'to keep people like you out of Canada.'" A photocopy of an immigration form was attached to one of the thirty-six cases, accompanied by a handwritten note from an immigration officer in Douglas, British Columbia, that read, "Note: wishes to apply for permanent admission, Ops Memo 117??" Still unbeknownst to the brief's authors, this note was an explicit reference to the instruction to immigration officers that initially required proof of discharge for admission to Canada, which was amended a short time later to list military status as possible grounds for exclusion from entry.[21]

The brief used the accumulation of cases as proof of a systemic problem. It argued that its "sample" could have been much larger, but that the cases had been selected to present a "gamut" of experiences. The brief called for changes in regulations to instruct immigration officers not to inquire regarding draft status; to make forms available upon request, along with a summary of criteria applied; and to process American applicants at the border. It also recommended closer supervision of immigration officers, clearer directives to the officers, and elimination of provisions that could be applied according to personal biases.[22]

The anti-draft movement found Tom Kent, then deputy minister of immigration, communicative; their correspondence began in 1966 and continued until 1968 when Kent became the deputy minister of the Department of Regional Economic Expansion, and was replaced as deputy minister by J.L.E. Couillard.[23] Kent replied to the Vancouver committee's brief at length in November 1967, issuing reassurances that were consistent with earlier statements. As Renée Kasinsky recounted in *Refugees from Militarism*, in 1966, Kent had penned a letter to *Ramparts Magazine* stating that potential draftees were not barred from entering Canada.[24] Perhaps he was merely expressing what he believed to be his own department's policy.

The Department of Immigration opened a "Draft Dodgers – Complaints and Criticisms" file in late 1967. The file at this time was full of newspaper clippings on the issue of draft dodgers and deserters.[25] At this point, immigration officers were still not directed not to inquire into draft status. In late 1967, with this increased public attention in mind, Kent wrote to his counterpart in the Department of External Affairs, Undersecretary of State Marcel Cadieux, to express his department's growing concern about the immigration of deserters: "There seems to be little doubt that public opinion is developing in a way that would make any deportation of a deserter highly controversial." Although deserters were not legally a prohibited class of immigrant, Kent worried to Cadieux that to allow American deserters to immigrate would provide uncomfortable comparisons for treatment of Canadian deserters, who faced "heavy penalties": "One can urge, of course, that the cases are not completely analogous; we are not engaged in a highly controversial war and we do not have a draft. But the distinction is a difficult one." Kent asked for advice about this apparent public relations quandary and for information regarding any indication of American government opinion about deserters immigrating to Canada. He noted that, as the numbers of deserters were likely to increase, it would be wise to think ahead.[26] Thus, Kent expressed his belief that the Department of External

Affairs had a role to play in setting policy, or at least that US government opinion was something to be taken into account.

Adding to this new immigration situation for deserters was the fact that, until January of 1968, proof of discharge had been required to process immigration applications. Between January and July of 1968, such proof was no longer required for applicants from within Canada, but was still required for applicants from outside the border. Deserters were able therefore to enter Canada as visitors and, once in Canada, apply for landed immigrant status. In July 1968, the government "withdrew" this practice and secretly replaced it with "discretion" by immigration officers on whether to consider or disregard military status.[27] The trouble was that reports from the border suggested that many, if not most, border officials were more frequently using their discretion to exclude draft dodgers and deserters from entering the country. In fact, internal departmental memos indicate that this regulation change was specifically intended to prevent deserters from entering Canada.[28] At first, this policy was not public, and anti-draft groups could only form suspicions. When the policy became public knowledge, immigration officials, especially the minister, found themselves under fire in the House of Commons and in the media for keeping the policy secret, and they were accused of circumventing public debate.

The lobbying efforts of the anti-draft movement were making themselves felt. In late January 1968, NDP MP for Kootenay West Herbert Herridge received a letter from Kent that stated,

People seeking admission to Canada must be examined either as immigrants or non-immigrants as defined in the Immigration Act. Those seeking permanent residence, as most deserters do, must be dealt with as prospective immigrants, and this means among other things that they must be able to meet the requirements set forth in Sections 31, 32, 33, or 34 of the Immigration Regulations, copies of which I am enclosing.

Section 34 of the Regulations ... makes admission contingent on various qualities which are objectively stated and assessed on a point rating basis. There is, however, no specific reference in this assessment to someone's military status in his home country. Therefore, if an applicant is otherwise able to meet normal immigration requirements he has nothing to fear from this department regarding his military status.[29]

Also in January of 1968, Herridge received a letter from the minister of manpower and immigration, Jean Marchand, which stated, in part, "It is not the policy of the Government to encourage the admission of military deserters or draft dodgers. However, if someone in either of these circumstances applies in Canada for immigrant status and otherwise meets the conditions set out in the Immigration Act and Regulations, there are no legally valid grounds under our present legislation for denying his application."[30] These letters coincided with the window, between January and July 1968, in which proof of discharge was not required at the border, and the instructions regarding legal, moral, and contractual obligations had not yet been issued. The situation was not to last long.

Both letters found their way into the files of the Vancouver Committee. The committee apparently communicated with BC members of Parliament as well as with Cabinet members such as Marchand.[31] The minister's and deputy minister's answers were very similar, which indicates that at this point, at least, there was a degree of internal coherence that was reflected in the department's public face.

Despite the earlier statements from the Ministry of Manpower and Immigration, experiences at the border did not change, and, in fact, they became worse after the secret directive was issued. The VCAAWO's predictions of bias appeared to be coming true. In 1969, the *New York Times* reported that Canada was considering closing the border to deserters completely and had already issued a memorandum to its personnel restricting entry for most deserters. The article reported that officials had been instructed on 29 July 1968 to consider whether applicants were currently serving members of the military. As a result, Toronto counsellors were encouraging applications from within Canada. The article went on to describe how immigration department officials were considering defining deserters as a prohibited class. In the article, James S. Cross of the Department of Immigration pointed out that military status was "only one of five guidelines laid down to help ... determine when to reject applicants who [meet] other criteria." The other examples included family desertion and debt.[32] A *Vancouver Sun* report stated that the Department of Immigration was denying any crackdown on deserters.[33] The instructions to immigration officers were also reported in the *Globe and Mail* on 30 January 1969. A *Baltimore Sun* report placed the first issuance of the instructions in January 1968.[34] Many of these reports were probably derived from reading other newspaper stories.

Internal Department of Immigration correspondence shows that the purpose of the guidelines directive issued in July of 1968 to immigration officers was to exclude draft dodgers.[35] As a May 1969 memo from Assistant Deputy Minister R.B. Curry later stated, "While 24.03 12(g) [immigration regulation] was designed to exclude deserters, the public posture has been that its purpose was to give examples of various 'substantial legal, contractual or moral obligations,' to our officers which they should take into account in the exercise of their discretion."[36] Several writers whose letters were filed by the Department of Immigration guessed as much. These letters, taken together, indicated a high degree of coordination of content, shared ideas about a Canadian tradition of pacifism, and awareness of media and pressure campaigns being waged by anti-draft groups. The two examples below indicate that members of the public suspected that bureaucrats operated separately from government, and that the practice of barring war resisters at the border was no accident:

"I suspect some bureaucrat with an inflated sense of his own wisdom has circulated a memorandum with the intention of bending the law to suit his own political views. I certainly hope this discrimination is not official government policy."
  – *Angus M. Taylor, Toronto, to MacEachen, 12 February 1969*

"Why are some bureaucrats in the Immigration Ministry able to enforce their petty decisions or feelings, over and above the apparent policy of the minister? I feel this needs looking into."
  – *Ray Morgan, Toronto, to Donald A. McDonald [sic], MP, Rosedale,*
    31 January 1969

Although the origins of the July 1968 guidelines to exclude deserters using immigration officers' discretionary powers are unclear, department records indicate, as suspected, that the decision was made by Kent shortly before he left the post at the Department of Immigration.[37] Indeed, internal memos suggest that, despite his public statements, Kent knew that even some draft dodgers were already being turned away if they did not intend to stay in Canada – that is, if they were using the possibility of entering as visitors as a way to seek refuge from the draft and nothing else.[38] In effect, the instructional memo issued in July 1968 was an endorsement of already existing, but less formal, practices of excluding war resisters from Canada. In any event, once the instructional memo became public (as a result of the anti-draft movement campaign), the department claimed that the decision had been made

> on the basis of a decision made by the former Deputy Minister, Mr. Kent, prior to his departure. He felt there was no basis under the Immigration Act or regulations to instruct immigration officers to refuse an application from a deserter and that the only way that their entry might be prevented was in the exercise of the discretion granted to them under ... the Regulations. As already stated, the purpose of the July 29 amendment was to provide the officers with guidelines on the use of their discretion.[39]

In January 1969, the VCAAWO prepared a third brief, "A Further Note on the Handling of Draft-Age Americans Who Apply for Entry into Canada." The brief formed a part of the campaign, now begun in earnest, to open the border. Like the earlier "Note on the Handling of Draft-Age Immigrants to Canada," it cited examples of biased behaviour by immigration officials in the treatment of American visitors and applicants for entry, and it included statements by American men and women that testified to their ill treatment by border officials and others. It called explicitly for the elimination of discrimination against deserters, since it was legal for them to enter if they were otherwise qualified.[40] The brief was delivered to MPs, followed by lobbying by Jim Wilcox of the Ottawa group and others.[41] This seems to have been the first brief that the VCAAWO used in coordination with other anti-draft groups. The Vancouver Committee probably led the campaign because of its experience in the development of such documents, although the other groups certainly engaged in lobbying of various kinds as well. This brief was part of the larger campaign to open the border to deserters.

Reacting to the media attention and to public pressure, in January 1969, MacEachen announced a review of policy regarding military status of potential immigrants.[42] Indeed, during the next few months, the pressure brought to bear on the department by the anti-draft movement and supporters of American war resisters was reflected in departmental statements, both public and internal.

Initially, draft communications and briefing notes to Cabinet by Department of Immigration staff, as well as other internal documents, consistently argued that deserters ought to be excluded on several grounds. These documents asserted that desertion was worse than draft dodging; deserters should have applied for conscientious objector status at home rather than dodge the draft by fleeing to Canada. Furthermore, to allow deserters to enter Canada could be interpreted as a judgment about American laws – specifically, the draft; and to pass judgment on American laws would be inappropriate from the government of another country. Officials also claimed that most Canadians opposed letting in deserters (although it is not clear where this information came from or if it was true). Overall, the direction of the discussion was towards their exclusion, and MacEachen's public statement in Washington on 25 March took that tentative position, as did a media release on 5 March, a public response to Moderator R.B. McClure of the United Church on 30 April, and a speech to the Committee on Labour, Manpower and Immigration on 8 May. A proposed revision of regulations was even prepared for legal review and was presented to Cabinet.[43] It is worth noting that these statements took place contemporaneously with a discussion about Canada's future role in the North Atlantic Treaty Organization (NATO) and the beginning of Richard Nixon's term as president, and Nixon had made an election promise to eliminate the draft.[44]

Taking note of the negative press the existing policy was receiving, the department eventually produced talking points for internal use and even met with reporters and journalists to clarify what they perceived as the actual situation of American war resisters in Canada. At this meeting, Department of Immigration communications staff, along with representatives from the Department of External Affairs Information Division, urged visiting American journalists to offer a more balanced, less sensational view of the war resister phenomenon.[45] The department also continued to monitor the anti-draft support groups and took note of pressures from the United Church – an indication that they were keeping track of the breadth of the movement and considering how seriously to take it.[46]

During the campaign to open the border to deserters, anti-draft groups were joined in their efforts by several committees whose sole purpose was to secure the revision of the immigration regulations to allow deserters to enter Canada. It is with the arrival of these specific committees in the campaign that the coordination of the overall efforts to have the border opened becomes most evident. There was some overlap in membership, and an important connection, between these committees and the anti-draft groups. For instance, as lawyer Paul Copeland remembered, "June Callwood ... did a bunch of stuff, we had been working with her on other issues than draft dodgers, and she was sympathetic to them."[47] In Ottawa, Jim Wilcox had a hand in promoting the committee's demands on Parliament Hill.[48] In Toronto, the Toronto Anti-Draft Programme's Bill Spira participated in the presentation of the committees' demands to immigration officials.[49] Further, the committees' demands were reflected both directly and indirectly in the letters written to the government.

One such committee was the Toronto Committee for a Fair Immigration Policy, formed in February 1969 by author June Callwood, journalist Dalton Camp, activist and intellectual Mel Watkins, and other prominent figures whose support lent legitimacy to the cause. The group sent a brief of its own to MacEachen and met with MPs.[50] The brief argued that Canadian policy should not discriminate against American deserters, and that to do so was unfair – a theme present in many of the letters the department received on the topic. It received media coverage in the *Vancouver Sun,* among other places, which reported that "a delegation made up of Members of Parliament and representatives of church groups, labour unions and the business, legal and academic communities" met with MacEachen and presented him with the document. The article described the contents of the brief and its Ottawa signatories, including Dr. Pauline Jewett of Carleton University, MPs NDP Andrew Brewin of Toronto-Greenwood, PC Gordon Fairweather of Fundy Royal, and Liberal Mark MacGuigan of Windsor-Walkerville, and Rev. John McRae of the Ottawa Anglican Church. The article outlined the group's contention that changes to the law were unnecessary and their suggestion that what were required were fair treatment and the application of existing laws.[51]

Following the Committee for a Fair Immigration Policy's brief and media release, the minister made a public statement on 5 March responding to the briefs and outlining the policy of discretionary powers. From late March until 12 May, this statement accompanied the department's responses to the letters they received. In the statement, MacEachen also tried to assert that the earlier public statements regarding deserters, made by Kent and others, had in fact applied only to draft dodgers.[52]

A few days after the 5 March statement, department officials began drafting a "Statement on Draft Dodgers and Military Deserters" for eventual presentation to Cabinet. The document went through several revisions, but it consistently called for deserters to be designated a prohibited class of immigrant.[53] This orientation was apparently the preferred position of J.L.E. Couillard, the new deputy minister of manpower and immigration.

The draft statement argued that the review of policy and procedures relating to draft dodgers and deserters was complete and that the policy on draft dodgers should remain the same. However, "military desertion must ... be clearly distinguished from draft evasion." It outlined the development of the revised instructions to immigration officers and asserted that a better policy was required to avoid requiring immigration officers to make difficult decisions and to be consistent in the application of policy for applicants from within or outside Canada. The draft statement said that "the Government believes it is in principle improper for Canada to admit military deserters from the armed forces of friendly countries" as both "detrimental to international interests" and inconsistent with past practice. It also highlighted the possible perception of unfairness, since Canadian deserters were punished.[54]

The document went on to take up, one at a time, potential arguments in favour of allowing deserters to enter Canada. To the argument that deserters are conscientious objectors, the document responded that individuals could have applied for conscientious objector status before serving. To the argument that to exclude deserters would make Canada an enforcer of the laws of other countries, the document responded that policy decisions should be made on the basis of politics, not on questions of legal technicalities.[55] The document concluded with the following unambiguous statement:

> The Government believes that it is not, on balance, in Canada's interest
> to accept military deserters from foreign countries. It has therefore been

decided to provide a regulation under the authority of section 61 of the Immigration Act which would limit admission to Canada of military personnel of foreign countries to those who are on authorized leave or official duty. This will have the effect of prohibiting military deserters from coming to Canada wherever they may apply.[56]

In effect, department officials were proposing that the past practice of excluding deserters through the use of secret guidelines taken as permission to exclude them be replaced by an explicit and public acknowledgment that they were excluded.

At around the same time, Department of Immigration personnel were working on responses to some of the more organized pressures that Minister MacEachen was experiencing. In late March 1969, Couillard sent a memo to MacEachen dealing with some of the arguments made in the brief submitted by the Committee for a Fair Immigration Policy. According to the memo, analysis had revealed, first, that the affidavits by war resisters, which formed part of the filed document, had little merit, and, second, that the group presenting the brief was the same as the Ottawa-based anti-draft group, Ottawa Assistance with Immigration and the Draft. Accordingly, the memo asserted, it appeared there was "an organized effort by certain persons in this country to help United States Army Deserters obtain permanent residence in Canada by any means possible. In this connection you will recall that I recently sent you a copy of an RCMP report dated March 3, concerning this matter."[57] The minister was unlikely to have found this organized effort surprising, given the number of letters he had personally received on the matter. Here, Couillard betrays a dismissive attitude towards pressure groups.

In April 1969, cabinet committee discussions about how to resolve the problem of ambiguity in the regulations regarding deserters revealed divisions in the Liberal caucus. An outline of one such meeting recounted how Jean Marchand, the previous minister of immigration, was puzzled because he felt he had already made it clear that no distinction was to be made between draft dodgers and deserters regarding admission; the current practices therefore seemed odd.[58] John Munro, former parliamentary secretary for manpower and immigration, said in the meeting that he thought earlier departmental public statements had applied to both groups.

In contrast, Marchand's successor, MacEachen, asserted that their statements had really only applied to draft dodgers. During this meeting, Marchand expressed his own strong feeling against banning deserters – a position that was not evident in internal departmental communications. MacEachen, for his part, noted that the impact of the current policy was to exclude only American deserters, and not necessarily deserters from other countries. In his view, the idea that some deserters, and not others, could be admitted was having the effect of making immigration policy dependent on foreign policy, because to exclude only American deserters could only be justified in terms of preserving good relations with the US government. (Remember that Tom Kent, formerly the deputy minister under Marchand, had written to the Department of External Affairs specifically to ascertain whether the policy regarding the treatment of American war resisters could have any impact on relations with the United States.) Marchand responded that it appeared the Department of Immigration wanted to be discretionary without asking the officers to exercise discretion. He suggested letting all deserters across the border and then excluding certain countries by way of an Order-in-Council.[59]

In the third week of April, Deputy Minister Couillard made one last attempt to persuade the minister once and for all against opening the border, and to fight for the recommendation in Cabinet. He acknowledged that some ministers were against the recommendations in the Department of Immigration's Cabinet submission and that there were concerns about "somewhat sweeping" legislation with no exceptions for "meritorious applicants." To address these concerns, he pointed out that an Order-in-Council might still let them in. Further, he asserted,

> in the meantime, the problem of US deserters is embarrassing for Canada, for the government, for you and your department. The matter is rife with inconsistencies and it places an unwarranted and unfair burden on our examining officers. We should not continue to drift and temporize, leaving these defects untouched on the rather blind assumption that the war will soon go away and with it our difficulties.[60]

Couillard reasserted that deserters were different from draft dodgers, despite contrary public perceptions. He dismissed the notion that Canadians would stop supporting the government if a decision was made to exclude deserters, calling the fear "questionable" and suggesting that most support for deserters came from "'protesters' in our society." Again, Couillard dismissed the movement's demands. The proposal that deserters should be allowed entry and then undesirables deported, he dismissed as unworkable; instead, he reaffirmed, ban them all and admit only deserters from specific countries for the plight of whom Canadians might have sympathy. Such a position could allow deserters from the USSR and not the United States, for example.[61]

Whether because of internal debates, external pressures, or a combination of the two, Jim Wilcox related that the Liberal caucus was rumoured, eventually, to have been split evenly, with MacEachen breaking the tie.[62] Interestingly, none of the recorded arguments in favour of open borders from the Cabinet meeting itself were overtly nationalist in nature. For example, there was no assertion that Canada must have an autonomous policy independent from American pressure. Instead, the arguments emphasized considerations such as international relations, legalities, and public opinion. The Cabinet discussions reflected both the influence of the movement and that of the Department of Immigration bureaucrats, including Couillard. In the end, the divisions in Cabinet, fortified by the efforts of activists and campaigners, resolved themselves in favour of opening the border to deserters. The decision was made on 15 May, and on 22 May 1969, MacEachen announced that henceforth deserter status would not be taken into consideration at the border.[63] A new revised instructional directive was sent to immigration officers directing them to state explicitly, should the subject arise, that military status was irrelevant, whether the information was volunteered or not: this was the part that changed. In keeping with earlier policy, neither proof of discharge nor proof of draft status was to be demanded. As long as applicants met the requirements for temporary entry, they were to be allowed in; if they met the requirements for landed immigrant status under the points system, then that status should be granted.[64] This revision was done with care not to expose the real motives behind the instruction: the exclusion of deserters. As Assistant Deputy Minister R.B. Curry urged, "To repeal the entire section at this time would indicate the true purpose of the July 29, 1968 amendment should it become known. For that reason I suggest we delete the example of membership in the armed forces and rewrite the final paragraph to make it clear that such membership is not to be taken into account."[65]

This resolution to the matter was not the result solely of internal departmental discussions. Although the movement had had its work cut out for it, this was a well-planned campaign that allowed for the change in policy to be made, which was a sign of a maturing social movement.

The Campaign to Open the Border to Deserters

The Committee for a Fair Immigration Policy and the briefs from Vancouver had formed part of a concerted effort, a campaign to open the border to deserters, undertaken by the anti-draft movement. While only the committee briefs and some movement lobbying efforts were directly reflected in the department's internal dialogue, other aspects of this public pressure campaign, including communications from citizens to the Department of Immigration and the movement's use of the media, were certainly felt as well. The campaign's messages regarding fairness and tradition came into conflict with most of the opinions expressed in the Department of Immigration discussions and with more conservative ideas about the Canadian nation, which were also expressed in some of the letters received by the department. The anti-draft movement invoked precedents of allowing war resisters into Canada; Couillard and others maintained that no such tradition existed. On principles and consistency, Couillard argued that it was unfair to Canadian military personnel not to punish American deserters, while the anti-draft movement advanced that it was unfair to discriminate against deserters among other immigrants at the border. Additionally, anti-draft activists did not consider the difference between draft dodgers and deserters to be a valid reason for different treatment at the border. Most Canadians supported draft dodgers, and by using an argument against distinction, the support could spread to include all war resisters. Taken together, the constellation of arguments made by the anti-draft movement shared themes with emerging left-wing notions of Canadian nationalism, in contrast to equally nationalist but more conservative ideas about deserters as criminal cowards.[66]

By late 1968, it had become clear among the anti-draft groups that the situation with deserters was getting urgent because of the regulatory changes already described. On 3 February 1969, activist Stephen Strauss of the Vancouver Committee to Aid American War Objectors (VCAAWO) asked activist Allen Mace of the Toronto Anti-Draft Programme (TADP) for better information to counsel deserters. The letter indicated that many more deserters than had previously been seen were coming across the border and were in need of help.[67] Strauss received five pages of single-spaced text in reply, which started,

> The deserter scene is complicated as hell and changing every day now ...
> the border from S.S. Marie [sic] east is bad all the way along for desert-
> ers. Not only are they having trouble with Canadian immigration, but it
> [is] becoming almost impossible for deserters to get out of Canada into
> the US ... Hence we have almost completely stopped sending d.'s [sic] to
> the border for the time being ... We are at present reduced to this: deserters
> with a potential 40 to 42 points [and not the required 50] without a job
> offer ... are being sent to Ottawa. This means that the rest are ... unlandable
> people ... The choices for those who don't have the points for Ottawa are
> three: (1) go underground (2) go back to the states or (3) go to Sweden.

Mace continued, explaining that even the deserters with adequate points were getting held up somehow in Ottawa. Mace's advice to Strauss makes clear how levels of education and work experience had a bearing on the deserter's ability to be landed under the points system.[68]

Eventually, it became clear that a campaign would be necessary because the changes in border policy to bar deserters from entry made it increasingly difficult, if not impossible, for deserters to live openly in Canada. In January and February of 1969, aid groups decided it was necessary to land deserters from within Canada and stop risking applications at the border, even though there was a higher requirement for employment offers when applying from within the country. The TADP's "sub-program" to help deserters came out in the open.[69] Bill Spira of the TADP suggested a year later that one reason the TADP went public with the deserters' issue was because, when the border closed, they had nothing to lose; Spira stated, "the Minister of Immigration simply denied that American deserters were treated differently from anybody else so the next phase was to prove that [MacEachen] lied. Not only lied to us but he lied to the press and to the public."[70]

The campaign began with an assessment of the current situation and continued with efforts to get the various anti-draft groups working together on the issue. In his letter to Strauss, Mace pointed to "[Department of I]mmigration [plans] to bar people with 'military obligations.' So we decided to fight it out with immigration. We are using legal briefs and the press." The campaign had three goals: stop discrimination at the border; return Ottawa to its (perceived) original policy on deserters; and shift public opinion so that any move to bar deserters would meet with a public outcry. "So there it is," continued Mace, "a head-on fight with immigration ... I don't like it at all, personally, because I don't like the media, but so far we are doing all right and probably in fact winning." Mace concluded, "At this point our best hope is to get Ottawa to back down. If possible, then deserters might continue to apply within with success ... One way or the other, if this fails, we will have to take more desperate measures ... we'll think of something."[71]

Another letter Mace sent around the same time asked Strauss to secure one or two resisters' testimonials of border experiences to attach to a brief that was to be presented to the government. A further letter, dated 25 February, provided an update on the campaign and referred to a "delegation" that met the minister later that week.[72] This coordination, initiated by the Toronto group, whose expertise was respected by other activists and supported by the experience of the Vancouver group was likely the first really substantial test of the network's strength. The Pan-Canadian Conference of US War Resisters in Montreal the following year recommended that such coordination be formalized among all of the groups, including the exile groups, and it placed the emphasis on communication, not action. The anti-draft groups were taking the lead.

Other anti-draft groups quickly joined the TADP and the VCAAWO. Jim Wilcox, a leader of the group Ottawa Assistance with Immigration and the Draft (AID), describes the campaign to improve the border situation in a chapter of *I Would Like to Dodge the Draft Dodgers, But ...* In his essay, "They Are Up against the Canadian Border," Wilcox details the campaign.[73] He recalls how anti-draft groups in 1967 and 1968 hid the fact they had helped deserters because they weren't sure their actions were legal. According to Wilcox, Ottawa, Toronto, and Montreal anti-draft groups subsequently engaged in a campaign of publicity and lobbying. In February 1969, the three groups sent fake immigration applicants across the border under the shared false identity of William John Heintzelman; the media coverage of the ambiguous results and questions in Parliament embarrassed the government.[74] Citizen petitions were signed and gathered across the country, on the initiative of the Victoria Voice of Women, and sent to the minister of immigration. Seven hundred and fifty signatures were filed. The signatures came from many different towns and cities, small and large, and were accompanied by the signees' occupations, which gave clear evidence of how broad the movement was.[75]

In Montreal, activists had their hands full as well. On 2 February 1969, a press release issued by the Montreal Council to Aid War Resisters (MCAWR) announced that a brief was being presented to government. The brief, compiled by Ottawa AID, included affidavits from the MCAWR, the TADP, and the VCAAWO. It was almost certainly the brief that the two Committees for a Fair Immigration Policy had presented. The press release also referred to the 1967 letter from Tom Kent, which had stated that military status was irrelevant to immigration.[76] At the same time, Ed Miller of the Montreal group issued a collective letter to "friends" to calm potential fears resulting from the press release that the border was about to be completely closed to deserters.[77] The release resulted in an article in *Le Devoir*, "Ottawa veut 'démoraliser' les déserteurs américains,'" which referred to the brief and mentioned the allegations of discrimination at the border and the secret memo.[78] A day later, an article in the *Montreal Star*, titled "Ottawa Accused of Prejudice," also referred to the brief submitted to Parliament.[79] The Montreal American Deserters Committee (ADC), meanwhile, organized a rally and press conferences in support of the campaign.[80]

In Toronto, the TADP distributed a flyer to garner public support for the campaign:

Another Case of Complicity

Due to American pressure, the Canadian Immigration Act is being bent to suit the wishes of the US Military. Immigration Minister MacEachen is justifying the refusal of border officials to let Americans who have deserted from the army immigrate into Canada.

The right of Canada to maintain its own immigration policy without outside interference and pressure must be actively defended by all those who are fighting against the war in Vietnam and all those who oppose the piecemeal sell-out of Canadian sovereignty.

It is crucial that you write or visit your MP, demanding the return to a fair immigration policy. And also that you send a letter of protest to

Minister of Manpower and Immigration Allan MacEachen and to Prime
Minister Trudeau. Our information indicates that a fairly large number of
MPs favour a non-discriminatory immigration policy as regards deserters, but others are undecided. If you fail to act, *you* may be responsible
for deserters being returned to the stockades.[81]

The references to American pressure and an independent foreign policy
in this leaflet were typical of the campaign. These documents followed the
lead of the 1967 VCAAWO brief, "A Note on Fugitives from Justice," which
had asserted that "one of Canada's oldest traditions" was to welcome deserters and that Canada should not be responsible to uphold American
law. These four ideas – independent foreign policy, American pressure, the
rule of Canadian law, and a tradition of haven for deserters – were about
to become the nucleus of the campaign, and the campaign gave them a
new coherence. The divisions among MPs, to which Warrian's flyer also
refers, were to become very important as well.

The campaign raised a few problems for anti-draft groups. First, there
was a fear that a public fight with the Immigration Department would
translate into rumours south of the border that the border was closed; such
rumours had already kept deserters underground. Similar fears had earlier
led the TADP and the Toronto Union of American Exiles, then based at
the University of Toronto Students' Administrative Council offices, to avoid
taking political action on the issue.[82] The campaign was further complicated
when the fairly new Montreal American Deserters Committee (ADC)
erroneously announced that it was easy to be a deserter in Canada. This
particular group had earlier antagonized others in the movement. The
ADC had not consulted anyone with experience counselling deserters
before issuing the statement that the deserter's life was easy. Perhaps as
deserters they thought they knew best. For their part, the TADP began
referring deserters to Montreal, possibly to force the ADC to deal with
the consequences of their statement.[83] A month later, the *New York Times*
confirmed that some anti-draft movement activists worried that anti-
deserter sentiment might grow as a result of the revolutionary rhetoric of
a Montreal ADC.

Despite these fears and problems, however, the movement found ways
to undertake the campaign. Along with letters and lobbying, the movement
made a particular effort to use the media to shift public opinion. The

campaign was conceived of as having three stages: a public relations stage, an exposure of government practice stage, and a stage in which high profile people lent their support. As Bill Spira recalled in 1970,

> Jim [Wilcox] in Ottawa spent a fantastic amount of time up on the hill; I spent some time lobbying and we got together about 26 of their votes, all of the NDP members and at least two in the conservatives ... In one day 4,000 cards and letters were sent to the House of Commons. This plus the expos[é] plus the fact that the media constantly gave it a very sympathetic show ... and the pressures simply started building up on that when we got to the third stage of our campaign – the first one was simply to meet your deserter, the second was to prove that MacEachen was a liar and the third one was where we got some very straight people that simply said they would disregard the Immigration Act.[84]

The campaign garnered a great deal of media attention, which was often "incredibly sympathetic," in the view of the editors of *AMEX Magazine*.[85] Part of this sympathetic response was directly due to the methods of the campaign by the anti-draft movement. The anti-draft movement employed deliberately dramatic tactics to garner media attention and to expose apparent government hypocrisy and secrecy. Perhaps the most sensational of the actions undertaken was the William John Heintzelman affair. On 9 February 1969, five students from Glendon College – Bob Waller, Graham Muir, John Thompson, Chris Wilson, and Jim Weston – crossed over the American side of the border at different points: two at Detroit, one at the Rainbow Bridge at Niagara Falls, one at the Peace Bridge at Buffalo, and one at the Queenston-Lewiston Bridge near Niagara-on-the-Lake. Each of them posed as the same American deserter, William John Heintzelman.[86] They had five different experiences but none were allowed through. Nonetheless, this act allowed them to compare their treatment at different border points. In several cases, they concluded that the Canadian authorities had called ahead to the American side to let American authorities know a deserter was headed their way. After a busy night, the five students went public with their experiences. Eventually, they signed affidavits that were filed as part of a package of material presented to government officials in lobbying efforts by anti-draft activists.[87] Lawyer Paul Copeland recalls his involvement as a lawyer representing the five students. As Copeland waited in a lawyer's office in Buffalo, the five men were turned back at the border. In one case, Copeland had to go in person to secure the release of one of the students, who was being detained by Canadian border officials. Copeland recounts,

When the TADP found the borders were closed to deserters, we then got involved in trying to figure out a strategy of how to deal with it ... I spent the day ... in a lawyer's office in Buffalo, and [law partner] Clay spent the day in ... Detroit ... in case anything got ugly.

They all hit the three Niagara frontier border points and the Detroit tunnel and bridge at the same time; that was part of the plan. They were all turned back ...

[I]t was finally decided the safer route for everybody was ... to use these photocopied documents from this American army deserter named William John Heintzelman. So he was actually a real person ...

For people immigrating ... it was much easier for people to come here, get a job offer, turn around, go back into the United States, and then apply. And that's basically what was done by the five guys who posed as William John Heintzelman. They all had a job offer; they had everything ... There was a whole organized group [helping them do that] ...

I was sitting in a lawyer's office in Buffalo playing bridge most of the day, and we were trying to keep track of where the people were, and ... when [Jim Weston] hit the Canadian border originally, [he] had been turned back ... and they wouldn't let him in, wouldn't really say why. He goes back to the American side. As he's going back across the bridge, he rips up all of his William John Heintzelman stuff, gets to the American side, and says, "Hi, I'd like to come in." And they said, "What's your name?" And he tells them, and they say, "Well, do you have any identification?" "Yeah." He shows them some identification, and they say, "Well, do you have any other identification?" "Yeah." And he pulls out his passport, and they say, "Well, it's a Saturday. We can't check to see if this is a valid passport." And they turn him back.

We, meanwhile, are sitting wondering what the hell had happened, and we call the [US personnel on the] American side and say, "Have you seen this guy using his Canadian name?" And they say, "Yeah, he just went back to the Canadian side." So we call the Canadian side and say, "Have you seen this guy?" "Oh yeah, he's here with us." I say I'll be right over [as his lawyer], and he had been detained for about an hour by this point. That's my recollection anyway. By the time I got there, they had let him out, but he had come back to the Canadian side, and the Canadians were sort of nice. They had just turned him away, and they said, "Mr. Heintzelman, you've come back." And he said, "Well no, actually that's not true," which is why they were interrogating him, and by the time we showed up, they had released him ...

In every case [the Canadian border officials] had tipped the Americans. [It] may well be true [that they routinely alerted the American side], but why you would [tell them] he was a US Army deserter is another question.[88]

The Canadian immigration officials' "tipping" the Americans was of great interest to the media because it seemed to indicate a situation in which Canadian officials were doing the Americans' work for them. They seemed, in effect, to be enforcing American laws, since no extradition agreements existed for military personnel unless they had deserted while on duty in Canada.[89]

A flurry of media coverage followed the incident.[90] As Copeland recalls, "The Heintzelman stuff was really critically important, because ... up till then, there was no publicity that Canada had closed the border. The guys, when they came back, did a press conference, and it was quite a bit of favourable media coverage."[91] One of the five students involved, Bob Waller, wrote an article for the *Toronto Star* to report in detail the results of the experiment. Waller claimed that his experience and the experience of one other student, Graham Muir, then editor of the Glendon College student newspaper *Pro Tem*, proved collusion between US and Canadian immigration authorities. Waller concluded, "The authorities actively turned me away while I was posing as a deserter, as were my four comrades. This is directly contrary to immigration department policy. The Canadian authorities unlawfully gave information of a private nature to officials of a foreign country. Had I really been a deserter, they would have been responsible for turning me in to the American authorities to suffer the consequences."[92]

On 10 February, national news coverage carried interviews with the five men, and the incident was often mentioned in media stories until the 22 May announcement by MacEachen that the border would, from that point forward, be open to deserters. In its coverage, also written by Waller, the *Montreal Star* quoted John Munro, the previous parliamentary secretary to the minister of manpower and immigration, who had publicly stated a year earlier that military status had no bearing on admissibility. The *Montreal Star* article went on to describe the Heintzelman incident in detail, in an account that matched the students' story, penned as it was by one of the five students; most remarkable was the publication of this account in a mainstream newspaper. The article suggested that "the government sanctions collusion between Canadian and American border guards."[93]

As a result of the Heintzelman events, in mid-February, Minister of Manpower and Immigration Allan MacEachen faced questions in the House of Commons from opposition MPs about the treatment of deserters at the border and about Canadian officials cooperating with American officials regarding their transfer to the US authorities. The news coverage had highlighted a main source of concern for MPs: the contradiction between previous public statements by the department and current statements and actions. Throughout February, March, and April, NDP MPs continued to ask for clarification of the policy and for the text of the directive to immigration officers regarding discretion. NDP MP for Winnipeg David Orlikow asked MacEachen if there was a policy against admission of deserters. In reply to this question, MacEachen referred to the July directive, after differentiating between draft dodgers and deserters.[94] It was the first explicit public reference to the directive made by the minister himself and took away any remaining doubts as to whether the border experiences of deserters were a matter of an express policy to exclude or merely of policy not properly upheld.

Thus, on 18 February, nine days following the Heintzelman event, MacEachen appeared to fully corroborate the conclusions war resister support groups had drawn from the Heintzelman affair, explaining publicly how deserter status could be grounds for denial of entry – at the discretion of the individual immigration officer. If the officer felt that a "contractual obligation" had been violated, he might then still deny the person entry, notwithstanding his qualification otherwise. MacEachen also stated that it was common practice for Canadian officials to notify American border officials that an American had been turned away – confirming accounts provided in the two briefs from the VCAAWO. *Toronto Star* reporter Robert

Stall, who covered the debate that day, observed that "previous government statements had implied that an individual's military status had no bearing on his admissibility to Canada." Stall reminded readers of the Heintzelman affair and suggested it had exposed the truth about border policy regarding deserters.[95] In his interview with Renée Kasinsky a year later, Bill Spira of the TADP recounted how well the campaign had worked: "Now we of course gave [the Heintzelman information] to the press and ... that, in my opinion, plus all the other things that we did to MacEachen, proved that we had an excellent lobby going."[96]

The NDP and the United Church took the results of the event seriously. In response to the Heintzelman incident, the Church passed a resolution later in February that stated "concern that the traditional admissibility of otherwise admissible persons to Canada without regard to military obligations abroad, except as provided in NATO agreements referring to forces in Canada or participating in NATO exercises, be continued."[97] On 30 April 1969, United Church Reverends Robert B. McClure and Ernest E. Long sent a telegram to Minister MacEachen, on behalf of the United Church General Council, denouncing the existence of secret regulations; they described these regulations an "immoral and intolerable evasion of public responsibility ... which we call upon the minister to abandon at once." Furthermore, they disagreed with the position, now made public, that desertion was a breach of a "contractual obligation," probably because of the existence of the draft. They also asserted that government actions to bend the law by issuing secret guidelines had resulted in immigration officials acting as enforcers for foreign powers. Finally, the two reverends invoked the tradition of allowing in dissenters and deserters. They argued that the present conditions of society gave a renewed importance to such traditions, and to government transparency:

In an age of vast complexity of social organization, it is all too easy for persons to be lost in the maze and human rights and values to disappear as victims of a nameless "they." In such an age the complete visibility of legislative and regulative process is essential and government by bureaucratic process and secret "guidelines" is both dangerous and evil.[98]

MacEachen responded by telegram and released both letters to the media. In his reply he accused McClure of "allegations ... ill-founded and erroneous to the point of irresponsibility"; in particular, he denied that the directive to immigration officers was secret.[99]

The action and its publicity also drew the support of Ontario's trade union federation, directly involving for the first time a constituency that had so far remained distant from the movement, at least in any visible way.[100] D.B. Archer, president of the Ontario Federation of Labour (OFL), wrote to MacEachen on 1 April informing him of a resolution of their executive council: "The OFL calls upon the Minister of Manpower and Immigration for an assurance that his dept. is applying with equity the Immigration Act." The federation also took the position that immigration officers should not be allowed to use discretion, and that discrimination should not be tolerated. Archer expressed the federation's desire to see such changes in policy debated by Parliament, and not adopted through regulatory changes by the minister or staff. Archer's use of the discrimination argument likely indicates either union members' direct involvement in the campaign, or lobbying of the OFL by activists to secure their support. MacEachen replied personally, which was unusual at this time due to the volume of letters he was receiving. He acknowledged and thanked Archer for the letter and stated that assurances were "hereby given" that the Department of Immigration was not discriminating. MacEachen ended by mentioning the policy review that was underway.[101]

Some MPs went so far as to threaten to break the law in order to protect resisters. As Spira also indicated in his 1970 interview, Liberal MP Marcel Prud'homme was prepared to harbour deserters in the name of fairness, which would have been illegal had the government decided to publicly close the border instead of opening it. Copeland recounts that "Prud'homme ... threatened to run an underground railway to bring the deserters in. Publicly. That was just after we had done the William John Heintzelman stuff."[102]

Taken together, the letters and other campaign tactics had an impact that exceeded the anti-draft movement's expectations. Campaign activists were not uniformly convinced of its potential success. For instance, Francis Marion of the VCAAWO even wrote to the Yugoslavian embassy in February, seeking assistance with taking in deserters should the campaign fail. This move was ostensibly a way to secure passage for resisters en route to Sweden.[103] The campaign succeeded, Spira believed, because it was able to exploit and further develop divisions among MPs on the treatment of deserters at the border. A year after the border was opened to deserters, Spira recalled,

> Cabinet then decided for MacEachen – we even knew from the [Members of] Parliament what the line-up in the Cabinet was and there was a majority so MacEachen had to back down. It was the first and only political action that I was ever engaged in that was successful. After we were successful we said, My God what did we do wrong, we've succeeded.[104]

Successful as they may have been, the anti-draft movement had mobilized ideas that could cut both ways when it came to criticizing Canadian immigration policy. At times, the growing use of "left nationalist" ideas, evident in the letters and telegrams sent to the Department of Immigration during the campaign, were very similar to other nationalist arguments used against war resisters; these arguments could be turned against other immigrants as well.

5

The Limits of Left Nationalism
The Campaign to Open the Border

In early 1969, hundreds of letters and telegrams calling for the border to be open to deserters reached the Department of Immigration from all regions of Canada. Although no information exists about how, or even to what extent, the letter writing was coordinated, so many of the communications quote directly from the ideas of the Committees for a Fair Immigration Policy that there is little doubt that the letters were part of the same campaign. The issues raised by the Heintzelman affair were reflected in the letters, as they were in the briefs to government officials. Why were immigration officials asking immigrants about their military status when, supposedly, that status was irrelevant? Were immigration officials acting without instructions? If not, then why was no one informed of the policy? And why did Canadian officials call the American side to warn them they would be sending back a war resister? These questions stirred nationalist sentiments, raising questions about independence from the United States and the use of secrecy to achieve the political goal of excluding deserters.

The relationship between nationalism and war resistance was contradictory. Proponents of an open border used left-wing nationalist arguments, while those opposed to war resisters could also use nationalist arguments, albeit of a right-wing variety. At times, the left nationalist arguments led to support for Canadian immigration policy that ran counter to the anti-draft movement's interests. Arguably, the use of nationalist arguments made possible the success of the campaign to open the border. However, at the same time, the left-wing nationalist position put deeper critiques of the Canadian state and its immigration policies out of reach.

This phenomenon can be framed as an example of Antonio Gramsci's exploration of common sense and ideology.[1] For Gramsci, ideology consists of a specific and fairly coherent set of ideas whose coherence arises from material application in social, political, and economic conventions and institutions. Understanding how these sets of ideas operate can help us understand the motivations underlying particular actions of the state, individuals, or groups because the ideas themselves, anchored in reality, enable historical actors to justify their actions.[2] Thus, the different perspectives expressed may contain some similar ideas yet may be attributed to groups that had dissimilar priorities. As I have explored elsewhere,[3] these commonalities between sets of ideas that served different interests may be explained through the application of Gramsci's notion of common sense. Itself a reformulation of the Marxist idea of contradictory consciousness, Gramsci's conception indicates that the buildup over time of accepted and often dominant practices – that is, applied ideologies – means that emergent or new sets of ideas have a better chance of succeeding if they have things in common with the current culture.[4] However, converting existing or emerging ideas or common sense into material change requires socialization through organization.[5] In the words of sociologist Stuart Hall, a "hegemonic moment is ... a process of unification (never totally achieved)."[6]

Contradictions within, and unexpected commonalities between, various ideas put forth to argue for or against allowing deserters to enter Canada had at least three observable material effects. First, the commonalities enabled and ultimately allowed for the stabilization of a common sense notion that deserters were just like any other person entering Canada. As Ian McKay argues in his influential article "The Liberal Order Framework" and his subsequent work *Rebels, Reds, Radicals: Rethinking Canada's Left History,* ideas, even if perhaps internally contradictory – whether liberalism or, in this case, specifically, nationalism – could be and were mobilized by social justice movements to achieve material goals.[7] Second, the internal contradictions reinforced the slippery zone between anti-American chauvinism aimed at individuals on one hand and opposition to American policy on the other. Third, the contradictions reinforced limits of the available critique of immigration policy.

Stephen Azzi establishes that left nationalism, also known as the "new nationalism," was well-entrenched by the late 1960s and had its roots in postwar debates about continentalism, economic and cultural protectionism, and foreign ownership.[8] Left nationalism in Canada has a long pedigree.[9] While its antecedents exist in the interwar years, a resurgence of interest in asserting an essentially progressive Canadian nation was marked by a commensurate resurgence in writing and theorizing about its various aspects. Arguably a seminal work in this resurgence of interest is George Grant's *Lament for a Nation,* a 1965 call for the defence of Canada in the Tory tradition; it expressed concerns about American cultural domination.[10] These calls were taken up by Walter Gordon, whose Committee for an Independent Canada focused largely on economic, but also on cultural, nationalism.[11] Similar concerns prompted Mel Watkins and others to form the Waffle, an internal caucus of the NDP that had sought to reform it into a socialist party.[12] In 1990, Watkins credited the Waffle for its role in establishing a viable left nationalist current in Canada: "Although we lost on free trade, we saw remarkable evidence of a strong, left nationalist sentiment as recently as one year ago. Let us, by all means, emphasize the Waffle's contribution to that legacy."[13]

Further works followed one of several strands: work documenting and implicitly supporting a conservative Canadian nationalism, as typified in Charles Taylor's *Radical Tories: The Conservative Tradition in Canada;* work implicitly supporting Canadian liberalism, as typified by Frank Underhill, *In Search of Canadian Liberalism;* and, more recently, a reconceptualization of Canadian nationalism as a cultural phenomenon, as typified in cultural theorist Erin Manning's *Ephemeral Territories: Representing Nation, Home, and Identity in Canada.*[14]

Nationalism as a historical phenomenon experienced a surge of interest in the first decade of the twenty-first century.[15] Ryan Edwardson in particular has attributed the rise of a "new nationalism" of the sixties to intellectuals:

English-Canadian new nationalism, then, was a reaction to economic continentalization and Americanization. An intelligentsia-based movement that sought to reclaim Canadian sovereignty through political and social activism, it was more than just a force of reconfiguration, it was an entire nation-building project seeking to construct and popularize new conceptions of Canadian identity.[16]

More recently, Ian McKay and Jamie Swift have explored how the idea of Canada as a peacekeeping nation, which they frame as part myth and part memory, is being replaced in the early twenty-first century by a very different and more militaristic mythology.[17] Theorists continue to debate typologies of nationalism, and a generally accepted definition of left nationalism remains elusive.[18] For the purposes of this work, I follow authors who define "left nationalism" in Canada as a perspective that ascribes several specific characteristics and values to Canada: the notion of a Canadian tradition of pacifism; an ingrained tolerance for cultural and linguistic minorities; a respect for individual and collective rights; and an adherence to a view of Canada as being in a colonial or subservient relationship to the United States. However, here it is important again to emphasize the distinction between the new nationalism or left nationalism, and anti-Americanism. If, as Azzi asserts, anti-Americanism is visceral, irrational, a monolithic association of individuals with the actions of their government, then the focus of left nationalism on the United States centres on its perceived hypocrisy – not on criticizing its citizens, or even its values.[19]

In the 1960s, then, a left nationalist movement made use of ideas to build momentum for positive reforms but also to assert Canadian sovereignty and to prioritize Canadian jobs for Canadians. Such a movement was limited by its reliance on essentialist notions of Canada, which prevented the deeper critique of Canada and its place in the world that other sections of the Left were calling for. The antiwar and anti-draft movements were to a large extent motivated by this kind of left nationalism. Many antiwar Canadians were concerned that Canadian foreign policy might be being shaped by American officials and pressures. The letters about the border, described below, illustrate that worries about American influence were centred on the actions of the US government, as opposed to the actions of individual Americans. Thus, the campaign can be seen as inherently internationalist – emphasizing that which ordinary people have in common across national categories over what they have in common with citizens of their own country – as well because it expressed solidarity with individuals and a movement in another country above the interests of its own government and elites.[20] In this case, an aspect of nationalism – the view of Canada as pacifist – became the justification for the internationalist actions of the Canadian anti-draft movement. This apparent contradiction did not appear to cause anyone to pause and reflect. At certain points, however, debates emerged, and some suggested that American immigrants were themselves bound to be an imperialist influence. The tensions between anti-American sentiment – defined as sentiment against American government actions and individual Americans – and solidarity with Americans were, later in the period, made more acute by the radicalism of the political orientation and actions of some of the American immigrants themselves.

The history of Canadian activism in the 1960s and 1970s runs in parallel with the development of the field of Canadian political economy (CPE) among intellectuals.[21] CPE scholars' preoccupation with and criticism of the prevailing idea of Canada as a country in need of protection from the United States has its roots in some of the same ideas circulating among intellectuals in the 1960s. In fact, these ideas played a role in shaping the movement to support resisters in substantial ways. Watkins, for instance, whose seminal economic nationalist report on foreign ownership in Canada took the country by storm in 1968, was also directly involved in the anti-draft movement.[22]

While left nationalism was centred on economic questions, it was not narrowly so; indeed, a distinguishing feature was its concern for the impact of economic dependence on domestic and foreign policy. Perhaps the best example of the concern for Canadian independence from the United States, from the antiwar movement beyond the anti-draft groups, was Claire Culhane's 1972 book *Why Is Canada in Vietnam? The Truth about Our Foreign Aid*.[23] Rather than look at Canada through rose-coloured glasses, Culhane, a nurse who had spent some time in Vietnam, considered Canada's foreign policy to be imperialist. She suggested that, if only Canada could be free of the yoke of American imperialism, it could play a decent role in the world. For Culhane, Canada was a "colony" of the United States. Here, we should not underestimate the significant impact of the Quiet Revolution on the consciousness of Quebeckers and, consequently, on the Left in Canada.[24] Echoes of this concern reverberate through the pages of Canadian political economy foundational texts such as *Capitalism and the National Question in Canada*, which called for a Canada of "independence and socialism":[25]

The appearance of autonomy ... is illusory ... Should capitalists from another country dominate the economy, political subservience shifts to favour the interests of the alien owners of capital. In this case, the nation whose economy is held in sway by foreign capital becomes, as well, a political satellite of the controlling state.[26]

Such concerns were also reflected in other Canadian political economy works, including Kari Levitt's *Silent Surrender* and Ian Lumsden's collection *Close the 49th Parallel*, among many others.[27] Similar arguments speckled the pages of *Canadian Dimension* magazine, founded in 1963 as a magazine of the Left.[28] The Canadianization movement, a movement that insisted on keeping Canadian university posts for Canadians, contributed later to the idea that American immigrants were taking Canadian jobs.[29]

These intellectuals can be seen as Gramscian "organic intellectuals."[30] They are both independent and connected to existing groups with existing material interests. Intellectuals organically connected to the social movements around the resisters contended with intellectuals and bureaucrats in the Department of Immigration whose ideas were shaped by, and in turn shaped, the concerns and responses of government.

Concerns about American influence and the preservation of the pacifist tradition were reflected in the campaign to open the border to deserters, particularly in the early 1969 letters and telegrams sent to the minister of manpower and immigration, Allan MacEachen, and to Prime Minister Trudeau. The letters were overwhelmingly in favour of opening up the border. The letter writing and telegram portion of the campaign was remarkable in its breadth and consistency. While they displayed a certain amount of confusion about the current policy and laws and about the difference between a deserter and a draft dodger, most letters on both sides of the issue mainly employed nationalism to make their points. There were, however, different understandings of nationalism. Those in favour of opening up the border appealed to a perceived tradition of hospitality towards political refugees and war resisters. They also insisted that Canada maintain an independent policy from the United States and referred to supposed American pressure to keep deserters out of the country. Those on the side of keeping deserters out, on the other hand, suggested that loyalty to the nation was the very definition of good character, and that those disloyal to the United States would not be loyal to Canada either.

The Department of Immigration's "Draft Dodgers – Complaints and Criticisms" file was opened in late 1967.[31] However, only two items appeared in that year, both in October. The trickle of letters did not increase substantially during 1968. Only four were filed, of which one was an individual citizen, Mrs. J.S. Allan of Bobcaygeon, Ontario, who expressed concern that Americans would take Canadian jobs and were "*causing* an *ill feeling* towards our good neighbor the States." By letting them in, she said, Canada was being charitable; but she expressed doubt the Americans would become good citizens of Canada. She wrote: "Please sir, stop military age men at the border our own men need help and jobs – and *charity begins at home*."[32] These letters were fairly similar to those received in 1969 in that they emphasized the negative effects of an influx of American deserters on Canadian society. The war resisters did not interact directly with the writers of these negative letters, but they should be seen as part of the political landscape in which the campaign to open the border took place.

Two of the letters in 1968 were from the anti-draft movement and were therefore supportive of the resisters. The Alexander Ross Society, an Edmonton group devoted to supporting war resisters, telexed the minister to ask for the transcript of a speech given in Calgary by Colonel Kossa, assistant director of the US Selective Service, on 5 August. The society suspected that "the FBI and the RCMP are working together to expose organizations that support draft dodgers in this country as well as the US." Jakob Letkemann, executive secretary of the Board of Christian Service of the Conference of Mennonites in Canada, wrote to insist that the borders should "remain open" to American immigrants. Referencing the postwar experience of Hungarian and Czech refugees who had fled wars in their countries, Letkemann praised Canada's current practice of "providing a new home for American draft age immigrants who are unable to support their nation in its present military policy." MacEachen replied to Letkemann to set the record straight: Canada was not, in fact, "providing a new home for American draft age immigrants who are unable to support their nation in its present military policy"; rather, no encouragement was given one way or another to war resisters.[33] Letkemann's letter in particular was a harbinger of the ideas used by supporters of war resister immigration in later letters, especially in its mention of Hungarian and Czech refugees.

These letters and the minister's replies foreshadowed both the flood of correspondence the department was to receive between 3 February and 23 May 1969 and the department's response. The Mennonites' concerns coincided with those held by hundreds of others whose engagement with the issue prompted them to write. For MacEachen's part, as the flood of letters increased, fewer and fewer received more than a brief acknowledgment from staff. But when MacEachen did take the time to respond, his missives also were consistent, often taking the shape of form letters, shifting only as events surrounding immigration policy progressed and reflecting the department's manifest desire to do damage control.

By far the largest group of letters was received in early 1969 – 391 were received before MacEachen's 22 May statement announcing the open border, an eighty-fold increase over 1968. Some were referred by the Prime Minister's Office. Between 3 February and 28 February alone, some eighty-two individual letters arrived in department mailboxes. Fifty-three arrived in March, seventy-nine in April, and 156 in May. Several dozen more arrived after the decision was announced; the last letters appeared in September 1969 and October 1970 from a previous writer who was attempting to secure a response. To explain the sudden increase in early 1969 one must look to events outside the Department of Immigration. The deluge was part of a campaign, as the activists involved in supporting war resisters asserted at the time and shortly thereafter; this was a coordinated effort to convince the government to open the border.

The Department of Immigration received a letter from Frank Epp, the editor of *I Would Like to Dodge the Draft-Dodgers, But ...* on 14 February and one from Ottawa Assistance with Immigration and the Draft's Jim Wilcox on 2 April. A memo to the minister by staff, with brief attached, referred to an earlier letter from Wilcox. That brief was also referred to in the submission by the Toronto Committee for a Fair Immigration Policy (CFIP).[34] Wilcox and CFIP member Mel Watkins were cited in numerous newspaper articles during this period.[35] In all, twenty or so letters made specific reference to the CFIP.

The letters showed signs of coordination in both wording and concepts.[36] A significant number of them included strikingly similar wording and expression of ideas. Many of the letters referred to a "tradition" in Canada of allowing deserters in, making specific reference to Hungarians and Czechs. The majority urged the government not to "bow to US pressure."

Since Canada was supposed to be more tolerant than the United States in general, it was significant that many of the letters, including those from university professors and organized groups, referred to the practice of excluding deserters as "discrimination." A subset of these referred to the practice of the immigration officers using discretion as illegal, an idea also set out in the briefs submitted by the anti-draft movement.

The arguments used in these letters were remarkable for their cohesion. The invocations of Canadian "traditions" of allowing war resisters to enter the country, or suggestions that to prevent American deserters from entering Canada was "discriminatory," were accompanied by other very common arguments. These included opposition to the Vietnam War; the position that the war resisters were making a moral decision that deserved admiration; and the opinion that they would likely make very good additions to Canada. "Humanitarian" and "liberal" values, such as universality and "fairness," were also mentioned; the campaign Committees for a Fair Immigration Policy referred to these values in their campaign name. Also very common was the argument that Canada's policy should be kept independent of "external pressures" from the American government.

The letters – their arrival and content – reflected the statements that MacEachen made in the media and Parliament. A few letters, for example, referred explicitly to MacEachen's 5 March statement, which asserted the right of immigration officers to exercise discretion. After a public radio address on or around 23 April, thirty-six telegrams arrived in a six-day period. The public exchange with R.B. McClure and Ernest E. Long of the United Church in late April received a great deal of attention, as did MacEachen's trial balloon around the same time about excluding deserters entirely. The last days of April and first days of May saw the arrival of petitions collected by individuals from British Columbia and Ontario, as well as letters and telegrams from individuals and groups, including peace groups, unions, and church officials. Many of the letters specifically stated their purpose in writing was to "support the aims of the Committee for a Fair Immigration Policy," the group that had submitted briefs and sent delegations to meet with MPs and the minister several times between February and May. Later in the spring, letters argued explicitly against MacEachen's public statements that military status should be considered an "outstanding legal, contractual or moral obligation," asserting that being drafted or inducted should not properly be considered a contract because it was signed under duress.

A left understanding of nationalism in the letters supporting an open border comes through quite clearly when they are read all at once. To give an idea of the impressions created by the letters, several of them are presented here as examples containing specific left nationalist ideas. While these ideas may arguably have made a victory possible for the anti-draft movement, they also contained contradictions that limited the extent of critique the movement could engage in.

Of the roughly 350 letters received by Manpower and Immigration Minister Allan MacEachen between February and May 1969, several dozen, including those below, expressed concern over Canadian autonomy from the United States, including at least fourteen that mentioned either sovereignty or independence:

"I have come to wonder recently whether Canada is an independent country in fact as well as in theory."
    – *Robert R. Kerton to MacEachen, 19 February 1969*

"Shocked and disgusted ... Why have the immigration officers not been instructed – ordered – to take a more liberal policy? ... I deeply regret this collaboration with American imperialism."
    – *Ken Carpenter, York University, to Trudeau, 10 February 1969*

"Such reprehensible actions move us further under the US thumb ... Is freedom to find no home in Canada at all? And do our northern islands go next?"
    – *Mrs. Muriel Luca, Foremost, Alberta, to Trudeau, 10 March 1969*

"Urge you to hold to Canada's sovereignty and permit entry US army draft dodgers just as you permit Czech immigrants."
    – *Dorothy Livesay, telegram to MacEachen, 26 April 1969*

"I urge you to keep our borders open to deserters from the American armed forces, as to all qualified immigrants. Let the American government

solve its own problems. It is not Canada's business to enforce America's policies."
- *Ronald D. Lambert, Dept. of Sociology, University of Waterloo, ON, telegram to Trudeau, 27 April 1969*

"We are thoroughly ashamed of the violation of the immigration act by Mr Maceachen [sic] and his department. American deserters must receive the same treatment as all other immigrants. Liberalism must not come to be equated with sell-outs to US pressure."
- *Bill Spira, John Levy, Bernard Jaffe, and Allen Mace, Toronto, 2279 Yonge St. [Toronto Anti-Draft Programme (TADP) office], telegram to Trudeau, 21 April 1969*

The letters also reflected left nationalist ideas by linking the "Just Society" with the rule of law. Even more intriguing was the letters' use of the idea of the "Just Society" to convince the Liberal government to change its attitude. The "Just Society" was a concept evoked by Trudeau in his leadership acceptance speech in 1968; it was a broad and vague enough concept to encapsulate many different ideas of social justice.[37] Letter writers using this rhetoric showed a level of political acumen, and also illustrated the ways in which the Liberal claim to stand for a "Just Society" could come back to bite them when their actions did not conform to expectations.[38] These letters were employing the nationalist idea of a good Canada. For their part, the letters regarding the deserters issue insisted that the government live up to its own claim to support the idea. Ten letters mentioned a "just policy," a "just society," or a "just decision," and thirty-two used the words "fair play" or simply "fair," while nineteen referred to their desire for an "open" immigration policy.

"Just what sort of a "Just Society" are *you* thinking of Mr. Immigration Minister?"
- *Mrs. Hilda J. Peterson, Merritt, BC, to MacEachen, March 1969*

"Where is the just society, when immigration laws are being violated by the immigration department to deny Americans entry into Canada?"
- *Malcolm Campbell, MJPJC, London ON, to MacEachen, 14 February 1969*

"If the immigration act is really framed in so sloppy a manner that national policy formation can so fortuitously slip into the hands of people who are not responsible to the electorate, then you should be more concerned with amending the act rather than justifying its more dicey provisions."
– *Mark Segal, Montreal, to MacEachen, 19 February 1969*

"We urge that Canadian law be adhered to and that officials therefore not take into account the military status of applicants for immigration into Canada."
– *Nancy and John Pocock, Toronto, telegram to MacEachen,*
ca. 5 March 1969

"I urgently request your continued support of an open border policy for the entry of qualified American deserters into Canada."
– *Marie Aprile, Scarborough, ON, telegram to Herb Gray, MP,*
Windsor West, 30 April 1969

Many of the letters made reference to Canada's tradition of pacifism, as well as its image abroad. Twenty-six mentioned a "tradition" either of "asylum" (mentioned by eleven writers), or of a destination for "political refugees" (mentioned forty-four times); twenty-seven letters referred to the waves of immigrants from Hungary in 1956 and Czechoslovakia in 1968 as examples of this tradition, and five or six mentioned the United Empire Loyalists.

"We support landed immigrant status for American draft resistors [sic] and deserters as a policy consistent with Canada's traditional acceptance of other refugee nationals."
– *T.M. Cox family, telegram to MacEachen, 27 April 1969*

"Dear Sir: If we wish to maintain our world image of a humanitarian nation we must grant asylum to US deserters. To do less would be to nullify the good we have done in aiding refugees from Czechoslovakia Hungary Germany Ukraine. We must never forsake this great tradition."
– *Rob Ward, telegram to MacEachen, 26 April 1969*

"As Canada has previously offered sanctuary to Hungarian Czechoslovakian and other refugees, we support a government policy offering on the same basis the status of landed immigrant to US deserters and draft resistors."
   – *Bruno Friesen, Rae Friesen, and eighty-nine others, telegram to MacEachen, 28 April 1969*

"Dismayed and shocked to hear of your proposal to restrict immigration of US soldiers and draftees protesting war in Viet Nam. Your proposal would flout Canada's tradition of political asylum and give aid and comfort to those favouring continued US fighting in Viet Nam."
   – *Dr. James Endicott, Canadian Peace Congress, Toronto, telegram to MacEachen, 24 April 1969*

The expression of the pacifist tradition went so far as to suggest that loyalists were war resisters and to encourage a similar treatment of those from the Vietnam War:

"As a Nova Scotian (are you not?) you know with what pride folks announce to less fortunate ones: 'We're descended from United Empire Loyalists, you know.' History books and teachers in the USA, however, depict those same early Canadians as Benedict Arnolds, or deserters ... For years I have watched the Liberal party sell Canada down the river to the USA, but your attitude does go a little far, wouldn't you agree?"
   – *A.H. Walkley, Toronto, to MacEachen, 19 February 1969*

Finally, the letters reflected the idea that Canada should return to a non-discriminatory policy towards deserters. Fully forty-three letters specifically demanded the elimination of "discrimination" from either immigration policy or its application. A further fifteen took issue with the discretionary powers applied by immigration officials, and a further eighteen explicitly linked the discretion with discrimination, such that, by the end of the period, discretion and discrimination were almost synonymous. Twenty-one of the letter writers also stated opposition to the fact that being drafted was considered a contractual obligation by current immigration regulations:

"It is most offensive to arrogate discretionary power to order functionaries."
- *Ronald D. Lambert, PhD, Assistant Professor of Sociology and Psychology, University of Waterloo, to MacEachen, 18 February 1969*

"[I am] opposed to any discrimination or tightening of laws or practices against draft dodgers or deserters from the US Army or other armed forces."
- *Rev. W. Grenfell Zwicker, United Church of Canada, Toronto, to MacEachen, 10 March 1969*

"[Immigration officers] being given greater 'discretion' ... [means] arbitrary exercise of bias, pique, and guile."
- *Dr. Eugene Kaellis, Saskatoon, to Trudeau, 7 March 1969*

"We strongly urge open immigration for American military deserters selective service is not repeat not a 'voluntary contract.'"
- *M.L. Benston and L. Foldhammer, telegram to MacEachen, 27 April 1969*

"Urge you declare Canada won't discriminate against US army deserters or draft resisters meeting landed immigrant qualifications. Precedent and sovereignty demand same. Alternative is national shame ... Betrayal of Americans who risk imprisonment."
- *Charles Boylan, telegram to MacEachen, 26 April 1969*

This sample is only a taste of the content of the letters. In the context of questioning in the House of Commons, media attention to the issue, and pressure through other means, such as lobbying and briefs, Minister MacEachen and his staff must increasingly have seen the letters as a reflection of public opinion. Then, on 9 May, the Committees for a Fair Immigration Policy simultaneously delivered copies of a "Petition to Concerned Canadians," apparently either the same or a very similar document to the briefs previously submitted, to the district administrator of immigration in Toronto, and in Ottawa to R.B. Curry, the assistant deputy minister of immigration. The document, which the committees requested be transmitted to the minister, read, in part,

Immigration officers should immediately be instructed to ignore military status in another country as a legal, moral or contractual factor – directly or indirectly – in determining an applicant's eligibility for immigration to Canada.

We invite concerned Canadians from across the country to write their Member of Parliament, the Minister of Immigration and the Prime Minister supporting this position.

– *Committee for a Fair Immigration Policy*[39]

Nearly 140 letters arrived in the department in the first two weeks of May. Perhaps it may be surmised from this deluge that the Committees for a Fair Immigration Policy's appeal for letters had been shared through the communication networks of the anti-draft groups. Letters had also increased immediately following media stories about the Heintzelman action, MacEachen's public statements about the discretionary powers of immigration officers, and the 5 March media release.

By the time of the last major submission to the department from the Committee for a Fair Immigration Policy, which was received just about the same time as the announcement of the open border, the momentum was clearly on the side of the campaign to open the border. The last set of signatures, date stamped 26 May, included:

Dr. A. Berland, Executive Secretary Designate, Canadian Association of University Teachers

Norm Bernstein, Civil Liberties Action Committee

Dr. Fred Caloren, Faculty of Social Sciences, University of Ottawa

Muriel Duckworth, Halifax, Fredericton Voice of Women

Dr. Frank Epp, Ottawa

Roy Faibish, Executive Assistant to Managing Director, Drama, CJOH

Dr. Allen Fenichel, Department of Economics, McGill; Treasurer, Civil Liberties Action Committee

Rev. Mr. Eilert Frerichs, Chaplain, University of Toronto

Irving Greenberg, Businessman, Ottawa

Mrs. Grace Hartman, Ottawa, National Secretary-Treasurer, Canadian Union of Public Employees

Rev. Mr. John G. Hilton, Chaplain, University of Toronto

Dr. Pauline Jewett, Department of Political Science, Carleton University

Dr. Gordon Kaplan, Department of Biology, University of Ottawa

Vincent Kelly, Lawyer

Dr. Laurier Lapierre, Director French Canada Studies Program, McGill University

Rev. Mr. Doug Lapp, Britannia United Church, Ottawa

John F. MacMillan, Ottawa, Director of Organizing, Canadian Union of Public Employees

Mrs. Kay Macpherson, Toronto, past President, Voice of Women

Rev. Prof. W.E. Mann, Department of Sociology, York University

Rev. Mr. John F. McRae, Deputy Director of Program, Anglican Diocese of Ottawa

Dr. Edward J. Monahan, Assistant Executive Secretary, Canadian Association of University Teachers

Mrs. Nancy Pocock, Society of Friends, Toronto

Rev. Father Louis Raby, O.M.I [Oblates of Mary Immaculate], Chaplain, University of Ottawa

Dr. Elliott Rose, Department of History, University of Toronto

Larry Sheffe, International Representative, United Auto Workers

Alex Sim, North Gower, Ontario

Dr. Percy Smith, Executive Secretary, Canadian Association of University Teachers

Dr. Frank Vallee, Department of Sociology, Carleton University

Dr. James Wilcox, Department of English, Carleton University

These signatures, some repeated from earlier iterations of the petitions, show both the breadth of the campaign and its impact among intellectuals, as well as connections to the left nationalist groups the Waffle and the Committee for an Independent Canada (CIC). Watkins was a founder of the Waffle, and Lapierre and Jewett were members of the CIC.[40] Letter writers included Lapierre and Kenneth McNaught of the CIC, who also wrote a section of the *Manual for Draft-Age Immigrants to Canada*.[41] All of the letters, combined with the impact of the prominent signatories to the Committee for a Fair Immigration Policy briefs and communications and the use of the media, had a significant and cumulative effect that the Department of Immigration, the minister, and Cabinet could not ignore. In the end, Cabinet decided to formally open the border to deserters in May 1969.

Before the announcement on 22 May 1969, sixty-four of 391 letters received were against opening the border. Like the letters supportive of the anti-draft movement, they arrived in clumps following media discussions. About ten were received following early March media statements and interviews about the review of policy underway and expressed conservative Canadian nationalist sentiments: "They are not refugees seeking sanctuary from oppression and tyranny but merely shirkers seeking a skunk-hole," said D. Patrick, MM (perhaps a military designation) of Foam Lake, Saskatchewan, on 11 May 1969. Not only the draft dodgers and deserters, but "student radicals, agitators and the hippie type crowd, the black power set and the professor[s] linked to subversive groups" should be kept out, suggested Harry Bagot of Edmonton, Alberta, on 15 April. On 12 May, A. MacAllistair of Cornwall, Ontario, wrote, "Through the aid of a number of pacifist centres, Marxist-oriented groups, so-called anti war, anti draft and anti imperialist and other narrow-minded anti American clubs, a continuous program is in effect to assist these deserters circumvent their duty." "No doubt on inspection the most of them will be long haired Johnnies with strong communistic tendency and would be a liability," argued Ms. Scott, who did not provide an address, on 6 May. For these writers, draft dodgers and deserters were part of an overarching threat to the social fabric.

Some of the arguments against opening the border were common to several letters. Many of these letters used the term "undesirable" to describe these potential immigrants. They argued that a propensity to break the law would be carried into Canada. Further, they argued that disloyalty to the United States would result in disloyalty to Canada. They often associated American war resisters with campus unrest, communism, drugs, and hippie culture. A good number of them also grouped American war resisters as part of an influx of non-Anglo Saxon stock, appealing to the government to prevent the entry of immigrants of colour: for instance, "you keep adding to our problems by admitting Hippies, Deserters and Negroes," wrote an anonymous correspondent on 6 June 1969. One writer, after the 22 May decision to open the border to deserters, said "I do not agree with present 'liberalising' of our former immigration policy any more than I can stomach the 'liberalising' of our laws on homosexuality." Another referred to herself as a reactionary. Others expressed anti-Quebec and anti-French views.

In general, all of the letters against the open border suggested that some aspect of the perceived character of war resisters was a threat to Canada and Canadian values. The following examples illustrate the strands of argument in these letters. Some were objections to the failings of the resisters as cowards, freeloaders, or subversives:

"Our whole existence is threatened if we continue to allow this type of rabble into our country ... I would like your assurance, sir, that the present government will not bow to pressure being brought forward by anarchists, and will continue to prohibit this cowardly element from polluting our Canadian security."
    – *G.H. Carley, Oakville, ON, to MacEachen, 17 February 1969*

"It is entirely proper that the questioning of would be immigrants by immigration officials should reveal other qualities than their job expectation. The word personal integrity is little used in Canada. By and large the desertes [sic] do not seem to raise the level of this desireable [sic] characteristic of Canadian citizen [sic]. Many of the landed deserte[r]s seem inclined to undertake highly undesireable activities. Therefore the grilling of Immigration minister ... by a combination of lawyers and churchmen is a proper political game, but not to the good of the well-being of Canada."
    – *Mrs. Henry Aruja, Don Mills, to MacEachen, 1 March 1969*

"Call it bias, discrimination or what you will. We don't need the deserters from the US here. We have enough of that type – people that want freedom without responsibility. Maybe just a free ride. Keep them out!"
    – *J.A. Brewster, Toronto, to MacEachen, 10 March 1969*

"With every particle of my being I commend you for your reply to Maclure [sic]. My only fault, and I do not mean this critically, with our Govt. is that they are not severe enough upon the dreadful horde of Yankee trash coming into our country, to evade the responsibilities of citizenship in their own country. More power to your arm."
    – *James M. Cameron, Ottawa, to MacEachen, 3 May 1969*

Some letters, like those below, expressed objections to specific aspects of the character of immigrants, such as cowardice and disloyalty. The letters did not make reference to intellectuals opposing the war resisters, although some did oppose them. They also tended to lump all of these intellectuals who had connections to social movements or the counterculture together in one category, rather than recognizing any differences of opinion that might exist among them. For these letter writers, the Left was a monolithic group of people. Remarkably few of the letters invoke citizenship, taxpayer status, or veteran status as a claim to a hearing for their view.

"I have never in my life ever seen such trash as these American Draft Dodgers in my life, whom we as Canadians have to support and cater to, after they haven't got the *guts* to fight for own country what in hell are they going to do for CANADA, the country I love so much."
   – *W.J. Arthur Fair, Jr., BA, Edmund Burke Society, to Peterborough*
   MP Hugh Faulkner and MPP Walter Pitman, 13 February 1969

"These draft dodgers and deserters are cowards and will not fight for their country ... Keep Canada a proud land, not a country that allow [sic] garbage in."
   – *J. Gadziola, Toronto, to MacEachen, 18 February 1969*

"Surely we have enough problems without welcoming men who do not have the courage to face up their convictions or fight for their country ... intellectuals say we should welcome such *men*!!!"
   – *Bedbrook, Winnipeg, to MacEachen, March 1969*

"What good would be served to Canada as a whole by granting Canadian citizenship to these unwashed cowards ... [who] have already taken part in the disruption of our educational institutions, which are being maintained by my taxes ... I would suggest, if you go underground, that you take Stanley Gray and Pierre Bourgault with you and, after due disruption of the democratic process, said gentlemen having had lots of experience in those tactics, that you all prevail upon the Canada Council (again functioning because of my taxes) to give these brave upstanding young deserters a Canada Council Grant ... [the] definition of a deserter is ... a 'rat.' Perhaps Mr. Trudeau will see fit to create a department headed by another Pied Piper of Hamelin who, together with his pipes, will get rid of the rats. Mr. MacEachen, a good Scotsman should know some good pipers.
   – *R.J. Perrier, veteran, Montreal, to Marcel Prud'homme, MP,*
   5 May 1969

References such as these to Stanley Gray, Pierre Bourgault, lawyers, churchmen, and other intellectuals call to mind the Gramscian idea of the influence of intellectuals in civil society. Gray, a leading intellectual in the movement Opération McGill to eliminate English control of McGill University in 1969,[42] and Bourgault, a militant Quebec activist for Quebec independence,[43] must have seemed to the author to be gaining momentum in the sixties political climate.

Finally, several letters took issue specifically with resisters' expected association with, and encouragement of, what the writers considered to be questionable elements within Canada:

"Why should we as Canadians continue to keep these 'BUMS' in our country when they have no loyalty to their own ... I say keep the 'BUMS' out. What good are they to Canada? Why have they not to pay income tax, etc., why do these homosexuals get special privileges?"
   – *W.J. Arthur Fair, Jr., BA, [Edmund Burke Society], Peterborough, to MacEachen, 21 February 1969*

"For every one who is honestly motivated, there are nine who are not. These nine I would consider are emotionally disturbed. They are anti-government, anti-authority, anti-religious, anti-school and anti-home ... [One I met] preaches love and flowers and is against anything that has any degree of organization or responsibility to it ... He associated with characters in Yorkville and made contact with strangers on the street or highway."
   – *Dr. E.S.A. Bartram, London, Ontario, to James S. Cross, Acting Director of Programs and Procedures, 31 January 1969*

"Carefully screen proposed immigrants. You are being badgered by various individuals who have allowed misguided humanitarianism and an inverted sense of values to distort their thinking ... professional troublemakers and dissidents ... a small but extremely vocal minority of misguided sentimentalists and professional do-gooders who go out of their way to champion the cause of the unworthy ... [I] will continue to agree that proposed immigrants be screened ... before being granted the privilege of immigrating to our country."
   – *V.T.B. Williams, P. Eng, Ottawa, to MacEachen, 7 May 1969*

David Surrey's 1980 study of class among war resisters in Canada describes the negative stigma that Canadians, whose sense of duty was affronted, attached to both draft dodging and deserting. According to Surrey, Canadians in general wanted war resisters to assimilate, although attitudes changed with time and shifts in antiwar sentiment.[44] The negative letters do not mention a desire to see war resisters assimilate, however, which may be accounted for by the fact that nearly all of them were written in response to a specific event – the public debate about deserters and the border – and not the separate question of how Americans should behave once they had arrived.

Despite the letters against the open border and Surrey's findings that Canadians wanted Americans to assimilate, the large majority of the letters – around five-sixths – were in favour of opening the border without qualification. What the letters against opening the border show is that opinion was not unanimously in favour of allowing war resisters to come to Canada, or allowing them to stay once they arrived. These views were reflected in some media reports as well. They also point to a fatal flaw in the left nationalist arguments: their organic linkages to more reactionary nationalist views. At their most basic, both sets of letters used nationalism to make their points. The line between left and right nationalism is very thin.

The letter-writing campaign and the other measures taken by anti-draft activists and supporters were successful in opening the border to deserters, but in at least two aspects the letters were also evidence of the limits imposed by a left nationalist orientation. First, hostile language was not limited to the anti-resister letters. In at least one case, the letters in favour of opening the border made use of racist ideas. The fact that letters could use such seemingly contradictory ideas in one argument was a comment on the murky border between left- and right-wing nationalism. Others, while not as reactionary, were at best contradictory to an open approach to immigration and ambivalent towards a universally open border, even for Americans:

"The one chance you get to obtain morally decent, well-educated immigrants from the US you immediately muff it and import uneducated ignorant and unequipped immigrants instead, i.e., [black] domestics from

Barbados. How would Mtr. MacEachen like to go to Vietnam? Or you, for that matter?"
  – *Rita Belkin, to Trudeau, 6 February 1969*

"Your ambiguous and, if I may say so, gutless, remarks re deserters from the American Armed Services surely please neither those eager to refuse entry to all save the lily-white and proven "patriotic," nor those who, in an excess of sympathy and mercy, would open the borders to any and all ... My husband and I would prefer that those who have made the soul-searing decision to leave family, friends and homeland forever, be allowed to come into Canada ... if they misbehave there are lots of people ready to report them."
  – *Mrs. A. Gibson, to MacEachen, March 1969*

Probably the clearest example of this ambivalence was the following letter from Robin Mathews, mentioned earlier. Mathews, an academic, CIC member, and leader of the left nationalist Canadianization movement, was a professor at Carleton University. His letter in support of an open border is worth restating as an effective example of the contradictions within left nationalism:

"I should like to make clear, as a Canadian publicly committed to the battle for Canadian viability that I hold the traditions of asylum as sacred to the definition of the country. Secondly, we must guard – within the legislation of the nation – against rigging or appearing to rig procedures that may in fact pervert the intention of legislation under which procedures exist.

The government, in my view, has never done enough to make guests and immigrants to this country aware of its uniqueness and of their responsibility to it.

Partly, problems of the present nature, arise from what is a general failure of consistency and purpose in immigration policy.

If the reasons for difficulty at the present time are that the Canadian government fears to offend the US govt., then the Canadian government deserves the criticism it is receiving. If the Canadian govt. fears the results of influx, then it had better set up citizenship courses that make possible

for immigrants some idea of Canada other than that it is a cow to be milked by whatever hand reaches for the udder."
   – *Robin Mathews, Ottawa, to MacEachen, May 1969*

Mathews's position on American war resisters evolved. This letter already showed how left nationalism could eventually lead to Mathews's later conclusion that Americans should assimilate, contribute meaningfully to Canadian society by getting jobs and learning about Canada, and not become a drain on social programs. From here, for Mathews, it would only be a short step to conclude that they should also not get privileged access to Canadian jobs – a clear contradiction from the position in this letter that resisters should not "milk" the "udder." Economic nationalism hovered just below the surface of these discussions.

Debates about assimilation permeated both the anti-draft movement and the resister community. Accounts vary on the question of whether anti-draft groups put pressure on Americans to assimilate into Canada or to maintain their American identity. Some have asserted that Canadians in general wanted Americans to assimilate, and certainly there is some evidence of such a viewpoint.[45] Further, while most participants in the campaign to open the border to deserters took issue with American government actions and not individual Americans, Mathews and others also came to believe that war resisters were part of American imperialism.

In 1970, Mathews, who had lent qualified support to the campaign to open the border to deserters in 1969, wrote an article for *AMEX* titled "The US Draft Dodger in Canada Is Part of US Imperialism in Canada." Critical of American immigrants for their contempt for Canadian citizenship, air of cultural superiority, and attitude of entitlement to positions of influence in Canada, he suggested that they represented cultural imperialism. This cultural imperialism made it "difficult" to "like US citizens, individually." Mathews criticized draft dodgers not for holding positions of influence per se, but for having the same accent, "to the Canadian ear," as those Americans in posts that should have gone to Canadians.[46] He further condemned them for distracting Canadian activists from Canadian problems by importing terms such as "pig" to describe police, and by insisting on focusing on such incidents as the Kent State massacre of students by national guardsmen. That focus, for Mathews, was associated with the

act of breaking windows at Eaton's, a Canadian company, in a demonstration at the time:

> That was such a bad tactic it was ludicrous. I don't believe it was a tac-
> tic. I believe it was the result of hell-raising, US style. Where were the
> window breakers when the Dunlop factory was being closed, putting
> hundreds of families out of work as a result of the imperial organization
> of the multi-national corporation? Window breakers who were trying
> to bring Canadian attention to US imperialism would surely not break
> the windows of one of the last Canadian companies of any size which
> has not yet been taken over by the US.[47]

Mathews concluded his article by disputing that the war resisters were
politically aware. Instead, for him,

> In Canadian intellectual history the American has always been recognized
> as a threat to survival. That is a fact ... The US citizen has in recent years
> done an immense amount to divert Canadian attention from Canadian
> interests. That is where the US draft dodger is today. He is part of US
> imperialism in Canada. His existence in Canada must cause many prob-
> lems – problems that he must face, problems that Canadians must face.
> It will not be easy. It will not be easy.[48]

Another left academic, sociologist Ron Lambert of the Kitchener-
Waterloo Anti-Draft Programme, debated with Mathews about the influence of war resisters. The pages of *AMEX* carried a debate between Lambert
and Mathews on whether the war resisters were a new wave of American
imperialism.[49] Lambert felt that Mathews was wrong in suggesting that
war resisters were an American issue, since the Vietnam War was not
solely an American issue. Lambert pointed out that American immigrants
had no particular power in Canada, and he rejected the implication that
Canada was inferior to the United States. He also took issue with the
equation of American ownership in the Canadian economy to "the radical
rhetoric of military resisters."[50]

At the same time, on one or two other points, Lambert agreed with
Mathews. He was most assuredly in favour of American immigrants

assimilating calmly and without confrontation into Canadian society. He objected to American resisters who uncritically drew parallels between the failures of American representative government and police behaviour and the corresponding Canadian institutions; and he agreed that most American exiles were "ignorant" about Canada and should approach Mathews and others, and presumably himself, for instruction. American objections to Canadian nationalism, for him, were similarly inappropriate. For Mathews and Lambert, Canadian nationalism and the Canadian Parliament were the only possible tools to subvert Canada's support for the American empire, and not American-style street demonstrations.[51]

The debate, published as it was in *AMEX*, had at least some influence. Renée Kasinsky's 1970 interview with Nancy Pocock of the Toronto Anti-Draft Programme shows the influence of left nationalist ideas on the leaders of the anti-draft movement. In response to a line of questioning about a perceived shift in the antiwar movement towards more violent tactics, she replied,

> Of the people that have passed through [my] house, very few of them are political because they find it very hard to fit into any Canadian thing, and I'm very disturbed about what's going on here. There's a copy, and I think it's a colonial copy of the movement in the US because I can't see how it helps the war in Vietnam to call a Canadian policeman a pig and kill him. It's irrelevant. It will do nothing to stop a war anywhere. It will only bring violence into Canadian cities. And it'll turn our policemen into pigs. And I feel very strongly that this is something very bad we're getting from the US and our Canadian youth are following along, and they're showing they're true colonialists instead of Canadians.[52]

Pocock may have been influenced by the article in *AMEX*, or perhaps by another article by Mathews on the same topic.[53]

Pocock went on to describe a meeting where participants discussed reaching out to the police after a recent demonstration that had turned violent; Americans at the meeting had refused to listen to the Canadians who wanted to argue that Canada was different.[54] She explained,

> I sometimes wonder ... why we work so hard at it, because some of them do bring their own pattern of life and their own violence and there is

Imperialism of the Left as well as of the Right. And there is a certain arrogance, and oh, blindness and insensitivity. I hope I don't hurt your feelings by saying that, but ... the US is a very ... strong country, I mean strong character, strong ideas, and Canada isn't. We are more quiet, reserved, and we've always been in a sort of colonial position. So, thank goodness we're not very patriotic. In fact we've only had a flag the last 2 or 3 years. That's what I like to point out to some of the boys. And we've escaped a lot of these things through our history.[55]

However, Pocock either did not see her sentiments as nationalist, or was troubled by the possibility that they were, because she soon added,

there is a wave of nationalism going through Canada which is a dangerous thing. I welcome it because I feel it myself. I feel we have something unique here we should preserve. And it's a real dilemma how we can preserve it, being so close to the States ... When you're faced with a human being who needs help, what can you do but help him? And hope that it turns out right! And this is why in our contact with the boys, we have taken time to talk to them ... But whether we'll keep [Canada the way it is] or not I don't know. Because we can't isolate ourselves, we can't be a little island in the world. So you just go on and do the best you can from day to day.[56]

The Toronto Anti-Draft Programme's *Manual for Draft-Age Immigrants to Canada* sported a maple leaf on its cover until its fifth edition was published in 1970. The sixth edition, published in spring 1971, abandoned all national symbolism for an engraving of a grieving mother figure holding two dead children. This last edition was largely typewritten and lower in production values than the previous five editions. It included a new section titled "Of Frying Pans and Fires," written by Lambert, outlining a debate between two streams of Canadian nationalism – one resistant to US domination, and one, "colonially-minded," justifying US foreign policy and its domination of Canadian decision making. And it encouraged readers to choose one or the other.[57] In effect, Lambert argued that the only effective path was to resist US domination.

Left nationalist ideas were perhaps not yet dominant on the left in the sixties, but they were certainly on the rise. There were also, however, other ideas available on the left, and many of these contended directly with left nationalist ideas about Canada and its policies. One of the more radical critiques of the Canadian anti-draft movement was its failure to engage with the way the immigration system channelled American immigrants of lower income backgrounds and with less education – and therefore, deserters more than draft dodgers – away from successfully obtaining landed immigrant status.[58]

In 1969, Melody Killian of the *Yankee Refugee* penned an article titled "Oh, Canada!," which provoked hostility from Toronto and Vancouver activists because of its assertion that anti-draft movement efforts to help Americans immigrate was "not anti-war work." Killian asserted that, while existing aid groups believed anti-draft counselling and support to be vital antiwar work that ought to be considered of utmost importance, the "Vancouver Yankee Refugee group," and Killian herself, had

> reached different conclusions ... [O]ur being here or helping others to come here is NOT anti-war work. Only work that aims at destroying the economic system that CAUSES the war (capitalism) is anti-war work. We know that we are allowed into Canada because of manpower needs of capitalism in Canada ... We also do not believe in the eminent danger of our activities causing a change in the immigration act or causing deportation of our members. If ... the Canadian government did undertake such moves, it would only reinforce our understanding of imperialism: that in fact there is no "refuge."[59]

The piece, and Goldie Josephy's indignant response,[60] reflected a debate about the relative value of certain kinds of antiwar work that may seem petty from the standpoint of the twenty-first century. Certainly, Killian's approach might have benefitted from a more generous appraisal of the legacy of the peace movement in Canada. However, in suggesting that the Canadian movement was missing some key points of analysis, she was correct. Killian pointed to economic motivations behind at least some of the American and Canadian governments' actions and policies. While there was some awareness of how the points system functioned to screen out deserters in particular, there was never a campaign on the scale of that to open the borders to deserters, aimed at removing economic and educational discrimination from the points system – only one to remove the discrimination against deserters as opposed to draft dodgers in the application process. Arguably, this analytical bias was at least partly due to the dominance of Canadian nationalism on the left in Canada. Because this left nationalism had at its heart the idea of Canada the good, it encouraged a view that, once Canada was free of American influence, its policies would be empty of discrimination. This is an example of common sense in Gramsci's theory of hegemony: at the level below the state, left nationalism was hegemonic among the anti-draft movement, and on the left more generally.

The flip side of this coin was that economics were driving immigration policy. At the same time, part and parcel of the prevalent top-down view of Canada was the common sense view of who was at least potentially a Canadian – despite the claim that the points system had ushered in a new tolerance and lack of discrimination. As Bruce Curtis has explored, administrative forms based upon measurements affect what they measure, encouraging people to fit the categories. The categories are shaped by interactions with the objects of measurement.[61] While the categories of the points system were not fundamentally altered by public pressure and interaction with immigrants between 1962 and 1972, the points system certainly shaped who could immigrate. The economic basis for immigration policy implied exclusion of immigrants without the proper skills; therefore, by virtue of their economic background and lack of access to education and skills, they could not become immigrants.

In fact, economic discrimination was a process that, for these young men, began with the Selective Service System in the United States and continued with the Canadian immigration points system. Economic and educational differences between draft dodgers and deserters determined their trajectory as war resisters and immigrants. Economic and educational stratification was part of life for American men while the Selective Service Program was in existence. Mark Phillips remembers the way the Selective Service system worked to select those with fewer resources:

> The overwhelming evil of the Selective Service program was that it was indeed selective. And in my Boston suburb, almost nobody went into the service. Most of my classmates at Harvard – likewise. I could have

gotten out. If you had the resources and the determination ... There was a struggle; people went through hell to make themselves unavailable, but they didn't go. So people that went were either working-class or gung ho.

In effect, working-class young men could expect either to be drafted or to see the military as their only option for a good job. Phillips recalls,

> I spent a year in Cambridge [MA] high school as a teaching assistant, as a volunteer ... I was teaching in a very tough class in a very tough school. Cambridge was a very poor town, and everyone I was teaching, they were all my own age; every day they had it on their record that that was what they were going to after Grade 12; they were going to join the army. It was a class thing. So people who went from my town were football players, gung ho, and of course it was a much tougher problem for [deserters] to turn around, and the penalties were much worse.[62]

Discussing the tendency of the Selective Service to encourage young men to make specific decisions, Phillips observed,

> I think you can dramatize [the political nature of the decision to avoid the draft or desert] too much. I think that people made very personal accommodations to a system that was always designed to control the lives of people who were never going to be in the army. That was the point; it wasn't a way of filling the ranks of the military; it was designed to control young men's lives ... The draft dodgers were a subset of the much, much bigger group of guys whose lives were distorted.[63]

Phillips touches on an issue that needs further study: the idea of the draft as social control. Social control analysis has been applied to public services but not to the American draft.[64] The notable exception is the numerous articles by New Left writers in the late 1960s and 1970s on the idea of "channelling." Their interest is no surprise given that social control analysis and debates about its utility were coming into vogue in academic circles at the time.[65]

There was also a much stronger reason for this analysis. The Selective Service was explicit in its own documents about the social control function of the draft. In a 1965 orientation document, excerpts of which were reproduced by *Ramparts Magazine* in 1967, the service affirmed,

One of the major products of the Selective Service classification process is the channelling of manpower into many endeavors, occupations and activities that are in the national interest.

While the best known purpose of Selective Service is to procure manpower for the armed forces, a variety of related processes take place outside delivery of manpower to the active armed forces ... The process of channelling manpower by deferment is entitled to much credit for the large number of graduate students in technical fields and for the fact that there is not a greater shortage of teachers, engineers and other scientists working in activities which are essential to the national interest.

The System has also induced needed people to remain in these professions and in industry engaged in defense activities or in the support of national health, safety or interest.

The meaning of the word "service," with its former restricted application to the armed forces, is certain to become widened much more in the future. This brings with it the ever increasing problem of how to control effectively the service of individuals who are not in the armed forces.

Throughout his career as a student, the pressure – the threat of loss of deferment – continues. It continues with equal intensity after graduation. His local board requires periodic reports to find out what he is up to. He is impelled to pursue his skill rather than embark upon some less important enterprise and is encouraged to apply his skill in an essential activity in the national interest.

Selective Service processes do not compel people by edict as in foreign systems to enter pursuits having to do with essentiality and progress. They go because they know that by going they will be deferred.[66]

The race and class bias of the Selective Service System, at least before 1971, is well documented.[67] American scholars, including sociologists and others, have examined the economic stratification among war resisters that divided deserters from others along class and racial lines.[68]

In Canada, this specific social control purpose or effect of the Selective Service Program were discussed by several New Left writers. So were the effects of the Canadian immigration points system on deserters, notably by Melody Killian and Rick Ayers. Their article "Nowhere to Run, Nowhere to Hide," in *The Movement,* June 1969, drew direct parallels between the two systems:

> The Canadian immigration regulations are paired almost perfectly to the Selective Service Act in its channelling effect. The poor, the non-white, the unskilled and "inarticulate" are denied entry to Canada and left to face the draft in the US, while skilled and educated middle-class (and therefore mostly white) young men are welcomed because they are potentially useful to the Canadian branch-plant economy. In general, immigration rules exclude those who could not have received deferments [for attending university] in the US.[69]

Killian and Ayers had a great impact on Renée Kasinsky, who included several sections on channelling in her 1976 book, *Refugees from Militarism.* She wrote,

> Certainly the most important feature of these provisions [the points system] was its continuation of the class-based, manpower channelling system that operated in the United States during most of the Vietnam War years through the Selective Service System. [The points system] would favour the middle-class draft dodger over his working-class deserter compatriot. Working-class youths were not able to meet the educational and occupational requirements sufficiently to raise their scores above the 50 points necessary to [become] landed immigrants. Since the bulk of the deserter population fell into this category, most of the exiles had great difficulty in moving from underground to landed status in Canada. Thus, the same youths who were channelled into the United States Army in the first place found that the same negative selection operated against them in their efforts to start life anew in Canada after desertion.[70]

While Killian, Ayers, and Kasinsky all made some questionable assumptions about class, their basic interest in the class-stratification effects of American and Canadian policy was well-placed. Lawyer Paul Copeland's memories of the question of deserter education levels also show how deserters continued to experience exclusion once they arrived in Canada, even after the explicit discrimination was removed from the application process, because the job offer made such a big difference to the points system:

> If you had pre-arranged employment when you made the application, you got ten points out of the fifty you needed. Inside the country, you didn't get the points for the pre-arranged employment, so it was much easier to apply at the border. Also, the immigration offices in Canada were generally swamped, so if you applied from inside the country, it might take you three, four, five, six months before you actually got interviewed. You couldn't work during that time – at least legally you couldn't.[71]

War resisters with higher education levels got more points to begin with. Those education levels, in turn, contributed to the possibility of a war resister being able to find employment. The job offer would also count towards the points required for getting landed. Thus, lower-educated immigrants had a harder time immigrating.

Although there is no statistical proof, enough anecdotal evidence exists to suggest that deserters in Canada did, in general, come from backgrounds with less education and/or less income than draft dodgers. Surrey found that, while deserters did generally have less education than draft dodgers, on average they came from fairly highly educated families.[72] Further, he argued that war resisters with "marginal" backgrounds were more often returned to the United States by border officials and immigration officers.[73] Black draft dodgers, he argued, found immigration particularly difficult and wished to return because they could "go underground" more easily – a claim remarkably similar to that made by anti-draft activists themselves.[74]

Surrey corroborates claims of discrimination at the border; he quotes an anonymous immigration officer who was threatened with transfer to the Maritimes if he let in too many deserters.[75] More importantly, Surrey emphasizes that while war resisters in Canada on the whole came from upper strata of income within their respective categories, deserters nonetheless did aggregate at the low end of the income data sample.[76]

Surrey's sample is quite small, and his conclusions could be explained by other factors – the availability of post-secondary education to one generation more than another, for instance. However, he is not alone in making such an assessment.[77] Additionally, the number of draft resisters and deserters who came to Canada was only a fraction of the total who resisted; even the highest estimates of American immigration numbers pale in comparison to the quarter million estimated to have avoided the draft by merely omitting to register on their eighteenth birthday.[78] In turn, the anti-draft movements were a sliver of the wider opposition to war in Vietnam. Further, the experiences of many war resisters interviewed for this work and others call into question Surrey's finding that negative stigma accrued to both draft dodging and desertion. However, Surrey's conclusions do support Joseph Jones's opinion that, despite the lower economic and education status of deserters, those deserters who managed to escape to Canada were from the upper stratum of that lower stratum.[79]

Killian, Ayers, and Kasinsky tended to see all draft dodgers as "middle-class" and deserters as "working-class." Using income stratification and educational background instead of uncritically using notions of working or middle class to discuss differences between groups of war resisters provides a clearer analysis of these categories. Moreover, it was a sweeping generalization – and false – to suggest that all non-white American war resisters who came to Canada were deserters. For instance, Kasinsky's records refer to at least three black draft dodgers: Mike Vance, mentioned in an article in *Race Relations Reporter;* Mac Elrod, a former civil rights activist from Georgia, mentioned in reference to a CBC interview in 1970; and "John," a draft dodger Kasinsky interviewed, who had arrived in Montreal in 1968.[80] Important questions of racial and economic discrimination were obfuscated by rigid terms such as those used by Kasinsky, Killian, and Ayers.

However, Kasinsky's, Killian's, and Ayers's general conclusions are valuable and merit further study. The points system certainly did, and does, favour more privileged strata of economic and educational backgrounds (although it was an improvement over the earlier race-based policy).[81] The racial and economic discrimination present in the points system was not a major focus of anti-draft activism; instead, the activism focused on removing explicit discrimination by immigration officials against deserters, which left the implicit discrimination more or less intact.

There were, of course, exceptions; after the success of the border campaign, some activists turned to other measures necessary in their view to permit all war resisters to enter the country whether they met the qualifications or not. John Pocock of the TADP told a 1970 Toronto public meeting that a category of political asylum was required to allow unqualified resisters to enter Canada. Because deserters were outnumbering draft dodgers, and the tendency was for deserters not to qualify under the points system, he argued, such a category was necessary.[82] In late 1969, the Regina Committee of American Deserters exchanged correspondence with the Calgary group to try to convince them to adopt a position in favour of a special provision for deserters, arguing that the points system was inherently discriminatory.[83] Other deserter groups probably felt the same.

Let us consider what might have been the outcome if the movement had rejected Canadian nationalism. Arguably, its campaign would have been less effective. What if it had more critically and carefully used left nationalist arguments as a well-considered and intentional strategy? Perhaps such a strategy would have perpetuated common sense left nationalism all the same. What if the movement had evolved out of left nationalism to demand that the points system be reformed to stop discriminating against immigrants with less education and money? None of these questions can be answered by history. However, there is no doubt that the idea that the points system was fair and without discrimination permeated the letters to the Department of Immigration. The problem, for the campaigners, was not the law, but how it was being applied at the border. The dominant ideas set limits on whether, and how, the anti-draft movement could provide a deeper critique of the Canadian system of immigration laws and regulations.

After the 22 May 1969 announcement by MacEachen, an additional flurry of letters, 73 of 119 of them against the decision to open the border, reached the department. However, the letters soon abated, which allowed department officials to deal with the pile of unacknowledged and unanswered correspondence. Two letters from this period – 23 May to late June 1969 – indicate that the department developed a strategy for dealing with the correspondence. The department divided the correspondence into that which required a response beyond an acknowledgment and that which required no further reply. To ensure that no reply was needed, the minister's statement of 22 May was broadcast and distributed as far and wide as possible. The vast majority of letters, therefore, received either a brief two-line acknowledgment or a brief two-line acknowledgment together with a copy of the statement. The exceptions were some peace groups, labour representatives, church officials, government MPs, and many of the negative responses received after the 22 May announcement. The negative responses received a two-page explanation of the decision and its justifications, which emphasized that the government was not encouraging desertion but merely upholding principles of universality. Finally, at the direction of the deputy minister, all correspondence originating in Nova Scotia, MacEachen's home province, was to receive a lengthier response.[84] Longer responses thus went to those who might be expected to be former Liberal voters whose votes could be lost, and to the leadership of social forces who had some influence on the political decisions of their members.

The inherent instability of the pre-May 1969 policy, with its contradictory approach of nominally allowing in deserters while unofficially barring their entry based on immigration officers' discretion, was a major factor in changing Canadian policy towards war resisters. So was the comparatively small but very vocal and politically able movement to support American war resisters, deserters, and draft dodgers. Not all Canadians supported or welcomed the war resisters, as shown in the letters placed on the draft dodgers file in the Department of Immigration. Moreover, left nationalism and anti-Americanism played a role in limiting the extent of the critiques levelled at the government and its attitude towards war resisters from all sides of the political spectrum. Be that as it may, the campaign had its intended effect. Working with activists in Ottawa, MPs, lawyers, and individual Canadian citizens, the Canadian anti-draft movement succeeded in its bid to have the border opened for deserters.

6

Hegemonic Reflections
Inside and Outside the Movement

Cops
were raiding every
dream, and I went all
night about the house looking
for sleep,

under the waning,
silver moon I took
for a manacle.

I was in a fever, fitful
for Peace,
                children
waking without mothers
or arms, holocaust, Hell
no, I wouldn't go.

– Joe Nickell, *"Hidden Places"*[1]

The inherent contradictions in the ideas at play in the campaign to open the border to deserters were reflected both in continued police surveillance of war resisters and their supporters, and in the debates that continued to strengthen in the movement between those engaged in advocacy campaigns and those attracted to more radical critiques of the system. While police surveillance reflected public fears about radicalism, inside the movement, debate raged about what radicalism really was.

The 22 May 1969 announcement of the open border for deserters, which might have been expected to have an impact on RCMP behaviour, neither quelled public fears about an influx of dangerous, shiftless, or unreliable young American men, as shown in some of the letters to the Department of Immigration in 1969, nor led the RCMP to cease targeting war resisters.

Debates about the political orientation and activity of groups and individuals centred most often on questions of tactics in the antiwar movement, radicalism, and American influence. Likely rooted in tensions between Old Left influences and New Left sensibilities, some of these discussions came to a head at a conference of war resisters in Montreal in late 1970. After that conference, the anti-draft groups found a new unity of purpose, which would not have been possible without the previous years of experience as a diverse and decentralized, yet more or less coordinated, movement.

Policing the Anti-Draft Movement: RCMP Surveillance and Legitimacy

Perhaps in part because of this new unity, partly brought about by a degree of radicalization, the RCMP continued its surveillance efforts well into the 1970s, despite the waning importance of the issue in the public arena. The 22 May announcement of an open border did nothing to slow these efforts. RCMP officers continued to conduct raids on war resister houses and those of their supporters. They also kept anti-draft groups and groups supportive of the cause under surveillance. Municipal police, federal politicians, and the legal system all played a role in widespread surveillance and occasional harassment of anti-draft groups and activists.

For example, on 12 August 1969, the Metropolitan Toronto Police narcotics squad and the RCMP narcotics squad raided the Toronto home of Donna Baron Fine, ostensibly to search for drugs and an alleged drug dealer (and war resister) named Bob Farrell. The officers questioned Farrell without a lawyer present for fifteen minutes. One officer called someone to check on Farrell's identity. Another officer made disparaging remarks about draft dodgers and deserters.[2] Subsequently, Fine filed complaints and took the matter public.[3] Similarly, Vancouver war resister aid groups reported seven raids between April and December of 1969 on a hostel they had set up. RCMP entered and searched personal documents and files while asserting they were looking for drugs. Steve Vernon of the Vancouver American Deserters Committee assumed they were doing work on behalf of the FBI.[4]

Interaction between immigration officials and the RCMP shows continued police preoccupation with US immigrants. It also suggests that tensions around the two departments' respective jurisdictions, about whose responsibility these potential troublemakers were, and about the efficacy of both organizations' actions, also continued. The jurisdictional conflict, marked by frustrated exchanges of correspondence, began shortly after an intense and more general discussion about the powers of the RCMP in the arena of security and secret policing and some limitation of those powers.[5] The fact that several bureaucrats in the Department of Immigration happened to agree with the RCMP about the trouble American immigrants could cause did nothing to alleviate the interdepartmental frustrations. The situation was, if anything, exacerbated by the change in border policy in May of 1969. As public policy changes took hold, Department of Immigration bureaucrats' attitudes towards the anti-draft groups slowly changed as well, increasing the differences in respective attitudes taken towards war resisters by the two departments. The jurisdictional struggle was, like earlier discussions, a part of the hegemonic process to develop an attitude towards war resisters that both complied with public perceptions of Canada as a refuge from militarism and legitimized sentiment against the war resisters and their activities in Canada.

After MacEachen's announcement, the RCMP continued to express concerns to Immigration Department officials about its apparent lack of commitment to enforcing its own regulations. Late 1969 correspondence from the assistant RCMP commissioner and director of security and intelligence, J.E.M. Barrette, suggested that the Department of Immigration had been reluctant to enforce immigration regulations, which banned the use of visitor status expressly in order to apply for landing once in Canada; made working before securing a permit from immigration illegal; and considered lying in an application to be grounds for barring entry. This lackadaisical approach, in the eyes of the RCMP, meant that Canada was "becoming a sanctuary for both political extremists and criminals." Al Gorman, chief of the Enforcement Section of the Department of Immigration's Home Services, assured RCMP Commissioner William Higgitt that such was not the case. Immigration officials, for their part, suspected the RCMP of being overzealous in their activities regarding American immigrants; a draft of Gorman's reply to the commissioner carried an admonishment that the RCMP should not be encouraged to use section 16 of the act (which stated that all statements made in the application for entry to Canada must be truthful), since that would eliminate the need for an arrest warrant and would invite abuse by the RCMP.[6]

Perhaps in an attempt to get the Department of Immigration to take the criminality of war resisters more seriously, the RCMP sometimes shared its information on draft dodgers support groups and activities with Department of Immigration officials. In 1970, the RCMP spied on the Pan-Canadian Conference of US War Resisters in Montreal. They interpreted the results of the conference as the movement's having "adopt[ed] a more militant attitude."[7] The coverage of the conference in *AMEX* magazine was filed by the RCMP, along with a list of participating groups and individuals. The information was discussed at the highest levels. On 2 July the RCMP notified the Privy Council, the Department of Manpower and Immigration, and the Department of External Affairs of the conference and the RCMP analysis.[8] On 17 July, a memo to the minister of immigration from Robert Adams, the assistant deputy minister of immigration, referred to a further RCMP report that "contain[ed] disquieting information": there were twenty-three anti-draft groups in Canada helping draft dodgers and deserters enter, and other unidentified organizations were doing the same. Some Canadian groups were working with US organizations. These groups were distributing information on immigration requirements, and some had set up "escape routes" to help deserters and, perhaps, "black power fugitives" come to Canada.[9] Finally, the memo indicated that American targets were becoming the focus of some antiwar protests.[10] It is likely this report was based in large part on the intelligence gathered at the pan-Canadian conference.

The RCMP's reports on the pan-Canadian conference and the war resister support groups had at least some impact on Department of Immigration attitudes. A handwritten note stated that "the draft-dodgers and deserter problem has every indication of becoming more of a problem. If the groups become more militant and conduct clandestine activities I would think this would force immediate remedial steps. It would seem more prudent to be quietly correcting a problem that appears to be developing than to wait for it to happen."[11]

In the campaign to open the border to deserters, the media had a significant impact on events and generally acted to reinforce the campaign. In the case of police harassment, the media role was more ambiguous and

did not consistently support the resisters. Some journalists rather uncritically reported the occasionally virulent anti-resister statements of public
figures in the justice system; others criticized the police. The *Globe and
Mail* encouraged critical scrutiny of the police in its 11 November 1969
article, "RCMP Checks 2259 on US Draft Status." Based on replies in
writing to questions asked by NDP .MP for Yorkton-Melville, Lorne
Nystrom, the article showed that police had targeted Americans for interviews, at the behest, at least in some cases, of "agencies of the United
States." The article was clipped and filed by the Department of Immigration.[12] Other cases, including illegal deportations and routine harassment,
were reported by both the mainstream and alternative news media in late
1969 and early 1970.[13]

Exiles and their supporters were highly conscious of police attention
and saw it as "repression." Aspects of this attention included RCMP cooperation with the FBI. The worst action the RCMP could take, in the eyes of
resisters and their supporters, was to hand over war resisters to American
police forces for prosecution, often in collaboration with immigration
officers. When Canadian officials accused war resisters of lying and brought
them before Canadian courts, resisters perceived it as persecution and a
waste of money spent on enforcing American laws. Judges were perceived
as biased against US war resisters.[14] But the worst offenders were the RCMP:
"collusion with the FBI is practically the RCMP's raison d'être," proclaimed
an *AMEX* feature in late 1970.[15]

Individual cases became legendary among resisters and the anti-draft
movement. One such case was that of David Lutz, a schoolteacher who lost
his job due to RCMP communication of false allegations of immoral behaviour to the school board in Fredericton, New Brunswick. Another was
the case of three deserters who were taken into RCMP custody in January
of 1970 and illegally deported to the United States. This case resulted in a
judicial inquiry that absolved the RCMP of blame and suggested that the
resisters were victims of circumstance, "misunderstanding, confusion, and
coincidence," and not the intentional actions of the police.[16]

Anti-draft groups noticed this police behaviour, and in some cases were
also targets. In March of 1970, as a war resister hostel run by the Vancouver
committee received continued visits by police, activist and deserter Pete
Maly claimed in the media that RCMP passed information to the FBI on a
regular basis.[17] A 1970 letter from Vance Gardner of the Montreal committee

to the Vancouver group indicated that deserters had been "hassled" by the RCMP, who had as much as admitted that the council's phones were tapped.[18] The Vancouver ADC hostel was also raided around this time; in that raid, officers told deserters present to "shut up or we'll smash your fucking heads in." The raid was officially for drugs, but officers reportedly recorded names of financial supporters and ransacked files.[19] Supporting groups outside the network of anti-draft groups were also the subjects of RCMP scrutiny. An RCMP brief written in 1970 about the University of Toronto Students' Administrative Council (SAC) noted that three years earlier, the SAC had given money to the "Toronto Anti-Draft Movement," adding that most students opposed the donation (although the president was re-elected almost immediately on a pro-draft dodger platform).[20]

The RCMP actions regarding war resisters suffered from particularly bad publicity on the occasion of the raid of the home of *Montreal Star* journalist, W.A. Wilson. Wilson was an outspoken supporter of the war resisters and critic of the RCMP. His wife had aided some war resisters in their home.[21] During a raid of their residence on 23 March 1970, when neither Wilson nor his wife was present, the RCMP questioned Wilson's children. The day after, Wilson reported on this fact in a feature article about RCMP targeting war resisters and colluding with the FBI.[22] Later that week, the issue was a topic of discussion in the House of Commons.[23] In early April, Wilson accused the RCMP of "taking a political role." He justified his earlier reports on RCMP activities as a necessary element of a democracy. "One of the great barriers to the effective scrutiny of established institutions is an unnecessarily respectful attitude towards them," he stated.[24] Wilson's views reflected public concerns about the potential political abuse of power by the RCMP.

Because of such examples of public concern and scrutiny, the RCMP could not act with complete impunity. In the late sixties and early seventies, events such as the Front de Libération du Québec crisis and student unrest on campuses led the RCMP Security Service to increase its activities, and even to set bombs to frame dissenting groups.[25] Among other trends and events, notably the implementation of the War Measures Act in October 1970, this heightened activity and the increased dissent to which the RCMP was reacting led to the convening of two Royal Commissions in the late 1960s and 1970s. The Royal Commission on Security, or the Mackenzie Commission, reported in 1969; the longer and more extensive Royal

Commission Concerning Certain Activities of the Royal Canadian Mounted Police, also known as the McDonald Commission, convened in 1978 and reported in 1981.[26] In some small way, the commissions might be understood as one of many reactions of the government to war resisters.[27]

At the same time, police actions were partially legitimized by the public statements of justice system figures and elected officials. One judge in a BC court room, committing a deserter to trial for assault, suggested (despite the right to be considered innocent until proven guilty) that "immigration should be more meticulous in accepting certain persons, especially draft dodgers ... This type of conscientious objector has no conscience."[28] The mayor of Vancouver, Tom Campbell, also weighed in: around October of 1970, he suggested using the War Measures Act to deal with draft dodgers:

> I'm not against dissent, but I believe the law should be used against any revolutionary whether he's a US draft dodger or a hippie if he is in an organization that advocates the overthrow of the government by force ... I don't like draft dodgers and I'll do anything within the law that allows me to get rid of them. The whole Communist theory is to corrupt youth and the country will follow. Somebody is sure doing a swell job of corrupting a minority of our youth. I want the border closed to radicals. I'm looking at more than the loss of a few civil liberties. I'm looking at freedom. Take a few liberties but give me freedom.[29]

These comments show that the fears of some in the movement – that a negative impact on public opinion would result from more radical politics – were not necessarily groundless.

Police behaviour was generally accepted until the mid-1970s, when the dirty tricks scandal that resulted in a commission of inquiry undermined public trust in the institution of the RCMP. Police harassment and surveillance behaviours reflected divisions at various strata of society. The surveillance also reflected public fears about Americans and their influence on Canadian society in general, and specifically on Canadian social justice movements. Further, it reflected debates among departmental officials about how to treat war resisters as their profile increased in the public arena. The 22 May 1969 announcement regarding opening the border to deserters was made, but surveillance and police targeting continued.

The war resisters of the Vietnam War era were not universally nor immediately welcomed in Canada – it took a campaign by pressure groups to achieve that, though not everyone involved in the campaign considered themselves to be part of the movement as a whole. Given these challenges, it is remarkable that they achieved what they did. But the activists of the 1960s and early 1970s were also participants in a discussion about Canadian nationalism, the internal contradictions of which, along with other debates in the movement, led to acrimonious scenes of conflict over whose tactics and strategy were more appropriate. After May of 1969, these conflicts were overcome, with difficulty, in time to allow the movement to take full advantage of its geographical diversity in participating and promoting aspects of 1972 and 1973 government programs to address emerging problems with the management of immigration to Canada.

"Politicized in a Canadian Way": "Anti-War Work" and Tactical Debates

Police surveillance of the anti-draft movement was a manifestation of public concerns about the role of Americans in Canadian society. These questions were also a major part of the movement's internal dialogue after May of 1969 in particular. Discussions about antiwar tactics, assimilation, radicalism, and nationalism were commonly subsumed under what was called, in the vernacular of the time, "politics." Although the debates made acting in concert at times difficult, ultimately, through discussion and compromise as well as a certain amount of radicalization, the movement was able to overcome these differences and offer a renewed commitment to work together for the cause.

Whether a person or a group qualified as "political" was a relative attribute that depended on the political orientation of the individual or group making the assessment. One excerpt from a Renée Kasinsky interviewee, Bill, describes well the tensions between the political aspirations of activists and their desire to help resisters. Bill describes his experience as a Vietnam veteran with the Montreal ADC:

> [At first] the meetings themselves were just general discussions on housing etc. and just supporting deserters when they came up, that's about all. There was a little controversy about politics but not much ...

Some of them were Canadians, there were ... deserters who had been there quite a while ...

There was a kind of [elitist] attitude, and there were a few people who formed kind of a [clique] and they all had good jobs and good places to live. [When] I became personally involved with them, I could take them aside ... and ask them for a favour ... Then there were some people ... [who] would put in all this work and effort and it would never be returned in any way so ... just quit. The people just kept doing that – working hard for a few months and then quitting ...

[Other people] didn't want it political, people who weren't radical. Like I was [a Marxist]... and a few other people were, but try as we would no-one would listen. They would just draw the line and would say well we don't want to get mixed up in that, it's too political ...

We wanted to effectively aid deserters, but at the same time provide to deserters to extend their political involvement in Canada ... People that came up ... figured well I'm in Canada now and I'm safe, and I don't want to discuss it any more – I don't want to hear about the army, and I don't want to hear about the war.[30]

The interviewee goes on to describe how a small group of American immigrants opposed to Communist ideas took over the ADC and renamed it the American Deserters Cooperative by dominating the volunteer force. The group that took over effectively split the ADC into warring and ineffective factions. Other deserters even went so far as to destroy some of the group's records. According to Bill, these conflicts damaged the public image of the ADC. The group had no supporters because it had become a "clique."[31] Bill describes how the divisions created by certain group members' adherence to one political ideology or another created a culture of cliques, which had, in turn, made the takeover possible. This clique effect was common, and so was the notion that adherence to a particular idea or mode of action was necessary to qualify as political. One possible root of these debates was the division between the Old and the New Left. Several observations here illustrate how perceived Old Left/New Left divisions might have affected the debates in the anti-draft movement.

First, a word on the Canadian New Left. As far as a New Left did exist in Canada, as Ian McKay, Bryan Palmer, and others certainly agree, it was shaped by the specificities of Canadian historical development, not least of which was the intellectual tradition of the staples thesis down through the Waffle, and even the NDP.[32] McKay argues that the New Left in Canada was a bona fide formation, differentiated from the "radical planners" of the 1930s such as the Co-operative Commonwealth Federation. But while divisions were perceived, and therefore had an impact, the New Left in Canada owed much to the Old Left as far as practices and ideas were concerned. Arguably, this was also the case for the American New Left.[33] In fact, one might go so far as to suggest that the "New Left," at least in Canada, was really more of a "renewed Left," especially considering two factors: the relatively small size of the groups normally identified with the Canadian New Left, namely, Student Union for Peace Action (SUPA) and related youth movements; and the close relationship with the new nationalist preoccupations of a broad section of civil society, including the Canadian Union of Students (CUS), whose flirtation with economic nationalism, while arriving comparatively late, was nonetheless strong.[34] Certainly for the anti-draft movement, the distinction between old and new is difficult to discern, since it was to such a large extent a multigenerational movement with influences from multiple sources – peace churches, pacifist traditions, and the crucible of radical ideas of the sixties born in the aftermath of the Cold War.

Anti-draft groups had links with draft counselling groups in the United States, and many of those groups had existed since long before the war on Vietnam. They were often staffed by activists from older pacifist strains of the peace movement. At the same time, as younger activists got involved in this counselling, they did not always recognize the historical contribution of the older activists to the pacifist movement. Mark Phillips, a draft counsellor before his move to Canada, recalls that

> there was always that division, between the traditional pacifists and Vietnam antiwar groups. In those days I was sort of supercilious about it, but now I'm chastened, because those people stayed [involved from a much earlier period]. They kept doing antiwar work in a way the rest of us didn't ... They produced the literature that we [counsellors] had [in the Oakland group he worked with], but they seemed to me at the time to be wholly apolitical ... There was this really strong division between

traditional pacifists, who had organized those earlier things I was involved with, SANE and all that, but the groups that I would have contacted [in Canada] were people like me who were doing anti-Vietnam War counselling. We got the [counselling] material from the old line pacifists.[35]

Phillips's experience was with both the older models of civil disobedience, like SANE, and with newer counselling groups who made use of the material, but focused on the Vietnam War specifically. His feelings about "traditional pacifists" seeming "apolitical" at the time are similar to those outlined earlier. Likewise, Hardy Scott, a draft dodger who got involved in the Vancouver group upon his arrival in 1967, was a former draft counsellor from 1964 to 1967 in New York City.[36] Groups such as the Central Committee for Conscientious Objectors coexisted with Students for a Democratic Society, the Boston Draft Resistance Group, and others, and shared common roots and experience in the anti-nuclear and civil rights movements.

The influence of old pacifist and socialist movements and groups on young people getting involved in anti-draft counselling in the context of the Vietnam War was considerable. As early as 1966, an American Quaker from the Central Committee for Conscientious Objectors in Philadelphia visited SUPA and the Canadian Quakers, likely in Toronto.[37] In addition, the files of the Toronto committee, in particular, but also others, contained multiple copies of American anti-draft counselling manuals and other publications. But many of the activists saw themselves as part of a new generation. Canadian activist Ken Fisher's experience bore some markings of encounters with Old Left activists. He remembers cultural differences between Old and New Left and a sense of a moment of transition:

First I met with some people from the old left. I can't remember them [clearly], but it was the first time I really woke up to the fact the new left was just the moment. There was a whole history of things before that ... And these guys [I met with] were communists. These guys were, I think, in the trade union movement somewhere in Ontario, and maybe they were retired, maybe still active.

[The] whole speech pattern was different in those days. [People] mimicked being stoned. We hesitated to say anything assertively. I can't even imagine imitating the way we talked, but it was a very slow cadence. But these guys, they didn't talk like that at all. They were like, here's the deal, here's the analysis, here's the situation. We're going to do this. And there was something about them. I felt like I was talking to something like a backwater or a political eddy. I remember thinking: this is really strange; this is a very strange culture that I'm playing with here. But it wasn't a church culture – *that* I was familiar with. It had a different imagination, and a different integrity, and a different certitude.[38]

Finally, lawyer Paul Copeland, who helped war resisters in Toronto and was involved in the campaign to open the border to deserters, shares an anecdote that sheds further light on the involvement of Old Left activists in the anti-draft movement. He jokingly suggests that he was unaware of the different political tendencies around him, but his words show that not only did he know about them, they all managed to work together in one way or another:

The day that the Americans actually leave Vietnam – you know, the helicopter taking off with people falling off it and stuff – I go down to the Wheat Sheaf tavern to meet with the people from the Anti-Draft Programme to celebrate the victory and a bunch of people I had worked with for years. And towards the end of the evening, [Canadian Communists] Nelson and Phyllis Clarke show up, and I sort of wonder, What are they doing here? And at the end of the evening, they all stand up and sing the Internationale. And I think, What the fuck? *[laughs]* These people are all part of the Communist Party? *[laughs]* We worked a lot with people from the Communist Party around the war stuff. There was a guy named "Rich Somebody" who had been a union organizer and who was a member of the CP who I did a fair bit of stuff with ... I always hated the CP and liked the new left because the CP was ... just way too serious ... I always thought that political work was important, but enjoying the political work was important, and enjoying life was important ...

There were a million Trot groups doing antiwar work ... There were the Young Socialists ... They did a lot of antiwar work [but not much anti-draft work]. You go to any antiwar demonstrations ... You had the Young Socialists carrying their flag; you had the League for Socialist

Action, which may have been the Young Socialists; you had the Spartacist League ... Just all sorts of people from all walks of life were involved in the antiwar movement, and it grew to be huge. And then there were sort of the new left groups floating around, doing both antiwar work and other work.

The CPC-ML [Communist Party of Canada (Marxist-Leninist)] did some antiwar work too – the CPC-ML, who we also acted for [as lawyers] and who would occasionally denounce me. I mean, we were [all] a little nutty.[39]

Of the traditions outlined above, the least significant in terms of direct influence was the communist or socialist tradition. Perhaps that was because communists focused on being effective, as Kasinsky's Bill suggested, and avoided the tactical discussions or perhaps because communists were mainly involved elsewhere in the antiwar movement. Other possible factors include lingering cold war doubts about communism among the public, and the fact that communism was not very fashionable among the new generation of activists. For whichever reason, their ideas do not figure prominently as influences on war resisters and their supporters. On the other hand, the traditions of nonviolent civil disobedience, churches and liberation theology, and pacifism, on the one hand, and the new approaches of the New Left and anti-imperialism on the other, were very present. And they were at loggerheads for much of the period, until 1970 when the conference in Montreal became the site of a new unity.

The many debates among anti-draft activists and deserter and exile groups were organized around the questions of violence, radicalism, and effectiveness. Some activists felt that a new strain of political action, one eschewing nonviolent traditions, was turning new immigrants away from getting involved. Nancy Pocock reflected on this possibility in her 1970 interview with Kasinsky:

I don't think the ones that come up here are very political. The political ones are staying down there and fighting ... And the pacifist ones are in jail ... [The ones who come up] think they can't do any good in jail, and they feel the movement is getting very violent, and they don't see how they can fit in ...

I think there was a movement for a long time before it became what it is now. There was a very strong movement. The civil rights movement grew out of a peace movement. And there still is a non-violent movement, as well as the other movement. And I know many people who are working down there in non-violent ways, and are not politicized.[40]

Pocock's concern to keep the movement non-violent and her conflation of politicization with violence were probably a response to mainstream media accounts of such incidents as the riots at the Chicago Democratic National Convention in 1968, Stonewall and the Days of Rage in 1969, and the Kent State events of May of 1970, as well as the Canadian example of Sir George Williams University in Montreal in January of 1969, where protesters occupied a computer lab over alleged mishandling of racism charges against the school.[41] It is easy to see how the idea of Canada as having a pacifist tradition may have played into these debates.

Here, "political" was defined in relation to violent and nonviolent strands of the movement. In effect, Pocock saw politicization as an Americanized strand of the Canadian movement, and a violent strand of the American movement:

> For instance, if they want to be political, I would like to see them taking on the problem of our complicity, of what factories do for the American war effort. I'd like to see them picketing those factories. I'd like to see them talking to those workers, interviewing the management ... I don't say I'm against their being politicized. I think it's a shame when they come here and lapse into nothing. But I'd like to see them politicized in a Canadian way. Not an American way. Heaven knows, I don't know what they can do. I don't know what *I* can do.[42]

On the other hand, for some American immigrants, being political meant being radical, as one deserter Kasinsky interviewed suggested: "I've seen a large percentage of deserters switch very quickly to becoming political. I remember one case, especially, where a guy came up – from Detroit – he came up one day, that night went off to listen to [Black Panther leader and American radical] Kathleen Cleaver, came back the next day rapping dialectics, and has steadily progressed leftward from there."[43] Similarly, the Vancouver ADC expressed its outlook as a political one. We have evolved a Five Point Program for deserters, which includes propaganda (both of action and of word), educational classes, pointing out Canada's colonial status and explaining the class bias of the selective service system in the States; a program to unify Canadian anti-draft organizations for great effectiveness; a pledge of support to all people and nations within North America fighting capitalist repression and imperialism. We have full information on the Canadian Immigration Act, and provide counsel and advice for anyone who needs it.[44]

The Montreal ADC listed, as one of its reasons for existing, "the cultural corruption and economic exploitation of the peoples and natural resources of Quebec, Canada, and of all the countries into which the US system extends." It decided in April of 1969 that it needed to be "more political and more public" to reach its constituency. But, for them, at this point, that meant becoming involved in the campaign, instigated by the Toronto Anti-Draft Programme (TADP), to open the border to deserters.[45]

The majority of the groups that adhered to these ideas emerged after the border was open to deserters. Because of their radical ideological approach, the exile groups sometimes alienated potential volunteers and those who might need help. For instance, Lee Zaslofsky, a deserter who arrived in 1970, wrote in *AMEX* that year that the Toronto ADC suspected him of being an FBI infiltrator because of his short hair. In the article, Zaslofsky was generally critical of exile groups.[46] Sometimes these tensions were resolved in public. Describing his own perspective on the incident described by (another) Bill above, Bill Murray of the Montreal American Deserters Co-op stated in an *AMEX* article, "[we have] no intention of ever going back to the US but the other group we belonged to [the ADC] and broke away from at their request, was more radical ... My men are neutral. We want to live here and because the Canadian government was decent in letting us come we don't want to spoil things." The ADC responded in the article that the "newcomers are either crazy, 'power-tripping' individuals, or cops."[47] Here, the ADC expressed the anti-authoritarian strain of the radical Left and fears about police infiltration of activist groups. The conflict between the American Deserters Committee and the American Deserters Co-op was apparently, in this instance, explicitly over ideological orientation. For the committee members, anyone who disagreed with their radical orientation must be mentally unstable or a police infiltrator. If nothing else, this episode gives a sense of how deeply felt were the sentiments on either side.

In contrast, the Toronto American Deserters Committee had little expressly political ambition. It initially sought to "provide deserters with the additional assistance needed for them to successfully conclude the immigration process and become contributing members of Canadian society." Similarly, the Toronto Union of American Exiles sought to "bring together exiled Americans for the purpose of self-help and social action" and to "complement and supplement the services of the Toronto Anti-Draft Programme."[48] For these two groups, the orientation of immigrants was not a deciding factor. Nor was political agreement with other groups a condition in order to work with them. The Union of American Exiles (UAE) came in for criticism for this less radical orientation. Said one movement journalist,

> The Union of American Exiles (UAE) is the largest, busiest and politically least effective exile group in Canada. It specifically defines itself not as a political group, but as a service organization committed to ameliorating problems such as loneliness, disorientation, the lack of housing and jobs ... The UAE has in the past addressed itself to questions such as whether the group, which has a formal membership and a constitution, should "Become Political." But ... the UAE has defined itself so far away from political self-consciousness that radical exiles living in Toronto usually cannot work with it ... Such an organization inevitably leads to Yankee chauvinism ... and can only alienate Canadians along national lines. Americans, as Americans, are hardly an oppressed minority in Canada. Their need to organize themselves can be rooted only in opposition to US imperialism, with the aim of liberating not only themselves, but Canadians also, from its grip.[49]

The debate expressed in the above excerpts appears to be ranged along the line between being a service organization and taking on an advocacy function that went beyond the assistance of individuals in securing landed immigrant status, jobs, and shelter. However, here again it is necessary to emphasize how subjective this judgment was, because to this date the largest advocacy campaign had been undertaken by the groups considered less political and more oriented to service. The advocacy the anti-draft groups undertook was not considered legitimate antiwar work by the more radical groupings, exactly because it was not sufficiently radical, ideologically speaking.

A good example of this argument about radicalism took place among BC activists and was also made public in the pages of movement publications. Some animosity existed between the TADP's Bill Spira and activists in other anti-draft groups, including Melody Killian of the *Yankee Refugee*. Killian was a war resister who was involved in organizing American "refugees." A letter dated 23 June 1969 from Steve Strauss of the Vancouver Committee to Aid American War Objectors (VCAAWO) to Allen Mace of the TADP stated, "It irritates me when I call long distance to be lectured for ten minutes about the misconduct of this office ... especially when it turns out that what Bill Spiro [sic] didn't like was the *Yankee Refugee* and Melody Killian, neither of whom are connected with the Committee. He says the trouble with us is that we aren't a liberal organization. Whatever the hell that means."[50] Here, liberal politics were opposed to radical politics. Spira probably saw liberal politics as a set of politics that sought change from within, while radicals sought to change the system fundamentally. This conflict was a symptom of the debate about politics within the anti-draft movement. Indeed, it was Killian's 1969 *Yankee Refugee* piece, "Oh, Canada!" that seems to have provoked hostility from Spira and others. In it, Killian asserted that

the belief of most counsellors [in existing aid groups] is the following: that anti-draft work decreases the size of the US military; that it is in some way anti-war work; that is it humanitarian and moral work and saves lives; that it is vital work which must take priority over political work; that in fact anyone doing political activity is jeopardizing the anti-draft programme and is threatening the lives of people because Americans doing political work in Canada could cause the "closing of the border."

Killian suggested that humanitarian work was not political. In contrast, the "Vancouver Yankee Refugee group" had decided that only anti-capitalist work was bona fide antiwar work: "The only justification for being out of jail or Vietnam is to fight the system more effectively from here. We will not remain quiet or complacent to protect work that is not really humanitarian in terms of our long-range goal of ending an anti-human system."[51]

Killian and *Yankee Refugee* were asserting a radical and anti-capitalist approach, suggesting that groups engaged in humanitarian work that did not relate war to capitalism were not really antiwar.

In the following issue of *Yankee Refugee,* Ottawa Assistance with Immigration and the Draft (AID) activist Goldie Josephy responded to Killian, stating,

> Some of us who helped form a viable peace movement in Canada might take exception to statements by Melody Killian that places like Ottawa etc. need "political groups ... to do real anti-war work." I think my dear children, you need to do a little homework, and then you will find that groups like mine have been active for nearly 10 years – you might also learn something useful in the process.

In reply, the editors gave their own educational advice, urging Josephy to read Herbert Marcuse on "repressive tolerance."[52] Marcuse argued that "within a repressive society, even progressive movements threaten to turn into their opposite to the degree to which they accept the rules of the game," and that movements that do not challenge the status quo are doomed to perpetuate it.[53] In this exchange, then, Josephy claimed that the underlying theme was one of experience over youth. By referring to her longer experience, Josephy invoked an older tradition of nonviolence and implicitly claimed the wisdom associated with that experience, effectively accusing the *Yankee Refugee* of being inexperienced hotheads. By invoking Marcuse, the *Yankee Refugee* claimed the debate was actually about repression, and accused Josephy of being part of the status quo. She could not be effective because she was not involved in fighting for fundamental changes within the system.

Killian's criticism of the anti-draft groups engaged in support work was sometimes shared by *AMEX*. In an early 1970 editorial, *AMEX* argued that Bill Spira and the TADP were using a too-narrow definition of antiwar work and accused them of being "liberal" – that is to say, accepting of the current democratic rule.[54] Bill Spira agreed, and, in fact, he thought that the Vancouver Committee was not liberal enough.

These debates had repercussions on the groups' funding. The January 1970 issue of *AMEX* reported on a meeting of clergy and resister aid groups in Windsor, Ontario, claiming that Spira had interfered in the event.[55] Later, the Montreal ADC wrote to *AMEX* that they had been denied funding from the Canadian Council of Churches because Spira had convinced them not to fund "political" groups.[56] In the next issue, Vance Gardner of the Montreal Council to Aid War Resisters suggested that the churches (likely referring to the Canadian Council of Churches) merely saw the aid groups as doing work more closely aligned with their approach.[57] A September 1970 letter to *AMEX* provided a "medium defence of Bill Spira ... where was the writer when Bill Spira started working with Toronto Anti-draft[?] Sure, Spira is not the easiest guy to get along with, but he's worked hard and has a lot of knowledge we benefited from. You must be pretty damn cock-sure to go around bad-mouthing ... So, can the bloody character assassination."[58]

In his 1970 interview with Kasinsky, Spira was explicit on the question of whether the counselling groups should be "political." Spira asserted that to place such a requirement would mean selecting volunteers for their political persuasions, which he regarded as "silly." Spira was forthrightly hostile at times to exile groups: "*AMEX* has no constituency at all. *AMEX* is two or three people who write a magazine. They have no constituency, they don't hold any meetings, etc." He was just as hostile in his opposition to the holding of an exile conference in Montreal in 1970.[59] For Spira, any group with no connection to a movement could not claim to represent anyone but its own members, narrowly defined. Therefore, it could not be effective.

However, Spira did not deny the political nature of war resistance: "I see the act of desertion as a highly political act. But that doesn't mean that the individual fully realizes the full implications of his act." Rather, his objection was to the expectation of a specific ideological orientation by aid groups and the potential effects that expectation could have on appropriate counselling. As he commented on the Montreal ADC's approach, "If [a counsellor] thinks politicizing a guy is more important than to get him landed obviously [he] will spend much less time on it and also the selection of counsellors will be different. You look for someone with 'the correct political line' instead of somebody who knows the immigration scene."[60] In May 1970, against Spira's position, movement journalist Fred Gardner expressed the idea that to advocate against the formation of exile groups, as Spira was doing, was to explicitly take a position against the political nature of desertion as an antiwar tactic: "To criticize deserters because they merely want to stay alive is inhumane; to dismiss them as apolitical is not only wrong, but has the elements of a self-fulfilling prophecy."[61]

As Joseph Jones noted, exile groups went through different phases of political orientation during their existence.[62] *AMEX* magazine reflected these changes. The mainstream media noticed its increasing politicization. A December 1970 *Toronto Star* editorial urged *AMEX* and American immigrants to fit into Canadian life, suggesting that the "revolution"-oriented American immigrants were in a minority.[63] The debate raged to a lesser degree in some places than others. In Ottawa, for instance, the ADC and Ottawa AID were staffed in 1970 by the same people – evidence that deserter groups and aid organizations could get along.[64] Even the *Yankee Refugee*, associated with the Vancouver ADC, went through different phases of orientation. One article by its staff suggested that "our constituency can only be the American community as long as it takes to dissolve that community – to effect meaningful assimilation into already existing groups or to create new groups that involve draft dodgers not as Americans but as new Canadians."[65] Here, instead of retaining American-ness, the *Yankee Refugee* argued for assimilation into the Canadian movement.

New Unity: The Montreal Conference, May–June 1970

In May 1969, the Toronto-based Union of American Exiles, one of the oldest American-identified groups, grew concerned about deterioration in the practice of sharing information among groups and a resulting inconsistency in counselling practices.[66] The group proposed a conference that would prove to be a turning point for the question of politics in the anti-draft movement.[67] The conference, dubbed the Pan-Canadian Conference of US War Resisters by *AMEX*, was planned for the purposes of improving consistency with counselling and other activities and generally improving communication.[68] Over the next few months, anti-draft groups discussed the proposal favourably.[69] Other groups worked to promote the conference once it was planned, and although the idea came from an exile group, the promoters cast a wide net. Voice of Women (VOW) received a letter from the ADC describing the conference and its purposes as being "cooperation" and sharing of resources. The ADC emphasized that the event was expected to be the largest ever conference of anti-draft groups and refugee or deserter groups, with twenty to twenty-five groups attending, as well as many individuals. The draft agenda included a roundtable;

discussions about information sharing, government relations, the political role of resisters, the formation of a "political coalition," and next steps; and the establishment of a means of coordination.[70] These agenda items were signs of a mature movement with experience working on behalf of resisters as individuals and as a group, and with the intention of overcoming political debates between liberal and radical orientations in order to move forward together in some unity.

The Pan-Canadian Conference of US War Resisters, held in Montreal in May and June of 1970, was attended by aid groups and exile organizations, as well as one or two international groups.[71] Other attendees included the main existing aid groups (except Calgary, Winnipeg, and Victoria); the antiwar and left activist groups the Front de libération populaire and Women's Liberation; American anti-draft groups; the Canadian Council of Churches (CCC); American church organizations; Unitarians and Quakers; and coffeehouse projects.[72]

In some ways, this conference was the logical next step for a social movement that had had a victory the year before and was looking for ways to be proactive in a unified way. Perhaps the unexpected victory had resulted in a lack of focus for the movement. It also coincided with tougher times for immigrants in Canada, with unemployment increasing and public opinion beginning to turn against immigrants for that reason. There was a need to work together in this new climate, instead of turning against one another.

The conference discussed the condition of employment and the impact the increase in the numbers of immigrants was having on the ability of aid groups to find work for the influx. Thunder Bay, Sudbury, Saskatoon, Edmonton, and Winnipeg were exceptions. Conference participants discussed the recent open border policy and factors that still restricted entry for deserters, including the potential impact of negative publicity regarding the political and other activities of war resisters.[73] The session also included the distribution of cheques from the CCC, including to the ADCs.[74] Canon Maurice P. Wilkinson of the CCC announced that, although money had been issued previously only to the TADP, now that the CCC knew about the other groups, money was being distributed more broadly. The months following the conference saw additional funds sent to the MCAWR, Montreal, Regina, and Toronto ADCs, the TADP, the VCAAWO, Winnipeg Committee to Assist American War Objectors, and RWB.[75] The CCC could no longer be accused of funding only "non-political" groups. The conference and the unity it displayed may have been the impetus for this shift in the CCC's policy.

At the conference, a document titled "Proposal from RWB and *AMEX* for Structure and Operating Procedure of a Pan-Canadian Information Centre" was circulated. The proposal aimed to establish a "clearing house" of information from the regions in Toronto, with a cost-shared publication; the idea was adopted.[76] Four regional information collection centres were established to funnel information to Toronto. RWB, *AMEX,* and *The Alternative* personnel formed the core group to publish the information as it was received. The groups also organized a publication schedule and contingency plans for the publication, which they named *EXNET.*[77] The first issue of *EXNET,* published on 16 June 1970, used updates, gathered by mail from Vancouver, New York, Montreal, the Toronto ADC, and RWB, that filled specific information needs including reports on border conditions and employment.[78]

The Vancouver representatives to the conference were Peter Maly and Peter Burton of the VCAAWO; Steve Vernon of the Vancouver ADC; and Renée Kasinsky, representing her research company and likely attending to gather information for her book. Afterwards, the four representatives wrote an eight-page report outlining the proceedings and the discussions about the state of the movement, the question of the "political role of American war refugees," and the implications for the movement in Vancouver. On the question of "politics," the Vancouver representatives reported that conference participants had discussed the role of Americans in Canada, how they could be more effective, and the relationship to the women's liberation movement. Tom Hayden and Carl Oglesby participated in this portion of the conference. The report stated that the "general and growing Canadian resentment of 'left imperialism' or 'cultural imperialism'" (by which they meant imperialism of American leftists in the Canadian movement) meant that American "exiles" needed to be active in ways that were not explicitly along the lines of current exile groups. Rather, Americans should work to learn about Canada and participate as immigrants in Canadian politics.[79]

At the same time, there had been "general agreement" that leaving the United States for Canada was an undesirable antiwar tactic; but despite that, the "exodus" had been changed positively by the increase in the numbers of deserters. Therefore, the conference attendees had agreed, draft dodgers should be encouraged to stay in the United States if possible, while deserters were the highest priority for action to improve border conditions for immigration: "[American immigrants] should become active in the exile scene to the extent of making it easier for deserters, whose act is of a much higher political nature and who are in greater need and under more pressure."[80] The conference was therefore a site of remarkable compromise and consensus, perhaps also because figures such as Bill Spira did not attend. This consensus could in part have been due to the pressure being put on the Americans, by writers like Robin Mathews, to assimilate or go home. At any rate, exile and deserter groups agreed to participate in Canadian movements, and, in turn, anti-draft groups agreed to promote the needs of deserters.

On "the issue of women," the conference discussed what was referred to as "male oppression" and how to combat it within the anti-draft movement. Suggested methods included the cessation of giving women the "secondary or less glamorous work" of the groups and acknowledging that their act of immigration was "of ... political consequence," rather than merely a by-product of actions taken by men.[81] The event occurred in a context of increasing women's activism and criticism of sexist ideas within social movements, as analyzed by such authors as Sara Evans.[82] As Evans notes, activist women in the sixties became disillusioned with their marginal role in social movements, and the resisters and anti-draft activists were no exception. A women's caucus meeting at the conference, critical of the common assumption that they were there only because their husbands or boyfriends were, made a "non-proposal" to respect women war resisters as equal to their male counterparts.[83]

AMEX's coverage of the event included a description of a debate between representatives from exile groups and aid groups, including the TADP and MCAWR. The coverage emphasized a unity of opinion that aid programs must be at least somewhat political.[84] News of the Pan-Canadian Conference of US War Resisters was also carried in the American alternative press, including the *Guardian*.[85] The Toronto delegates returned thinking that perhaps it might no longer be "enough to have just refused to go ... We are hardly free of the United States up here ... [P]erhaps it is our role to lead the fight, physically, against the US from our exile." However, the resolutions passed at the conference did not deviate from the core activities of aid groups: communication, visibility, fundraising, and political involvement to protect the refuge Canada now represented.[86]

Aspects of the more political outlook adopted by the conference had implications for the TADP's ability to reach those it wanted to help. The April issue of *AMEX* reported that war resisters in Toronto were worried by reports that the TADP was telling people to stay in the military to "resist from within," or turning people away in a policy of "priority counselling." Danny Zimmerman of the TADP clarified that the practice referred to a triage process to help deserters and delinquent resisters first.[87] The TADP was not turning resisters away, but merely responding to an influx of deserters, likely the direct result of the movement's victory in May of 1969.

Differences in the anti-draft movement about tactics and legitimate activity may have had their roots in different political cultures from earlier in the century. These differences could have resulted in the fracturing and further splintering of the movement; but instead, the Pan-Canadian Conference of US War Resisters in Montreal developed a unified vision. The unity was brought about in part by the rise of left nationalism, but also by the pressures on the movement brought about by economic and political conditions and police activity as well as the need to work together effectively to resist the negative effects of those pressures.

In 1972, larger problems besetting the Department of Immigration – namely, backlogs of appeals and thousands of "visitors" living illegally in Canada – prompted new immigration policies that affected war resisters and their supporters. These visitors' presence was the result of 1967 changes to immigration regulations that allowed foreign nationals to apply from within Canada to become landed immigrants. Those entering Canada as visitors could subsequently apply for landed status. The backlog in the appeals program and the large number of visitors prompted the government to cease this practice. In 1972, the very policy that the war resisters used to their advantage was eliminated. The newly forged unity in the movement would prove essential to ongoing efforts to assist war resisters in Canada.

7

"Last Chance to Get Landed"
Immigration Department Strategies, Anti-Draft Movement Responses, 1971-73

His date to report has come
and gone, he can not leave now,
and although I think about it often,
I can't either. So, we adjust. Find,
and lose jobs; move from place
to place. Come to terms, gradually,
with the decision we so quickly
made. "You must live with the consequences
of your actions," my father
offers again and again
over crackly long distance lines.

We stay in this country
that is not home, until,
eventually, it becomes home.

– Ronnie R. Brown, "XIII. Home" [1]

The uneasy relationship between the government and war resister supporters changed as the new measures abolishing the policy on visitors were
enacted. The 1972 Administrative Measures and 1973 Adjustment of Status
Program, created to clear the backlog and address the problem of illegal
visitors, at first provoked new tensions. Eventually, however, these programs
elicited outright promotion by anti-draft groups, greater interaction between Department of Immigration officials and anti-draft group activists,

and a general entente as the war wound down and the anti-draft movement's focus shifted to new priorities. While RCMP agents continued to keep files on the groups well into the 1970s, the Department of Immigration could view the anti-draft groups as a part of the solution.

By January of 1971 the changing political landscape, including rising unemployment in Canada and the evolving antiwar mood in the United States, which encouraged resisters to stay there, combined to reduce the general number of American immigrants in Toronto. Naomi Wall of the Toronto Anti-Draft Programme guessed that the availability of legal advice on draft avoidance in the United States, the memory of the previous year's War Measures Act in Canada, and a "'stay-and-fight-the-draft' mood among the US young" were also factors. The proportion of deserters among the war resisters who came to Canada was also higher.[2]

A major episode in the history of immigration after 1972 was the decision by Minister of Immigration Bryce Mackasey to introduce new policy that ceased the practice of landing prospective immigrants from within Canada under section 34 of the regulations.[3] The 1967 rule that had allowed application for landing from within Canada or at the border under the points system had resulted in an influx of self-identified "visitors" who had actually intended to immigrate. The same rule allowed appeals of deportation orders, which enabled many "visitors" who had been thereafter denied landed status from within Canada to stay even longer. By 1971, the result was a backlog of thousands of appeals, from immigrants from all over the world, which put enormous pressure on the Immigration Appeal Board. First, Mackasey announced administrative measures to address the backlog. Subsequently, he revoked section 34 of the regulations, effectively putting a stop to the practice of landing from within Canada. Mackasey was succeeded in late 1972 by Robert Andras, who added punitive regulations that included fines and jail sentences for visitors who intended to stay in Canada longer than three months, but who had not registered this intention with the department. To address the problem of the thousands of visitors who were "stranded" by these changes, Andras later introduced the Adjustment of Status Program, under which thousands of illegal visitors were landed. The development and implementation of the Adjustment of Status Program was marked by government interaction with immigrant groups and cooperation with, among others, anti-draft groups.[4]

These new policies heralded renewed tensions between war resister supporters and the government. Mackasey's administrative measures to allow those awaiting appeals to have their cases heard more quickly and with relaxed criteria were met with skepticism from anti-draft groups. Matters did not improve when section 34, which allowed for entrance to Canada as a visitor, was revoked altogether in November. However, when Andras's 1973 program was announced, the anti-draft groups undertook to actively promote it. In some cases, immigration officials and anti-draft activists, as well as other immigration activists, worked together to maximize the number of landings. These interactions showed how the social movement in support of war resisters could, when necessary, take on some of the role of the government. The interaction between the anti-draft movement and the government was marked by changing levels of mutual influence. The social movement and the government influenced each other in a dance reminiscent of Bruce Curtis's "circular process" of government.[5] The relationship was predominantly adversarial. However, by the end of the period, the groups were undertaking the same work as that of the government, while still maintaining their autonomy and their roles as advocates for American immigrants. The border between government institutions or functions and pressure groups or even individuals is constantly in transition and, like hegemony, never completely settled.

Anti-draft activists and war resisters were generally skeptical towards the regulatory changes in 1972. In the months following the November 1972 revocation of section 34, the anti-draft movement pressed the government for solutions to the new problems facing war resisters who had not acquired status as landed immigrants. The 1973 Adjustment of Status Program was shaped both by internal Department of Immigration discussions and by anti-draft movement campaign efforts. Perhaps because of this interactive process, the anti-draft movement ended by promoting the 1973 program, albeit on their own terms.[6]

By late 1969, the worsening backlog in immigration appeals necessitated the opening of a department file on the matter.[7] A year later, in September of 1970, outgoing Minister of Manpower and Immigration Allan MacEachen announced plans to review the three-year-old policy of allowing visitors to apply for landed status from within Canada. The policy, combined with a liberal appeals policy, which allowed anyone to appeal once they had been denied landed immigrant status, was creating a backlog of epic proportions.[8]

Over the following months, the media took notice of the backlog.[9] By early 1972, the media also documented conflicts internal to the government about how to address the situation. A *Toronto Sun* article titled "Immigration Heads to Quit Over Scrapped Amendments," for instance, indicated that Prime Minister Trudeau was balking at proposed amendments to the immigration policy, and that some immigration officials were so frustrated at this inaction that they were considering leaving the department.[10] The media were not always friendly to the Department of Immigration. In this case, they appeared to be rallying to the call for reform of the regulations. That the issue was controversial probably helped encourage the media to pay attention, further fanning the flames of public opinion.

The aforementioned articles probably came from leaked information about Cabinet-level discussions that took place in January and February of 1972. In January 1972, Deputy Minister of Immigration J.L.E. Couillard made several suggestions to the brand new Minister of Immigration Bryce Mackasey aimed at addressing "alternative measures for dealing with current major immigration problems." The suggestions included eliminating the "handicap" of ten points from within Canada, whereby applicants at the border received ten points for having a job offer in hand, but applicants from within Canada did not get the ten points. Eliminating this measure to award the points within the country would make attaining landed status from within Canada easier if the application was accompanied by a job offer. This would in turn lessen the need for an appeal. Couillard also suggested introducing new humanitarian criteria for admission, and, significantly for our story, offering "special transitional arrangements to permit inquiry officers to land immigrants who have submitted late applications or have taken unauthorized employment if they meet other provisions of the Act and regulations and if they were in Canada on a current date such as April 1, 1972." Further suggestions in the same spirit concerned the appeals of deportation: to "re-examine applicants for landing who are awaiting hearing of their appeals in the light of the provisions contained in [the above] proposals" and to "secure the cooperation of the Appeal Board to land with a minimum of formal proceedings appellants who on re-examination are found to be admissible."[11] Many of these measures were eventually taken up.

A month later, Minister Mackasey brought these ideas to Cabinet, proposing an "Administrative Program to Reduce the Size and Growth of Immigration Inquiry Backlogs."[12] Mackasey was aware that Cabinet had decided in December 1971 to try to resolve the immigration problems without passing legislation, probably to avoid a contentious issue in a period leading up to an election, and a period of rising unemployment. Mackasey argued that changes of a strictly administrative nature would be important, but limited in their effect, and he sought to get Cabinet to agree to some legislative changes and to provide additional resources.

The administrative measures he proposed broadly coincided with Couillard's suggestions. They included broadening the discretion of immigration officials to grant landed status; allowing the consideration of humanitarian reasons; and retroactively applying looser guidelines for addressing appeals. In the legislative field, Mackasey suggested that Cabinet consider a suspension of section 34 of the regulations, which allowed for application to land from within Canada, for non-immigrants from "non-contiguous territories." Such a policy would have the effect of allowing only American visitors to apply for landing, he stated, without explaining why this would be a good thing.

Mackasey's recommendations included several suggestions from Couillard, such as the removal of the ten-point penalty for employment if within Canada, and the revocation of certain other regulations to allow for expedited consideration of landing of those in the country illegally or having taken illegal employment.[13] Two months later, in April of 1972, a directive was issued by Cabinet to implement an Administrative Measures Program through a review of cases already in backlog on the basis of employment prospects, financial stability, efforts made by applicants to establish themselves in Canada, language improvements, and the length of their residence to date.[14] Cabinet was implementing the administrative changes. They did not implement the suggestion to exclude "non-contiguous" countries from section 34, and the legal changes would have to wait.

Preparations were made throughout May with the intent of launching the program on 1 July. The ideas discussed by Couillard, the minister, and Cabinet formed the core of the Administrative Measures Program announced publicly in June 1972 to deal with the backlog of appeals. The announcement coincided with the declaration of the government's intention to repeal section 34 of the regulations altogether – an administrative change as well – eliminating the possibility of landing from within Canada or at the border.[15] Despite the declaration, however, the revocation of section 34 would not occur for several more months.

On 22 June 1972, standing in the House of Commons, Minister of Immigration Bryce Mackasey announced "New Measures to Expedite Immigration Inquiry Cases" through a review of current appeals cases in an expedited way. These measures were along the lines suggested in the internal communications of previous months.[16] Special inquiry officers would review the current situation of applicants, considering such factors as employment, family, and letters of reference. After 1 January 1973, no more inquiries would be added to the backlog. The appeal process would be eliminated. The criteria of review, and the focus on the appeals backlog, meant that this was not a "general amnesty" but a short-term measure taken as part of a set of steps to fix the situation created by the 1967 regulations.[17] The next day, Mackasey announced further details to the public: the measures would only be available to those physically in the country as of midnight 23 June; those who had already been referred to an inquiry officer; those whose application for Landed Immigrant status was registered by midnight of 23 June; and those legally in Canada who subsequently filed applications for Landed Immigrant status before the expiry of their non-immigrant status – that is, those who were bona fide visitors.[18]

The Administrative Measures Program, sometimes known in the Department of Immigration as Project P-80 (perhaps a financial account number) and sometimes as the "Task Force for the Implementation of Administrative Measures," had mixed results.[19] All outstanding appeals were scheduled to be dealt with by an immigration officer. Many war resisters did not turn up for appointments, and did not reschedule, by the December deadline.[20] Some thought the program was a trap to get them deported; immigrants from other countries likely thought the same. At the same time, the mere anticipation of a potential revocation of section 34 was resulting in huge increases in the numbers of applicants for landing. At first, the treatment of section 34 was ambiguous; the department seemed to indicate that the intended revocation might only be temporary. Even so, a secret memo from Deputy Minister J.M. Desroches to Minister Mackasey indicated that, while the backlog of immigration appeals was being worked out, the stated intention to revoke section 34 had resulted in an enormous influx of people attempting "to become entrenched in

Canada" before the changes were implemented. At the end of September 1972, new applications for landed status had reached forty-four thousand in nine months, compared to 35,326 in all of 1971. The record number of applicants in one year, set in 1969, had already been exceeded by 3 percent. Extrapolation of the data indicated that the department might well receive up to seventy-five thousand applications in 1972. According to Desroches, the influx was "evidence that the increase in applications is, at least from certain countries, an abuse of Canada's Immigration policies." Indeed, there were reports from overseas of ads in newspapers encouraging emigration, and reports of "commercial trafficking in Immigration to Canada." The Toronto airport office was barely coping with the levels of applications. Desroches urged Mackasey not to reinstate section 34.[21]

In February of 1973, "Project P-80 – Progress Report on Review Cases" was officially deemed successful by the Programs and Procedures branch.[22] The permanent revocation of section 34 called for by Desroches had been under review in the department for several months. In June 1972, James Cross, director of the Department of Immigration Programs and Procedures Branch, sent a memo to the assistant deputy minister, Robert M. Adams. A "submission to the Minister respecting procedures for applicants from the United States" was being prepared, which included a recommendation to eliminate altogether the allowed-forward-under-examination procedure (AFUE) under section 34. Cross warned that, while it was recommended, such an action could create problems by introducing situations where applicants turned away within Canada would have to be deported, which, in turn, could negatively affect public perceptions of the government. Cross specifically mentioned possible ramifications stemming from the response of supporters of draft dodgers and deserters. Preparations should be made to deal with such negative consequences, Cross implied.[23] Five months later, on 3 November 1972, Mackasey followed the recommendations of his staff and announced the revocation of section 34 of the regulations.[24] The negative attention by the press and the response of anti-draft groups and others soon coalesced into public pressure on the department to take further steps to address the situation that illegal visitors inside the country's borders now faced.

An unanticipated consequence of the revocation of section 34 was that a large number of visitors and illegal immigrants who had either not yet received a deportation order at the time of the Administrative Measures

Program, or who had not come forward out of fear that the program was a trap, were effectively stranded in the country with no recourse. The anti-draft groups had immediately begun informing their contacts in Canada and in the United States about the change in policy and helped increase public pressure on the department to do something to allow this stranded group to remain in the country. In December 1972, a meeting of "concerned members of the Toronto community" regarding "the current immigration crisis for war resisters" took place. The meeting resolved to send a "deputation" to Mackasey, with a brief and a proposal for re-opening the border for war resisters, thereby reversing the unfairness of the sudden 3 November announcement. Nancy Pocock of the Toronto Anti-Draft Programme, Dee Knight and Jack Colhoun of *AMEX,* and lawyer Paul Copeland were present. Toronto area MPs were also targeted for lobbying.[25]

The public pressure came from many different quarters, and media voices also increased. Many of the media reports reflected the myth, by now well-entrenched, of Canada as a haven, not only for war resisters but for immigrants from around the world. For instance, in March of 1973, a *Toronto Star* article endorsed a suggestion by the "Session of the Bloor Street United Church" that those "caught in the middle" ought to be allowed to stay if they had entered as visitors between June and mid-November of 1972.[26] A few days later, a *Toronto Star* editorial asserted that "Stranded 'Visitors' Deserve[d] Justice." The article indicted Canada's contradictory policy and invoked the country's international reputation for an open immigration policy. Having first attracted immigrant workers, the editors argued, and then effectively stranded them in Canada, the policy had forced some to work illegally, and for very little, to survive. The editorial called for those stranded by the change to be allowed to apply from within Canada for landed status; otherwise, "the world's 'kindest' immigration policy [would be] a failure." It added that the suddenness of the 3 November announcement had meant that policy was effectively retroactive and had caused additional problems by initiating a flood of last-minute applicants from around the world who were now forced to hurry their applications in order to move to Canada before the policy change.[27]

In May, the Quaker Social Concerns Committee of Vancouver lent their voice to the cause. In a letter to the prime minister, they asked for "special consideration" for Americans facing deportation who entered before the November 1972 announcement and who did not apply in time.[28] In June, Richard Brown of the Toronto Anti-Draft Programme (TADP) wrote a letter to Andrew Brewin, NDP MP for Toronto-Greenwood, raising concerns about illegal Americans in Canada who couldn't return to the United States due to threats of felony charges, but couldn't be landed, either, due to the elimination of section 34.[29]

Other groups of war resisters also paid attention to the new rules and began pressing for remedies to the situation of stranded illegal immigrants. A letter from a Miriam Pearson to the Nova Scotia Committee to Aid War Resistors, undated and unaddressed, outlined a resolution passed by the General Council of United Churches regarding the 3 November 1972 announcement and highlighting what they perceived to be the racist effect of the policy. The resolution appealed to the government to allow for a retro-active application of the rules to allow those who entered before 3 November to use the old rules.[30]

Thus, between 3 November 1972 and the summer 1973 announcement of an Adjustment of Status Program six months later, anti-draft groups and supporters pressed for a solution. Meanwhile, the policy change did not mean the war resisters stopped applying for landing. For instance, the Halifax committee files included copies of correspondence between American immigrants whose applications for landed status had been rejected and the Department of Manpower and Immigration Canada. One such rejection was from December 1970; the other two were from 19 January and 31 October 1972.[31] The Canadian Council of Churches (CCC) Ministry to Draft-Age US Immigrants in Canada continued its funding and advocacy on behalf of war resisters. The Ministry's Accountability Committee meetings in 1972 and 1973 heard a story of dwindling applications and the need to readjust. Internal landings were now a "thing of the past"; Montreal's caseload was down, as was Toronto's and Winnipeg's. In the first quarter of 1973, the total allocation of funding for the four main groups was only $3,400, down from about $8,000 per quarter in 1971 and 1972.[32] At the 29 March meeting of the CCC Accountability Committee, member Gordon Walker reported on a meeting with immigration officials at which he had pressed for a solution to the problem of dealing with the cases of applicants who fell between the 3 November announcement and the actual implementation of the Order-in-Council on 5 November.[33]

Meanwhile, the new regime also affected American groups who supported war resisters. A 13 November 1972 letter from the American Friends Service Committee, Chicago Regional Office for Illinois and Wisconsin, perhaps acting in concert with Canadian Quakers, asked why it had been so long between communications, and whether the anti-draft groups were still operating; the draft had continued, and war resisters still needed support.[34] The TADP responded, outlining the new rules and stating that application would have to be made through a consulate with a waiting period of three to six months. Visitor status was still possible, but it could no longer easily be transformed into a successful application for landed immigrant status.[35]

Eventually, public pressure was felt at the ministerial level, where shifts were occurring.[36] These discussions were taking place at the beginning of a period of growing popularity of Canadian multiculturalism as policy and practice. Multiculturalism had gained in popularity in the public mind due partially to the work of the Royal Commission on Bilingualism and Biculturalism. It also probably owed something to left nationalism, which, in part, sought to distinguish Canadian society from US policies and an American culture that was perceived as less tolerant.[37]

In this climate, deciding what to do about illegal immigrants became a more and more sensitive issue. Department of Immigration staff briefed the new minister as of 27 November, Robert Andras, in memos titled "The Immigration Situation" and "Briefing Paper for Minister: Non-Immigrant Control and Non-Immigrant Applicants for Landing in Canada." The memos provided an overview of recent developments from the department's perspective. The Administrative Measures Program had been initially successful, but it had resulted in a huge influx of applicants who were fearful of the changes; "visitors" abused the opportunity to apply for landed immigrant status from inside Canada in the lead-up to the implementation of the revocation of section 34. The "Revocation of Regulation 34" had been announced on 3 November 1972 by the previous minister upon Cabinet consultation. Public pressure, the memo mentioned, had then increased to deal with so-called visitors who had been stranded as a result. The possible solutions to this issue and their potential effects were listed for the minister's consideration.

One of the possible solutions, to stand firm on current policy, would require a great deal of public image damage control, staff suggested: "There is ... the outside possibility, considering some of the people involved, of some desperate protest act such as suicide, which would not help the Department's image at all," the memo said. Earlier that summer, a Polish woman facing deportation had committed suicide, casting attention on the appeals backlog.[38] Subsequent news reports had indicated that Minister Mackasey suspected his staff of providing him with misleading information about the status of the woman's case, suggesting she had not succeeded in achieving the necessary fifty points, when in fact she had been denied a work permit and the appeal board had declined to allow her to stay in Canada on humanitarian grounds. Mackasey had appeared to suspect the department's staff of seeking to have the immigration policies applied in the strictest manner possible, instead of honouring the "small-l liberal" application Mackasey supported.[39]

On the other hand, the memos went on, to increase the variety of exceptions under the act – categories of immigrants allowed in by virtue of their membership in a designated group – would set another dangerous precedent like that set by section 34 in the first place. Further, to allow those who had arrived before 5 November to be considered would add hundreds or thousands to the backlog. Finally, to allow a future amnesty to those who had been working in Canada for a year would not be good policy as it would encourage people to work without permits.[40] Staff appeared to be taking the opportunity of the ministerial changes to press for a less "liberal" approach to immigration, and to urge the minister not to allow current illegal immigrants to become landed. They did so by presenting a variety of options and pointing out their weaknesses.

In April of 1973, departmental discussions of proposals for an Adjustment of Status Program to address the problem of the stranded immigrants began in earnest. Essentially, the minister had decided to allow those in Canada illegally to become landed immigrants by means of a special program. Appearing to respond to staff concerns about leniency towards illegal immigrants, Andras expressed concerns to his staff about visitors who had entered prior to 3 November being in "limbo," and sought recommendations on how to address their situation, "keeping in mind our international image and the concerns many have (rightly or wrongly) that our November 3 action had elements of unfairness." The minister intended to talk about the issue of stranded immigrants in an upcoming speech announcing Bill C-197, legislation to amend the Immigration Act, and hoped to introduce a program before an anticipated "assault on us by people trying to beat the appeal deadline under existing legislation." A program included in the new legislation to eliminate the appeal process might mitigate the anticipated rush of last-minute appeals before the law was passed.[41] On 18 June 1973, Andras announced that his department was planning to initiate a grace period to land illegal immigrants, eliminate the remaining appeals backlog, and eliminate "loopholes," which invited abuse.[42] Two days later, in the House of Commons, Andras announced his plans to review all immigration policy. The immediate need, however, was to adjust the status of illegal immigrants, now that applying for landed immigrant status was no longer permitted from within Canada.[43]

From there, things moved fairly quickly. This time, staff had presented a variety of options, unlike in 1969, when Department of Immigration staff had taken a uniform and firm position against opening the border until a political decision was made by Cabinet. Immigration officials now turned to making recommendations about how the program should be shaped and implemented and, in doing so, also responded to some movement criticisms. For instance, on 20 June 1973, Deputy Minister A.E. Gotlieb made strong recommendations to the minister on placing a time limit on the program.[44] Gotlieb anticipated pressure to keep the program open-ended; the department had already received some correspondence in this direction. He insisted that options existed for any potential immigrants to apply for landed status in larger immigration centres and ports of entry and by mail from more remote areas and, therefore, that any claims that the program would be inaccessible were baseless. Additionally, he pointed out, the department would be "advertising widely in the ethnic and daily press. This, combined with the grapevine of the ethnic community, [would] make it unlikely that those eligible for the program will not get the message." In short, Gotlieb urged Andras to resist public pressure. If a longer period of time were to be chosen, at least the time frame should remain fixed.[45]

On 21 June, Gotlieb sent the minister draft regulations for the program. As proposed, the program, under relaxed criteria, would allow the landing of sponsored dependants; anyone who would be given a visa if applying from overseas; refugees; anyone dependent on a Canadian citizen or permanent resident for support, or who was depended upon for support by a Canadian citizen or permanent resident; and anyone over eighteen who had "demonstrated the ability to become established" in Canada, as judged by immigration officials based on employment, financial stability, efforts made to establish themselves in the country, their conduct in Canada, the presence of relatives in Canada, or their having established a business in the country.[46] These criteria were in line with the criteria in the points system and existing sponsorship processes; they could be expected to be received favourably and perceived as fair.

When the new law was introduced in June and debate began, there was an immediate increase in the number of applicants at immigration offices. The Vancouver immigration office, for instance, telexed on 22 June to report the registration of fifteen people and a high number of telephone inquiries. Later that day, Adams reported to the minister that as of close of business on 21 June, 357 people had notified immigration offices of their intent to register, clogging the phone lines to do so.[47] However, unlike the Administrative Measures Program, Andras's Adjustment of Status Program was well-planned, and the regional directors general were prepared for the deluge. For financial purposes, the program was assigned project number 97. On 22 June, J.R. Robillard, director of operations (immigration), telexed directors general in Halifax, Montreal, Toronto, Vancouver, and Winnipeg, asking all immigration offices to report numbers daily and regularly communicate the anticipated breakdown of dispensation of applications.[48] On 19 July, Robillard reported to J.E. McKenna, Home Services Branch director, that the proclamation of Bill C-197 was not anticipated to cause any problems in the regions.[49] However, the process would not prove universally smooth. For example, on 18 July a report reached the deputy minister that the Ontario immigration office had 170 cases on file of individuals who would be ineligible for the Adjustment of Status Program because they entered Canada after 30 November. Of these, about forty were still insisting on an appeal.[50] The RCMP had concerns about the coming program, worrying that individuals they perceived as subversives might use the opportunity to get landed status; an undated memo to the minister from Gotlieb mentioned this anxiety, citing a list of about thirty "persons of concern," including Hardial Singh Bains, leader of the Communist Party of Canada – Marxist-Leninist, and eight lecturers or professors at Canadian universities.[51]

As the program's parameters developed, the question of how to address the specific situation of students arose. July correspondence between the Programs and Procedures and Home Services Branch mentioned that the

International Students Organization had made inquiries about the status of students who went home for the holidays.[52] Officials considered allowing students to apply if they were due back in September; landing students by special Order-in-Council; and disallowing anyone who had been absent from the country for any reason from benefitting from the Adjustment of Status Program. McKenna communicated his position to the assistant deputy minister of immigration that any indication that a person had been out of the country for any reason whatsoever on a passport since 30 November 1972 meant they were not admissible.[53] Domestic pressure had more impact. On 20 July, the assistant deputy minister's office received an unusual phone call from the Association of Universities and Colleges of Canada expressing concern over the impact of the new law on the university community; on 27 July, Deputy Minister Gotlieb suggested, and received agreement from the minister, that leniency would be appropriate in dealing with students who might have crossed the border for short periods of time since 30 November.[54]

Bill C-197, assented to on 27 July 1973, abolished the right of appeal for individuals who had applied for landed status and been denied.[55] Although the program's proclamation was on file on 31 July, it took two more weeks before the Adjustment of Status program was officially launched on 15 August.[56] As of 29 August, 12,383 individuals had registered their intent to apply for landing, with a total of 9,461 dependants.[57] The program was billed as a "once-and-for-all opportunity" for anyone in Canada, legally or illegally, as of 30 November 1972, to apply for Landed Immigrant status. The "relaxed selection criteria" eventually resulted in about fifty thousand people being landed, while the appeals backlog was effectively solved, for the time being.[58] The program was monitored by the House of Commons. Reports on the debates, along with statistics about the program, were sent to directors of immigration offices.[59]

To ensure the program would be effective, the Department of Immigration used the media to promote it. Immigration staff were advised that, through the office of Information Services, advertising was to be undertaken in daily, weekly, weekend, English, French, and "ethnic" newspapers; magazines, including foreign and religious publications; English, French, and "ethnic" television and radio; cinema; and transit and subway advertising spaces. For broad appeal, "Regional Information Service Managers can highlight human interest cases, [and] work with local political and community leaders." One million brochures and fifty thousand "counter cards" (flyers) were anticipated. The department encouraged regional offices to set up information booths and vans in parking lots and to organize poster campaigns. Visiting remote areas and workplaces "like construction sites and mines" was also part of the plan for outreach.[60]

Some of the Department of Immigration materials found their way into anti-draft group offices. One Department of Immigration pamphlet declared, "If you were in Canada by November 30, 1972 and have remained here since, as a visitor or without legal status, we're going to give until midnight, October 15, 1973 to make our country your country." The pamphlet went on to outline the process for applying, emphasizing the leniency in applying the rules during this period.[61] A war resister support organization secured a copy of "Regulations Respecting the Adjustment of Immigration Status of Certain Persons in Canada," also referred to as the "Immigration Adjustment of Status Regulations," a blank form affidavit attesting to the immigrant's presence in Canada by 30 November, and a listing of acceptable types of proof.[62] The Department of Immigration certainly made significant efforts to get the information out. *AMEX* magazine reported that the department had spent $1.2 million on advertising.[63]

Perhaps because, unlike in November of 1972, they knew the program was coming and had time to prepare, the anti-draft movement responded decisively to the announcement and the program itself. In 1972, the anti-draft groups had only been able to react to the regulatory change, trying to improve matters after the fact. In contrast, in 1973, the movement was able to share information among groups and resisters; intervene in the debate about how the program should be shaped; and plan, and wage, a significant media campaign of their own to first shape, and then promote, the program in their own way and in their own words.

The Anti-Draft Movement Responds to the Adjustment of Status Program

As soon as the program was announced, the anti-draft groups began to share information on the new situation. For instance, the TADP sent out information on the proposed legislation to other anti-draft groups. They estimated that ten to twenty thousand Americans might qualify for the program, and exhorted activists to spread the word to unlanded Americans about the sixty-day window of opportunity.[64] The memo, with the headline

"Sixty Days of Grace: Your Last Chance," outlined the grace period of 15 August to 15 October. It suggested that, partly due to pressure from the anti-draft movement, the program had been introduced to help those who had had no recourse after the "arbitrary cancellation last November [1972] of applications for landed status from within Canada and cancellation of the right to apply at Canada-US border points," leaving many "caught stranded." The document also described the temporary application criteria under the current program as "noticeably far more relaxed."[65]

To help Americans take advantage of the program, the TADP also produced a thirteen-page document titled "Sixty Days of Grace: Your Last Chance, Aug. 15, 1973 through Oct. 15, 1973." The Table of Contents read as follows:

It's Now or Never
People eligible for the 60-Day Grace Period
Admissibility Criteria
Rights of Appeal
Documentation
The Process of Applying
Helpful Folks[66]

This document was probably inspired by the positive impact of past publications such as the *Manual for Draft-Age Immigrants to Canada*. It might also have been calculated to mimic government pamphlets. The last section indicated which anti-draft groups were still active during 1973, after the official end of the Vietnam War and the elimination of the US Selective Service Draft. It listed the Calgary Committee on War Immigrants, Regina Committee to Aid American War Objectors (likely the successor to the Regina Committee of American Deserters), Alexander Ross Society, Ottawa Committee to Aid War Objectors, the Halifax Committee to Aid War Objectors, the TADP, the Montreal Council to Aid War Resisters, the Vancouver Committee to Aid American War Objectors, and the Winnipeg Committee to Assist War Objectors. The TADP also issued corrections to the *Manual for Draft-Age Immigrants to Canada*.[67]

As the campaign for registration geared up, the Canadian Council of Churches once again worked with anti-draft groups to promote it. The council met with anti-draft groups to allocate new funding for the program's promotion. At an ad hoc meeting in Winnipeg on 2 July, a publicity campaign with two proposed budgets was discussed, one set at $80,000, and the other proposal for $110,000. The funds would be sent directly to aid centres, not through the council, to save time, given the limited duration of the Adjustment of Status Program. The discussion showed awareness and a willingness to help on the part of the CCC.[68] The money was to pay for a lawyer; national staff to do a media campaign, liaison, and maintain contacts; meetings; aid centre casework; and materials.[69] Other groups looked for resources to help as well; for instance, in mid-July, Voice of Women asked their "contacts and friends from [the US-based] Women Strike for Peace" for funding assistance to help with applications during the sixty days.[70] The day after the program's announcement, the United Church announced its support for the "government olive branch to illegal immigrants," noting that fifteen to twenty thousand Americans were among the estimated two hundred thousand illegal immigrants in Canada.[71]

As the Adjustment of Status Program neared its launch date, anti-draft groups began agitating for better regulations. In late July of 1973, several of the aid groups united to form the Canadian Coalition of War Resisters under the slogan "a unified voice in the struggle." A media release, "War Resister's Aide [sic] Centres Launch 60 Day Immigration Drive," declared that, after a period in which several groups had slowed or ceased operations, "the national network of war resister aide [sic] centres has re-opened this week in response to the government's new immigration legislation allowing for the 'adjustment of status' of unlanded immigrants in Canada." The release quoted from Andras's speech in Parliament. The Canadian Coalition of War Resisters responded by implementing its own program: nine centres opened, five of which had closed their doors after the November 1972 revocation of section 34, and after the US ceasefire had been signed in January 1973. As part of a sixty-day campaign, fundraising was planned, and so were additional media work, lobbying, and ad campaigns. The release also warned that, after the program wound down, a crackdown could occur as stricter rules came into effect.[72]

The next undertaking was a pressure campaign to close an expected "loophole" that could prevent landing. Upon their arrival to register for the new program, applicants without proof on their person of having entered by the 30 November 1972 date were in danger of immediate deportation. In their announcement of a sixty-day campaign the same day as the Adjustment of Status Program was announced, the groups pointed out that the standard of proof of entry was unknown because only immigration officers had access to the precise criteria.[73] This demand for openness was reminiscent of the successful campaign used to cast doubt on the practice of "discretion" at the border in early 1969. Without such clarity, Americans in Canada illegally still hesitated to come forward, fearing that the program was actually a trap laid to deport them.

The campaign to improve the program continued until its launch. A 6 August 1973 media release from the Toronto group raised the same concerns about the standard of proof of residence, which had likely resulted in multiple immediate deportations. The group promised legal assistance and protection from such deportation, but expressed worry about immigrants who might apply without first consulting them.[74] It was also concerned that this lack of clarity regarding proof would mean that counselling would be necessary before registering. Because many might assume no proof was required upon reporting to register, based on past experiences with the department, there was a danger of immediate deportation.[75] Ironically, such communications might have contributed to wariness of a trap on the part of some resisters. While this phase of the anti-draft movement's attempts to shape the program were largely ineffective, later the government appeared to relent and agreed to measures to reassure immigrants fearing a trap.

Despite their misgivings, once the program started, the anti-draft groups actively encouraged war resisters to apply. However, the misgivings remained strong enough for them to insist on the importance of registering through the committees, to secure pre-counselling. Anti-draft groups used the media, poster campaigns, and word of mouth to make sure war resisters got the message. They also, eventually, engaged directly with the program to improve the number of applicants.

The anti-draft groups, including the TADP, promoted the program widely in the media with funding from the CCC. The TADP ran fifty-one ads on Toronto's CHUM AM and FM radio stations, public service announcements on other stations, and ads in the *Varsity* newspaper, as well as in *7 News*, the Ward 7 community newspaper:

UNLANDED WAR RESISTER?
OR JUST NOT LANDED YET???

Your last chance – that's right – your LAST CHANCE to get landed immigrant status in Canada has already begun.

If you have been in Canada since Nov. 30, 1972, you have until Oct. 15 to register with the government.

The incredibly easy standards to get landed are for real, but the paperwork is quite tricky.

So see us first before you go to the government – it's in the interest of your own safety.

Be sure to register.

And be sure to contact us first.

Toronto Anti-Draft Programme
11-½ Spadina Road (just North of Bloor)
Toronto M5R 2S9 920-0241[76]

TADP ads also appeared in other Ontario regions on the first day of the program, in newspapers such as the *Mountain News, Dundas Star, Ancaster News,* and *Stoney Creek News*.[77] Eric Stine of the Halifax Committee wrote an article regarding the program and asked local newspapers to print it, but it is not clear whether any did.[78] The Nova Scotia group placed ads in several regional papers, including the *Hants Journal* (Windsor, Nova Scotia), the Charlottetown *Guardian-Patriot,* the *Brunswickan* student newspaper at the University of New Brunswick (Fredericton), and the *Amherst Daily News* (Nova Scotia).[79] These newspapers were likely less expensive to advertise in and could reach communities where resisters might not regularly listen to or read the major dailies. The anti-draft groups also attempted to shape the media coverage of the program; for instance, a TADP letter praised CBC Radio for its coverage but encouraged them in future to refer immigrants to counselling groups.[80] This interaction with the media was typical of previous campaigns as well. The Canadian Council of Churches used its influence to try to secure free airtime for radio public service announcements recorded with the voices of popular singers Ian Tyson, Joan Baez, and Jesse Winchester.[81]

The groups monitored their success in the media. They saw headlines like the *Globe and Mail*'s on 7 August, "Draft Evaders Fear No-appeal Deportation," and 11 September, "Offer of Landed Status No Trap, Andras Assures Illegal Immigrants," as direct evidence of their impact on the government.[82]

Posters were also used to promote the campaign. A Halifax poster on yellow paper announced "American War Resistors [sic], your last chance to become a legally landed immigrant from inside Canada ends on October 15. For free counselling and information on complying with the special regulations call or visit us immediately, the Halifax Committee to Aid War Resistors [sic]." Another poster read:

Potential Immigrants or War Resistors

Now is your last chance to become a landed immigrant from within Canada.

The government has granted sixty day amnesty period for those people living in Canada without legal status. Anyone who has been in Canada since on or before November 30, 1972, may apply during the period August 15 to October 15, 1973 to become a legally landed immigrant.

The government has stated that those who come forward now will be free "from prosecution for the manner in which they came in or remained in Canada." For more information contact: The Halifax Committee to Aid War Resistors[83]

The text was followed by contact information and office hours for the committee. Other materials, such as leaflets, were produced with similar messages.[84] Montreal's poster used the image of a beaver holding a placard that read "IMMIGRATE": "Illegal immigrants: you must immigrate now or never. Do not register until you are fully prepared. Free expert counselling at American refugee service yellow door – 3625 Aylmer St. 843-3132 August 15 to October 15."[85] In order to reach as many potential immigrants as possible, the Canadian Coalition of War Resisters hired a driver from 15 August to 26 September to drive around in a school bus on a tour of Canada to find unlanded American immigrants living outside urban centres.[86] Activists also paid visits to nearby towns.[87]

The groups also continued their casework. The TADP, for instance, tracked potential registrants, the number of visits they had made to the TADP offices, and the number of times they had called, and ranked them by priority. The fact that they also divided them into American and non-American inquiries indicates that the campaign had reached further than the immediate American immigrant community. Between 15 August and 28 September, the TADP alone recorded 401 first visits, 77 repeat visits, 248 first calls, and 41 repeat calls from Americans. They kept weekly reports and meticulous daily records.[88] In the end, many of those counselled were immigrants from countries other than the United States. An *AMEX* report stated,

> It breaks down like this: the Vancouver Committee to Aid American War Objectors had counselled some 520 people at the half-way point [of the program's duration]; 450 were Americans and 100 of these were war resisters. The Winnipeg Committee to Assist War Objectors counselled 175 people; 130 were Americans and 70 were war resisters. The TADP has counselled 800 people; 650 were Americans, and 400 were war resisters. Ottawa counsellors saw 170 people; 42 were Americans and 30 were war resisters. The Montreal American Refugee Service counselled 300 people; 150 were Americans and 75 were war resisters. All these figures were approximations made by the counselling centres. No reports were available from the Alexander Ross Society in Edmonton, the Calgary Committee on War Immigrants, the Thunder Bay Aid Committee or the Halifax Committee to Aid War Objectors.[89]

Thus, the anti-draft groups, at the point in the program where these numbers were amassed, had counselled a total of over two thousand people, of which only 1,422 were Americans, and fewer were war resisters.

Meanwhile, anti-draft groups continued efforts to find ways to keep the border open to American war resisters. On 30 August 1973, Immigration Minister Robert Andras sent a letter to Prime Minister Trudeau:

> Recently I received representations to allow American war resisters (draft dodgers and deserters) in Canada to apply for landed immigrant status despite the fact that on November 3, 1972, the Government announced

that the right of an individual to apply for immigration status while temporarily in Canada had been revoked. The representations maintained that such persons were political refugees and hence deserving of special treatment. I thought that you might be interested in my stand in this matter.[90]

Andras did not see conscription as persecution or discrimination and therefore did not consider war resisters to be refugees under the international conventions adopted by Canada in 1969.[91] Andras pointed out to Trudeau that war resisters could still qualify under C-197, the Adjustment of Status Program.[92]

The movement also pressed the government to double the duration of the program. On 10 October 1973, the Nova Scotia Committee to Aid American War Objectors, Halifax Committee to Aid War Resistors, Halifax Neighbourhood Committee, Black United Front of Nova Scotia, Sign of the Fish – Halifax, Canadian Council of Christians and Jews for the Atlantic Region, and the Coalition for Development sent a telegram to Andras requesting a sixty-day extension of the grace period to allow for fears of deportation to be allayed and information to be disseminated to harder-to-reach regions. The Halifax Friends Meeting also supported the initiative, passing a resolution to that effect. A media release was distributed about the telegram and the Friends resolution.[93] The Vancouver committee also called for an extension; once again, they highlighted fears of a "trap" and expressed worries that information was not reaching all affected people.[94]

With the $110,000 provided by the CCC to publicize the program, the campaign was significant. But despite these efforts and those of the Department of Immigration, many potential registrants at first feared to come forward, perhaps, paradoxically, because of the very intensity of the promotional efforts being made. In early September of 1973, an advice column in the *Ottawa Citizen* printed a letter headlined, "Illegal Immigrant's Fear Unjustified." The author of the letter explained that "this campaign scares me. I fear it is a ploy to have illegal immigrants expose themselves so they can be arrested and deported." Advice columnist Roger Appleton assured the writer that "if you are a draft dodger from the United States, don't worry. That won't be held against you here." Appleton offered in his column to act as a "middle man" to protect illegal American immigrants in the application process.[95]

By mid-September, war resister supporters were sounding the alarm about the effectiveness of the program. Reverend Richard Killmer and Tim Maloney of Winnipeg wrote to the Department of Immigration to express concerns regarding the credibility of the program among "illegals"; their research indicated that only 25 percent of registrants were bona fide illegal immigrants, while 58 percent were students taking advantage of the program to fast-track their own plans to immigrate. In response to such concerns, and "as a result of an experiment [using anti-draft counsellors to pre-screen registrants] conducted in the Pacific region and recent consultations with the War Objectors Committee at Toronto," Deputy Minister of Immigration A.E. Gotlieb recommended to Minister Andras the establishment of a "commitment officer" process for pre-screening cases where immigrants fear to come forward. An officer would pre-screen, without prejudice, the documentation provided by potential registrants and tell them what they needed to bring to their appointment to be registered. He also re-emphasized the need to deal leniently with short absences from Canada.[96] The commitment officer suggestion was adopted.

To do some damage control in the media, Gotlieb recommended that the minister talk about the practice with regard to short absences from Canada, and to remind the public that the sixty-day period, under fire from some quarters as inadequate, was firm and legislated and could not be changed. Intriguingly, he also recommended soliciting support for the program from the Canadian Labour Congress and the Canadian Chamber of Commerce, probably to illustrate the breadth of the program's public support.[97] A media release quoted Minister Andras's statement that the "government of Canada has shown its complete sincerity in the processing of those already registered and the relaxed criteria being applied to these cases mean that almost all of the applicants will be granted permanent residence."[98] Further media statements promoted the commitment officer process. The coverage indicated that the war resister support groups had played a decisive role in the decision to try it:

> The federal government is stepping up its campaign to convince the public that [the Adjustment of Status Program] is not a trap. Starting this weekend, a system of pre-registration is being introduced into Toronto's ethnic communities so that illegal immigrants can find out in advance if they are going to be accepted ... Unofficially, the Immigration

Department had already established links with organizations concerned with US draft-resisters to provide the kind of reassurance the mediators [commitment officers] will be able to offer. An Immigration Department Spokesman said that the Toronto anti-draft program [sic] has been phoning the department with details of anonymous cases, and getting a kind of pre-clearance before the individual came in to report officially.[99]

Here again, the war resisters' supporters had an impact not only on American immigrants but also on the entire immigration picture.

Starting in early October, regional offices of immigration began directly reporting to each other on the progress being made with the program, in a process similar to the one used by war resister support groups to keep each other informed. This process was likely launched at an Assistant Directors General Conference held in Winnipeg, 1 October 1973. At the conference, reports were heard on actions being taken in each region. In Ontario, "special offers [of cooperation] were made to Mr. Dick Brown of the Toronto Anti-Draft Program [sic] but he has yet to come up with any applicants [for a job promoting the program]." The Ontario office also reported that it was not receiving a high volume of applicants, possibly because the 1972 Administrative Measures Program had dealt with "a lot of problem cases," and there was not a large pool of potential registrants. Ontario reported that they intended to "continue with their Commitment Officers, particularly with the War Resistors [sic] groups." In the Pacific Region,

> four persons have been hired to aid the War Resistors [sic] ... [A]ccording to the T.V. Hour Glass [sic] Program there were 2,500 resistors in the Vancouver area but they have not been able to turn up more than about 250. Another claim was that there were some 5,000 visitors in the Sloakum Valley [sic] area, but a visit does not turn up many – in fact Sloakum Valley does not have that much of a population ... [We] believe we underestimated the results of project 80 [the Administrative Measures] on the Adjustment of Status Program.[100]

After the conference of assistant directors general, the regional promotion of the program was reported back to headquarters and then sent back out to the regions. In early October, Director of Information Services

Allan Duckett reported to the directors general in all regions, the directors of home services and of programs and procedures, and the director general, foreign service, on "Information progress for Thursday, October 4, 1973." Regional information was provided. The report documented how immigration officials were working directly with, among others, anti-draft groups, to promote the Adjustment of Status Program: "Ontario – a meeting in Toronto between acting Director of Immigration Operations, Peter Murray, and members of the war resistors [sic] group was taped by radio stations CHIN, CHUM and CBC. The *Toronto Star* published a story on the Adjustment of Status Program."[101] A similar report for Tuesday, 9 October 1973 stated that in Ontario, "a mobile unit is currently travelling through Innisville, Golden Lake, Barry's Bay and Pembroke." In the Prairies, "assurances are also being given to a number of Americans who are afraid to register for fear of being turned back to the United States where warrants may be out for their arrests."[102]

Anticipating the end of the sixty-day period, and perhaps in response to pressure from anti-draft groups to extend it, the department decided to accept registrations by mail or telegram if they were postmarked by midnight 15 October, instead of requiring a form and an interview.[103] On 12 October, the director of Home Services Branch reported to the assistant deputy minister that no regions were reporting significantly higher numbers of applications that day; but, the memo continued, the Winnipeg War Resisters group was planning to meet with "ethnic groups [outside the American immigrant community]," "to coordinate efforts to prevail upon Immigration authorities that persons ... apprehended after October 16 will be dealt with as leniently as those who register [under the program]."[104] The Vancouver Committee to Aid American War Objectors asked Minister Andras for an extension of the program, but because Parliament did not sit again until 15 October, the last day of the program, an extension was impossible, even had the minister wished to consider it. Instead, applicants who would have qualified under the program after the sixty-day period were treated as requests for consideration on humanitarian grounds.[105] In the end, about fifty thousand people attained landed status under the program.[106]

The cooperation between the Department of Immigration and the anti-draft group network was unprecedented. Dick Brown of the Toronto group even received a thank-you letter on 19 October from G.D.A. Reid, director general, Ontario region, manpower and immigration.[107] However, the Administrative Measures and the Adjustment of Status Program did not figure heavily in the memories of war resisters, with a few exceptions. Joseph Jones recalls,

> I remember discussions at *AMEX* about the sixty-day grace period from August to October 1973. Concerns included the limited time for publicity, the way in which church and perhaps government money was directed to politically dubious individuals and groups, the possibility that applicants would be rejected and deported, the possibility that the paranoia of life underground would keep people from applying, and the anticipation that Canadian immigration officials might attempt a program of deporting those who failed to apply.[108]

"Daniel," whose recollections were vague on the matter, remarked, "I didn't know that they called them that. If this refers to no longer being able to gain 'landed immigrant' status by application from within Canada after September, 1972, I remember it, but I managed to get landed just before they cut off this option."[109] Paul Copeland also had some recollection of Administrative Measures and the Adjustment of Status Program:

> I vaguely remember the adjustment of status program. I think there were a couple of in-effect amnesties. I think the appeals board would get so backed up. Certainly, in some of the later refugee stuff, they got so backed up that they did reviews and adjustment of status programs. Anyone who was here long-term, in the adjustment of status program, they could get landed.[110]

This comparative lack of collective memory about these two government measures shows that, for the anti-draft movement and war resisters, they mostly figured in the minds of those directly engaged in policy work or case work.

Thus, the effects of these programs on draft dodgers and deserters did not get incorporated into the mainstream narrative about draft dodgers in Canada. This is likely partly because the narrative about immigration writ large tends to exclude Americans. Further, just as exact numbers of American war resisters coming to Canada are elusive, it remains unclear how many Americans were among those landed during the programs. The Adjustment of Status Program is promoted by the Canadian government as a part of the story of Canada's open immigration policy and is generally understood – or criticized – as such, not as part of the story of war resisters specifically.[111]

At the time, the response from the war resister community was ambivalent. "Immigration's 'Last Chance' Ends: Get Back Jack!" announced a Vancouver American Exiles Association (VAEA) newsletter issued after the program ended. Although 49,230 immigrants had registered, the newsletter claimed that perhaps hundreds of thousands remained illegal. "Perhaps when one has lived underground anywhere from 2 [to] 10 years, a '60 day Immigration Act' is not as convincing as the immigration dept. would like," the newsletter quipped. The article told of "the looming prospect of a 'deportation drive' by Immigration authorities and RCMP." The VAEA stated its commitment to "win a special refugee status for American war resisters."[112]

While Mackasey's administrative measures to address the problems of a large appeals backlog and the subsequent move to remove the rule allowing visitors to apply for landed immigrant status from within Canada were viewed with suspicion by the anti-draft movement, the programs to allow for faster processes were actively promoted by the groups. The interaction between the anti-draft groups and government officials is an example of how the permeable barrier between the "state" and civil society sometimes allows for social movements to take on roles normally played by government agencies and officials. The mutual influence of the movement and government, while predominantly adversarial, allowed for positive steps to be taken for American immigrants, while the groups were still able to maintain their autonomy and their roles as advocates.

Conclusion
A Contested Refuge from Militarism

Let Freedom Ring
it would be nice if it did ring,
but it doesn't
it explodes and makes a mess

– Poets Against the War, Red Cloud, "Let Freedom Ring"[1]

Was Canada, as so many implied at the time and many continue to believe to this day, a refuge from militarism? Departmental debates about the border, the existence of Operational Memo 117 encouraging the exclusion of deserters from Canada, discrimination at the border, and the behaviour of public figures and the police all indicate that, if Canada was such a refuge, it was a hard-fought and bitterly defended refuge as well as a contingent and partial one, at best. Media scrutiny of police behaviour and the interplay between those discussions and events such as raids and deportations meant that the anti-draft movement could express its side of the discussion. But the discussion never ended; the conflict never resolved in one direction or the other.

The American and Canadian Vietnam-era anti-draft movements got organized at the same time, around 1966-67.[2] Between 1967 and 1972, about forty thousand Americans immigrated to Canada, many of them war resisters. Many Canadians supported the war resisters. Others were not so welcoming. Canadian government officials were ambivalent towards these immigrants. They viewed them as both a potential source of trained labour and a potential source of social disorder. The politically broad movement to support American war resisters was united in its support, but it also contained divergences of opinion, especially when the difference between draft dodgers and deserters was considered.

The anti-draft movement in Canada was a social movement that shared a complex relationship with the government of the day. More generally, this movement played a role in, and was influenced by, debates about the changing role of immigration, the influence of old movements on new ones, and nationalism. This book examines the interaction of government officials, police, anti-draft groups, individual activists, and war resisters through the lens of a multidisciplinary theory, which allows for a consideration of the complexity of social interactions, including the relationship between material experience and culture. This approach yields a rich understanding of this episode in Canadian history. Some of its elements had never been told in written form before, especially from the ground up. It is useful to view the story as a battle for hegemony between ideas and perceptions of war resisters and between different ideas of Canadian nationalism. It also represents an interesting case of a movement's relationship to the government – and shows especially well how a movement may act in ways that are usually considered the domain of government institutions.

The Canadian anti-draft movement existed for only about seven years. During this time, it experienced problems of unity stemming from internal debates, first about the relative effectiveness of draft dodging and deserting as antiwar actions and, later, about strategy, which manifested itself most tellingly as a debate about radicalism.

The decentralized network of anti-draft groups, rooted in the New Left, was well-suited to the needs of a movement aimed at supporting American immigrants who could cross the border anywhere. Groups in the United States provided assistance in distributing materials and information; in Canada, lawyers, intellectuals, politicians, and church groups helped pave the way. The groups and individuals shaped, and were shaped by, the perceptions held by war resisters of Canada and the Canadian anti-draft movement.

Using methods partly taken from pacifist tradition, this movement reached out to potential immigrants. Social work methods combined with those of political advocacy. Their juxtaposition contributed to tensions within the movement, but they also often provided successful techniques of communication and information sharing and helped maintain the strength that comes from a shared commitment to a cause. Maturing over time, this movement developed an ability to face new situations critically and used imagination and open-mindedness to adjust their methods accordingly. Reliance on such varied traditions prepared the movement well to overcome both geographical and ideological obstacles to help individual war resisters and to effect changes to immigration policy. It was also strengthened by links with groups of an equally varied nature in the United States.

The movement's campaigns made an especially effective use of the media, lobbying, and letter-writing campaigns. These methods, first put to good use in 1969 to open the border to deserters, worked well a second time in attempts to influence the two programs undertaken by the Department of Immigration in 1972 and 1973 to address backlogs in the appeals system and to address the large number of illegal immigrants in the country. At the same time, negative police attention, seen as harassment by anti-draft activists and war resisters alike, was significant. Behind such police behaviour, and underlying police interactions with immigration officials, were divisions both at the top and at the bottom of society. Accordingly, the media at large was also to play a significant role in the public scrutiny of police behaviour. The surveillance itself reflected wider fears in Canadian society of American influence on Canadian society in general and on Canadian social justice movements in particular. In this context, the interplay between institutions of government at many levels and the movement was part of a struggle for hegemony over perceptions of war resisters and their influence on Canadian society.

Initially, most Canadian activists refrained from discriminating between the varieties of draft resistance tactics among Americans. Eventually, however, the formation of intransigent American exile groups, which valorized desertion and radicalism, provoked important debates among Canadian supporters. They resulted in a general preference, among Canadian supporters, for American actions geared towards assimilating to Canadian institutions and ideas. For the most part, such preferences were expressed as a desire for Canadian independence, and not as anti-American sentiment aimed at individual Americans. To be sure, vocal elements of anti-Americanism emerged among the Canadian Left in connection to this push for assimilation and were at times aimed at individuals, but they were the expressions of a minority.

These ideas about Canadian independence were part of an emergent new nationalism, a portion of which I categorize as "left nationalist." While promotion of Canadian independence and of a Canada with a tradition of asylum allowed for gains to be made on behalf of resisters, it limited, to some degree, the movement's ability to challenge fundamental assumptions about Canada and its immigration policy. These internal contradictions reflected back on debates in the movement about nationalism, strategy, and tactics. These contradictions complicated existing differences about tactics in the anti-draft movement that had their roots in divergences between political cultures from earlier in the century.

As the movement matured, it began to engage more directly and assertively with government policy. In 1972 and 1973, it actively intervened and, once programs were in place, promoted government actions to help visitors get landed. By so doing, the movement became a concrete example of the permeable boundary between state and society, which also showed the state as in constant formation, change, and interaction.

As the anti-draft movement wound down, American exile groups and deserter committees continued with a new focus: winning an unconditional amnesty from the United States government. This focus was evidently one that privileged the desires of Americans who wished to return to the United States. Two amnesties, one by President Gerald Ford, and one by President Jimmy Carter, were eventually decreed. Meanwhile, the new and newly reforged movements of the sixties – women's liberation, Black Power and Red Power, anti-imperialism – continued well into the seventies. For some, entry into these movements was via the antiwar and anti-draft movements.

The anti-draft movement managed to effectively help war resisters from 1966 to 1973. The movement was uneven, and it enjoyed its ups and downs in terms of effectiveness. It also carried out debates centred on questions about citizenship, engagement, and nationalism. Despite the complexity of the scene, the anti-draft movement helped thousands of war resisters successfully immigrate to Canada. Its story is one of perseverance and tenacity. Almost entirely because of the efforts of its activists, Canada came to represent a refuge for Vietnam-era American war resisters.

Appendices

APPENDIX 1: Groups and Abbreviations
(in alphabetical order)

Anti-Draft Groups and Exile Groups

Alexander Ross Society, AB

American Deserters Committee (ADC). *See also individual ADCs under name of city (Montreal, Toronto, Vancouver)*

American Immigrants Employment Service, Toronto

American Refugee Service, Montreal

Black Anti-Draft Programme, Afro-American Brotherhood, Toronto

Black Refugee Committee, Toronto

Black Refugee Organization (BRO), Toronto

Calgary Committee on War Immigrants

Calgary Committee to Aid War Immigrants

Canadian Assistance to War Objectors (CATWO, CAWO)

Committee to Aid Refugees from Militarism, Toronto (CARM)

Ebony Social Services, Toronto

Edmonton Committee to Aid American War Objectors

Guelph Anti-Draft Programme

Information '68, Windsor, ON

Information '68-'69, Windsor, ON

Inter-Church Committee on Refugees

Jewish Immigrant Aid Service

Kitchener-Waterloo Anti-Draft Programme

Lakehead Committee to Aid American War Objectors

London Information Committee for Draft Refugees, ON

Montreal American Deserters Committee (Montreal ADC)

Montreal American Deserters Co-op

Montreal Council to Aid War Resisters (MCAWR)
New Brunswick Committee to Aid American War Objectors, Sackville
New Brunswick Committee to Aid War Resisters
Newfoundland Committee to Aid American War Objectors
Nova Scotia Committee to Aid American War Objectors (NSCAAWO)
Oshawa Anti-Draft Programme
Ottawa AID: Assistance with Immigration and the Draft (AID)
PEI Committee to Aid War Objectors
Red White & Black (RWB)
Regina Committee of American Deserters (RCAD)
Regina Committee to Aid Immigrants
Saint John Anti-Draft Programme
Saskatoon Immigrant and Refugee Society
Southern Ontario Committee on War Immigrants, Hamilton
Teach-in Committee Against the War, Charlottetown
Toronto American Deserters Committee (TADC)
Toronto Anti-Draft Programme (TADP)
Union of American Exiles (UAE), Toronto
Union of New Canadians, Toronto
University of Toronto Anti-Draft Program
Vancouver American Deserters Committee (Vancouver ADC)
Vancouver American Exiles' Association (VAEA)
Vancouver Committee to Aid American War Objectors (VCAAWO)
Vancouver Co-ordinating Council for American Refugees
Victoria Committee to Aid Draft Resisters
Victoria Committee to Aid War Resisters
Winnipeg Committee to Assist War Objectors
Yankee Refugee group

Anti-Draft Activist Contacts

Nelson Adams, Fredericton, NB
Rev. Jim Allman, Peterborough, ON
Dunc Blewett, Regina, SK
Goldie Josephy, Ottawa, ON
Martha and Peter Kellerman, Moncton, NB
Joan Mackenzie, Kingston, ON
Roy Officer, Walter Klaasen, or Dr. Ronald D. Lambert, Kitchener-Waterloo, ON
Don Pentland, Winnipeg, MB
Glen Tenpenny, London, ON
John Warnock Jr., Saskatoon, SK

Other War Resister Supporting Groups

Canadian Campaign for Nuclear Disarmament (CCND)
Canadian Council of Churches (CCC)
Canadian Friends Service Committee
Canadian Peace Research Institute
Canadian Union of Students (CUS)
Carleton Committee to End the War in Vietnam
Combined Universities Campaign for Nuclear Disarmament (CUCND)
Ottawa Committee for Peace and Liberation
Student Association to End the War in Vietnam
Student Union for Peace Action (SUPA)
University of Toronto Faculty Committee to End the War in Vietnam
University of Toronto Students' Administrative Council
Vancouver Vietnam Action Committee (VVAC)
Voice of Women (VOW)

American and Other Non-Canadian Groups

British Committee for American War Resisters
Central Committee for Conscientious Objectors (CCCO)
Fellowship for Peace and Reconciliation
Students for a Democratic Society (SDS)
War Resisters League (WRL)

APPENDIX 2: Shifts in Immigration Regulations and Tactics of Counselling and Border Crossing

Date	Minister of Manpower and Immigration	Regulatory factors	Border conditions	Counselling and services	Possible immigration tactic
1967	Jean Marchand	Points system introduced; immigrants answer a questionnaire about their education, skills, etc. and are awarded points on that basis; some points are awarded at the discretion of immigration officers			
	Jean Marchand	Applications for landed immigrant status permitted at border points, at consulates, or from within Canada Those entering originally as visitors can therefore apply for landed immigrant status from within Canada	Proof of discharge required for military, but not consistently queried Draft status not a factor Job offer at the border gains ten points more than with an application from within Canada	Job placement, advice on how to get maximum points	Resisters enter Canada at border points as visitors; get counselling; return to the US, make a U-turn and re-cross the border with a job offer to get landed immigrant status Deserters less likely to succeed; may go underground

Date	Minister of Manpower and Immigration	Regulatory factors	Border conditions	Counselling and services	Possible immigration tactic
January 1968	Jean Marchand (continuing from Lester Pearson's administration into Trudeau's, as of April 1968)	Proof of discharge no longer required for applicants from within Canada; remains a requirement at the border		Job placement, advice on how to get maximum points	Deserters now encouraged to enter as visitors and apply for landed immigrant status from within Canada
July 1968	Allan MacEachen	Immigration officers can use "discretion" to prevent entry of individuals judged to have significant legal, moral or contractual obligations in their country of origin. List of examples includes military obligations. Intended as instruction to immigration officers to exclude deserters	Deserters routinely denied entry at border points; multiple examples of informing US officials that deserter is returning to the US side of the border crossing	Deserters counselled separately; many go underground, at least temporarily	Deserters tend to withhold their status, leading to legal problems later

May 1969	Allan MacEachen	"Discretion" clause revised to delete the example of military status; MacEachen announces border is now open to anyone regardless of military status	Discrimination against all resisters continues, but no longer systematic	Deserters counselled separately because of their tendency to score fewer points on immigration questionnaire	Many resisters enter as visitors and never get around to applying for status, especially deserters
July–August 1972	Bryce Mackasey	Administrative Measures Program allows relaxed criteria for the consideration of appeals		Focus becomes counselling individual resisters through the appeals backlog processing; anticipating revocation of section 34 of the regulations, groups encourage as many as possible to get landed quickly	
November 1972	Bryce Mackasey, 3 to 26 November 1972; Bob Andras, 27 November 1972	Section 34 of the Immigration Regulations repealed; landing at the border or from within Canada no longer allowed	Selective Service draft ends December 1972; last draftees inducted in 1973	Immigration no longer a viable option for resisters; those already in Canada now illegal	Resisters continue to use the appeals process to get special consideration

▷

Date	Minister of Manpower and Immigration	Regulatory factors	Border conditions	Counselling and services	Possible immigration tactic
June 1973	Bob Andras	Bill C-197 debated and adopted, eliminating universal right to appeal and announcing Adjustment of Status Program		Anti-draft groups actively promote the Adjustment of Status Program, encouraging resisters to be pre-examined by counsellors before meeting with immigration officers	"Last chance to get landed"
15 August to 15 October 1973		Adjustment of Status Program			

Notes

Preface

1 See, for instance, the journal *The Sixties: A Journal of History, Politics and Culture* (Routledge); Bryan Palmer, *Canada's 1960s: The Ironies of Identity in a Rebellious Era* (Toronto: University of Toronto Press, 2009); and Karen Dubinsky et al., eds., *New World Coming: The Sixties and the Shaping of Global Consciousness* (Toronto: Between the Lines, 2009), from the conference of the same name that took place 13-16 June 2007 at Queen's University.

2 Daniel Francis, *National Dreams: Myth, Memory, and Canadian History* (Vancouver: Arsenal Pulp Press, 1997), 11.

3 These interviews were conducted in accordance with the Tri-Council Policy on Ethical Conduct for Research Involving Humans. They were solicited through a snowball method: a combination of searching for living individuals mentioned in the documentary evidence; an email broadcast to acquaintances involved in movement activities today and in academic and non-academic conferences; and through word-of-mouth contacts elicited from these methods. The sample is not intended to be statistically representative; rather, it is meant to include women and men, Canadians and Americans, and a range of involvement and political opinion. Early on, I attempted to secure interviews with Allan MacEachen and Marcel Prud'homme, but neither of them replied to my letters, emails, or phone calls. The work does not rely on their perspective, however, since the focus is on the campaign and the activists within it, not on government representatives.

4 Under the Selective Service Program, American males were (and are today) required to register on their eighteenth birthday. During the Vietnam War, a draft that placed the names of registered Americans into a lottery for military service was in effect. Those whose names were drawn were sent an induction notice.

5 To be precise, at the time the interviews were conducted, two of my interview subjects were involved in the War Resister Support Campaign that supported American

war resisters from the Iraq and Afghanistan conflicts: one man and one woman, both American war resisters in the 1960s.

6 Bernard S. Cohn, *An Anthropologist among Historians and Other Essays* (Delhi and New York: Oxford University Press, 1990).

7 David Lowenthal, *The Past Is a Foreign Country* (Cambridge: Cambridge University Press, 1985), 190.

8 C.J. Fuller, review of *An Anthropologist among the Historians and Other Essays*, by Bernard Cohn, *Man* 26, 4 (December 1991): 762-63.

9 Donald A. Ritchie, *Doing Oral History: A Practical Guide* (New York: Oxford University Press, 2003), 27, quoting David Lodge, *Out of the Shelter*.

10 Ibid., 30.

11 Ibid., 31-32; Alessandro Portelli, *The Death of Luigi Trastulli, and Other Stories: Form and Meaning in Oral History* (New York: SUNY Press, 1991), 50.

12 See also Richard Rodger and Joanna Herbert, "Frameworks: Testimony, Representation and Interpretation," in *Testimonies of the City: Identity, Community and Change in a Contemporary Urban World* (Surrey, UK: Ashgate Publishing, 2007), 1-22.

13 For more information on the War Resisters Support Campaign, see "War Resisters Support Campaign," War Resisters Support Campaign, accessed 20 March 2011, http://www.resisters.ca. The Pentagon admitted to 5,500 AWOLs in 2004 alone. Tom Reeves, "A Draft By Any Other Name ... Is Still Wrong: Exposing the Coming Draft," *Counterpunch*, Weekend Edition, 19-21 March 2005, http://www.counterpunch.org/.

Introduction

1 This epigraph is an excerpt of a song that was published on the day of the defeat of the French in Vietnam at Điện Biên Phủ. The song was banned in France until 1962. See *Antiwar Songs*, http://www.antiwarsongs.org/.

2 Douglas T. Miller, *On Our Own: Americans in the Sixties* (Toronto: D.C. Heath and Company, 1996); Todd Gitlin, *The Sixties: Years of Hope, Days of Rage* (New York: Bantam Books, 1993).

3 Miller, *On Our Own*, 196-97.

4 John Hagan, *Northern Passage: American Vietnam War Resisters in Canada* (Cambridge: Harvard University Press, 2001), 170-75.

5 Draft dodgers were avoiding their induction into the US military; deserters were inducted and subsequently fled their posts.

6 Hagan, *Northern Passage*, 3, 241-42. For a good overview of the issues and previous attempts at estimating numbers, see Joseph Jones, *Contending Statistics: The Numbers for US Vietnam War Resisters in Canada* (Vancouver: Quarter Sheaf, 2005).

7 Miller, *On Our Own*, 196.

8 The extent to which this myth is shared can be seen in Dan Springer, "Canada Plans Draft-Dodger Monument," *Fox News*, 21 September 2004, http://www.foxnews.com/ and Valerie Knowles's official history on Citizenship and Immigration

Canada's website, which states, "Starting in 1965, Canada became a choice haven for American draft-dodgers and deserters." "Draft-Age Americans in Canada," in *Forging Our Legacy: Canadian Citizenship and Immigration, 1900-1977,* Public Works and Government Services Canada, 2000, http://www.cic.gc.ca/.

9 Julian Bell, ed., *We Did Not Fight: 1914-18 Experiences of War Resisters* (London: Cobden-Sanderson, 1935), vii. See also Peter Brock, ed., *"These Strange Criminals": An Anthology of Prison Memoirs by Conscientious Objectors from the Great War to the Cold War* (Toronto: University of Toronto Press, 2004).

10 Renée G. Kasinsky, *Refugees from Militarism: Draft-Age Americans in Canada* (New Brunswick, NJ: Transaction Books, 1976), 83; Hagan, *Northern Passage,* frontispiece. See also Roger Neville Williams, *The New Exiles: American War Resisters in Canada* (New York: Liveright Publishers, 1971), 89. Kasinsky was an American immigrant and sociologist who secured her status as a landed immigrant in 1969 and who was involved with the Vancouver Committee to Aid American War Objectors (VCAAWO). She also conducted dozens of rigorously documented interviews and questionnaires.

11 Mark Nykanen, "Canada Still a 'Refuge from Militarism?'" *Seattle Post-Intelligencer,* 10 March 2006, http://www.commondreams.org/; Reuben Apple, "War Resisters Welcome," *Eye Weekly* (Toronto), 5 April 2007, http://www.eyeweekly.com/; War Resisters Support Campaign, accessed 23 October 2007, http://www.resisters.ca/. Many of these references merely repeat the quotation without sourcing it; one or two mention Hagan's book.

12 Joseph Jones, *Happenstance and Misquotation: Canadian Immigration Policy 1966-1974, the Arrival of US Vietnam War Resisters in Canada, and the Views of Pierre Trudeau* (Vancouver: Quarter Sheaf, 2008).

13 Library and Archives Canada (hereafter LAC), Department of Employment and Immigration fonds, RG 76, vol. 983, file 5660-1, "Military Personnel – Draft Dodgers – General," Office of the Minister of Manpower and Immigration, press release and House of Commons Statement by Allan MacEachen, 22 May 1969; CBC Archives, "Seeking Sanctuary: Draft Dodgers: Trudeau Opens the Door to Draft Dodgers," original air date 25 March 1969, http://archives.cbc.ca/.

14 See Sara Speicher and Donald F. Durnbaugh, "Historic Peace Churches," World Council of Churches, "Ecumenical Dictionary: 'Article of the Month' Series," August 2003, http://www.wcc-coe.org/. They write, "Historic Peace Churches (HPC) is a term popularized in 1935 to refer to the Church of the Brethren, the Religious Society of Friends (Quakers), and the Mennonite churches which share a common witness against war ... All have held an official witness that peace is an essential aspect of the gospel and all have rejected the use of force and violence. Their common position on peace has brought the three traditions into many cooperative relationships, not only during times of war but also in worldwide service and relief projects." In Canada, the Quakers, Mennonites, Hutterites, and Doukhobors were historically guaranteed the right to live according to their pacifist beliefs. Thomas P. Socknat,

Canadian Encyclopedia, s.v. "Pacifism," 2012, http://www.thecanadianencyclopedia. com.

15 See, for instance, Reginald C. Stuart, "Continentalism Revisited: Recent Narratives on the History of Canadian-American Relations," *Diplomatic History* 18, 3 (1994): 405-14.

16 I encountered the idea of Canadian movements as derivative of American ones when I presented earlier drafts of this work to a Canadian Historical Association meeting in 2005 and again at the "New World Coming: The Sixties and the Shaping of Global Consciousness" conference at Queen's University in the summer of 2007. On transnationalism, see Patricia Clavin, "Defining Transnationalism," *Contemporary European History* 14, 4 (2005): 421-39.

17 Other possible theoretical contexts and perspectives, such as regional considerations, philosophical questions of morality and pacifism, women war resisters, racism, the impact that other "classes" of immigrants excluded by the Immigration Act may have had in this movement, are either set aside for future research or left for others to explore. For instance, Lara Campbell (Simon Fraser University) has explored war resisters and gender; Donald W. Maxwell (Indiana University) has conducted an examination of the involvement of churches.

18 A. Paul Pross, *Group Politics and Public Policy*, 2nd ed. (Toronto: Oxford University Press, 1992), 4.

19 David A. Snow, Sarah Anne Soule, and Hanspeter Kriesi, *The Blackwell Companion to Social Movements* (Malden, MA: Blackwell Publishing, 2004), 6-11. See also Miriam Smith, *A Civil Society? Collective Actors in Canadian Political Life* (Peterborough, ON: Broadview Press, 2005).

20 Robert Cox, "Social Forces, States and World Orders: Beyond International Relations Theory," in *Neorealism and Its Critics*, ed. Robert Keohane (New York: Columbia University Press, 1986), 207.

21 Theda Skocpol, "Bringing the State Back In: Strategies of Analysis in Current Research," in *Bringing the State Back In*, ed. Peter R. Evans, Dietrich Ruesdchemeyer, and Theda Skocpol (Cambridge: Cambridge University Press, 1985), 3-37.

22 This poem appears by kind permission of Chris Faiers. The poem appears in *Crossing Lines: Poets Who Came to Canada in the Vietnam War Era*, ed. Allan Briesmaster and Steven Michael Berzensky (Hamilton, ON: Seraphim Editions, 2008), 80.

23 A detailed reading of even the most pivotal works on the period – for example, Greg Donaghy, *Tolerant Allies: Canada and the United States, 1963-1968* (Montreal and Kingston: McGill-Queen's University Press, 2002); J.L. Granatstein and Norman Hillmer, *For Better or For Worse: Canada and the United States to the 1990s* (Toronto: Copp Clark Pitman, 1991); Robert Bothwell, Ian Drummond, and John English, *Canada since 1945* (Toronto: University of Toronto Press, 1991), to name but a few – reveal that these works devote less than a page and usually only a paragraph or so to the draft dodgers, as part of explorations of international relations or cultural history

at the level of states. Other examples include Alvin Finkel, *Our Lives: Canada after 1945* (Toronto: James Lorimer, 1997); J.L. Granatstein, *Canada 1957-1967: The Years of Uncertainty and Innovation* (Toronto: McClelland and Stewart, 1986); Douglas A. Ross, *In the Interests of Peace: Canada and Vietnam, 1954-1973* (Toronto: University of Toronto Press, 1984); and J.L. Granatstein and Robert Bothwell, *Pirouette: Pierre Trudeau and Canadian Foreign Policy* (Toronto: University of Toronto Press, 1990).

24 Robert Bothwell, *Alliance and Illusion: Canada and the World, 1945-1984* (Vancouver: UBC Press, 2007); Robert Bothwell, *The Big Chill: Canada and the Cold War* (Toronto: Canadian Institute of International Affairs, 1998); Robert Bothwell, *Canada and the United States: The Politics of Partnership* (Toronto: University of Toronto Press, 1992); J.L. Granatstein, *Yankee Go Home? Canadians and Anti-Americanism* (Toronto: Harper Collins, 1996); John Herd Thompson and Stephen J. Randall, *Canada and the United States: Ambivalent Allies* (Montreal and Kingston: McGill-Queen's University Press, 1994).

25 Bothwell, *Alliance and Illusion*, 212-13, 318.

26 Victor Levant, *Quiet Complicity: Canadian Involvement in the Vietnam War* (Toronto: Between the Lines, 1986).

27 Alan Haig-Brown, *Hell No We Won't Go: Vietnam Draft Resisters in Canada* (Vancouver: Raincoast Books, 1996); Frank Kusch, *All American Boys: Draft Dodgers in Canada from the Vietnam War* (Westport, CT: Praeger Publishers, 2001); Williams, *The New Exiles*.

28 Hagan, *Northern Passage*. Hagan was one of Haig-Brown's twenty interviews. Hagan is now researching the influence and activities of the descendants of draft dodgers in Canadian society.

29 David S. Churchill, "An Ambiguous Welcome: Vietnam Draft Resistance, the Canadian State, and Cold War Containment," *Social History/Histoire sociale* 27, 73 (2004): 1-26. See also Churchill's PhD dissertation, "When Home Became Away: American Expatriates and New Social Movements in Toronto, 1965-1977" (University of Chicago, 2001).

30 As Michael S. Foley notes, there is a curious symmetry in that draft resistance is not often treated as part of American histories of the Vietnam War. Michael S. Foley, *Confronting the War Machine: Draft Resistance during the Vietnam War* (Chapel Hill: University of North Carolina Press, 2003), 13.

31 Two exceptions are Dan Malleck (Brock University), "Crossing the Line: The American Drinker in Ontario Border Communities, 1927–1944" (paper presented at the British Association of Canadian Studies conference, Kent, UK, 13 April 2005); and Dan Malleck, "The Bureaucratization of Moral Regulation: The LCBO and (Not-So) Standard Hotel Licensing in Niagara, 1927-1944," *Social History/Histoire sociale* 38, 75 (2005): 59-77.

32 Valerie Knowles, *Forging Our Legacy: Canadian Citizenship and Immigration, 1900-1977* (Ottawa: Citizenship and Immigration Canada, 2000).

33   Anna Triandafyllidou, "Nations, Migrants and Transnational Identifications: An Interactive Approach to Nationalism," in *The Sage Handbook of Nations and Nationalism*, ed. Gerard Delanty and Krishan Kumar (London: Sage, 2001), 287.

34   Himani Bannerji, "On the Dark Side of the Nation: Politics of Multiculturalism and the State of 'Canada,'" in *Literary Pluralities*, ed. Crystal Verduyn (Peterborough, ON: Broadview Press, 1998), 125-51.

35   Ibid., 143.

36   Rose Baaba Folson, "Representation of the Immigrant," in *Calculated Kindness: Global Restructuring, Immigration and Settlement in Canada*, ed. Rose Baaba Folson (Halifax: Fernwood Publishing, 2004), 21-32. See also Tania Das Gupta and Franca Iacovetta, eds., "Whose Canada Is It? Immigrant Women, Women of Colour and Feminist Critiques of 'Multiculturalism,'" special issue, *Atlantis: A Women's Studies Journal* 24, 2 (2000): 1-4.

37   Bannerji, "On the Dark Side of the Nation," 144.

38   On "whiteness" in the United States and the racialization of immigrants, see David R. Roediger, *Working toward Whiteness: How America's Immigrants Became White: The Strange Journey from Ellis Island to the Suburbs* (New York: Basic Books, 1999); Matthew Frye Jacobson, *Whiteness of a Different Color: European Immigrants and The Alchemy of Race* (Cambridge, MA: Harvard University Press, 1999); Eileen Boris, "The Racialized Gendered State: Constructions of Citizenship in the United States," *Social Politics* 2, 2 (1995): 160-80; Héctor R. Cordero-Guzmán, Robert C. Smith, and Ramón Grosfoguel, eds., *Migration, Transnationalization, and Race in a Changing New York* (Philadelphia: Temple University Press, 2001).

39   The question of racism and black war resisters remains a topic deserving a great deal more study, although it is addressed briefly throughout this work. Authors considering this topic in passing include David Cortwright, *Soldiers in Revolt: GI Resistance during the Vietnam War* (1975, repr., Chicago: Haymarket Books, 2005); Christian Appy, *Working-Class War: American Combat Soldiers and Vietnam* (Chapel Hill, NC: University of North Carolina Press, 1993); and Robert Buzzanco, *Vietnam and the Transformation of American Life* (Malden, MA: Blackwell, 1999).

40   See, for instance, Reginald C. Stuart, *Dispersed Relations: Americans and Canadians in Upper North America* (Baltimore: Johns Hopkins University Press, 2007); John J. Bukowczyk, Randy William Widdis, Nora Faires, and David R. Smith, *Permeable Border: The Great Lakes Basin as Transnational Region, 1650-1990* (Pittsburgh: University of Pittsburgh Press, 2005). Studies of transnational migration and social movements include David D. Harvey, "Garrison Duty: Canada's Retention of the American Migrant, 1901-1981," *American Review of Canadian Studies* 15, 2 (1985): 169-87; Mildred A. Schwartz, "Cross-Border Ties among Protest Movements: The Great Plains Connection," *Great Plains Quarterly* 17, 2 (1997): 119-30; Randy William Widdis, "Borders, Borderlands and Canadian Identity: A Canadian Perspective," *International Journal of Canadian Studies* 15 (1997): 49-66; Barry Carr, "Globalization from Below:

Labour Internationalism Under NAFTA," *International Social Science Journal* 51, 1 (1999): 49-59; Karen Andrea Balcom, "The Traffic in Babies: Cross-Border Adoption, Baby-Selling and the Development of Child Welfare Systems in the United States and Canada, 1930-1960" (PhD diss., Rutgers State University, 2002); Joel Stillerman, "Transnational Activist Networks and the Emergence of Labor Internationalism in the NAFTA Countries," *Social Science History* 27, 4 (2003): 577-601.

41 For good overviews of this history from both the war resister and the pacifist perspective, see Foley, *Confronting the War Machine,* 61-67; Thomas Socknat, *Witness against War: Pacifism in Canada, 1900-1945* (Toronto: University of Toronto Press, 1987), 289-291, 295; Peter Brock and Nigel Young, *Pacifism in the Twentieth Century* (Syracuse, NY: Syracuse University Press, 1999), 266-67, 281-86, 289-95.

42 Cox, "Social Forces, States and World Orders," 205, 215-16.

43 Theda Skocpol, *States and Social Revolutions: A Comparative Analysis of France, Russia and China* (New York: Cambridge University Press, 1979), 32.

44 For additional material considering the role and nature of the state, see Allan Greer and Ian Radforth, eds., *Colonial Leviathan: State Formation in Mid-Nineteenth Century Canada* (Toronto: University of Toronto Press, 1992) as well as the debates between Ralph Miliband and Nicos Poulantzas between 1969 and 1976, principally Nicos Poulantzas, "The Problem of the Capitalist State," *New Left Review* 58 (1969): 67-78; and Ralph Miliband, "The Capitalist State: Reply to Nicos Poulantzas," *New Left Review* 59 (1970): 53-60.

45 Dominique Marshall, *The Social Origins of the Welfare State: Quebec Families, Compulsory Education, and Family Allowances, 1940-1955,* trans. Nicola Doone Danby (Waterloo, ON: Wilfrid Laurier University Press, 2006), xi-xii.

46 Theda Skocpol, "Why I Am an Historical Institutionalist," *Polity* 28, 1 (1995): 103-6.

47 Antonio Gramsci, "The Study of Philosophy," in *Selections from the Prison Notebooks of Antonio Gramsci,* trans. and ed. Quintin Hoare and Geoffrey Nowell Smith (New York: International Publishers, 1971), 328-33. See also Stuart Hall, "Gramsci's Relevance for the Study of Race and Ethnicity," in *Stuart Hall: Critical Dialogues in Cultural Studies,* ed. David Morley and Kuan-Hsing Chen (New York: Routledge, 1996), 431.

48 Hall, "Gramsci's Relevance," 439; Gramsci, "The Study of Philosophy," 330-33.

49 Hall, "Gramsci's Relevance," 423-24, 432; Antonio Gramsci, "The Modern Prince," in *Selections from the Prison Notebooks of Antonio Gramsci,* trans. and ed. Quintin Hoare and Geoffrey Nowell Smith (New York: International Publishers, 1971), 182.

50 Gramsci, "The Study of Philosophy," 323-33.

51 Ian McKay, *Rebels, Reds, Radicals: Rethinking Canada's Left History* (Toronto: Between the Lines, 2005), 61-62.

52 Antonio Gramsci, "The Intellectuals," in *Selections from the Prison Notebooks of Antonio Gramsci,* trans. and ed. Quintin Hoare and Geoffrey Nowell Smith (New York: International Publishers, 1971), 9-13; Gramsci, "The Modern Prince," 185.

53 Gramsci, "The Modern Prince," 184-85; Gramsci, "State and Civil Society," 245-46, 254.

54   Gramsci, "The Study of Philosophy," 330, 344-45.

55   Max Weber, *The Theory of Social and Economic Organization*, ed. Talcott Parsons (New York: Oxford University Press, 1966), 324-341. Of course, the implication is that the only rational legal system is one that upholds the class interests of the propertied class, because the right to own property is upheld. For further analysis on bureaucracies as historical actors or agents of change, see James D. Thompson, *Organizations in Action* (New York: McGraw-Hill, 1967).

56   Bruce Curtis, *The Politics of Population: State Formation, Statistics, and the Census of Canada, 1849-1875* (Toronto: University of Toronto Press, 2001), 309-10. See also James C. Scott, *Seeing Like a State: How Certain Schemes to Improve the Human Condition Have Failed* (New Haven: Yale University Press, 1998).

57   Michel Foucault, "Governmentality," in *The Foucault Effect: Studies in Governmentality*, ed. Graham Burchell, Colin Gordon, and Peter Miller (Toronto: Harvester Wheatsheaf, 1991), 91.

58   Allan Greer, "The Birth of the Police in Canada," in *Colonial Leviathan: State Formation in Mid-Nineteenth Century Canada*, ed. Allan Greer and Ian Radforth (Toronto: University of Toronto Press, 1992), 17.

59   Steve Hewitt, *Spying 101: The RCMP's Secret Activities at Canadian Universities, 1917-1997* (Toronto: University of Toronto Press, 2002); Tina Loo and Carolyn Strange, *Making Good: Law and Moral Regulation in Canada, 1867-1939* (Toronto: University of Toronto Press, 1997); Gary Kinsman, Dieter K. Buse, and Mercedes Steedman, eds., *Whose National Security? Canadian State Surveillance and the Creation of Enemies* (Toronto: Between the Lines, 2000); Reg Whitaker and Gary Marcuse, *Cold War Canada: The Making of a National Insecurity State, 1945-1957* (Toronto: University of Toronto Press, 1994); and John C. Weaver, *Crimes, Constables, and Courts: Order and Transgression in a Canadian City, 1816-1970* (Montreal: McGill-Queen's University Press, 1995).

60   Irving Lester Janis, *Victims of Groupthink: A Psychological Study of Foreign-Policy Decisions and Fiascoes* (Boston: Houghton, Mifflin, 1972); Irving Lester Janis, *Groupthink: Psychological Studies of Policy Decisions and Fiascoes*, 2nd ed. (Boston: Houghton Mifflin, 1982); Paul 't Hart, *Groupthink in Government: A Study of Small Groups and Policy Failure* (Rockland, MA: Swets and Zeitlinger, 1990).

61   Hewitt, *Spying 101*.

62   Curtis, *The Politics of Population*, and Scott, *Seeing Like a State*, take this approach.

63   The global aspect of this shift is explicitly accepted and theorized by contributors to *New World Coming: The Sixties and the Shaping of Global Consciousness*, ed. Karen Dubinsky et al. (Toronto: Between the Lines, 2009). The hegemonic crisis or "crisis of authority" is explored in Gramsci, *Prison Notebooks*, 210-11, 275-76.

Chapter 1: "We Help Them Because Their Need Is Great"

1   Tom Earley (1911-98) was a poet from South Wales and a Second World War conscientious objector. The date of this poem is unknown. This poem is used by kind

permission of Gomer Press. It appears in Tom Early, *Rebel's Progress* (Llandysul, Dyfed [Wales]: Gomer Press, 1979). Dennis McIntyre, *International Who's Who in Poetry and Poets' Encyclopaedia* (New York: Routledge, 2001), 158.

2 Phillip B. Davidson, *Vietnam at War: The History, 1946-1975* (London: Oxford University Press, 1986), 333.

3 Davidson, *Vietnam at War*, 342; David Cortwright, *Soldiers in Revolt: GI Resistance during the Vietnam War* (1975; repr., Chicago: Haymarket Books, 2005), 93.

4 F.H. Leacy, ed., *Historical Statistics of Canada*, 2nd ed. (Ottawa: Statistics Canada, 1983), series D223-247 and D491-497.

5 Library and Archives Canada (hereafter LAC), Canadian Security Intelligence Service fonds, RG 146, vol. 765, Students Against War in Vietnam Toronto, ON, flyer, "International Student-faculty Strike Against the War in Vietnam, Racial Oppression, and The Draft on April 27"; LAC, Canadian Security Intelligence Service fonds, RG 146, vol. 765, Students Against War in Vietnam Toronto, ON, flyer, "International Student-faculty Strike Against the War in Vietnam, Racial Oppression, and The Draft on April 27." These two flyers may have advertised events occurring in successive years, as years were not included in the dates of the events advertised.

6 LAC, Canadian Security Intelligence Service fonds, RG 146, vol. 2804, "Brief 325 - Student Administrative Council, University of Toronto," 1970-71, page 16. The report suggests that most students opposed the donation, but there is no indication of the source of that idea.

7 LAC, Peter Warrian fonds, MG 31, D 66, vol. 1, file 5, "CUS – 32nd Congress," Brief, Barry McPeake, "The Vietnam War," for Congress held at Guelph, 28 August–4 September 1968; LAC, Peter Warrian fonds, MG 31, D 66, vol. 1, file 20, "CUS – Correspondence, Memoranda 1968-69," memo, 8 October 1968, regarding "Secretariat Meeting, September 28, 29 and 30," from Lib Spry; LAC, Peter Warrian fonds, MG 31, D 66, vol. 1, file 6, "CUS - 33rd Congress and Rebuilding Conference"; LAC, Peter Warrian fonds, MG 31, D 66, vol. 1, file 19, "CUS – Correspondence 1968-69," n.d. A possible reason for the need to rebuild (as indicated in the title of their thirty-third congress) could have been that Quebec student groups had largely left the organization in 1965, a part of a larger trend of the Quiet Revolution. Robert Frederick Clift, "The Fullest Development of Human Potential: The Canadian Union of Students, 1963-1969" (MA thesis, Simon Fraser University, 2002), 23, cited in Roberta Lexier, "'The Backdrop against Which Everything Happened:' English-Canadian Student Movements and Off-Campus Movements for Change," *History of Intellectual Culture* 7, 1 (2007), http://www.ucalgary.ca/. However, this demise was probably due to several factors, including political divisions and debates about priorities. Doug Nesbitt, "The 'Radical Trip' of the Canadian Union of Students, 1963-69" (MA thesis, Trent University, 2009).

8 LAC, Canadian Security Intelligence Service fonds, RG 146, vol. 765, "Students Against War in Vietnam Toronto, ON," flyer, "March on October 26th," 26 October 1968.

9 Appendix 1, "Groups and Abbreviations," lists the various groups mentioned in the text.
10 Mark Satin, ed. *Manual for Draft-Age Immigrants to Canada,* 3rd and 4th eds. (Toronto: Toronto Anti-Draft Programme and House of Anansi, 1969).
11 Renée G. Kasinsky, *Refugees from Militarism: Draft-Age Americans in Canada* (New Brunswick, NJ: Transaction Books, 1976), 77, 85.
12 Kenneth Fred Emerick, *War Resisters Canada: The World of the American Military-Political Refugees* (Knox, PA: Knox, Pennsylvania Free Press, 1972), 229, 233.
13 Ibid., 232.
14 This view was held by at least some resisters who attended the "Our Way Home Reunion" conference in Castlegar, BC, in July 2006. It is also the view presented by Roger Neville Williams, *The New Exiles: American War Resisters in Canada* (New York: Liveright Publishers, 1971), 33-89.
15 *Sanity* was a publication of the Combined Universities Campaign for Nuclear Disarmament (CUCND) until 1965. Its publication ended in 1968. Jacquetta A. Newman, "Continuing Commitment: The Durability of Social Movements – Project Ploughshares in the 1990s" (PhD diss., Queen's University, 1998), 48-49.
16 McMaster University, William Ready Division of Archives and Research Collections (hereafter WR), Canadian student social and political organizations (CSSPO), box 4, file 13, "Committee to American War Objectors," undated correspondence between Glenn Sinclair, collections librarian at McMaster University, and Francis Marion [later an activist with the Vancouver group]; University of British Columbia Library, Rare Books and Special Collections (hereafter UBCL, RBSC), Renée Kasinsky fonds, box 1, file 2, "Correspondence – VCAAWO."
17 Thomas Socknat, *Witness against War: Pacifism in Canada, 1900-1945* (Toronto: University of Toronto Press, 1987); Patricia I. McMahon, "The Politics of Canada's Nuclear Policy, 1957-1963" (PhD diss., University of Toronto, 1999); Newman, "Continuing Commitment"; and, for an American focus, Michael Foley, *Confronting the War Machine: Draft Resistance during the Vietnam War* (Chapel Hill: University of North Carolina Press, 2003).
18 WR, Doug Ward fonds, box 1, file 1, "Student Action," Philip Smith, "US Draft Dodgers Tell Why They Chose Canada," in *Weekend Magazine,* 26 November 1966, 18.
19 WR, Hans Sinn fonds, box 1, file 2, "Correspondence with Potential Draftees"; WR, Hans Sinn fonds, box 1, file 8, "*Sanity: Peace Oriented News and Comment,*" 1965-67. Alternative service was an option offered to American men who successfully applied for conscientious objector status. It typically involved non-military service for two years.
20 WR, Hans Sinn fonds, box 1, file 2, "Correspondence with Potential Draftees"; WR, Hans Sinn fonds, box 1, file 8, "*Sanity: Peace Oriented News and Comment,*" 1965-67.
21 WR, Hans Sinn fonds, box 1, file 2, "Correspondence with Potential Draftees"; WR, Hans Sinn fonds, box 1, file 3, "Immigration Procedures and the Fact Sheet on Immigration to Canada," 1967. These facts are corroborated in *Peace Magazine*'s online

edition, http://archive.peacemagazine.org/; accessed 11 July 2007; and in the entirety of the fonds, as described by William Ready Division of Archives and Research Collections archivists in the fonds-level description at http://library.mcmaster.ca/.

22 WR, Hans Sinn fonds, box 1, file 2, "Correspondence with Potential Draftees"; WR, Hans Sinn fonds, box 1, file 8, "*Sanity: Peace Oriented News and Comment,*" 1965-67.

23 WR, Hans Sinn fonds, box 1, file 2, "Correspondence with Potential Draftees." The Toronto names to which Sinn referred were Bill Spira, Robert McNamee, and Rev. A.M. Little.

24 Ibid.

25 Ibid. SDS history is outlined in Todd Gitlin, *The Sixties: Years of Hope, Days of Rage* (New York: Bantam Books, 1993), Helen Garvy, *Rebels with a Cause* (Los Gatos, CA: Shire Press, 2007), and Kirkpatrick Sale, *SDS: Ten Years toward a Revolution* (New York: Random House, 1973). For more on the New Left see Doug Owram, *Born at the Right Time: A History of the Baby Boom Generation* (Toronto: University of Toronto Press, 1997), 216-47.

26 WR, Hans Sinn fonds, box 1, file 8, "*Sanity: Peace Oriented News and Comment,*" 1965-67.

27 Ibid.

28 WR, Hans Sinn fonds, box 1, file 2, "Correspondence with Potential Draftees." Sinn corresponded with Benson and Meg Brown; Nancy Pocock, later of the Toronto committee; Don Pentland of Winnipeg; Olive Johnson of the BC Canadian Campaign for Nuclear Disarmament, among others.

29 Ibid.

30 WR, Hans Sinn fonds, box 1, file 2, "Correspondence with Potential Draftees"; WR, Hans Sinn fonds, box 1, file 8, "*Sanity: Peace Oriented News and Comment,*" 1965-67. For overviews of American war resister experiences in Sweden – there were approximately 450 resisters there – see Thomas Lee Hayes, *American Deserters in Sweden: The Men and Their Challenge* (New York, Association Press, 1971); James Dickerson, *North to Canada: Men and Women against the Vietnam War* (Westport, CT: Praeger, 1999), 2; John Cooney and Dana Spitzer, "Hell, No, We Won't Go!" in *The American Military*, ed. Martin Oppenheimer (Chicago: Aldine, 1971), 123.

31 Kasinsky, *Refugees from Militarism*, 96; Emerick, *War Resisters Canada*, 229.

32 WR, Quebec social and political organizations, file 9, "Montreal Council to Aid War Resisters," ca. 1968.

33 UBCL, RBSC, Renée Kasinsky fonds, box 1, file 3, "Correspondence – Other Canadian Organizations with Committee," various letters, 1967-68.

34 UBCL, RBSC, Renée Kasinsky fonds, box 5, file 20, "Canadian Aid Groups," form letter and letter to Friends of the Council, 1967-68.

35 UBCL, RBSC, Renée Kasinsky fonds, box 1, file 3, "Correspondence – Other Canadian Organizations with Committee"; WR, Quebec social and political organizations, file 9, "Montreal Council to Aid War Resisters." Those involved over the first few

years included Nardo Castillo, John Callender, Ed Miller, Vance Gardner, Bill Mullen, and Bruce Garside.

36 Ibid.

37 Dalhousie University Archives and Special Collections, Halifax, Nova Scotia, Canada (hereafter DAL), Nova Scotia Committee to Aid American War Objectors fonds, MS-10-7, box 1, folder 5, "Communications with the Press, Community and Affiliated Organizations," CCC Newsletter to Aid Centres, 19 July 1971; Yellow Door Coffeehouse, Montreal, QC, file "Montreal Council/Programme, American Refugee Service," newsletter, American Refugee Service, March 1972. See also Gary W. Davis, "The Montreal Council to Aid War Resisters and the American Refugee Service," personal website, http://www.nuclearmidnight.com/C/TheMontrealCouncil.html, 1 May 2008; Bruce Garside, "Montreal Council to Aid War Resisters – My Involvement," personal website, 26 March 2011, http://brucethoughtsblog.blogspot.ca.

38 This one sentence cannot do justice to the complexity and thoroughness of Mills's treatment: Sean Mills, *The Empire Within: Postcolonial Thought and Political Activism in Sixties Montreal* (Montreal and Kingston: McGill-Queen's University Press, 2010).

39 A better picture of the role the MCAWR played in this vibrant scene could be possible with access to the papers of the council, which were not available at the time of writing. Gary W. Davis, author of a website on the group, has an "old beaten up cardboard box that lies buried in my office closet." Requests to consult these documents have been refused: Gary W. Davis, "The Montreal Council to Aid War Resisters and the American Refugee Service: My Years (1972-75) as the Director of the Montreal Council to Aid War Resisters and the American Refugee Service," accessed 3 March 2011, http://www.nuclearmidnight.com. See also Bruce Garside, "Montreal Council to Aid War Resisters – My Involvement," personal website, 26 March 2011, http://brucethoughtsblog.blogspot.ca.

40 A search of the 1966-68 pages of *Quartier Latin,* the main French-language student newspaper in Montreal at that time, showed a deep concern about the Vietnam War but no mention of American war resisters. A search of *Parti pris,* a journal of the Quebec Left that ceased publication in 1968, yielded the same results. Similarly, a search of the main Montreal archives of social movements and left groups at the Université du Québec à Montréal showed the same concerns about Vietnam, but no mention in the papers of either anglophone or francophone groups of the war resisters in the city. Université du Québec à Montréal Service des archives et de gestion des documents, Collection de publications de groupes de gauche et de groupes populaires, 21P-900:01, 21P-900:04, 21P-900:05.

41 Kasinsky, *Refugees from Militarism,* 92-94; WR, CSSPO, box 4, file 13, "Committee to Aid American War Objectors."

42 UBCL, RBSC, Vancouver Vietnam Action Committee fonds, box 1, file 27, "Committee to Aid American War Objectors: correspondence, circulars," 1966-67.

43 Kasinsky, *Refugees from Militarism*, 92-94; WR, CSSPO, box 4, file 13, "Committee to Aid American War Objectors."

44 LAC, Voice of Women fonds, MG 28, I 218, vol. 12, file 3, "Draft Resistance: Correspondence; Printed Material; Clippings," 1966-73. Renunciation of citizenship would only void military obligations pre-conscription. Deserters would not have benefitted legally from this act.

45 It was not necessary to renounce American citizenship in order to be landed in Canada or to gain Canadian citizenship; renouncing American citizenship only had the benefit of voiding any military obligations to the United States.

46 Kasinsky, *Refugees from Militarism*, 93.

47 UBCL, RBSC, Renée Kasinsky fonds, box 5, file 20, "Canadian Aid Groups."

48 WR, CSSPO, box 4, file 13, "Committee to Aid American War Objectors."

49 Hardy Scott, interview with author by mail, 31 October 2006. Philadelphia's *Ladies' Home Journal* – published by Curtis Publishing Company until 1968 – with its largely white, largely prosperous readership, may be seen here as part of a continuum with the Canadian magazine *Chatelaine*; Valerie J. Korinek has broken the dichotomous analytical mould of magazine as vehicle for either pleasure or ideological indoctrination; see Valerie J. Korinek, *Roughing It in the Suburbs: Reading Chatelaine Magazine in the Fifties and Sixties* (Toronto: University of Toronto Press, 2000). Korinek convincingly asserts that *Chatelaine* was first to promote feminist ideas and was first to shift its demographic appeal to women of average aspirations (59-65). In this context, sympathy to the war resisters is not surprising.

50 WR, CSSPO, box 4, file 13, "Committee to Aid American War Objectors"; UBCL, RBSC, Renée Kasinsky fonds, box 1, file 3, "Correspondence – Other Canadian Organizations with Committee." By February of 1969, Meg Brown's (and perhaps Benson Brown's) and Myra Riddell's tenure at the VCAAWO was over, and Stephen Strauss had taken over, likely overlapping with Betty Tillotson's involvement. Francis Marion replied to letters to the VCAAWO in 1969.

51 See note above for sources.

52 UBCL, RBSC, Renée Kasinsky fonds, box 1, file 2, "Correspondence – VCAAWO."

53 UBCL, RBSC, Renée Kasinsky fonds, box 8, file 8, "A Note on the Handling of Draft-Age Americans Who Apply for Entry Into Canada"; vol. 7, file 13, "A Further Note on the Handling of Draft-Age Americans Who Apply for Entry Into Canada."

54 Jack Todd, *Desertion: In the Time of Vietnam* (New York: Houghton Mifflin Company, 2001), 171.

55 Michael Goldberg, interview with the author by telephone, 11 July 2006.

56 DAL, Nova Scotia Committee to Aid American War Objectors fonds, MS-10-7, box 1, folder 2, "Various Organizations That Aided American Draft-Dodgers," "So You're Having a War Resister"; UBCL, RBSC, Renée Kasinsky fonds, box 7, file 29, "Minutes – Canadian Assistance to War Objectors – Steering Committee," "On Being a Kept Person," CAWO, 1968.

57 Churches and religious communities played a large role in the anti-draft movement. See Donald W. Maxwell, "Religion and Politics at the Border: Canadian Church Support for American Vietnam War Resisters," *Journal of Church and State* 48 (Autumn 2006): 807-30.

58 Renée Kasinsky fonds, box 7, file 29, "Minutes – Canadian Assistance to War Objectors – Steering Committee," "The Care and Feeding of War Objectors," CAWO, 1968. "The Care and Feeding of [Such-and-Such]" is a phrase that may have been coined in 1913. Marion Balfour Chalmers, "The Care and Feeding of Babies," *American Journal of Nursing* 13, 6 (1913): 357-65 and 424-27. "So You're Having a Baby" is ubiquitous in popular culture as a title for advice to new mothers. If war resisters were socially gendered as male, as Lara Campbell posits, then support activity in these two flyers appears to have been assigned female gender. Lara Campbell, "'Women United against the War:' Gender Politics, Feminism, and Vietnam Draft Resistance in Canada," in *New World Coming: The Sixties and the Shaping of Global Consciousness*, ed. Karen Dubinsky et al. (Toronto: Between the Lines, 2009), 339-48.

59 UBCL, RBSC, Renée Kasinsky fonds, box 7, file 29, "Minutes – Canadian Assistance to War Objectors – Steering Committee."

60 UBCL, RBSC, Renée Kasinsky fonds, box 7, file 29, "Minutes – Canadian Assistance to War Objectors – Steering Committee," "Seventh Meeting of the Steering Committee."

61 LAC, Goldie Josephy fonds, MG 31, I 4, file 4, "Ottawa Committee for Peace and Liberation"; Emerick, *War Resisters Canada,* 227; Joan Wilcox, interview with the author, Ottawa, ON, 17 May 2006.

62 Emerick, *War Resisters Canada,* 231; UBCL, RBSC, Renée Kasinsky fonds, box 6, file 4, "Canadian Publications – *AMEX,*" "Ottawa: Amexiles Who Settle in Ottawa Easily Forget from Whence They Came," *AMEX* 2, 6 (October-November 1970). Janzen's wife's name was not provided. Mennonites are one of the peace churches. Emerick makes reference to a francophone Anglican church, which seems highly unlikely; the *AMEX* reference is probably accurate, especially since there is today a francophone United church at Elgin and Lewis streets in Ottawa. "L'Église Unie St-Marc," accessed 10 September 2008, http://st-marc.freehosting.net/.

63 Wilcox, interview.

64 Campbell, "Women United against the War," 339-48; Lara Campbell, "Women's Liberation and 'US Chauvinism:' Vietnam War Resistance and Feminist Activism," and Robin Folvik, "'They Followed Their Men into Canada?' American Women in Canada during the Vietnam War Era" (papers presented at "New World Coming: The Sixties and the Shaping of Global Consciousness" conference, Queen's University, 16 June 2007).

65 Wilcox, interview.

66 Ibid.

67   WR, CCND, box 1, file 8, "Board of Directors minutes," 1965. SUPA was originally connected to the Canadian University Campaign for Nuclear Disarmament, acting as student wing, but had broken from it by 1965.

68   WR, Doug Ward fonds, box 1, file 1, "Student Action," Philip Smith, "US Draft Dodgers Tell Why They Chose Canada," in *Weekend Magazine*, 26 November 1966, 12-14, 16-18.

69   Kasinsky, *Refugees from Militarism*, 96-97.

70   WR, Doug Ward fonds, box 1, file 1, "Student Action," Philip Smith, "US Draft Dodgers Tell Why They Chose Canada," in *Weekend Magazine*, 26 November 1966, 12-14, 16-18.

71   *Escape from Freedom, or, I Didn't Raise My Boy to Be a Canadian* (Toronto: SUPA, 1967). *Escape from Freedom* was penned by Richard Paterak, a University of Toronto student and draft dodger. David Churchill, "When Home Became Away: American Expatriates and New Social Movements in Toronto, 1965-1977" (PhD diss., University of Chicago, 2001), 188-89.

72   During the Second World War, an arrangement had existed to allow for the return of "deserters and draft evaders," but, in 1952, an exchange of diplomatic notes eventually deemed the arrangement to have ceased as of the signing of the Treaty of Peace with Japan. This position was affirmed by the Department of National Defence in 1960, to the effect that NATO members would not apprehend deserters unless they desert from a visiting force. If deserters entered a NATO member country after their desertion, no action could be taken under NATO regulations. LAC, Department of External Affairs fonds, RG 25, vol. 2851, file 1539-B-40, pt. 3, "Arrangements Between United States and Canada re Return of Deserters and Draft Evaders – General File," memo to the Deputy Minister, Department of National Defence, from USSEA KJ Burbridge (for the) "Exchange of Notes, Canada and the United States – Apprehension of Deserters from United States armed Forces," 10 March 1952; and ensuing correspondence between the Deputy Minister, Department of National Defence, the Canadian embassy in the US, and the USSEA; LAC, Department of External Affairs fonds, RG 25, vol. 8045, file 1539-B-2-40 pt. 2, "Mutual Assistance in the Arrest of Deserters and Defaulters among NATO Countries," memo to The Delegation of Canada to the Atlantic Council, Paris, France, from the Department of External Affairs, "NATO status of forces Agreement – Apprehension of Deserters," 9 December 1960, signed G.C. Langille, Under-Secretary of State for External Affairs; LAC, Department of External Affairs fonds, RG 25, vol. 2851, file 1539-B-40, pt. 2, "Mutual Assistance in the Arrest of Deserters and Defaulters among NATO Countries," numbered letter L-844 from the Under-Secretary of State for External Affairs, to the Delegation of Canada to the North Atlantic Council, Paris, France, 9 December 1960; LAC, Department of External Affairs fonds, RG 25, vol. 2851, file 1539-B-40, pt. 2, "Mutual Assistance in the Arrest of Deserters and Defaulters among

NATO Countries," letter from the Deputy Minister of DND, to Under-Secretary of State for External Affairs, attention Mr. G. Sicotte, 22 August 1960, "NATO Status of Forces Agreement – Apprehension of Deserters"; LAC, Department of External Affairs fonds, RG 25, vol. 2851, file 1539-B-40, pt. 2, "Mutual Assistance in the Arrest of Deserters and Defaulters among NATO Countries," letter from Legal Division to Deputy Minister of the Department of National Defence, 22 July 1960, "NATO Status of Forces Agreement - Apprehension of Deserters"; LAC, Department of External Affairs fonds, RG 25, vol. 2851, file 1539-B-40, pt. 2, "Mutual Assistance in the Arrest of Deserters and Defaulters among NATO Countries," numbered letter N-201 to the Under-Secretary of State for External Affairs, from the Delegation of Canada to the North Atlantic Council, Paris, France, 8 February 1960.

73 WR, CSSPO, box 7, file 17, "Toronto Anti-draft programme [sic]."

74 See Paul Breines, ed., *Critical Interruptions: New Left Perspectives on Herbert Marcuse* (New York: Herder and Herder, 1971); Douglas Kellner, ed., *The New Left and the 1960s*, vol. 3, *Collected Papers of Herbert Marcuse* (New York: Routledge, 2005); and Angela Davis, "Preface: Marcuse's Legacies," in *The New Left and the 1960s*, ed. Kellner, vii-xiv.

75 WR, Doug Ward fonds, box 1, file 1, "Student Action," Philip Smith, "US Draft Dodgers Tell Why They Chose Canada," in *Weekend Magazine*, 26 November 1966, 12-14, 16-18.

76 Kasinsky, *Refugees from Militarism*, 97-98; WR, Doug Ward fonds, box 1, file 1, "Student Action," *Sanity* magazine 2, 7 (February 1965), "CUCND disbanded; SUPA-men Emerge"; WR Doug Ward fonds, box 1, file 1, "Student Action," Donald McKelvey, "Report on Federal Council Meeting," 9 November 1966.

77 Emerick, *War Resisters Canada*, 229.

78 UBCL, RBSC, Renée Kasinsky fonds, box 7, file 11, "Exile Group Publications: Toronto, Montreal."

79 Quakers were one of the peace churches.

80 UBCL, RBSC, Renée Kasinsky fonds, box 4, file 12, "Interview with Nancy Pokhawk [sic], May 1970, Toronto, Quaker, Active in Exile Movement since 1965." Quaker social justice activism is the subject of a huge literature. See Peter Brock, *The Quaker Peace Testimony, 1660 to 1914* (Syracuse, NY: Syracuse University Press, 1990).

81 UBCL, RBSC, Renée Kasinsky fonds, box 4, file 12, "Interview with Nancy Pokhawk [sic], May 1970, Toronto, Quaker, Active in Exile Movement since 1965."

82 Mark Satin, ed. *Manual for Draft-Age Immigrants to Canada*, 3rd ed. (Toronto: Toronto Anti-Draft Programme, 1969), back cover.

83 UBCL, RBSC, Renée Kasinsky fonds, box 4, file 14, "Interview with Bill Spira of the Toronto Anti-Draft Program [sic], June 1970."

84 Other works include Kasinsky, *Refugees from Militarism;* Emerick, *War Resisters Canada*. Emerick was an American academic who spent several months in Canada living with and among American war resisters.

85 The involvement of historians in this process is a demonstration of the blurry line between public and private history, as Margaret Conrad has addressed. See Margaret Conrad, "2007 Presidential Address of the CHA: Public History and its Discontents or History in the Age of Wikipedia," *Journal of the Canadian Historical Association* 18, 1 (2007): 1-26.

86 There was also a *Manual for Draft-Age Americans in Europe*, published by War Resister International. It is not clear which pamphlet was published first. WR, Doug Ward fonds, box 3, file 3, "Vietnam 2," pamphlet, "Literature List 1969," War Resisters League, NY. A copy can be found at the Modern Record Centre, Warwick University, UK, in the papers of the group Release. For additional analysis of the content of the *Manual* see Churchill, "When Home Became Away," 188-92.

87 DAL, Nova Scotia Committee to Aid American War Objectors fonds, MS-10-7, box 1, folder 2, "Various Organizations That Aided American Draft-Dodgers," Byron Wall, *Manual for Draft-Age Immigrants to Canada*, 5th ed. (Toronto: House of Anansi, 1970).

88 The first four editions were edited by Mark Satin and published by House of Anansi, with the involvement of the TADP. House of Anansi was later briefly housed at Rochdale College, a bastion of the Toronto New Left. WR, CSSPO, box 6, file 31-2, "Rochdale College." See also Stuart Henderson, "Off the Streets and into the Fortress: Experiments in Hip Separatism at Toronto's Rochdale College, 1968–1975," *Canadian Historical Review* 92, 1 (2011): 107-33.

89 University of Toronto, Thomas Fisher Rare Book Library (hereafter TF), Pocock (Jack) Memorial Collection, box 29, "Various [printed items]."

90 DAL, Nova Scotia Committee to Aid American War Objectors fonds, MS-10-7, box 1, folder 2, "Various Organizations That Aided American Draft-Dodgers"; Satin, *Manual* 3rd ed.; Satin, *Manual for Draft-Age Immigrants to Canada*, 4th ed.; Wall, *Manual*, 5th ed.; Toronto Anti-Draft Programme, ed., *Manual for Draft-Age Immigrants to Canada*, 6th ed. (Toronto: Toronto Anti-Draft Programme), 1971; UBCL, RBSC, Renée Kasinsky fonds, box 6, file 4, "Canadian Publications: *AMEX*," "New Manual Due Soon," *AMEX* 2, 8 (April 1971). The manual described the TADP as the largest of the anti-draft groups and credited the Vancouver Committee with starting the movement. TF, Pocock (Jack) Memorial Collection, box 29, printed items.

91 WR, CSSPO, box 7, file 17, "Toronto Anti-Draft Programme."

92 Mark Satin, ed. *Manual for Draft-Age Immigrants to Canada* (Toronto: Toronto Anti-Draft Programme and House of Anansi), 4th ed., 1970.

93 DAL, Nova Scotia Committee to Aid American War Objectors fonds, MS-10-7, box 1, folder 2, "Various Organizations That Aided American Draft-Dodgers," Toronto Anti-Draft Programme, *Manual*, 6th ed., 32-36.

94 J.M.S. Careless, "culture," in *Manual*, 4th ed., 68-71; Elliott Rose, "You're Not the First," in *Manual*, 4th ed., 88-89. Some of these professors, including Elliott Rose, were also connected with the University of Toronto Faculty Committee to End the War in Vietnam.

95   Satin, *Manual,* 4th ed. Lawyers included Vincent Kelly and Robert D. Katz; church officials included Rev. Roy G. de Marsh, Secretary, Board of Colleges, United Church of Canada.

96   TF, Pocock (Jack) Memorial Collection, box 12, "Central Committee for Conscientious Objectors (CCCO) publications"; TF, Pocock (Jack) Memorial Collection, box 9, "Counselling Materials – US Legal Publications"; TF, Pocock (Jack) Memorial Collection, box 7, "Counselling Materials – US Legal Publications"; TF, Pocock (Jack) Memorial Collection, box 5, "Counselling Materials," file 1, "Handbook for Training Draft Counsellors"; TF, Pocock (Jack) Memorial Collection, box 3, "Counselling Materials," "Counselling Resource Binder 2"; TF, Pocock (Jack) Memorial Collection, box 3, "Counselling Materials," "Counselling Resource Binder 1."

97   TF, Pocock (Jack) Memorial Collection, box 6, "Canadian Legal Publications."

98   WR, CSSPO, box 7, file 17, "Toronto Anti-Draft Programme," "Many More Draft-Resisters Expected This Summer."

99   WR, CSSPO, box 7, file 17, "Toronto Anti-Draft Programme."

100   TF, Pocock (Jack) Memorial Collection, box 25, "TADP Administrative Files," folders 3-9, "Donor letters."

101   TF, Pocock (Jack) Memorial Collection, box 2, "TADP Intake Records, Sales Records, Stationery, and Other Materials," folder 1-4, "Front Desk Inquiry records," 1972-73.

102   TF, Pocock (Jack) Memorial Collection, box 13, "Lobbying and Public Relations," folder 1, "TADP Statements and Lobbying"; TF, Pocock (Jack) Memorial Collection, box 2, "TADP Intake Records, Sales Records, Stationery, and Other Materials," folders 1-4, "Front Desk Inquiry records," 1972-73.

103   Kasinsky, *Refugees from Militarism,* 101.

104   Emerick, *War Resisters Canada,* 231.

105   Kasinsky, *Refugees from Militarism,* 101-2. The origin of the name of the group (RWB) is unknown, but participants in the "Our Way Home Reunion" conference in 2007 in Castlegar, BC, shared two theories with me. One is that the colours of the American flag had been shifted to reflect the darkness of the period – black replacing blue. The other, which is probably more likely, was that the name reflected a desire in the group to bring together white people, black people, and Aboriginal people in common cause. *EXNET* was also referred to in some movement literature as *Exnet.* This book uses *EXNET.*

106   WR, CSSPO, box 6, file 30, "Red White and Black [sic]"; LAC, Judith Merril fonds, MG 30, D 326, vol. 14, file 14-24, "Red White and Black [sic]," 1970.

107   LAC, Voice of Women fonds, MG 28, I 218, vol. 12, file 3, "Draft Resistance: Correspondence; Printed Material; Clippings," 1966-73.

108   LAC, Judith Merril fonds, MG 30, D 326, vol. 14, file 24, "Red White and Black," poster, 1970.

109 UBCL, RBSC, Renée Kasinsky fonds, box 6, file 4, "Canadian Publications: *AMEX*," "Toronto: Groups Amalgamate and Begin Struggle for Asylum; Second Conference Tentatively Planned for Late October," *AMEX* 2, 5 (August-September 1970), 15.

110 Emerick, *War Resisters Canada,* 231.

111 DAL, Nova Scotia Committee to Aid American War Objectors fonds, MS-10-7, box 1, folder 4, "Newspaper Clippings," "American Draft Dodgers Receive Information, Help at Halifax Office," *Chronicle-Herald* (Saturday, 7 February 1971).

112 DAL, Nova Scotia Committee to Aid American War Objectors fonds, MS-10-7, box 2, folder 2, "Counselling Records"; DAL, Nova Scotia Committee to Aid American War Objectors fonds, MS-10-7, box 1, folder 4, "Newspaper Clippings," "Expatriates in Halifax: A Reasonable Alternative," *The Phoenix* (31 August 1971); DAL, Nova Scotia Committee to Aid American War Objectors fonds, MS-10-7, box 1, folder 5, "Communications with the Press, Community and Affiliated Organizations"; DAL, Nova Scotia Committee to Aid American War Objectors fonds, MS-10-7, box 2, folder 7, "Organizational Correspondence." Personnel in 1971 included Lind, Eric Stine, and counselling volunteers Brad and Margot Sorrell and Mike Panella.

113 DAL, Nova Scotia Committee to Aid American War Objectors fonds, MS-10-7, box 2, folder 3, "Requests for Help or Information on How to Emigrate," correspondence from American immigrants; DAL, Nova Scotia Committee to Aid American War Objectors fonds, MS-10-7, box 2, folder 7, "Organizational Correspondence," correspondence with various anti-draft and peace groups.

114 DAL, Nova Scotia Committee to Aid American War Objectors fonds, MS-10-7, box 2, folder 11, "Directories," Department of Immigration, "Who Can Come to Canada" (Ottawa: Queen's Printer, 1969), and "Admission of University Students to Canada" (Ottawa: Information Canada, 1971); DAL, Nova Scotia Committee to Aid American War Objectors fonds, MS-10-7, box 1, folder 1, "Department of Manpower and Immigration Publications," Department of Manpower and Immigration, "Immigration Manual" and "Copy of the Act and Regulations," August 1971, 49-82; DAL, Nova Scotia Committee to Aid American War Objectors fonds, MS-10-7, box 1, folder 2, "Various Organizations That Aided American Draft-Dodgers."

115 DAL, Nova Scotia Committee to Aid American War Objectors fonds, MS-10-7, box 2, folder 2, "Counselling Records"; DAL, Nova Scotia Committee to Aid American War Objectors fonds, MS-10-7, box 1, folder 4, "Newspaper Clippings."

116 DAL, Nova Scotia Committee to Aid American War Objectors fonds, MS-10-7, box 1, folder 5, "Communications with the Press, Community and Affiliated Organizations," various correspondence.

117 DAL, Nova Scotia Committee to Aid American War Objectors fonds, MS-10-7, box 2, folder 2, "Counselling Records"; DAL, Nova Scotia Committee to Aid American War Objectors fonds, MS-10-7, box 1, folder 5, "Communications with the Press, Community and Affiliated Organizations," correspondence.

118 DAL, Nova Scotia Committee to Aid American War Objectors fonds, MS-10-7, file 1.5, "Communications with the Press, Community and Affiliated Organizations," various correspondence.

119 DAL, Nova Scotia Committee to Aid American War Objectors fonds, MS-10-7, box 2, folder 7, "Organizational Correspondence," various correspondence.

120 UBCL, RBSC, Renée Kasinsky fonds, box 5, file 13, "Assorted Articles," "Thunder Bay, Ont.; A New City and a Reorganized War Immigrant Committee," *AMEX,* n.d.

121 UBCL, RBSC, Renée Kasinsky fonds, box 6, file 6, "Canadian Publications: *AMEX,*" "Winnipeg Committee Closes Its Doors," *AMEX* 4, 7 (January 1974).

122 UBCL, RBSC, Renée Kasinsky fonds, box 7, file 29, "Minutes – Canadian Assistance to War Objectors – Steering Committee," "Fifth Meeting of the Steering Committee"; WR, CSSPO, box 1, file 6, "Alexander Ross Society." An in-depth study of the histories of these groups is not part of this study primarily because their records are thin or nonexistent. Additionally, it is likely that much of their material and information would have matched that found in the files of the major groups. Some groups' records are in better condition because the groups existed longer, were in a more central location, and had greater access to resources.

123 UBCL, RBSC, Renée Kasinsky fonds, box 8, file 4, "Newspaper Articles," "Black Draft Dodger Speaks Out on Canada," *AMEX,* n.d.

124 See, especially, G. David Curry, *Sunshine Patriots: Punishment and the Vietnam Offender* (Notre Dame, IN: University of Notre Dame Press, 1985). See also Kasinsky, *Refugees from Militarism;* Kusch, *All American Boys;* and David Sterling Surrey, *Choice of Conscience: Vietnam Era Military and Draft Resisters in Canada* (New York: Praeger, 1982).

125 UBCL, RBSC, Renée Kasinsky fonds, box 3, file 12, "Interview with Johnny, Southern Black Draft Dodger Montreal 1970," May 1970. For a good overview of the race bias in Canadian immigration policy see Yasmeen Abu-Laban, "Keeping 'Em Out: Gender, Race, and Class Biases in Canadian Immigration Policy," in *Painting the Maple: Essays on Race, Gender, and the Construction of Canada,* ed. Veronica Strong-Boag, Sherrill Grace, Avigail Eisenberg, and Joan Anderson (Vancouver: UBC Press, 1998), 69-82.

126 UBCL, RBSC, Renée Kasinsky fonds, box 5, file 14, "Black Draft Dodgers," "Black Deserters in Canada," *Race Relations Reporter,* 19 (2 November 1970).

127 UBCL, RBSC, Renée Kasinsky fonds, box 4, file 5, "Interview Black Draft Dodgers; EJ, Toronto, May 1970 and Fred"; and box 7, file 11, "Exile Group Publications: Toronto, Montreal," flyer, RWB press.

128 UBCL, RBSC, Renée Kasinsky fonds, box 4, file 14, "Interview with Bill Spira of the Toronto Anti-Draft Program [sic]," June 1970.

129 UBCL, RBSC, Renée Kasinsky fonds, box 5, file 14, "Black Draft Dodgers," "Black Deserters in Canada," *Race Relations Reporter,* 19 (2 November 1970). *Race Relations*

Reporter was a newsletter of the Race Relations Information Centre, based in Nashville, Tennessee. It was issued from 1970 until 1974. Pennsylvania State University, Dickinson School of Law Library, "Race, Racism, and American Law Bibliography," accessed 17 July 2007, http://www.dsl.psu.edu/.

130 LAC, MG 28, I 218, Voice of Women fonds, vol. 12, file 3, "Draft Resistance: Correspondence; Printed Material; Clippings," 1966-73, letter from Olin L. Tillotson, Clerk, Vancouver Monthly Meeting Religious Society of Friends, 22 June 1969.

131 UBCL, RBSC, Renée Kasinsky fonds, box 6, file 4, "Canadian Publications – *AMEX*," "Women Exiles Organize Group," *AMEX* 2, 3 (April-May 1970). To the extent that the draft applied only to men, and women serving in Vietnam were few in number in comparison to men, it is somewhat understandable that the groups focused on men. However, at least one woman marine deserter did come to Canada. See "Amnesty for the War Exiles?" *Newsweek*, 79, 3 (17 January 1972): 19-20, 23-26. Thanks to Joseph Jones for this information.

132 UBCL, RBSC, Renée Kasinsky fonds, box 6, file 4, "Canadian Publications: *AMEX*," "The Parley in Montreal," *AMEX* 2, 4 (June 1970).

133 UBCL, RBSC, Renée Kasinsky fonds, box 6, file 4, "Canadian Publications: *AMEX*," "Male Chauvinists," *AMEX* 2, 6 (June 1970).

134 Carolyn Egan, interview with the author, Toronto, 1 June 2006.

135 Judy Rebick, though she does not much address the Vietnam War, makes it clear how complex the broader women's movement was in her book *Ten Thousand Roses: The Making of a Feminist Revolution* (Toronto: Penguin, 2005). The experience of women as war resisters and as anti-draft activists is important, but a full exploration is left to other researchers. For a general overview of women's experience in Canada in this period, see Alison Prentice et al., *Canadian Women: A History* (Toronto: Harcourt Brace Jovanovich, 1988), esp. 319-66. For an exploration of the roots of women's movements in earlier movements such as civil rights and the antiwar movement, see Sara Evans, *Personal Politics: The Roots of Women's Liberation in the Civil Rights Movement and the New Left* (New York: Alfred A. Knopf, 1979).

136 The activities of these groups are important for this study insofar as they played a role in debates within the anti-draft movement in Canada about political approach and Canadian politics more broadly. Their history and impact deserve broader study beyond the analysis provide here. For more on the exile groups see Kasinsky, *Refugees from Militarism*, 99-101, 105-7; 148-50. See also Jason Young, "'To Define a Community in Exile:' Producers, Readers, and War Resister Communication in *AMEX* Magazine, 1968-1977" (MA major research paper, York University, 2006). Young argues *AMEX* promoted a sense of community among war resisters, who generally shared a political outlook.

137 UBCL, RBSC, Renée Kasinsky fonds, box 7, file 30, "Minutes and Notes: Union of New Canadians."

138   WR, CSSPO, box 1, file 8, "Union of American Exiles."

139   Ibid.

140   Dick Perrin, interview with the author by email, 12 December 2006.

141   Joseph Healey Library, University of Massachusetts, Boston, Perrin, Richard, Papers, 1966-2001, series V, "Regina Committee of American Deserters (RCAD)," 1969.

142   WR, CSSPO, box 1, file 7, American Deserters Committee of Toronto, TADC Newsletter 1.

143   WR, CSSPO, 1, file 7, American Deserters Committee of Toronto, "The Totality of Desertion," 1 March 1970.

144   UBCL, RBSC, Renée Kasinsky fonds, box 6, file 2, "Canadian Press on Emigrants, Deserters, Exiles," Melody Killian, "American Deserters Committee Program," *Yankee Refugee*, 8 (1969).

145   Killian also wrote at least one article about the VCAAWO that was positive. See Melody Killian, "Canadians Know, Even if Germans Didn't," *Ubyssey* (14 March 1969). It is unknown if Killian wrote this article with the knowledge of VCAAWO activists.

146   UBCL, RBSC, Renée Kasinsky fonds, box 6, file 2, "Canadian Press on Emigrants, Deserters, Exiles," Melody Killian, "American Deserters Committee Program," *Yankee Refugee* 8 (1969).

147   UBCL, RBSC, Renée Kasinsky fonds, box 5, file 8, "Analysis of Desertion – ADC's Political Activity," "American Deserters Committee Running," *The Peak* (15 October 1969).

148   LAC, MG 28, I 218, Voice of Women fonds, vol. 12, file 3, "Draft Resistance: Correspondence; Printed Material; Clippings," 1966-73.

149   UBCL, RBSC, Renée Kasinsky fonds, box 6, file 4, " Publications – *AMEX*," "Ottawa," AMEX 2, 4 (June 1970).

Chapter 2: Transnational Connections

1   As Franca Iacovetta has argued, immigration is a consciousness-changing experience. Bruce Elliott's understanding of "chain migration" also has some relevance for a class of immigrants who often followed friends over the border. Bruce S. Elliott, *Irish Migrants in the Canadas: A New Approach* (Montreal and Kingston: McGill-Queen's University Press, 1988); Franca Iacovetta, *The Writing of English Canadian Immigrant History* (Ottawa: Canadian Historical Association, 1997). However, as I explain in the Introduction, I do not see the American war resisters as immigrants.

2   Mark Satin, ed. *Manual for Draft-Age Immigrants to Canada*, 4th ed. (Toronto: Toronto Anti-Draft Programme and House of Anansi, 1969), 72-76.

3   Heather Dean, "It Has Politics," *Manual*, 4th ed., 85-89.

4   John Hagan, *Northern Passage: American Vietnam War Resisters in Canada* (Cambridge, MA: Harvard University Press, 2001), 75; Mark Satin, "About the Editor (Mark

Satin bio)," *The Radical Middle Newsletter,* accessed 26 April 2005, http://www. radicalmiddle.com/editor.htm.

5 Hagan, *Northern Passage,* 140.

6 Satin, *Manual,* 4th ed., 72-76. The pamphlet is listed on the War Resisters League 1969 literature list. McMaster University, William Ready Division of Archives and Research Collections (hereafter WR), Doug Ward fonds, box 3, file 3, "Vietnam 2," pamphlet, "Literature List 1969," War Resisters League, NY, NY.

7 WR, CCND, box 15, file 11, War Resisters League, *War Resisters League News* (July-August 1963).

8 University of British Columbia Library, Rare Books and Special Collections (hereafter UBCL, RBSC), Renée Kasinsky fonds, box 7, file 11, "Exile Group Publications: Toronto, Montreal."

9 Kenneth Fred Emerick, *War Resisters Canada: The World of the American Military-Political Refugees* (Knox, PA: Knox, Pennsylvania Free Press, 1972), 229.

10 Satin, *Manual,* 4th ed., 1-2.

11 Rubin and Hoffman were prominent anti-establishment figures in the 1960s United States, associated with the Yippies movement, Berkeley, and the protest against the Vietnam War. See, for instance, Robert Buzzanco, *Vietnam and the Transformation of American Life* (Malden, MA: Blackwell, 1999), 98-99, 236-37. For an unsympathetic view, see Gerard J. De Groot, *A Noble Cause? America and the Vietnam War* (Harlow: Longman, 2000). See also Marty Jezer, *Abbie Hoffman: American Rebel* (New Brunswick, NJ: Rutgers University Press, 1992); and, by fellow Yippie, Jonah Raskin, *For the Hell of It: The Life and Times of Abbie Hoffman* (Berkeley: University of California Press, 1996).

12 Paul Copeland, interview with the author, Ottawa, ON, 5 June 2006.

13 For a good overview of church pacifism see Peter Brock and Nigel Young, *Pacifism in the Twentieth Century* (Syracuse, NY: Syracuse University Press, 1999), 332-65. Church involvement in this movement is a vast topic deserving of a great deal more research, for which I do not have space here. Donald Maxwell has made a beginning.

14 Donald W. Maxwell, "Religion and Politics at the Border: Canadian Church Support for American Vietnam War Resisters," *Journal of Church and State* 48 (Autumn 2006): 807-30.

15 Copeland, interview.

16 UBCL, RBSC, Renée Kasinsky fonds, box 4, file 12, "Interview with Nancy Pokhawk [sic], May 1970, Toronto, Quaker, Active in Exile Movement since 1965." For background on Skedaddle Ridge, see Bill Hamilton, *Place Names of Atlantic Canada* (Toronto: University of Toronto Press, 1996), 139. See also Peter Gzowski/Canadian Broadcasting Corporation, "From Naked Man Hill to Skedaddle Ridge," *Morningside,*

broadcast 25 October 1996, http://archives.cbc.ca/. In an online article, Bill Hamilton explains, "In the 19th century there were three New Brunswick communities named Skedaddle Ridge: two in York County and one in Carleton. All had the same origin. During the American Civil War (1861-65), isolated areas of the province became a haven for the first American draft dodgers ... Of the three, only the last mentioned, located southeast of Knowlesville, is on contemporary maps." See Bill Hamilton, "The Lost Names of New Brunswick," *Moncton Forum*, accessed 25 June 2008, http://www.moncton.net/forum/thread/69689.aspx.

17 CALCAV was a multi-faith group founded in 1965, in which Martin Luther King was involved. See Mitchell K. Hall, *Because of Their Faith: CALCAV and Religious Opposition to the Vietnam War* (New York: Columbia University Press, 1990).

18 UBCL, RBSC, Renée Kasinsky fonds, box 6, file 13, "CBC *Weekend* Transcript: Deserters Deportment Case; Interview with D. Rosenbloom," "transcript of CBC *Weekend,* February 8 [1970]."

19 The terminology may seem confusing, but terms like "exile" and "draft resister" were fairly interchangeable at the time.

20 University of Toronto, Thomas Fisher Rare Book Library (hereafter TF), Pocock (Jack) Memorial Collection, box 21, "Canadian Council of Churches," folder 25, "Other Anti-War Religious Groups."

21 Frank H. Epp, ed., *I Would Like to Dodge the Draft-Dodgers, But ...* (Waterloo, ON and Winnipeg: Conrad Press, 1970), 68-76.

22 Ibid., 8, 68.

23 Ibid., 70.

24 Ibid., 71.

25 Renée G. Kasinsky, *Refugees from Militarism: Draft-Age Americans in Canada* (New Brunswick, NJ: Transaction Books, 1976), 82-83.

26 The Mennonite tradition in particular places an emphasis on conscientious objection and pacifism, as do the other historic peace churches. Mennonites were attracted to Canada because of its guarantee of exemption from military service. Waves of immigrants arrived from Eastern Europe due to religious persecution, and then from the US to avoid conscription. Frank H. Epp and Leo Driedger, s.v. "Mennonites," *Canadian Encyclopedia,* http://www.thecanadianencyclopedia.com, 2012. There is a huge bibliography on Mennonite pacifism. See for instance Marlene Epp, *Women without Men: Mennonite Refugees of the Second World War* (Toronto: University of Toronto Press, 1999). See also Maxwell, "Religion and Politics at the Border"; Michael S. Foley, *Confronting the War Machine: Draft Resistance during the Vietnam War* (Chapel Hill, NC: University of North Carolina Press, 2003); Thomas Socknat, *Witness against War: Pacifism in Canada, 1900-1945* (Toronto: University of Toronto Press, 1987); Peter Brock and Nigel Young, *Pacifism in the Twentieth Century* (Syracuse, NY: Syracuse University Press, 1999).

27 UBCL, RBSC, Renée Kasinsky fonds, box 1, file 3, "Correspondence – Other Canadian Organizations with Committee," letter from Bill Spira, TADP, to Betty Tillotson, VCAAWO, December 1969.

28 Dalhousie University Archives and Special Collections, Halifax, Nova Scotia, Canada (hereafter DAL), Nova Scotia Committee to Aid American War Objectors fonds, MS-10-7, file 2.7, "Organizational Correspondence."

29 According to council records, in attendance were the Reverends Gordon K. Stewart, Chairman of the Canadian Affairs Commission; Elmer Stainton; Dr. Charles Forsyth; D.C. Candy; Roy Hamilton; Dr. T.E. Floyd Honey; Dr. A.B.B. Moore; Dr. R.M. Bennett; Canon M.P. Wilkinson, Secretary; Mr. Fred Haslam; and Miss Anne Davison. A visitor, the Reverend Richard Killmer, attended on behalf of Clergy and Laity [sic] Concerned about Vietnam. Regrets were sent from the Baptists' Reverend A. Coe, and from Lt. Col. Wm. Gibson of the Salvation Army. Library and Archives Canada (hereafter LAC), Canadian Council of Churches fonds, MG 28, I 327, box 39, file 6, "Commission on Canadian Affairs Minutes – Ministry to Draft-Age US Immigrants – Accountability Committee and Others," 1969-73.

30 The World Council of Churches is an international umbrella group of churches from over a hundred countries. World Council of Churches, 2013, http://www.oikoumene.org/.

31 LAC, Canadian Council of Churches fonds, MG 28, I 327, box 39, file 6, "Commission on Canadian Affairs Minutes – Ministry to Draft-Age US Immigrants – Accountability Committee and Others," 1969-73.

32 Ibid.

33 Emerick, *War Resisters Canada*, 234.

34 Ibid., 234.

35 Ibid., 234-35.

36 LAC, Voice of Women fonds, MG 28, I 218, vol. 12, file 3, "Draft Resistance: Correspondence; Printed Material; Clippings," 1966-73, First Unitarian Congregation of Toronto, Appeal for funds, 1 February 1970.

37 Emerick, *War Resisters Canada*, 235.

38 Maxwell, "Religion and Politics at the Border," 819. Since church support was not forthcoming in any major official way until 1970, it cannot be argued that the Canadian movement arose in order to spend American money. However, as Maxwell indicates, there is an interesting phenomenon that could be explored: both the National Council of Churches in the United States and the Canadian Council of Churches received some funding from their respective governments' international aid agencies (respectively, the US Agency for International Development and the Canadian International Development Agency). Thus, indirectly, the war resisters support groups received funding from the two governments.

39 Socknat argues the "religious factor" in the peace movement is uniquely Canadian. Socknat, *Witness against War*, 295.

40   DAL, Nova Scotia Committee to Aid American War Objectors fonds, MS-10-7, box 2, folder 7, "Organizational Correspondence."

41   Ibid. To put these amounts in context, the approximate cost of a car in 1968 was $2,500.

42   UBCL, RBSC, Renée Kasinsky fonds, box 8, file 4, "Newspaper Articles," "Churches Aid Deserters in Canada," editorial, *Fellowship Magazine,* July 1970.

43   Maxwell, "Religion and Politics at the Border," 827.

44   Ibid., 808, 823-26.

45   Marlene Legates, *In Their Time: A History of Feminism in Western Society* (New York: Routledge, 1991), 337-38; Christine Ball, "The History of the Voice of Women/Les Voix des Femmes – The Early Years" (PhD diss., University of Toronto, 1994), 1-33; Joanna Dean, "The Gendered Politics of Nuclear Fallout" (paper presented at Ottawa Historical Association, April 2008).

46   LAC, Voice of Women fonds, MG 28, I 218, vol. 12, file 3, "Draft Resistance: Correspondence; Printed Material; Clippings," 1966-73.

47   Kay Macpherson and Sara Good, "Canadian Voice of Women for Peace," *Peace Magazine,* October/November 1987, 26, http://archive.peacemagazine.org/. See also "Canadian Voice of Women for Peace," http://vowpeace.org/about/. According to Macpherson and Good, international linkages included an International Women's Conference in September 1962, organized by VOW, which included women from the Soviet Union; support for the international call for a Test Ban Treaty, which resulted in the Partial Test Ban in 1963; hosted delegations from the Soviet Union and Indochina; and a conference of Women for Peace during Canada's Centennial Year, attended by women from thirty countries. It also organized exchanges with Vietnamese women and "a close bond with American 'peace' women," as well as women from Greece, Cyprus, Indochina, Chile, Bolivia, Africa, Japan, and Britain.

48   LAC, Voice of Women fonds, MG 28, I 218, vol. 12, file 3, "Draft Resistance: Correspondence; Printed Material; Clippings," 1966-73, letter from Mrs. Matthew T. Corso to VOW Toronto, Canada, 22 January 1970.

49   LAC, Voice of Women fonds, MG 28, I 218, vol. 12, file 3, "Draft Resistance: Correspondence; Printed Material; Clippings," 1966-73, "Voice of Women: Deserters and Draft Resisters," policy statement drafted after executive meeting, 11 January 1970, Toronto.

50   LAC, Voice of Women fonds, MG 28, I 218, vol. 12, file 3, "Draft Resistance: Correspondence; Printed Material; Clippings," 1966-73. For background on Muriel Duckworth see Marion Kerans, "Muriel Duckworth: the Peace Movement's Best Friend," *Peace Magazine,* October/November 1988, 8, http://archive.peacemagazine. org/; and Marion Kerans, *Muriel Duckworth: A Very Active Pacifist* (Halifax: Fernwood Publishing, 1996).

51   LAC, Voice of Women fonds, MG 28, I 218, vol. 40, file 20, "Duckworth, Muriel – Correspondence," 1969-70.

52 Ibid.

53 LAC, Voice of Women fonds, MG 28, I 218, vol. 12, file 3, "Draft Resistance: Correspondence; Printed Material; Clippings," 1966-73, "Excerpt: Voice of Women, British Columbia, Interim Report from Special Committee on Draft Dodgers and Deserters," 18 February 1970.

54 LAC, Voice of Women fonds, MG 28, I 218, vol. 12, file 3, "Draft Resistance: Correspondence; Printed Material; Clippings," 1966-73.

55 LAC, Voice of Women fonds, MG 28, I 218, vol. 12, file 3, "Draft Resistance: Correspondence; Printed Material; Clippings," 1966-73. Pryce previously reported on VOW involvement with war resisters in her January letter.

56 UBCL, RBSC, Renée Kasinsky fonds, box 6, file 4, "Canadian Publications – *AMEX*," "At TADP ... Priority Counselling," *AMEX* 2, 8 (April 1971).

57 WR, Hans Sinn fonds, box 1, file 2, Correspondence with Potential Draftees; WR, Hans Sinn fonds, box 1, file 8, "*Sanity: Peace Oriented News and Comment,*" 1965-67.

58 Joseph Jones, interview with the author by email, 21 November 2006.

59 UBCL, RBSC, Renée Kasinsky fonds, box 4, file 14, "Interview with Bill Spira of the Toronto Anti-Draft Program [sic], June 1970."

60 Marvin Work, interview with the author by email, 28 November 2006.

61 Michael Goldberg, interview with the author by telephone, 11 July 2006.

62 Emerick, *War Resisters Canada,* 238.

63 Ibid., 239.

64 UBCL, RBSC, Renée Kasinsky fonds, box 1, file 3, "Correspondence – Other Canadian Organizations with Committee."

65 Ibid.

66 Joan Wilcox, interview with the author, Ottawa, ON, 17 May 2006.

67 WR, Doug Ward fonds, box 1, file 1, Student Action, Philip Smith, "US Draft Dodgers Tell Why They Chose Canada," in *Weekend Magazine,* 26 November 1966, 12-14, 16-18. It is typical of the time that the men's wives were not identified nor interviewed.

68 UBCL, RBSC, Renée Kasinsky fonds, box 1, file 2, "Correspondence – VCAAWO."

69 DAL, Nova Scotia Committee to Aid American War Objectors fonds, MS-10-7, file 2.3, "Requests for Help or Information on How to Emigrate," various correspondence from Americans, 1970; "So You Want to Teach Public School in Canada?," WR, Canadian student social and political organizations, box 7, file 17, "Toronto Anti-Draft Programme." Emphasis on teaching jobs coincided with the shift to service work in the Canadian economy. By late 1969, the beginning of the end of the postwar boom meant unemployment was on the rise, albeit slowly.

70 DAL, Nova Scotia Committee to Aid American War Objectors fonds, MS-10-7, box 2, folder 3, "Requests for Help or Information on How to Emigrate," correspondence, 1970; DAL, Nova Scotia Committee to Aid American War Objectors fonds, MS-10-7, box 2, folder 4, "Requests for Help or Information on How to Emigrate," correspondence, 1971; DAL, Nova Scotia Committee to Aid American War Objectors fonds,

MS-10-7, box 2, folder 5, "Requests for Help or Information on How to Emigrate," correspondence, 1972.

71 UBCL, RBSC, Renée Kasinsky fonds, box 2, file 7, "Interview Analysis/Questionnaire Analysis and Code." According to one handwritten note, 341 draft dodgers were tabulated, of which twenty-three had corresponded with a committee; and 110 deserters were counted, of which seven had corresponded with a committee.

72 UBCL, RBSC, Renée Kasinsky fonds, box 3, file 11, "Interview with Bill, Vietnam Vet, Montreal," [1970].

73 UBCL, RBSC, Renée Kasinsky fonds, box 6, file 4, "Canadian Publications: *AMEX*," *AMEX* 2, 3 (April-May 1970): 39.

74 UBCL, RBSC, Renée Kasinsky fonds, box 7, file 20, "It's Your Choice: Guide to Opportunities Open to Volunteers for Military Service," 1968.

75 "James," interview with the author by telephone, 10 July 2006.

76 Donald Duncan, "Sanctuary," *Ramparts Magazine* 5, 10, April 1967, 29-33.

77 "Ben," interview with the author by email, 4 November 2006.

78 Carolyn Egan, interview with the author, Toronto, 1 June 2006.

79 For a Canadian exploration of the concept of chain migration see Elliott, *Irish Migrants in the Canadas.*

80 Work, interview.

81 David Brown, interview with the author by email, 6 November 2006.

82 Mark Phillips, interview with the author, Ottawa, ON, 11 July 2006.

83 Although all American men were required to register for the draft, the process of choosing who would actually be drafted was a lottery process based on drawing birthdates and initials from a drum.

84 Jones, interview. Jones probably recollected these experiences so clearly partly because his research focus at the time of the interview was on the anti-draft movement.

85 "Daniel," interview with the author by email, 2 November 2006.

86 Goldberg, interview.

87 Lee Zaslofsky, interview with the author by email, 30 October 2006.

88 Hardy Scott, interview with the author by mail, 31 October 2006.

89 Dick Perrin, interview with the author by email, 12 December 2006.

90 Joseph Healey Library, U. Massachusetts, Boston, "Perrin, Richard: Papers, 1966-2001," archives' description, http://www.lib.umb.edu/.

91 Examining the transnational dimension of the anti-draft movement also raises the question of whether, generally speaking, chain migration in the postwar period was encouraged and/or augmented by involvement with or by immigrant advocacy groups.

92 Kasinsky, *Refugees from Militarism,* 81-82.

93 Theda Skocpol, *Diminished Democracy: From Membership to Management in American Civic Life* (Norman: University of Oklahoma Press, 2003), 17.

Chapter 3: Deserters

1　Kaneko Mitsuharu, *Opposition*, circa 1917, cited in Donald Keene, *Dawn to the West: Japanese Literature of the Modern Era, Poetry, Drama, Criticism* (New York: Columbia University Press, 1999), 358.

2　Renée Kasinsky holds that the groups did not see themselves as part of the antiwar movement, but cites no evidence to support this statement. Renée Kasinsky, *Refugees from Militarism: Draft-Age Americans in Canada* (New Brunswick, NJ: Transaction Books, 1976), 77-78.

3　"History of the Committee to Aid American War Objectors," VCAAWO, 1970, cited in Kasinsky, *Refugees from Militarism*, 104; McMaster University, William Ready Division of Archives and Research Collections (hereafter WR), Canadian student social and political organizations, box 4, file 13, "Committee to Aid American War Objectors"; University of British Columbia Library, Rare Books and Special Collections (hereafter UBCL, RBSC), Renée Kasinsky fonds, box 1, file 2, "Correspondence – VCAAWO."

4　Lee Zaslofsky, interview with the author by email, 30 October 2006.

5　"James," interview with the author by telephone, 10 July 2006.

6　"Ben," interview with the author by email, 4 November 2006.

7　Marvin Work, interview with the author by email, 28 November 2006. About half of the world's Doukhobors live in Canada; a few hundred live in the United States. Koozma J. Tarasoff, "Doukhobors – An Overview," revised and updated 28 February 2006, www.spirit-wrestlers.com.

8　Hardy Scott, interview with the author by mail, 31 October 2006.

9　Alan G. Green and David A. Green, "The Economic Goals of Canada's Immigration Policy: Past and Present," *Canadian Public Policy/Analyse de Politiques* 25, 4 (1999): 432-33.

10　Michael Goldberg, interview with the author by telephone, 11 July 2006.

11　Joan Wilcox, interview with the author, Ottawa, ON, 17 May 2006.

12　Ibid.

13　Ken Fisher, interview with the author, Gatineau, QC, 9 June 2006.

14　Doug Owram, *Born at the Right Time: A History of the Baby Boom Generation* (Toronto: University of Toronto Press, 1997), 217, 218.

15　Cynthia Comacchio, *The Dominion of Youth: Adolescence and the Making of a Modern Canada, 1920-1950* (Waterloo, ON: Wilfrid Laurier University Press, 2006), 7.

16　Ibid., 1-4.

17　UBCL, RBSC, Renée Kasinsky fonds, box 4, file 12, "Interview with Nancy Pokhawk [sic], May 1970, Toronto, Quaker, Active in Exile Movement since 1965."

18　Ibid.

19　UBCL, RBSC, Renée Kasinsky fonds, box 4, file 14, "Interview with Bill Spira of the Toronto Anti-Draft Program [sic], June 1970."

20　Wilcox, interview.

21 Paul Copeland, interview with the author, Ottawa, ON, 5 June 2006.

22 Kenneth Fred Emerick, *War Resisters Canada: The World of the American Military-Political Refugees* (Knox, PA: Knox, Pennsylvania Free Press, 1972), 236-37.

23 Wilcox, interview.

24 Walter Gordon was the chair of a Royal Commission that produced a controversial report on tariff policy for the Canadian economy. It was followed almost a decade later by the equally controversial Watkins report; then Liberal-leaning Mel Watkins had chaired a task force for Gordon. For a good overview of these concerns see Stephen Azzi's study of the left-wing strain of "new nationalism," *Walter Gordon and the Rise of Canadian Nationalism* (Montreal and Kingston: McGill-Queen's University Press, 1999). See also Chapters 5 and 6 in this volume.

25 Zaslofsky, interview. It seems unlikely, if the event Zaslofsky recalls was a Waffle meeting, that Walter Gordon was in attendance, although the event would have taken place after he left office in 1968. Perhaps it was a meeting put on by the Waffle, with guests, or perhaps it was a meeting of the Committee for an Independent Canada, which Watkins and Gordon helped found.

26 "Daniel," interview with the author by email, 2 November 2006.

27 Goldberg, interview.

28 UBCL, RBSC, Renée Kasinsky fonds, box 4, file 14, "Interview with Bill Spira of the Toronto Anti-Draft Program [sic], June 1970."

29 David Cortwright, *Soldiers in Revolt: GI Resistance during the Vietnam War* (1975; repr., Chicago: Haymarket Books, 1995), 14.

30 WR, Doug Ward fonds, box 1, file 1, Student Action, Philip Smith, "US Draft Dodgers Tell Why They Chose Canada," *Weekend Magazine,* 26 November 1966, 12-14, 16-18.

31 Joseph Jones, interview with the author by email, 21 November 2006.

32 On Vietnam veterans see, for instance, Jennifer L. Price, "Fact Sheet: Findings from the National Vietnam Veterans' Readjustment Study," 1 January 2007, United States Department of Veterans Affairs National Center for Posttraumatic Stress Disorder, http://www.ptsd.va.gov/. See also Christian Appy, *Working-Class War: American Combat Soldiers and Vietnam* (Chapel Hill, NC: University of North Carolina Press, 1993); Christian Appy, "From Working-Class War: American Combat Soldiers and Vietnam," in *American Identities: An Introductory Textbook,* ed. Lois Rudnick, Judith E. Smith, and Rachel Lee Rubin (Boston: Blackwell, 1995), 138-42.

33 Wilcox, interview. Wilcox's views are corroborated by, for instance, Cortwright, especially Chapter 10, "The Recruitment Racket," in *Soldiers in Revolt* (Chicago: Haymarket, 2005), 187-200; and his own recollected experiences, "Past as Present: Further Reflections on GI Resistance," in *Soldiers in Revolt,* Postscript to the 2005 edition, esp. 245-49. This streaming aspect of the Selective Service System, while less familiar to many, is well-documented. See Gerard J. De Groot, *A Noble Cause? America and the Vietnam War* (Harlow: Longman, 2000), 312, and discussion of channelling in Chapter 5 in this volume.

34 Work, interview.

35 Goldberg, interview.

36 Fisher, interview.

37 Zaslofsky, interview.

38 Dick Perrin and Tim McCarthy, *G.I. Resister: The Story of How One American Soldier and His Family Fought the War in Vietnam* (Victoria, BC: Trafford Publishing, 2001), 130-32.

39 UBCL, RBSC, Renée Kasinsky fonds, box 4, file 12, "Interview with Nancy Pokhawk [sic], May 1970, Toronto, Quaker, Active in Exile Movement since 1965."

40 UBCL, RBSC, Renée Kasinsky fonds, box 4, file 14, "Interview with Bill Spira of the Toronto Anti-Draft Program [sic], June 1970."

41 Ibid. For an excellent overview of the many ways resisters in the US could avoid the draft see Michael S. Foley, *Confronting the War Machine: Draft Resistance during the Vietnam War* (Chapel Hill, NC: University of North Carolina Press, 2003).

42 University of Toronto, Thomas Fisher Rare Book Library (hereafter TF), Pocock (Jack) Memorial Collection, box 13, "Lobbying and Public Relations," folder 1, "TADP Statements and Lobbying."

43 Wilcox, interview.

44 Goldberg, interview.

45 Jones, interview.

46 Work, interview.

47 "Daniel," interview.

48 Emerick, *War Resisters Canada*, 240.

49 Ibid., 235-36.

50 Ibid., 236.

51 WR, Quebec social and political organizations, file 9, "Montreal Council to Aid War Resisters," letter from Bill Mullen to Glenn Sinclair, 10 March 1970.

52 Library and Archives Canada (hereafter LAC), Voice of Women fonds, MG 28, I 218, vol. 12, file 3, "Draft Resistance: Correspondence; Printed Material; Clippings," 1966-73.

53 UBCL, RBSC, Edward Starkins fonds. Starkins's resignation letter states that the VAEA started in 1972.

54 Ibid. The Ford amnesty was announced on 16 September 1974; it "required up to two years of community service and a 'reaffirmation of allegiance to the United States.'" John Hagan, *Northern Passage: American Vietnam War Resisters in Canada* (Cambridge, MA: Harvard University Press, 2001), 161.

55 UBCL, RBSC, Edward Starkins fonds.

56 Ibid.

57 Ibid., letter to Mr. Kilmer, ca. 1974.

58 UBCL, RBSC, Edward Starkins fonds. John Hagan has done some analysis on the question of American war resister responses to the debate about amnesty in the

United States. Hagan, *Northern Passage*, 138-79. See also Kasinsky, *Refugees from Militarism*, 237-68.

59 "Ben," interview. To achieve "conscientious objector" status, a possibility in the United States in some form since the First World War, applicants had to go through a rigorous process of questionnaires and interviews, secure reference letters, and complete a lengthy form. The military frequently did not inform soldiers of the possibility of applying. Despite this, applications increased rapidly during the Vietnam War. For a good introduction to this process and its employment as a resistance tactic see Cortwright, *Soldiers in Revolt*, 15-17. The internal debate that "Ben" went through reflected contemporary ideas about masculinity and heroism, which is an important aspect of the broader history of war resistance.

60 Mark Phillips, interview with the author, Ottawa, ON, 11 July 2006.

61 Zaslofsky, interview; UBCL, RBSC, Renée Kasinsky fonds, box 2, file 7, "Interview Analysis/Questionnaire Analysis and Code."

62 David Brown, interview with the author by email, 6 November 2006.

63 See Appendix 2, "Shifts in Immigration Regulations and Tactics of Counselling and Border Crossing."

64 Scott, interview.

65 Hagan also addresses this discussion, framing it as a moral choice, but only in passing. Hagan, *Northern Passage*, 23-24.

66 See, for instance, Hagan, *Northern Passage*, esp. 135-37.

67 See Andrew L. Johns, review of *Northern Passage: American Vietnam War Resisters in Canada* by John Hagan, *Journal of Cold War Studies* 5, 2 (2003): 86-89.

68 Phillips, interview.

69 "James," interview.

70 UBCL, RBSC, Renée Kasinsky fonds, box 1, file 3, "Correspondence – Other Canadian Organizations with Committee."

71 Jones, interview.

72 In fact, early on, anti-draft literature explained how to renounce one's American citizenship, but it was only effective if done prior to committing an offence, and it carried the disadvantage of cutting off any chance of return. Kasinsky, *Refugees from Militarism*, 25-26. It is unclear how Phillips knew it was possible to do so. Renouncing one's citizenship was the only way to avoid being drafted, since residence in another country did not matter to the Selective Service.

73 Phillips, interview.

74 Wilcox, interview.

75 Goldberg, interview. There was a waiting period of two years after attaining landed immigrant status before one could become a citizen.

76 Scott, interview.

77 UBCL, RBSC, Renée Kasinsky fonds, box 4, file 12, "Interview with Nancy Pokhawk [sic], May 1970, Toronto, Quaker, Active in Exile Movement since 1965."

78 Ibid.

79 UBCL, RBSC, Renée Kasinsky fonds, box 4, file 11, "Interview with Larry Lynch (Officer), Deserter, Toronto, Summer 1969."

80 UBCL, RBSC, Renée Kasinsky fonds, box 4, file 14, "Interview with Bill Spira of the Toronto Anti-Draft Program [sic], June 1970."

81 UBCL, RBSC, Renée Kasinsky fonds, box 5, file 8, "Analysis of desertion – ADC's Political Activity," Fred Gardner, "The Future of Desertion," *Hard Times,* 4-11 May 1970.

82 Jones, interview.

83 UBCL, RBSC, Renée Kasinsky fonds, box 4, file 15, "Interview with Tom, Draft dodger, Toronto."

84 UBCL, RBSC, Renée Kasinsky fonds, box 5, file 8, "Analysis of Desertion – ADC's Political Activity," Vladimir B. Brown, "Uncle \$am, Canadian Independence and the American Exile," *AMEX* 1, 6 (1969): 5-8. The *Watkins Report* was a document prepared to expose foreign ownership and control of Canadian corporations. (The formal title of the report was *Foreign Ownership and the Structure of Canadian Industry: Report of the Task Force on the Structure of Canadian Industry,* Task Force on the Structure of Canadian Industry [Ottawa: Queen's Printer, 1968].) One of a handful of foundational texts in left economic nationalism in Canada, its conclusions that Canada was inordinately foreign controlled have since been questioned.

85 UBCL, RBSC, Renée Kasinsky fonds, box 5, file 8, "Analysis of Desertion – ADC's Political Activity," Vladimir B. Brown, "Uncle \$am, Canadian Independence and the American Exile," *AMEX* 1, 6 (1968): 5-8.

86 David Sterling Surrey, "The Assimilation of Vietnam-Era Draft Dodgers and Deserters into Canada: A Matter of Class" (PhD diss., New School for Social Research, 1980), 170.

87 This was certainly the case, at least, for economic nationalism – born of concerns about foreign, and more specifically American, investment and control of the Canadian economy. See Norman Hillmer and Adam Chapnick, eds., *Canadas of the Mind: The Making and Unmaking of Canadian Nationalisms in the Twentieth Century* (Montreal and Kingston: McGill-Queen's University Press, 2007), esp. Stephen Azzi, "Foreign Investment and the Paradox of Economic Nationalism," in *Canadas of the Mind,* 63-88.

88 LAC, Department of External Affairs fonds, RG 76, vol. 725, file 5660-2, "Military Personnel - Draft Dodgers – Complaints and Criticisms - General," Robin Mathews, Ottawa, to Minister of Manpower and Immigration Alan MacEachen, May 1969. For more on Mathews and the Canadianization movement, see Jeffrey Cormier, *The Canadianization Movement: Emergence, Survival, and Success* (University of Toronto Press, 2004). Mathews and his contemporary, James Steele, criticized Cormier's book for omitting significant facts and distorting others. See Robin Mathews and James Steele, "Canadianization Revisited: A Comment on Cormier's 'The Canadianization Movement in Context,'" *Canadian Journal of Sociology* 31 (2006): 491-508. In his

review of the same book, Bryan Palmer questions whether Mathews really led a social movement or had much influence; Bryan D. Palmer, review of *The Canadianization Movement,* by Jeffrey Cormier, *Pacific Historical Review* 75, 2 (2006): 369-71. Both reviews granted that Cormier was researching important areas but suggested there were gaps in his research.

89 Zaslofsky, interview.

90 Ibid.

91 Jones, interview.

92 Work, interview.

93 "Daniel," interview.

94 Phillips, interview.

95 Carolyn Egan, interview with the author, Toronto, 1 June 2006.

96 I have examined the question of police and government surveillance of the anti-draft movement and war resisters in detail elsewhere. See Jessica Squires, "The Canadian Anti-draft Movement, American War Resisters, and the State," in *War Resisters in Retrospect,* ed. Joseph Jones and Lori Olafson (Ottawa: National Research Council of Canada, 2009), 97-108. There are undoubtedly others. In 1972, the *Georgia Straight* reported that Vancouver area American immigrants were being harassed by police regarding their use of welfare. UBCL, RBSC, Renée Kasinsky fonds, box 8, file 5, "Newspaper Articles – Dodgers and Deserters," "Immigration Hassle," *Georgia Straight* (January 1972): 20-27. For a good overview of RCMP surveillance of university campus peace groups and conclusions about the RCMP's lack of inhibitions in spying on Canadians, see Steve Hewitt, *Spying 101: The RCMP's Secret Activities at Canadian Universities, 1917-1997* (Toronto: University of Toronto Press, 2002), 93-172.

97 Goldberg, interview.

98 LAC, Canadian Security Intelligence Service fonds, RG 146, file "Vancouver Committee to Aid American War Objectors," "RCMP Admits FBI Agents are Operating in Canada," unknown newspaper publication, circa April 1966.

99 LAC, Department of External Affairs fonds, RG 25, vol. 10842, file 20-1-2-USA, pt. 3, "Political Affairs – Policy and Background – Canadian External Policy and Relations – United States of America." Certainty on this statement is not possible partly because the following documents were exempted from release under Access to Information legislation from the file on FBI-RCMP cooperation – the existence and titles of which are themselves a strong indication that such collaboration took place:

  - "Memorandum from USA division re Canada-US Relations, 31 March 1966," 3 pages
  - "For Mr. Wall, Privy Council Office re RCMP – FBI Cooperation April 18, 1966," 2 pages
  - "From DC (2) division to USA Division April 21, 1966," 1 page

- "Telegram from External Affairs to Washington re RCP-FBI cooperation April 22, 1966," 2 pages
- "Letter External Affairs to US embassy re RCMP-FBI cooperation, April 22, 1966," 1 page
- "Memo for the Minister, May 9, 1966," 5 pages
- "Memo for the Under-Secretary May 9, 1966," 1 page
- "Memorandum from the Office of the Secretary for External Affairs, May 13, 1966," 1 page
- "Memorandum for the Under-Secretary, May 14, 1966," 2 pages
- "Memorandum for the Minister, May 30, 1966," 4 pages
- "Hansard, April 25, 1966, re activities of FBI in Canada"
- "Aide-Memoire, April 22, 1966," 2 pages
- "Memorandum for the Secretary of State for External Affairs re Canada-US Relations, June 24, 1965," 17 pages

What is certain, however, is that the US and Canadian governments had earlier sought a reciprocal arrangement that allowed for the FBI and RCMP to work together to arrest deserters. LAC, Department of External Affairs fonds, RG 25, vol. 8045, file 1539-B-2-40, pt. 2, "Mutual Assistance in the Arrest of Deserters and Defaulters among NATO Countries," "Summary of a Meeting Held in Room 117 East Block Monday, September 26, 1955, 10:00 AM."

100 "Ottawa Told FBI Hunts Draft Dodgers in Canada," *Toronto Star,* 1 April 1966, 1.

101 LAC, Department of External Affairs fonds, RG 25, vol. 10842, file 20-1-2-USA, pt. 3, "Political Affairs – Policy and Background – Canadian External Policy and Relations – United States of America," July 5/65 – July 13/66, Hansard, Wednesday, March 30, 1966, Question 1,151, Mr. Basford, March 24; "Ottawa Told FBI Hunts Draft Dodgers in Canada," *Toronto Star,* 1 April 1966, 1.

102 LAC, Department of External Affairs fonds, RG 25, vol. 10842, file 20-1-2-USA, pt. 4, "Political Affairs – Policy and Background – Canadian External Policy and Relations – United States of America," memo to Mr. Ritchie from USA Division, signed by Hicks, "Canada-US Relations: Cases of Alleged Draft Evasion," 31 March 1966.

103 Ibid.

104 LAC, Department of External Affairs fonds, RG 25, vol. 10842, file 20-1-2-USA, pt. 3, "Political Affairs – Policy and Background – Canadian External Policy and Relations – United States of America," "Additional questions which may rise on the House when the solicitor General Makes the Statement in reply to Question 1,151 With Suggested Answers," 25 April 1966. The instructions in question were contained in an Aide-Memoire signed by Secretary of State for External Affairs Paul Martin Sr. on 22 April 1966. Paul Martin Sr. was a career politician who had served in three previous Cabinets. He left Parliament for the Senate shortly after these events.

105   LAC, Department of External Affairs fonds, RG 25, vol. 10842, file 20-1-2-USA, "Political Affairs – Policy and Background – Canadian External Policy and Relations – United States of America," "Aide-Memoire," 22 April 1966.

106   LAC, Department of External Affairs fonds, RG 25, vol. 10842, file 20-1-2-USA, pt. 4, "Political Affairs – Policy and Background – Canadian External Policy and Relations – United States of America," Hansard, 25 April 1966; Memorandum for the Minister, "Questions on the House on FBI Activities in Canada," 30 May 1966.

107   LAC, Department of External Affairs fonds, RG 25, vol. 10842, file 20-1-2-USA, pt. 3, "Political Affairs – Policy and Background – Canadian External Policy and Relations – United States of America," Memorandum for the Minister from M. Cadieux, "Possible Question in the House Regarding US Citizens Using Canada as a Haven from US Selective Service," 11 May 1966. The report in question was by Larry Bondy, CBC Television News, "Safe Haven in Toronto – Yorkville Village," Broadcast 10 May 1966, 02:49, http://archives.cbc.ca.

108   LAC, Department of External Affairs fonds, RG 25, vol. 10842, file 20-1-2-USA, pt. 3, "Political Affairs – Policy and Background – Canadian External Policy and Relations – United States of America," Memorandum for the Minister from M. Cadieux, "Possible Question in the House Regarding US Citizens Using Canada as a Haven from US Selective Service," May 11, 1966.

109   LAC, Department of External Affairs fonds, RG 25, vol. 10842, file 20-1-2-USA, pt. 4, "Political Affairs – Policy and Background – Canadian External Policy and Relations – United States of America," memo to Mr. Goldschag, Far Eastern Division, from USA Division, "Canadian M.P.s and Vietnam," 19 July 1966; "Brief for Minister's Press Conference In Boston – October 26, 1966: US Draft Dodgers Coming to Canada," 24 October 1966. The synchronization had been informed to some extent by a 1955 agreement between the two departments that sought an arrangement with the United States to apprehend deserters, which would both allow for FBI and RCMP to work together to arrest deserters to relieve Immigration of the responsibility, and for Canadian deserters to be deported by the US government. However, this earlier decision was never acted upon. LAC, Department of External Affairs fonds, RG 25, vol. 8045, file 1539-B-2-40, pt. 2, "Mutual Assistance in the Arrest of Deserters and Defaulters among NATO Countries," numbered letter N-201 to Under-Secretary of State for External Affairs from the Delegation of Canada to the North Atlantic Council, Paris, France, 8 February 1960; letter from Legal Division to Deputy Min DND, "NATO Status of Forces Agreement - Apprehension of Deserters," 22 July 1960; letter from the Deputy Minister of the Department of National Defence to the Under-Secretary of State for External Affairs, attn. Mr. G. Sicotte, "NATO Status of Forces Agreement - Apprehension of Deserters," 22 August 1960; Numbered letter L-844 from Under-Secretary of State for External Affairs to the Delegation of Canada to the North Atlantic Council, Paris, France, 9 December 1960; Memo to the Delegation of Canada to the Atlantic Council, Paris, France from G.C. Langille, Under-Secretary

of State for External Affairs, "NATO Status of Forces Agreement – Apprehension of Deserters," 9 December 1960.

110 Perrin and McCarthy, *G.I. Resister,* 130-32.

111 LAC, Department of Employment and Immigration fonds, RG 76, vol. 983, file 5660-1, pt. 1, "Military Personnel – Draft Dodgers – General," Office of the Commissioner, RCMP, to Director, Home Branch, Canadian Immigration Division, Department of Manpower and Immigration, "Re: Co-operation with the Department of Manpower and Immigration – Canada Immigration Division," 24 October 1967. Nadon replaced William Higgitt as RCMP commissioner in 1973.

Chapter 4: Opening the Border

1 The poem in the epigraph appears by kind permission of Wayne Padgett. Wayne Padgett, "Do People in Canada Write on Bathroom Walls Less?" Vancouver, BC, 21 March 1970, in *Crossing Lines: Poets Who Came to Canada in the Vietnam War Era,* ed. Allan Briesmaster and Steven Michael Berzensky (Hamilton, ON: Seraphim Editions, 2008), 178.

2 Criminal charges pending, deserted heads of families, child support, and debts without arrangements were the other listed examples of moral, legal, or contractual obligations that might prevent an immigrant from properly settling in Canada. See Library and Archives Canada (hereafter LAC), Department of External Affairs fonds, RG 76, vol. 983, file 5660-1, "Military Personnel – Draft Dodgers – General," Memorandum to the Minister from the Deputy Minister's Office file, 30 January 1969.

3 Antonio Gramsci, "State and Civil Society," in *Selections from the Prison Notebooks of Antonio Gramsci,* trans. and ed. Quintin Hoare and Geoffrey Nowell Smith (New York: International Publishers, 1971), 238-39.

4 Appendix 2, "Shifts in Immigration Regulations and Tactics of Counselling and Border Crossing," helps navigate the somewhat complex events described in this section.

5 LAC, Department of External Affairs fonds, RG 25, vol. 830, file 552-1-637, "Immigration from USA – Policy and Instructions," "Brief on Aide Memoire" and "Aide Memoire – Changes to Canadian Immigration Regulations," 23 January 1962. For an overview of the shift in the 1962 immigration regulations, see William L. Marr, "Canadian Immigration Policies since 1962," *Canadian Public Policy/Analyse de Politiques* 1, 2 (1975): 196-203; Louis Parai, "Canada's Immigration Policy, 1962-74," *International Migration Review* 9, 4 (1975): 449-77; and Ravi Pendakur, *Immigrants and the Labour Force: Policy Regulation, and Impact* (Montreal: McGill-Queen's University Press, 2000).

6 LAC, Department of External Affairs fonds, RG 25, vol. 830, file 552-1-637, "Immigration from USA – Policy and Instructions," memo, Deputy Minister to R.B. Curry, 16 June 1965; "Brief on Aide Memoire" and "Aide Memoire – Changes to Canadian Immigration Regulations," 23 January 1962. Couillard had spent some time at the Department of External Affairs in the 1950s, but little else is publicly known

about him. See "Documents on Canadian External Relations," vol. 23, Chapter VII, "Atomic Energy," Part 2, "Export of Uranium: Policy," DEA/14002-2-6-40, item 806, "Problems Relating to the Export of Uranium, Memorandum from JLE Couillard, Head, Economic Division, to Under-Secretary of State for External Affairs, 23 April 1957, http://www.international.gc.ca/. No information was readily available regarding R.B. Curry.

7 LAC, Department of External Affairs fonds, RG 25, vol. 830, file 552-1-637, "Immigration from USA – Policy and Instructions."

8 Ibid., letter from Executive Assistant to R.B. Curry, Assistant Deputy Minister (Immigration), 13 September 1966.

9 Ibid., 1966 report summary, in memo from R.B. Curry, Assistant Deputy Minister (Immigration) to Information Division, Economic and Social Research Division, Planning Branch, Foreign Branch, Head of Secretariat. It was not the first time Canada had benefitted from political tensions in the United States. See J.L. Granatstein and Norman Hillmer, *For Better or For Worse: Canada and the United States to the 1990s* (Toronto: Copp Clark Pitman, 1991).

10 For a good overview of immigration policy shifts through this period, see Donald H. Avery, "Immigrant Workers and Canada's Changing Immigration Policy, 1952-1980," in *Reluctant Hosts: Canada's Response to Immigrant Workers, 1896-1994* (Toronto: McClelland and Stewart, 1995), 170-97, esp. 178-92. See also Pendakur, *Immigrants and the Labour Force*, esp. 75-81; Reg Whitaker, *Canadian Immigration Policy since Confederation* (Ottawa: Canadian Historical Association, 1991); Freda Hawkins, *Canada and Immigration: Public Policy and Public Concern*, 2nd ed. (Montreal and Kingston: McGill-Queen's University Press, 1988); Reg Whitaker, *Double Standard: The Secret History of Canadian Immigration* (Toronto: Lester and Orpen Dennys, 1987).

11 Alan G. Green and David A. Green, "The Economic Goals of Canada's Immigration Policy: Past and Present," *Canadian Public Policy/Analyse de Politiques* 25, 4 (1999): 432-33.

12 Pendakur, *Immigrants and the Labour Force*, 79-81.

13 Ibid., 82-83.

14 University of British Columbia Library, Rare Books and Special Collections (hereafter UBCL, RBSC), Renée Kasinsky fonds, box 6, file 17, "Communication with High Officials – Fugitives from Justice Submission," 1967.

15 Ibid.

16 Ibid.

17 It was illegal to desert from the Canadian military, but not illegal in Canada to desert from the military of another country.

18 LAC, Department of External Affairs fonds, RG 25, vol. 8045, file 1539-B-2-40, pt. 2, "Mutual Assistance in the Arrest of Deserters and Defaulters among NATO Countries,"

numbered letter L-844 from Under-Secretary of State for External Affairs to the Delegation of Canada to the North Atlantic Council, Paris, France, 9 December 1960.

19 For a description of how independent high-level bureaucrats have in fact been in the Canadian government, see J.L. Granatstein, *The Ottawa Men: The Civil Service Mandarins, 1935-1957* (Toronto: Oxford University Press, 1982). For more on this aspect of bureaucracy, see Max Weber, *The Theory of Social and Economic Organization,* ed. Talcott Parsons (New York: Oxford University Press, 1966), 324-41, and Colin Campbell, "The Political Roles of Senior Government Officials in Advanced Democracies," *British Journal of Political Science* 18, 2 (1988): 243-72.

20 UBCL, RBSC, Renée Kasinsky fonds, box 8, file 8, "A Note on the Handling of Draft-Age Americans Who Apply for Entry into Canada," [1967].

21 Ibid.

22 Ibid.

23 Tom Kent, *A Public Purpose: An Experience of Liberal Opposition and Canadian Government* (Montreal and Kingston: McGill-Queen's University Press), 1988. Tom Kent, an Oxford scholar and journalist, lifetime public servant, and businessman, was a policy adviser to Prime Minister Lester Pearson from 1963 to 1966. As such, he was a transitional figure in the Liberal Party as power shifted to the Trudeau leadership.

24 *Ramparts Magazine,* 26 September 1966, cited in Renée Kasinsky, *Refugees from Militarism: Draft-Age Americans in Canada* (New Brunswick, NJ: Transaction Books, 1976), 62-63.

25 LAC, Department of External Affairs fonds, RG 76, vol. 983, file 5660-1, "Military Personnel – Draft Dodgers – General."

26 Ibid., memo from Tom Kent to M. Cadieux, Undersecretary of State for External Affairs, re "Deserters – United States and Armed Forces," 17 November 1967.

27 Ibid., Office of the Minister of Manpower and Immigration, press release and House of Commons Statement by Allan McEachen, 22 May 1969.

28 Ibid., Memorandum to the Minister from Deputy Minister's office file, January 30, 1969; LAC, Department of External Affairs fonds, RG 76, vol. 1209, file 5665-1, "Military Personnel – Draft Dodgers – General," letter from J.C. Morrison to L.R. Vachon, 9 January 1968. See also Churchill, "When Home Became Away," 201-2.

29 UBCL, RBSC, Renée Kasinsky fonds, box 6, file 19, "Copies of letters from Deputy Minister, Dept. of Manpower and Immigration," letter from Tom Kent, Deputy Minister, Ministry of Manpower and Immigration to Herbert Herridge, MP, 31 January 1968.

30 UBCL, RBSC, Renée Kasinsky fonds, box 6, file 17, "Communication with High Officials – Fugitives from Justice Submission," letter from Minister of Manpower and Immigration Jean Marchand to Herbert Herridge, MP, 1968.

31 Herridge may also have been seeking to help potential immigrants in his area of BC, the Kootenays, today known as a common destination for war resisters from the

Vietnam era. Statnet[.ca] Productions, "Our Way Home Peace Event and Reunion," 2006, http://www.ourwayhomereunion.com/home.php.

32   LAC, Department of External Affairs fonds, RG 76, vol. 983, file 5660-1, "Military Personnel – Draft Dodgers – General," H. Ross Munro, "Ottawa Said Taking Hard Line on Deserters," *Globe and Mail*, 30 January 1969, appended to Memorandum to the Minister from Deputy Minister's office file, 30 January 1969; UBCL, RBSC, Renée Kasinsky fonds, box 8, file 5, "Newspaper Articles – Dodgers and Deserters," "Canada Moves to Deny a Haven to US Deserters," *New York Times*, 31 January 1969.

33   UBCL, RBSC, Renée Kasinsky fonds, box 8, file 5, "Newspaper Articles – Dodgers and Deserters," "Crackdown Denied," *Vancouver Sun*, 1 February 1969.

34   UBCL, RBSC, Renée Kasinsky fonds, box 8, file 5, "Newspaper Articles – Dodgers and Deserters," "Number of US Deserters Played Down by Canada," *Baltimore Sun*, 23 March 1969.

35   LAC, Department of External Affairs fonds, RG 76, vol. 983, file 5660-1, "Military Personnel – Draft Dodgers – General," Memorandum to the Minister from Deputy Minister's office file, 30 January 1969.

36   LAC, Department of External Affairs fonds, RG 76, vol. 983, file 5660-1, "Military Personnel – Draft Dodgers – General," Memorandum to the Minister from Deputy Minister's office file, 30 January 1969; LAC, RG 76, vol. 983, file 5660-1, "Military Personnel – Draft Dodgers – General," Memorandum from Assistant Deputy Minister (Immigration) signed by James S. Cross for [R.B. Curry] to Deputy Minister [Couillard], 23 May 1969.

37   LAC, Department of External Affairs fonds, RG 76, vol. 983, file 5660-1, "Military Personnel – Draft Dodgers – General," Memorandum to the Minister from Deputy Minister's office file, 30 January 1969.

38   LAC, Department of External Affairs fonds, RG 76, vol. 983, file 5660-1, "Military Personnel – Draft Dodgers – General," memo to Assistant Deputy Minister, Immigration from Director, Planning Branch, "Divisional Instructions on US Draft Dodgers," and "Operations Memorandum to All Holders of Immigration Manual" 117 (revised), 24 August 1967.

39   Discretionary power was contained in sections 32 and 33 of the regulations. The elements to consider in exercising discretion were the subject of the instructional memo. See LAC, Department of External Affairs fonds, RG 76, vol. 983, file 5660-1, "Military Personnel – Draft Dodgers – General," Memorandum to the Minister from Deputy Minister's Office file, 30 January 1969.

40   UBCL, RBSC, Renée Kasinsky fonds, box 7, file 13, "A Further Note on the Handling of Draft-Age Americans Who Apply for Entry to Canada," 1969.

41   Frank H. Epp, ed., *I Would Like to Dodge the Draft-Dodgers, But ...* (Waterloo and Winnipeg: Conrad Press, 1970), 53-54.

42   LAC, Department of External Affairs fonds, RG 76, vol. 983, file 5660-1, "Military Personnel – Draft Dodgers – General."

43 LAC, Department of External Affairs fonds, RG 76, vol. 983, file 5660-1, "Military Personnel – Draft Dodgers – General," "Draft: Memorandum to Cabinet: Draft Dodgers and Military Deserters," 10 March 1969; Conrad Black, *Richard M. Nixon: A Life in Full* (New York: Public Affairs, 2008), 543.

44 Mary Halloran, John Hilliker, and Greg Donaghy, Historical Section, Foreign Affairs Canada, "The White Paper Impulse: Reviewing Foreign Policy under Trudeau and Clark" (paper presented at the Canadian Political Science Association conference, Waterloo, Ontario, June 3 2005), http://www.cpsa-acsp.ca/papers-2005/Halloran.pdf.

45 LAC, Department of External Affairs fonds, RG 76, vol. 983, file 5660-1, "Military Personnel – Draft Dodgers – General," "Report on Visiting Washington Correspondents," circa 13 March 1969.

46 LAC, Department of External Affairs fonds, RG 76, vol. 983, file 5660-1, "Military Personnel – Draft Dodgers – General," "Background Paper: Draft Resistance/Deserters, Background to May 1968," undated; Memorandum to the Minister from R.B. Curry, "Re: United Church Board of Evangelism, Toronto, 20 February 1969," 24 February 1969.

47 Paul Copeland, interview with the author, Ottawa, ON, 5 June 2006.

48 Epp, *I Would Like to Dodge*, 50-54; LAC, Department of Employment and Immigration fonds, RG 76, vol. 725, file 5600-2, "Draft Dodgers and Deserters – Complaints and Criticisms," press release, Toronto Committee for a Fair Immigration Policy, signed by D. Camp, J. Ludwig, F. Mowat, R. Fulford, B. Frum, J. Callwood, D. Anderson, H. Adelman, W. Kilbourn, V. Kelly, S. Clarkson, Mel Watkins, C. Templeton, Watson, Russell, M. Moore, Rev. Gordon Stewart, Jane Jacobs, W. Spira, Allen Linden, attached to memo from District Admin., Toronto, to Director, Home Services Branch, Ottawa, subject: "Military Deserters – Petition by Committee for Fair Immigration Policy," 9 May 1969.

49 LAC, Department of Employment and Immigration fonds, RG 76, vol. 725, file 5660-2, Military Personnel – Draft Dodgers – Complaints and Criticisms, Memo from District Administrator, Toronto, to Director, Home Services Branch, Department of Immigration, "Military Deserters – Petition by Committee for Fair Immigration Policy," 9 May 1969.

50 Epp, *I Would Like to Dodge*, 50-54; LAC, Department of Employment and Immigration fonds, RG 76, vol. 725, file 5600-2, Draft Dodgers and Deserters – Complaints and Criticisms, press release, from Toronto Committee for a Fair Immigration Policy, signed by D. Camp, J. Ludwig, F. Mowat, R. Fulford, B. Frum, J. Callwood, D. Anderson, H. Adelman, W. Kilbourn, V. Kelly, S. Clarkson, Mel Watkins, C. Templeton, Watson, Russell, M. Moore. Rev. Gordon Stewart, Jane Jacobs, W. Spira, Allen Linden, attached to memo from District Admin., Toronto, to Director, Home Services Branch, Otttawa, subject: "Military Deserters – Petition by Committee for Fair Immigration Policy," 9 May 1969.

51 UBCL, RBSC, Renée Kasinsky fonds, box 8, file 5, "Newspaper Articles – Dodgers and Deserters," "Discrimination Alleged at Border," *Vancouver Sun,* 5 March 1969.

52 LAC, Department of External Affairs fonds, RG 76, vol. 983, file 5660-1, "Military Personnel – Draft Dodgers – General," Office of the Minister of Manpower and Immigration, press release, 5 March 1969.

53 LAC, Department of External Affairs fonds, RG 76, vol. 983, file 5660-1, "Military Personnel – Draft Dodgers – General," Memorandum from A.J. Banerd, Senior Planning Officer, Programs and Procedures Branch, to Director General of Operations, Attention of J.R. Robillard, "Statement on Draft Dodgers and Military Deserters," 24 March 1969.

54 Ibid.

55 Ibid.

56 Ibid.

57 LAC, Department of External Affairs fonds, RG 76, vol. 983, file 5660-1, "Military Personnel – Draft Dodgers – General," Memorandum to the Minister from Deputy Minister of Manpower and Immigration, Subject: "Draft Dodgers and Military Deserters from the United States," 28 March 1969. This RCMP exchange was part of a jurisdictional disagreement between the RCMP and the Department of Immigration regarding enforcement.

58 After a brief stint as Trudeau's secretary of state, Marchand moved on, first, to the Department of Forestry and Rural Development and then to a post as the minister of regional economic expansion. Privy Council Office, "Guide to Ministries since Confederation: Twentieth Ministry," modified 20 January 2013, http://www.pco-bcp. gc.ca/.

59 LAC, Department of External Affairs fonds, RG 76, vol. 983, file 5660-1, "Military Personnel – Draft Dodgers – General," Memorandum from R.B. Curry, Assistant Deputy Minister (Immigration), to Deputy Minister, 15 April 1969; Memorandum from W.R. Dymond, Assistant Deputy Minister (Program Development), to L.E. Couillard, Deputy Minister, ca. 15 April 1969.

60 LAC, Department of External Affairs fonds, RG 76, vol. 983, file 5660-1, "Military Personnel – Draft Dodgers – General," Memorandum to the Minister from L.E. Couillard, "Submission on Deserters," 22 April 1969.

61 Ibid.

62 Epp, *I Would Like to Dodge,* 57.

63 LAC, Privy Council Office, RG 2, vol. 6340, "Cabinet Conclusions," "Admission to Canada of Draft Dodgers and Military Deserters," 15 May 1969.

64 LAC, Department of External Affairs fonds, RG 76, vol. 983, file 5660-1, "Military Personnel – Draft Dodgers – General," Operations Memorandum to All Holders of Immigration Manual, 117 (Rev.), 31 July 1969.

65 LAC, Department of External Affairs fonds, RG 76, vol. 983, file 5660-1, "Military Personnel – Draft Dodgers – General," Memorandum to the Minister from Deputy

Minister's office file, January 30, 1969; RG 76, vol. 983, file 5660-1, "Military Personnel – Draft Dodgers – General," Memorandum from Assistant Deputy Minister (Immigration) signed by James S. Cross for [R.B. Curry] to Deputy Minister [Couillard], 23 May 1969.

66 For a good overview of the broad strokes of the debate about Canadian nationalism, see Alvin Finkel, *Our Lives: Canada after 1945* (Toronto: James Lorimer, 1997), esp. Chapter 6, "English-Canadian Nationalism," 157-75. See also Robert Bothwell, Ian Drummond, and John English, *Canada since 1945* (Toronto: University of Toronto Press, 1991), 307-9.

67 UBCL, RBSC, Renée Kasinsky fonds, box 1, file 3, "Correspondence – Other Canadian Organizations with Committee," letter to Allen from "S.," 3 February 1969.

68 Ibid., letter to Steve from "A.," February 1969.

69 UBCL, RBSC, Renée Kasinsky fonds, box 6, file 4, "Canadian Publications: *AMEX*," "Is the Honeymoon Over? US Deserters and Canadian Immigration," *AMEX* 1, 12, 9 March 1969.

70 UBCL, RBSC, Renée Kasinsky fonds, box 4, file 14, "Interview with Bill Spira of the Toronto Anti-Draft Program [sic], June 1970."

71 UBCL, RBSC, Renée Kasinsky fonds, box 1, file 3, "Correspondence – Other Canadian Organizations with Committee," letter to Steve from "A.," February 1969.

72 UBCL, RBSC, Renée Kasinsky fonds, box 1, file 3, "Correspondence – Other Canadian Organizations with Committee," letter to Steve from Allen, TADP, 25 February 1969.

73 Jim Wilcox, "They Are Up against the Canadian Border" [sic], in *I Would Like to Dodge*, 49-60.

74 "6 Pose as Deserters, Can't Enter Canada," *Toronto Star,* undated; Graham Muir, "'Deserters' Were Refused Entry at Border," *Pro Tem* (Toronto), 8, 19, 13 February 1969; LAC, Department of External Affairs fonds, RG 76, vol. 983, file 5660-1, "Military Personnel – Draft Dodgers – General," "Deserter, Don't Darken My Door," *Canso Breeze and Victoria-Inverness Bulletin* (Truro, NS), 5 March 1969; "US Deserters Dumped," *The Ubyssey* (Vancouver, BC), 18 February 1969; LAC, Department of External Affairs fonds, RG 76, vol. 725, file 5660-2, "Military Personnel – Draft Dodgers – Complaints and Criticisms," George Orr, "York Exposes Deserters' Persecution," *Excalibur* (Toronto, ON), 13 February 1969; *Toronto Star,* "MacEachen Backs Barring US Deserters," 18 February 1969. Jim Wilcox was wrong about the timing of the action; in his chapter, he wrote that the campaign occurred in the summer of 1968. Movement lawyer Paul Copeland also recalls the events occurring in 1968. However, newspaper and Hansard accounts leave no doubt that the events transpired in February of 1969.

75 LAC, Department of External Affairs fonds, RG 76, vol. 725, file 5660-2, "Military Personnel – Draft Dodgers – Complaints and Criticisms."

76 McMaster University, William Ready Division of Archives and Research Collections (hereafter WR), Quebec social and political organizations, file 9, "Montreal Council to Aid War Resisters."

77   WR, Quebec social and political organizations, file 9, "Montreal Council to Aid War Resisters," letter from Ed Miller to "Friends," 3 February 1969.

78   WR, Quebec social and political organizations, file 9, "Montreal Council to Aid War Resisters," "Ottawa veut 'démoraliser' les déserteurs américains," *Le Devoir,* 5 February 1969.

79   WR, Quebec social and political organizations, file 9, "Montreal Council to Aid War Resisters," Brian McKenna, "Ottawa Accused of Prejudice," *Montreal Star,* 6 February 1969.

80   UBCL, RBSC, Renée Kasinsky fonds, box 7, file 1, "Declaration of Purpose and History of American Deserters Committee – Montreal," 1969.

81   WR, Canadian student social and political organizations, box 7, file 17, "Toronto Anti-Draft Programme."

82   UBCL, RBSC, Renée Kasinsky fonds, box 8, file 5, "Newspaper Articles – Dodgers and Deserters," "Canada Moves to Deny a Haven to US Deserters," *Vancouver Sun,* 31 January 1969.

83   UBCL, RBSC, Renée Kasinsky fonds, box 1, file 3, "Correspondence – Other Canadian Organizations with Committee."

84   UBCL, RBSC, Renée Kasinsky fonds, box 4, file 14, "Interview with Bill Spira of the Toronto Anti-Draft Program [sic], June 1970." One such favourable report appeared in the *Globe and Mail,* editorial page, George Bain, "Too Much to Swallow," 20 May 1969. Bain took issue with MacEachen's reasons for not publishing the instructions to immigration officers regarding deserters.

85   UBCL, RBSC, Renée Kasinsky fonds, box 6, file 4, "Canadian Publications: *AMEX,*" "Is the Honeymoon Over? US Deserters and Canadian Immigration," *AMEX* 1, 12 (9 March 1969).

86   Graham Muir, "'Deserters' Were Refused Entry at Border," *Pro Tem* (Toronto) 8, 19, 13 February 1969.

87   UBCL, RBSC, Renée Kasinsky fonds, box 4, file 14, "Interview with Bill Spira of the Toronto Anti-Draft Program [sic], June 1970."

88   Copeland, interview.

89   LAC, Department of External Affairs fonds, RG 25, vol. 8045, file 1539-B-2-40, pt. 2, "Mutual Assistance in the Arrest of Deserters and Defaulters among NATO Countries," numbered letter L-844 from Undersecretary of State for External Affairs to the Delegation of Canada to the North Atlantic Council, Paris, France, 9 December 1960. The state of affairs was the result of a decision made to consider all such war-time agreements to have ceased as of the signing of the Treaty of Peace with Japan in April of 1952. See LAC, Department of External Affairs fonds, RG 25, vol. 8045, file 1539-B-2-40, pt. 2, "Mutual Assistance in the Arrest of Deserters and Defaulters among NATO Countries," memo from Canadian Embassy to Undersecretary of State for External Affairs, 1 August 1952.

90 UBCL, RBSC, Renée Kasinsky fonds, box 8, file 5, "Newspaper Articles – Dodgers and Deserters," "'Deserters Turned Back,'" Canadian Press, 10 February 1969.

91 Copeland, interview.

92 UBCL, RBSC, Renée Kasinsky fonds, box 8, file 5, "Newspaper Articles – Dodgers and Deserters," Bob Waller, "Students Expose Border Ban – Masqueraded as Deserters to Test Immigration," *Montreal Star,* 10 February 1969.

93 UBCL, RBSC, Renée Kasinsky fonds, box 8, file 5, "Newspaper Articles – Dodgers and Deserters," Bob Waller, "Students Expose Border Ban – Masqueraded as Deserters to Test Immigration," *Montreal Star,* 10 February 1969; LAC, Department of External Affairs fonds, RG 76, vol. 725, file 5660-2, "Military Personnel – Draft Dodgers – Complaints and Criticisms," telex from unspecified Toronto office to Frank Fredman, Information Service, Department of Manpower and Immigration, 10 February 1969, "We'll Treat US Deserters Like Anyone Else, MPs Told," *Toronto Star,* 23 May 1969; LAC, Department of External Affairs fonds, RG 76, vol. 983, file 5660-1, "Military Personnel – Draft Dodgers – General," Memorandum to the Minister from the Deputy Minister of Manpower and Immigration, subject: "Draft Dodgers and Military Deserters from the United States," 28 March 1969.

94 UBCL, RBSC, Renée Kasinsky fonds, box 8, file 5, "Newspaper Articles – Dodgers and Deserters," "Collusion at Border Admitted," *Montreal Star,* 14 February 1969.

95 UBCL, RBSC, Renée Kasinsky fonds, box 8, file 5, "Newspaper Articles – Dodgers and Deserters," Robert Stall, "US Army Deserters Find Canada Closed," *Montreal Star,* 18 February 1969.

96 UBCL, RBSC, Renée Kasinsky fonds, box 4, file 14, "Interview with Bill Spira of the Toronto Anti-Draft Program [sic], June 1970."

97 LAC, Department of External Affairs fonds, RG 76, vol. 983, file 5660-1, "Military Personnel – Draft Dodgers – General," Memorandum to the Deputy Minister from Minister MacEachen, 21 February 1969, accompanying document.

98 LAC, Department of External Affairs fonds, RG 76, vol. 725, file 5660-2, pt. 5, "Military Personnel – Draft Dodgers – Complaints and Criticisms," telegram from Robert B. McClure, Moderator, and Reverend Ernest E. Long, Secretary, General Council, United Church of Canada, Toronto, to MacEachen and Trudeau, April 30, 1969.

99 Frank Jones, "MacEachen Rows with United Church Over Deserter Policy," *Toronto Star,* 1 May 1969, 1, 4.

100 At least one anti-draft activist, Katie McGovern of the TADP, was involved in unions. Matthew McKenzie Bryant Roth, "Crossing Borders: The Toronto Anti-Draft Programme and the Canadian Anti-Vietnam War Movement" (MA thesis, University of Waterloo, 2008), 15-16, http://hdl.handle.net/10012/4108.

101 LAC, Department of External Affairs fonds, RG 76, vol. 725, file 5660-2, pt. 5, "Military Personnel – Draft Dodgers – Complaints and Criticisms," telegram from Archer, President, Ontario Federation of Labour, Don Mills, to MacEachen, 1 April 1969, and reply, MacEachen to Archer, 17 April 1969.

102   Copeland, interview.
103   UBCL, RBSC, Renée Kasinsky fonds, box 1, file 3, "Correspondence – Other Canadian Organizations with Committee," letter from Francis Marion, VCAAWO, to Branko Milojanovic, Embassy of Yugoslavia, Ottawa, ON, February 1969.
104   UBCL, RBSC, Renée Kasinsky fonds, box 4, file 14, "Interview with Bill Spira of the Toronto Anti-Draft Program [sic], June 1970."

Chapter 5: The Limits of Left Nationalism

1   Antonio Gramsci, "The Study of Philosophy," in *Selections from the Prison Notebooks of Antonio Gramsci,* trans. and ed. Quintin Hoare and Geoffrey Nowell Smith (New York: International Publishers, 1971), 323-27, 333, 375-77.
2   Ibid., 328.
3   Jessica Squires, "Creating Hegemony: Consensus by Exclusion in the Rowell-Sirois Commission," *Studies in Political Economy* 81 (2008): 159-90.
4   Gramsci, "The Study of Philosophy," 333. See also Karl Marx and Frederick Engels, *The Communist Manifesto,* New York: International Publishers, 1998 edition: "Does it require deep intuition to comprehend that man's ideas, views, and conceptions, in one word, man's consciousness, changes with every change in the conditions of his material existence, in his social relations and in his social life? ... When people speak of ideas that revolutionize society, they do but express the fact within the old society the elements of a new one have been created, and that the dissolution of the old ideas keeps even pace with the dissolution of the old conditions of existence ... But whatever form they may have taken, one fact is common to all past ages, viz., the exploitation of one part of society by the other. No wonder, then, that the social consciousness of past ages ... cannot completely vanish except with the total disappearance of class antagonisms" (28-29).
5   Gramsci, "The Study of Philosophy," 325.
6   Stuart Hall, "Gramsci's Relevance for the Study of Race and Ethnicity," in *Stuart Hall: Critical Dialogues in Cultural Studies,* ed. David Morley and Kuan-Hsing Chen (New York: Routledge, 1996), 437.
7   Ian McKay, "The Liberal Order Framework: A Prospectus for a Reconnaissance of Canadian History," *Canadian Historical Review* 81, 4 (2000): 617-45. See also his *Rebels, Reds, Radicals: Rethinking Canada's Left History* (Toronto: Between the Lines, 2005).
8   Stephen Azzi, *Walter Gordon and the Rise of Canadian Nationalism* (Montreal and Kingston: McGill-Queen's University Press, 1999), 167-88.
9   I am not including Quebec nationalism here for several reasons, not least of which is a problem of scope, but also because whether Quebec nationalism and Canadian nationalism can really be seen as the same phenomenon, or even the same type of phenomenon, is contentious, and an exploration that would do it justice, while valuable, is not pertinent to the topic at hand.

10   George Grant, *Lament for a Nation: The Defeat of Canadian Nationalism* (Toronto: McClelland and Stewart, 1965). It is interesting to note the number of times the book has been re-issued, most recently in 2005 by McGill-Queen's University Press, a fortieth anniversary edition. David Tough argues that Grant's work cannot be categorized as left- or right-wing. David Tough, "A Global Introduction to George Grant's Lament for a Nation" (paper presented at "New World Coming: The Sixties and the Shaping of Global Consciousness" conference, Queen's University, Kingston, ON, 15 June 2007).

11   Azzi, *Walter Gordon*, 176-80.

12   For discussions of the influence of the Waffle, see Mel Watkins, "The Waffle and the National Question," *Studies in Political Economy* 32 (Summer 1990): 173-76; John Smart, "The Waffle's Impact on the New Democratic Party," *Studies in Political Economy* 32 (Summer 1990): 177-86. See also Azzi, *Walter Gordon*, 170-72.

13   Watkins, "Waffle," 176. A good primary source on the development of the "new nationalism" is Philip Resnick, *Land of Cain: Class and Nationalism in English Canada, 1945-1975* (Vancouver: New Star Books, 1977). Resnick concludes that nationalism is generally progressive because it encourages social movements to form around democratic demands. See also Ken Wyman, "A Report from the Tip of the Iceberg," Robin Mathews, "Economy and Nationhood," and George Lermer, "The Task Force Report: An Economic Notebook," all in *Canadian Dimension* 5, 4 (April-May 1968), 15-20.

14   Charles Taylor, *Radical Tories: The Conservative Tradition in Canada* (Toronto: House of Anansi Press, 1982); Frank H. Underhill, *In Search of Canadian Liberalism* (Toronto: Macmillan, 1960); Erin Manning, *Ephemeral Territories: Representing Nation, Home, and Identity in Canada* (Minneapolis: University of Minnesota Press, 2003). See also Philip Massolin, *Canadian Intellectuals, the Tory Tradition and the Challenge of Modernity, 1939-1970* (Toronto: University of Toronto Press, 2001).

15   Scholarship includes Norman Hillmer and Adam Chapnick, eds., *Canadas of the Mind: The Making and Unmaking of Canadian Nationalisms in the Twentieth Century* (Montreal and Kingston: McGill-Queen's University Press, 2007); Stephen Azzi's study of the left-wing strain or "new nationalism," *Walter Gordon and the Rise of Canadian Nationalism* (Montreal and Kingston: McGill-Queen's University Press, 1999); Patricia K. Wood, who examines the exclusionary ethnicity embedded in the anti-Americanism of John A. Macdonald in "Defining 'Canadian': Anti-Americanism and Identity in Sir John A. Macdonald's Nationalism," *Journal of Canadian Studies* 36 2 (2001): 49-60; Ryan Edwardson, "'Kicking Uncle Sam out of the Peaceable Kingdom': English-Canadian 'New Nationalism' and Americanization," *Journal of Canadian Studies* 37, 4 (2003): 131-52.

16   Edwardson, "'Kicking Uncle Sam,'" 145.

17   Ian McKay and Jamie Swift, *Warrior Nation: Rebranding Canada in an Age of Anxiety* (Toronto: Between the Lines, 2012).

18 The debate is evident in Paul Kellogg, "State, Capital and World Economy: Bukharin's Marxism and the Dependency/Class Controversy in Canadian Political Economy," *Canadian Journal of Political Science* 22, 2 (1989): 337-62; Paul Kellogg, "Kari Levitt and the Long Detour of Canadian Political Economy," *Studies in Political Economy: A Socialist Review* 76 (Autumn 2005): 31-60; Mel Watkins, "Staples Redux," *Studies in Political Economy: A Socialist Review,* 79 (Spring 2007): 213-26; and William K. Carroll, *Corporate Power and Canadian Capitalism* (Vancouver: UBC Press, 1986).

19 Stephen Azzi, "Americanism and Anti-Americanism in English Canadian Nationalism, 1965-1975" (paper presented at "The Sixties Canadian-Style: Where Have all the Sixties Gone?" 24th Annual Two Days of Canada conference, Brock University, St. Catharines, ON, 4-5 November 2010).

20 Contrast this to John Hagan's framing of the letters as part of a stark Canadian sovereignty vs. personal suitability debate. John Hagan, *Northern Passage: American Vietnam War Resisters in Canada* (Cambridge, MA: Harvard University Press, 2001), 49.

21 For a good historical overview of the development of the field of Canadian political economy, see Wallace Clement and Glen Williams's Introduction to *The New Canadian Political Economy* (Montreal and Kingston: McGill-Queen's University Press, 1989), 3-15.

22 Mel Watkins, *Foreign Ownership and the Structure of Canadian Industry: Report of the Task Force on the Structure of Canadian Industry* (Task Force on the Structure of Canadian Industry, Ottawa: Queen's Printer, 1968). Another key figure in the production of this report was Walter Gordon, as Stephen Azzi examines in *Walter Gordon.*

23 Claire Culhane, *Why Is Canada in Vietnam? The Truth about Our Foreign Aid* (Toronto: New Canada Press, 1972). See also Stephen Clarkson, ed., *An Independent Foreign Policy for Canada?* (Toronto: McClelland and Stewart, 1968).

24 Examples of this influence include Gary Teeple, ed., *Capitalism and the National Question in Canada* (Toronto: University of Toronto Press, 1972); Steve Moore and Debi Wells, *Imperialism and the National Question in Canada* (Toronto: S. Moore, 1975).

25 Teeple, ed. *Capitalism and the National Question in Canada,* xv.

26 Ibid., x.

27 Kari Levitt, *Silent Surrender* (Toronto: Macmillan, 1970); Ian Lumsden, ed., *Close the 49th Parallel* (Toronto: University of Toronto Press, 1970).

28 See, for instance, John Warnock, review of *An Independent Foreign Policy for Canada* by Stephen Clarkson, ed., *Canadian Dimension* 5, 5 (June-July 1968), 36-37.

29 Sociologist Jeffrey Cormier has studied this "social movement of intellectuals" among university professors in the late 1960s and early 1970s. *The Canadianization Movement: Emergence, Survival, and Success* takes a fairly straightforward social movement theory approach and outlines the involvement of professors in a largely successful campaign to prevent university teaching positions from being taken by (primarily)

Americans. For a good overview of social movement theory see also Miriam Smith, *A Civil Society? Collective Actors in Canadian Political Life* (Peterborough, ON: Broadview Press, 2005), 25-39.

30 Gramsci, "The Study of Philosophy," 330-31.

31 A series of complaints files on various topics was apparently opened in the 1960s, based on a cursory search of the holdings of RG 76 at Library and Archives Canada. However, more research is necessary in order to determine if this was a shift in the political methods and "openness" of the department or of government in general; a reflection of new tactics used by pressure groups; or some combination of the two; or perhaps a reflection of the recently determined policy to "make available to the public as large a portion of the records of the government as was consistent with the national interest." Robert J. Hayward, "Federal Access and Privacy Legislation and the Public Archives of Canada," *Archivaria* 18 (Summer 1984): 47-57.

32 Emphasis in original. This letter and all others hereinafter, except as otherwise noted, are from Library and Archives Canada (hereafter LAC), Department of External Affairs fonds, RG 76, vol. 725, file 5660-2, parts 1-13, "Military Personnel – Draft Dodgers – Complaints and Criticisms," 1968-69.

33 LAC, Department of External Affairs fonds, RG 76, vol. 725, file 5660-2, "Military Personnel – Draft Dodgers – Complaints and Criticisms."

34 Frank H. Epp, ed., *I Would Like to Dodge the Draft-Dodgers, But ...* (Waterloo, ON and Winnipeg, MB: Conrad Press, 1970), 50-54; LAC, RG 76, Department of Employment and Immigration fonds, vol. 725, file 5600-2, "Draft Dodgers and Deserters – Complaints and Criticisms," press release from Toronto Committee for a Fair Immigration Policy, signed by D. Camp, J. Ludwig, F. Mowat, R. Fulford, B. Frum, J. Callwood, D. Anderson, H. Adelman, W. Kilbourn, V. Kelly, S. Clarkson, Mel Watkins, C. Templeton, Watson, Russell, M. Moore. Rev. Gordon Stewart, Jane Jacobs, W. Spira, Allen Linden, attached to memo from District Admin, Toronto, to Director, Home Services Branch, Ottawa, "Military Deserters – Petition by Committee for Fair Immigration Policy," 9 May 1969.

35 LAC, Department of External Affairs fonds, RG 76, vol. 725, file 5660-2, "Military Personnel – Draft Dodgers – Complaints and Criticisms," clipping attached to letter from Herbert Compton, Alf Chaiton, "Canadian Gov't [sic] Powerless against US: Watkins," *The Varsity*, February 1969.

36 LAC, Department of External Affairs fonds, RG 76, vol. 725, file 5660-2, "Military Personnel – Draft Dodgers – Complaints and Criticisms."

37 CBC Television, "Pierre Elliott Trudeau: Swinger, Philosopher, Prime Minister," "Canada Must Be a Just Society," originally aired 9 September 1968, http://archives.cbc.ca/.

38 Ian McKay makes a similar argument in his *Rebels, Reds, Radicals*, with reference to liberalism in general. Ian McKay, *Rebels, Reds, Radicals: Rethinking Canada's Left History* (Toronto: Between the Lines, 2005).

39 LAC, Department of External Affairs fonds, RG 76, vol. 725, file 5660-2, "Military Personnel – Draft Dodgers – Complaints and Criticisms," memo to the Minister from L.E. Couillard, Subject: Committee for a Fair Immigration Policy, 14 May 1969.

40 Resnick, *Land of Cain,* 226-27.

41 Mark Satin, ed. *Manual for Draft-Age Immigrants to Canada* (Toronto: Toronto Anti-Draft Programme and House of Anansi), 2nd ed., 1968, 64-67. Although not a signatory here, James Laxer, a Waffle co-founder, also wrote a section (pages 82-84) of the *Manual,* 4th ed. Mark Satin, ed. *Manual for Draft-Age Immigrants to Canada* (Toronto: Toronto Anti-Draft Programme and House of Anansi), 4th ed., 1970.

42 McMaster University, William Ready Division of Archives and Research Collections (hereafter WR), Stanley Gray fonds, fonds-level description, http://library.mcmaster.ca/archives/.

43 Jean Dion, "Pierre Bourgault (1934-2003) – Mort d'un homme libre," *Le Devoir,* 17 June 2003.

44 David Sterling Surrey, "The Assimilation of Vietnam-Era Draft Dodgers and Deserters into Canada: A Matter of Class" (PhD diss., New School for Social Research, 1980), 162-70, 176-77.

45 Ibid., 170.

46 University of British Columbia Library, Rare Books and Special Collections (hereafter UBCL, RBSC), Renée Kasinsky fonds, box 6, file 4, "Canadian Publications – *AMEX,*" "The US Draft Dodger in Canada Is Part of US Imperialism in Canada," *AMEX* 2, 4 (June 1970), 24-25. See also David Churchill, "When Home Became Away: American Expatriates and New Social Movements in Toronto, 1965-1977" (PhD diss., University of Chicago, 2001), 225.

47 UBCL, RBSC, Renée Kasinsky fonds, box 6, file 4, "Canadian Publications – *AMEX,*" "The US Draft Dodger in Canada Is Part of US Imperialism in Canada," *AMEX* 2, 4 (June 1970), 24-25.

48 Ibid.

49 UBCL, RBSC, Renée Kasinsky fonds, box 6, file 4, "Canadian Publications: *AMEX,*" Robin Mathews, "The US Draft Dodger in Canada Is Part of US Imperialism in Canada," *AMEX* 2, 4 (June 1970), 24-25; UBCL, RBSC, Renée Kasinsky fonds, box 6, file 4, "Canadian Publications: *AMEX,*" Ron Lambert, "Answering Mr. Mathews," *AMEX* 2, 5 (August-September 1970), 8-9.

50 UBCL, RBSC, Renée Kasinsky fonds, box 6, file 4, "Canadian Publications: *AMEX,*" Ron Lambert, "Answering Mr. Mathews," *AMEX* 2, 5 (August-September 1970), 8-9.

51 Ibid.

52 UBCL, RBSC, Renée Kasinsky fonds, box 4, file 12, "Interview with Nancy Pokhawk [sic], May 1970, Toronto, Quaker, Active in Exile Movement since 1965."

53 Robin Mathews, "The Americanization of Canada Means Precisely the Takeover of Canadian Culture by its Citizens," *Saturday Night,* May 1971, 20-22, cited in Churchill, "When Home Became Away," 227-28.

54 Ibid.

55 Ibid.

56 Ibid.

57 Dalhousie University Archives and Special Collections, Halifax, Nova Scotia, Canada (hereafter DAL), Nova Scotia Committee to Aid American War Objectors fonds, MS-10-7, box 1, folder 2, "Various Organizations That Aided American Draft-Dodgers," various publications.

58 UBCL, RBSC, Renée Kasinsky fonds, box 6, file 2, "Canadian Press on Emigrants, Deserters, Exiles," Melody Killian, "Oh, Canada!," *Yankee Refugee*, 4, 1969.

59 Ibid.

60 UBCL, RBSC, Renée Kasinsky fonds, box 6, file 3, "Canadian Publications," letter from Goldie Josephy and reply from the editors, *Yankee Refugee*, 5, 1969.

61 Bruce Curtis, *The Politics of Population: State Formation, Statistics, and the Census of Canada, 1849-1875* (Toronto: University of Toronto Press, 2001), 30, 309-10. See also James Scott, *Seeing Like a State: How Certain Schemes to Improve the Human Condition Have Failed* (New Haven: Yale University Press, 1998). Curtis is also drawing from a theory developed in Bruno Latour, *Science in Action* (Cambridge, MA: Harvard University Press, 1987), called "black-boxing." For a social science application and critique of Latour, see Susan Sturman, "On Black-boxing Gender: Some Social Questions for Bruno Latour," *Social Epistemology* 20, 2 (2006): 181-84.

62 Mark Phillips, interview with the author, Ottawa, ON, 11 July 2006.

63 Ibid.

64 The sole more recent exception appears to be John Whiteclay Chambers II, *To Raise an Army: The Draft Comes to Modern America* (New York: The Free Press, 1987).

65 See, for instance, Morris Janowitz, "Sociological Theory and Social Control," *American Journal of Sociology* 81, 1 (1975): 82-108; Joseph S. Roucek, ed., *Social Control for the 1980s: A Handbook for Order in a Democratic Society* (Westport, CT: Greenwood Press, 1978). Janowitz was also, interestingly, author of a foundational text in sociology and the military; see Morris Janowitz, in collaboration with Roger W. Little, *Sociology and the Military Establishment* (Beverly Hills, CA: Sage Publications, 1959). The social control thesis has been reformed, revised, and criticized; see Dany Lacombe, "Reforming Foucault: A Critique of the Social Control Thesis," *British Journal of Sociology* 47, 2 (1996): 332-52.

66 "Channeling," in *Ramparts Magazine* 6, 5 (December 1967), 34-35. For assessments of the practice of channelling see Roger W. Little, ed., *Selective Service and American Society* (New York: Russell Sage Foundation, 1969), 22-23; Steven L. Canby, *Military Manpower Procurement: A Policy Analysis* (Toronto: Lexington Books, 1972), 84-85; Eliot A. Cohen, *Citizens and Soldiers: The Dilemmas of Military Service* (Ithaca, NY: Cornell University Press, 1985), 163-64; and Michael S. Foley, *Confronting the War Machine: Draft Resistance during the Vietnam War* (Chapel Hill: University of North Carolina Press, 2003), 61-62.

67   See Gerard J. De Groot, *A Noble Cause? America and the Vietnam War* (Harlow: Longman, 2000), 312; Christian Appy, *Working-Class War: American Combat Soldiers and Vietnam* (Chapel Hill, NC: University of North Carolina Press, 1993); Robert Buzzanco, *Vietnam and the Transformation of American Life* (Malden, MA: Blackwell, 1999), 90-92, 220.

68   See, for instance, G. David Curry, *Sunshine Patriots: Punishment and the Vietnam Offender* (Notre Dame: University of Notre Dame Press, 1985), esp. 23, 25-27, 41-42, 70-71.

69   UBCL, RBSC, Renée Kasinsky fonds, box 5, file 10, "Articles on Channeling Analysis," Rick Ayers and Melody Killian, "Nowhere to Run, Nowhere to Hide," *The Movement*, June 1969, 14.

70   Kasinsky, *Refugees from Militarism*, 71. See also Kasinsky, *Refugees from Militarism*, 65-68, 71-74. See also Veronica Strong-Boag, Joan Anderson, Sherrill E. Grace, and Avigail Eisenberg, *Painting the Maple: Essays on Race, Gender, and the Construction of Canada* (Vancouver: UBC Press, 1998).

71   Paul Copeland, interview with the author, Ottawa, ON, 5 June 2006.

72   Surrey, "The Assimilation of Vietnam-Era Draft Dodgers," 80.

73   Ibid., 82; David S. Surrey, *Choice of Conscience: Vietnam Era Military and Draft Resisters in Canada* (New York: Praeger, 1982), 76.

74   Surrey, "The Assimilation of Vietnam-Era Draft Dodgers," 85.

75   Ibid., 161.

76   Surrey, *Choice of Conscience*, esp. 73-74.

77   See, for instance, Frank Kusch, *All American Boys: Draft Dodgers in Canada from the Vietnam War* (Westport, CT: Praeger Publishers, 2001), 75-77.

78   Douglas T. Miller, *On Our Own: Americans in the Sixties* (Toronto: D.C. Heath and Company, 1996), 196.

79   Joseph Jones, interview with the author by email, 21 November 2006.

80   UBCL, RBSC, Renée Kasinsky fonds, box 5, file 14, "Black Draft Dodgers"; and box 4, file 5, "Interviews – Black Draft Dodgers; E.J. Toronto, May 1970, and Fred."

81   For scholarly accounts that agree with this analysis, see Yasmeen Abu-Laban, "Keeping 'Em Out: Gender, Race, and Class Biases in Canadian Immigration Policy," in *Painting the Maple: Essays on Race, Gender, and the Construction of Canada*, ed. Veronica Strong-Boag et al. (Vancouver: UBC Press, 1998), 69-82.

82   UBCL, RBSC, Renée Kasinsky fonds, box 8, file 5, "Newspaper Articles – Dodgers and Deserters," "Political Asylum Is Demanded If Deserter Can't Enter Otherwise," *Toronto Daily Star*, 24 February 1970.

83   Joseph Healey Library, University of Massachusetts, Boston, Perrin, Richard, Papers, 1966-2001, series V, "Regina Committee of American Deserters (RCAD)," 1969.

84   LAC, Department of External Affairs fonds, RG 76, vol. 725, file 5660-2, "Military Personnel – Draft Dodgers – Complaints and Criticisms."

Chapter 6: Hegemonic Reflections

1 The poem in the epigraph appears by kind permission of Joe Nickell. Excerpt from Joe Nickell, "Hidden Places," in *Crossing Lines: Poets Who Came to Canada in the Vietnam War Era,* ed. Allan Briesmaster and Steven Michael Berzensky (Hamilton, ON: Seraphim Editions, 2008), 162.

2 University of British Columbia Library, Rare Books and Special Collections (hereafter UBCL, RBSC), Renée Kasinsky fonds, box 7, file 21, "Law Enforcement: RCMP Role re: American Exiles," Statement of D.B. Fine, 12 August 1969.

3 UBCL, RBSC, Renée Kasinsky fonds, box 7, file 21, "Law Enforcement: RCMP Role re: American Exiles," Donna Fine, "Action Taken after Police visit of August 12, 1969."

4 UBCL, RBSC, Renée Kasinsky fonds, box 6, file 13, "CBC *Weekend* transcript: Deserters Deportment Case; Interview with Rosenbloom," "Transcript of CBC *Weekend,* February 8 [1970]."

5 Reg Whitaker, *Double Standard: The Secret History of Canadian Immigration* (Toronto: Lester and Orpen Dennys, 1987), esp. 218-33.

6 Library and Archives Canada (hereafter LAC), Department of External Affairs fonds, RG 76, vol. 983, file 5660-1, "Military Personnel – Draft Dodgers – General," letter from Al Gorman, Chief of the Enforcement Section of the Department of Immigration's Home Services, to Commissioner W.L. Higgitt, RCMP, 26 November 1969; handwritten note from unsigned to "Al" [Gorman, Chief Enforcement Section of Home Services]; letter from Home Services Div., Immigration, to Barrette; handwritten notes, 22, 23, and 24 April 1970.

7 LAC, Canadian Security Intelligence Service fonds, RG 146, vol. 812, file "Pan-Canadian Conference for Deserters and Anti-War Organizations," memo from J.E.M. Barrette, Assistant Commissioner and Director of Security and Intelligence, RCMP, to A. Butroid, Special Assistant, Office of the Deputy Minister, Immigration Division, Department of Manpower and Immigration, 2 July 1970; UBCL, RBSC, Renée Kasinsky fonds, box 6, file 4, "Canadian Publications: *AMEX,*" "The Parley in Montreal," *AMEX* 2, 4 (June 1970): 5-11.

8 LAC, Canadian Security Intelligence Service fonds, RG 146, vol. 812, file "Pan-Canadian Conference of Deserters and Anti-War Organizations – Montreal, Que.," memo from J.E.M. Barrette, Assistant Commissioner and Director of Security and Intelligence, RCMP, to A. Butroid, Special Assistant, Office of the Deputy Minister, Immigration Division, Department of Manpower and Immigration, 2 July 1970, and copies to other officials.

9 As the memo itself was not released by LAC for public use, in accordance with the Access to Information Act, only the summary in the covering memo is available for reference.

10 LAC, Department of External Affairs fonds, RG 76, vol. 983, file 5660-1, "Military Personnel – Draft Dodgers - General," memo to the Minister from Robert Adams, "Draft dodgers and deserters – USA," 17 July 1970.

11 LAC, Department of External Affairs fonds, RG 76, vol. 983, file 5660-1, "Military Personnel – Draft Dodgers - General," handwritten note [names illegible], 6 July 1970.

12 LAC, RG 76, Department of Employment and Immigration fonds, vol. 1210, file 5660-1, "Military Personnel – Draft Dodgers – General."

13 UBCL, RBSC, Renée Kasinsky fonds, box 7, file 21, "Law Enforcement: RCMP Role re: American Exiles," "Voluntarily or Else," *Georgia Straight,* 11 November [1970]; UBCL, RBSC, Renée Kasinsky fonds, box 6, file 13, "CBC *Weekend* Transcript: Deserters Deportment Case; Interview with Rosenbloom," "transcript of CBC *Weekend,* February 8 [1970]"; UBCL, RBSC, Renée Kasinsky fonds, box 7, file 21, "Law Enforcement: RCMP Role re: American Exiles," "Inquiry Told RCMP Were There at Handing Over of US Deserters," *Montreal Star,* 26 March 1970; UBCL, RBSC, Renée Kasinsky fonds, box 1, file 4, "Questionnaire Code and Identification."

14 UBCL, RBSC, Renée Kasinsky fonds, box 6, file 4, "Canadian Publications: *AMEX,*" "RCMP Harassment of US Deserters: A Three-Year History," *AMEX* 2, 6 (October–November 1970).

15 UBCL, RBSC, Renée Kasinsky fonds, box 6, file 4, "Canadian Publications: *AMEX,*" "RCMP Harassment of US Deserters: A Three-Year History," *AMEX* 2, 6 (October–November 1970).

16 Ibid.; Renée G. Kasinsky, *Refugees from Militarism: Draft-Age Americans in Canada* (New Brunswick, NJ: Transaction Books, 1976), 3.

17 UBCL, RBSC, Renée Kasinsky fonds, box 7, file 21, "Law Enforcement: RCMP Role re: American Exiles," "Dusty House in B.C. Is End of Road for Draft Dodgers," *Montreal Star,* 26 March 1970.

18 UBCL, RBSC, Renée Kasinsky fonds, box 1, file 3, "Correspondence – Other Canadian Organizations with Committee."

19 UBCL, RBSC, Renée Kasinsky fonds, box 7, file 21, "Law Enforcement: RCMP Role re: American Exiles," "Cops Raid Deserters' Home: Ransack Files, Letters," *Georgia Straight,* n.d. Telephone tapping was already commonplace as an RCMP spying tactic, although as a practice it was regulated. Steve Hewitt, *Spying 101: The RCMP's Secret Activities at Canadian Universities, 1917-1997* (Toronto: University of Toronto Press, 2002), 146-70.

20 LAC, Canadian Security Intelligence Service fonds, RG 146, vol. 2804, file "Brief 325 - Student Administrative Council," University of Toronto, 6 October 1970, addressed to "D.G.S.I. [an unnamed RCMP official]," 16; LAC, Canadian Security Intelligence Service fonds, RG 146, vol. 2991, file "New Left Caucus, Toronto, ON."

21 Despite her clear involvement in the case, Wilson's spouse was not identified or interviewed.

22 UBCL, RBSC, Renée Kasinsky fonds, box 7, file 21, "Law Enforcement: RCMP Role re: American Exiles," "Police Power Creates Unease," *Montreal Star,* 24 March 1970; "McIlwraith Denies RCMP Harassed *Montreal Star* Newsman," *Montreal Star,*

26 March 1970; "RCMP Told to Stop Probing US Deserters," *Montreal Star,* 24 April 1970.

23 UBCL, RBSC, Renée Kasinsky fonds, box 7, file 21, "Law Enforcement: RCMP Role re: American Exiles," "McIlwraith Denies RCMP Harassed *Montreal Star* Newsman," *Montreal Star,* 26 March 1970.

24 UBCL, RBSC, Renée Kasinsky fonds, box 7, file 21, "Law Enforcement: RCMP Role re: American Exiles," "RCMP Seizing a Political Role," *Montreal Star,* 7 April 1970.

25 Steve Hewitt refers to these years as "The Crisis Years," suggesting both the crisis of legitimacy of the RCMP and a political crisis to which the RCMP needed to respond. Hewitt, *Spying 101,* 146-70.

26 Hewitt, *Spying 101,* 25; Canadian Security Intelligence Service, "ARCHIVED: Backgrounder No. 5 – A Historical Perspective on CSIS," http://www.csis-scrs.gc.ca; LAC, Royal Commissions of Inquiry [archived content], "Commission of Inquiry Concerning Certain Activities of the Royal Canadian Mounted Police, 1977-1981," http://epe.lac-bac.gc.ca.

27 Two books, the publication of which coincided with the RCMP's centennial, illustrate the competing views of police behaviour in the early 1970s: Nora Kelly and William Kelly, *The Royal Canadian Mounted Police: A Century of History, 1873-1973* (Edmonton, AB: Hurtig Publishers, 1973); and Lorne Brown and Caroline Brown, *An Unauthorized History of the RCMP* (Toronto: James Lewis and Samuel, 1973). The Kellys' book, taking an institutional approach, accents the nobility of the RCMP's mission and calling; the Browns' polemical work depicts RCMP officers as violent strike breakers.

28 UBCL, RBSC, Renée Kasinsky fonds, box 7, file 21, "Law Enforcement: RCMP Role re: American Exiles," "Deserter Suspects Committed to Trial," *Montreal Star,* 3 April 1970.

29 UBCL, RBSC, Renée Kasinsky fonds, box 9, file 12, "Vancouver Support for Dodgers and Deserters," "Vancouver's Mayor 'Not Against Dissent,'" *Toronto Daily Star,* 26 October 1970.

30 UBCL, RBSC, Renée Kasinsky fonds, box 3, file 11, "Interviews," "Interview with Bill, Vietnam Vet, Montreal, [1970]."

31 Ibid.

32 Ian McKay, *Rebels, Reds, Radicals: Rethinking Canada's Left History* (Toronto: Between the Lines, 2005), 185-89; Bryan Palmer, *Canada's 1960s: The Ironies of Identity in a Rebellious Era* (Toronto: University of Toronto Press, 2009), 245-310.

33 McKay, *Rebels, Reds, Radicals,* 185-89.

34 Douglas Nesbitt, "The 'Radical Trip' of the Canadian Union of Students, 1963-69" (MA thesis, Trent University, 2009), 151-52 and footnotes, citing LAC, Canadian Union of Students fonds, MG 28, I 61, box 11, July 1968, Bob Baldwin, "An Analysis of US Imperialism," and August 1968, Peter Warrian, "Capitalism and the Underdevelopment of Canada." Nesbitt also provides insights into SUPA connections with CUS.

35 Mark Phillips, interview with the author, Ottawa, ON, 11 July 2006.
36 Hardy Scott, interview with the author by mail, 31 October 2006.
37 LAC, RG 76, Department of Employment and Immigration fonds, vol. 983, file 5660-1, "Military Personnel – Draft Dodgers – General," "Pacifist Adviser," *Globe and Mail*, 6 May 1966.
38 Ken Fisher, interview with the author, Gatineau, QC, 9 June 2006.
39 Paul Copeland, interview with the author, Ottawa, ON, 5 June 2006.
40 UBCL, RBSC, Renée Kasinsky fonds, box 4, file 12, "Interview with Nancy Pokhawk [sic], May 1970, Toronto, Quaker, Active in Exile Movement since 1965."
41 Ibid.
42 Ibid.
43 UBCL, RBSC, Renée Kasinsky fonds, box 4, file 7, "Interview with Doyle, Deserter, Toronto, A.E. Union," n.d.
44 UBCL, RBSC, Renée Kasinsky fonds, box 5, file 8, "Analysis of Desertion – ADC's Political Activity," clippings and articles, "American Deserters Committee Running," *The Peak*, 15 October 1969.
45 UBCL, RBSC, Renée Kasinsky fonds, box 7, file 1, "Declaration of Purpose and History of American Deserters Committee – Montreal," 1969.
46 UBCL, RBSC, Renée Kasinsky fonds, box 6, file 4, "Canadian Publications – *AMEX*," "Toronto ADC plays Spy Games," *AMEX* 2, 4 (June 1970).
47 UBCL, RBSC, Renée Kasinsky fonds, box 5, file 13, "Assorted Articles," "Montreal, P.Q.: An Organizational Split (Now There Are Three Immigrant Groups There) and a Bombing of One of the Groups," *AMEX*, unknown date.
48 UBCL, RBSC, Renée Kasinsky fonds, box 5, file 8, "Analysis of Desertion – ADC's Political Activity," clippings and articles.
49 UBCL, RBSC, Renée Kasinsky fonds, box 5, file 11, "Articles on Deserters," *The Movement*, June 1969.
50 UBCL, RBSC, Renée Kasinsky fonds, box 1, file 3, "Correspondence – Other Canadian Organizations with Committee."
51 UBCL, RBSC, Renée Kasinsky fonds, box 6, file 2, "Canadian Press on Emigrants, Deserters, Exiles," Melody Killian, "Oh, Canada!," *Yankee Refugee*, 4, 1969.
52 UBCL, RBSC, Renée Kasinsky fonds, box 6, file 3, "Canadian Publications," letter from Goldie Josephy and reply from the editors, *Yankee Refugee*, 5, [1970].
53 Herbert Marcuse, *Repressive Tolerance*, 1965, http://www.marcuse.org/.
54 UBCL, RBSC, Renée Kasinsky fonds, box 6, file 4, "Canadian Publications – *AMEX*," "Like Washington, Some People Are Only Interested in Body Counts," *AMEX* 2, 2 ([February-March] 1970).
55 UBCL, RBSC, Renée Kasinsky fonds, box 6, file 4, "Canadian Publications: *AMEX*," letter from Vance Gardner, Montreal Council to Aid War Resisters, Montreal, 25 February 1970, *AMEX* 2, 3 (April-May 1970).

56 UBCL, RBSC, Renée Kasinsky fonds, box 6, file 4, "Canadian Publications: *AMEX*," letter from R. Whitteair, American Deserters Committee, Montreal, 3 February 1970, in *AMEX* 2, 3 (April-May 1970).

57 UBCL, RBSC, Renée Kasinsky fonds, box 6, file 4, "Canadian Publications: *AMEX*," letter from Vance Gardner, Montreal Council to Aid War Resisters, Montreal, 25 February 1970, in *AMEX* 2, 3 (April-May 1970).

58 UBCL, RBSC, Renée Kasinsky fonds, box 6, file 4, "Canadian Publications: *AMEX*," Sol Burrows (Winnipeg Committee to Assist War Objectors), "Lay Off Bill Spira," *AMEX* 2, 5 (September 1970).

59 UBCL, RBSC, Renée Kasinsky fonds, box 4, file 14, "Interview with Bill Spira of the Toronto Anti-Draft Program [sic], June 1970."

60 Ibid.

61 UBCL, RBSC, Renée Kasinsky fonds, box 5, file 8, "Analysis of Desertion – ADC's Political Activity," Fred Gardner, "The Future of Desertion," *Hard Times*, 4-11 May 1970.

62 Joseph Jones, interview with the author by email, 21 November 2006.

63 UBCL, RBSC, Renée Kasinsky fonds, box 8, file 5, "Newspaper Articles – Dodgers and Deserters," "Some US Exiles Here Have Faulty Priorities," *Vancouver Sun*, 25 September 1970.

64 UBCL, RBSC, Renée Kasinsky fonds, box 6, file 4, "Canadian Publications – *AMEX*," "Ottawa: Amexiles Who Settle in Ottawa Easily Forget from Whence They Came," *AMEX* 2, 6 (October–November 1970).

65 UBCL, RBSC, Renée Kasinsky fonds, box 5, file 8, "Analysis of Desertion – ADC's Political Activity," *Yankee Refugee* staff, "Americans in Canada," n.d.

66 UBCL, RBSC, Renée Kasinsky fonds, box 1, file 3, "Correspondence – Other Canadian Organizations with Committee," letter from Union of American Exiles, received by TADP on 15 May 1969.

67 UBCL, RBSC, Renée Kasinsky fonds, box 6, file 4, "Canadian Publications – *AMEX*," "The Parley in Montreal," *AMEX* 2, 4 (June 1970), 5-11; and box 7, file 25, "Materials for Chapters VII to IX," "Report on the Pan-Canada Deserter/Resistor [sic] Conference."

68 UBCL, RBSC, Renée Kasinsky fonds, box 1, file 3, "Correspondence – Other Canadian Organizations with Committee," letter from Union of American Exiles, received by TADP on 15 May 1969. The conference was referred to in various ways, sometimes referring to pan-Canada and sometimes pan-Canadian. At times the title included the word "Deserters." This book uses *AMEX*'s title.

69 University of Toronto, Thomas Fisher Rare Book Library (hereafter TF), Pocock (Jack) Memorial Collection, box 13, "Lobbying and Public Relations," Folder 3, "TADP Statements and Lobbying," various correspondence.

70 LAC, Voice of Women fonds, MG 28, I 218, vol. 12, file 3, "Draft Resistance: Correspondence; Printed Material; Clippings," 1966-73.

71   UBCL, RBSC, Renée Kasinsky fonds, box 6, file 4, "Canadian Publications: *AMEX*," "The Parley in Montreal," *AMEX* 2, 4 (June 1970), 5-11; and box 7, file 25, "Materials for Chapters VII to IX," "Report on the Pan-Canada Deserter/Resistor [sic] Conference."

72   UBCL, RBSC, Renée Kasinsky fonds, box 7, file 25, "Materials for Chapters VII to IX," "Report on the Pan-Canada Deserter/Resistor [sic] Conference." The presence of the Front de libération populaire is one of very few hints of linkages between francophones in Quebec and war resisters.

73   Ibid.

74   UBCL, RBSC, Renée Kasinsky fonds, box 6, file 4, "Canadian Publications: *AMEX*," "The Parley in Montreal," *AMEX* 2, 4 (June 1970), 5-11; and box 7, file 25, "Materials for Chapters VII to IX," "Report on the Pan-Canada Deserter/Resistor [sic] Conference."

75   UBCL, RBSC, Renée Kasinsky fonds, box 6, file 4, "Canadian Publications: *AMEX*," "The Parley in Montreal," *AMEX* 2, 4 (June 1970), 5-11; and box 7, file 25, "Materials for Chapters VII to IX," "Report on the Pan-Canada Deserter/Resistor [sic] Conference." *AMEX* also noted the absence of Spira and one or two others.

76   LAC, MG 30, D 326, Judith Merril fonds, vol. 33, file "Anti-War Movement in Toronto," "Proposal from RWB and *AMEX* for Structure and Operating Procedure of a Pan-Canadian Information Centre," n.d.

77   UBCL, RBSC, Renée Kasinsky fonds, box 7, file 25, "Materials for Chapters VII to IX," "Report on the Pan-Canada Deserter/Resistor [sic] Conference"; UBCL, RBSC, Renée Kasinsky fonds, box 7, file 10, "*EXNET Bulletin*," *EXNET* issues 3, 4, 5, and 7, 28 July 1970.

78   LAC, MG 30, D 326, Judith Merril fonds, vol. 33, file "Anti-War Movement in Toronto," letter from *EXNET*/RWB, Toronto, to "all groups in Canada Assisting American Exiles", n.d., and enclosure, "Type of Information Required"; LAC, MG 30, D 326, Judith Merril fonds, vol. 33, file unnumbered, "Anti-war Movement in Toronto," *EXNET Bulletin*, 1 (16 June 1970).

79   UBCL, RBSC, Renée Kasinsky fonds, box 7, file 25, "Materials for Chapters VII to IX," "Report on the Pan-Canada Deserter/Resistor [sic] Conference."

80   Ibid.

81   Ibid.

82   See Sara Evans, *Personal Politics: The Roots of Women's Liberation in the Civil Rights Movement and the New Left* (New York: Alfred A. Knopf, 1979); and Alison Prentice et al., *Canadian Women: A History* (Toronto: Harcourt Brace Jovanovich, 1988), esp. 343-66.

83   UBCL, RBSC, Renée Kasinsky fonds, box 6, file 4, "Canadian Publications: *AMEX*," "The Parley in Montreal," *AMEX* 2, 4 (June 1970), 8-9. Anti-draft activist Naomi Wall's recollection of an antiwar conference, mentioned and cited in Prentice et al., may in fact be a recollection of the Pan-Canadian Conference of US War Resisters. See Prentice et al., *Canadian Women*, 352-53.

84 UBCL, RBSC, Renée Kasinsky fonds, box 6, file 4, "Canadian Publications: *AMEX*," "The Parley in Montreal," *AMEX* 2, 4 (June 1970), 5-11; and box 7, file 25, "Materials for Chapters VII to IX," "Report on the Pan-Canada Deserter/Resistor [sic] Conference."

85 UBCL, RBSC, Renée Kasinsky fonds, box 7, file 25, "Materials for Chapters VII to IX," "GI Movement News," *National Guardian* (New York, NY), May 1970.

86 UBCL, RBSC, Renée Kasinsky fonds, box 6, file 4, "Canadian Publications: *AMEX*," "The Parley in Montreal," *AMEX* 2, 4 (June 1970), 11; and box 7, file 25, "Materials for Chapters VII to IX," "Report on the Pan-Canada Deserter/Resistor [sic] Conference."

87 UBCL, RBSC, Renée Kasinsky fonds, box 6, file 4, "Canadian Publications: *AMEX*," "At TADP ... Priority Counselling," *AMEX* 2, 8 (April 1971), 30.

Chapter 7: "Last Chance to Get Landed"

1 The poem in the epigraph appears by kind permission of Ronnie R. Brown. Ronnie R. Brown, "XIII. Home," excerpt from "Un-Deferred: A Draft Dodger's Wife Remembers" in *Crossing Lines: Poets Who Came to Canada in the Vietnam War Era*, ed. Allan Briesmaster and Steven Michael Berzensky (Hamilton, ON: Seraphim Editions, 2008), 55.

2 University of British Columbia Library, Rare Books and Special Collections (hereafter UBCL, RBSC), Renée Kasinsky fonds, box 8, file 5, "Newspaper Articles – Dodgers and Deserters," "Far Fewer Seek Canadian Refuge," *Vancouver Sun*, 25 September 1970.

3 See Valerie Knowles, *Strangers at Our Gates: Canadian Immigration and Immigration Policy, 1540-1990* (Toronto: Dundurn Press, 1992), esp. 161-65, 173.

4 Renée Kasinsky, *Refugees from Militarism: Draft-Age Americans in Canada* (New Brunswick, NJ: Transaction Books, 1976), 69.

5 Bruce Curtis, *The Politics of Population: State Formation, Statistics, and the Census of Canada, 1849-1875* (Toronto: University of Toronto Press, 2001), 309.

6 The story of these regulations is touched upon (although never studied in depth) in other immigration histories. One exception is an international study by political scientist Freda Hawkins: *Critical Years in Immigration: Canada and Australia Compared* (Montreal and Kingston: McGill-Queen's Press, 1991).

7 Library and Archives Canada (hereafter LAC), RG 76, Department of Employment and Immigration fonds, vol. 1135, file 5235-6, pt. 1, "Deportation – Appeals Backlog," memo from Assistant Deputy Minister (Immigration) to Deputy Minister, 14 November 1969.

8 UBCL, RBSC, Renée Kasinsky fonds, box 8, file 5, "Newspaper Articles – Dodgers and Deserters," "Immigration Department Reviews 'Draft Dodger Rule,'" *Vancouver Sun*, 25 September 1970.

9 LAC, Department of External Affairs fonds, RG 76, vol. 1135, file 5235-6, pt. 1, "Deportation – Appeals Backlog," "Migration Logjam Worsens," *Edmonton Journal*, 28 May 1971; noted on sheet in blue pen, "same in *Ottawa Journal*."

10 LAC, Department of External Affairs fonds, RG 76, vol. 1135, file 5235-6, pt. 1, "Deportation – Appeals Backlog," *Toronto Sun,* "Immigration Heads to Quit over Scrapped Amendments," 23 February 1972.

11 LAC, Department of External Affairs fonds, RG 76, vol. 1135, file 5235-6, pt. 1, "Deportation – Appeals Backlog," memo to the Minister from Deputy Minister L.E. Couillard, "Alternative Measures for Dealing with Current Major Immigration Problems," 15 January 1972.

12 LAC, Department of External Affairs fonds, RG 76, vol. 1135, file 5235-6, pt. 1, "Deportation – Appeals Backlog," memorandum to the Cabinet from Minister of Manpower and Immigration Bryce Mackasey, "Administrative Program to Reduce the Size and Growth of Immigration Inquiry and Appeal Backlogs," 17 February 1972.

13 LAC, Department of External Affairs fonds, RG 76, vol. 1135, file 5235-6, pt. 1, "Deportation – Appeals Backlog," memorandum to the Cabinet from Minister of Manpower and Immigration Bryce Mackasey, "Administrative Program to Reduce the Size and Growth of Immigration Inquiry and Appeal Backlogs," 17 February 1972.

14 LAC, Department of External Affairs fonds, RG 76, vol. 1135, file 5235-6, pt. 1, "Deportation – Appeals Backlog," memo to the Minister from J.M. Desroches, Assistant Deputy Minister, "April 27 directive from Cabinet," 8 May 1972.

15 LAC, Department of External Affairs fonds, RG 76, vol. 1135, file 5235-6, pt. 1, "Deportation – Appeals Backlog," memorandum to the Minister, from J.M. Desroches, Assistant Deputy Minister, "Progress Report on Implementation of Administrative Program," 18 May 1972.

16 LAC, Department of External Affairs fonds, RG 76, vol. 1135, file 5235-6, pt. 1, "Deportation – Appeals Backlog," Office of Manpower and Immigration, press release, 22 June 1972.

17 LAC, Department of External Affairs fonds, RG 76, vol. 1135, file 5235-6, pt. 1, "Deportation – Appeals Backlog," "Statement by the Honourable Bryce Mackasey, Minister of Manpower and Immigration, in the House of Commons, June 22, 1972: New Measures to Expedite Immigration Inquiry Cases."

18 LAC, Department of External Affairs fonds, RG 76, vol. 1135, file 5235-6, pt. 1, "Deportation – Appeals Backlog," Office of Manpower and Immigration, press release, 23 June 1972.

19 LAC, Department of External Affairs fonds, RG 76, vol. 1135, file 5235-6, pt. 1, "Deportation – Appeals Backlog," memo to the Minister from the Deputy Minister, 9 August 1972; Memo to the Assistant Deputy Minister, from the Director, Home Services Branch, 25 August 1972.

20 LAC, Department of External Affairs fonds, RG 76, vol. 994, file 5855-12-7-2, "Selection and Processing – Applications – Revocation of Sec. 34 of the Regulations – Statistics," Toronto International Airport, Officer-in-Charge, to Director – Home Services, Attn. Mr. McKenna, 9 December 1972.

21 LAC, Department of External Affairs fonds, RG 76, vol. 994, file 5855-12-7-2, "Selection and Processing – Applications – Revocation of Sec. 34 of the Regulations – Statistics," secret memo to the Minister from J.M. Desroches.

22 LAC, Department of External Affairs fonds, RG 76, vol. 1135, file 5235-6, pt. 1, "Deportation – Appeals Backlog," memorandum from Director, Programs and Procedures Branch, to Assistant Deputy Minister, Immigration, "Project P-80 – Progress Report on Review Cases," 6 February 1973.

23 LAC, Department of External Affairs fonds, RG 76, vol. 983, file 5660-1, "Military Personnel – Draft Dodgers – General," memo from James S. Cross to Robert M. Adams, "Submission to the Minister Respecting Procedures for Applicants from the United States," 13 June 1972.

24 LAC, Department of External Affairs fonds, RG 76, vol. 1135, file 5235-6, pt. 1, "Deportation – Appeals Backlog," memorandum to the Deputy Minister from the Assistant Deputy Minister (Immigration), "Developments in Immigration Legislation and Policy," 11 December 1973; University of Toronto, Thomas Fisher Rare Book Library (hereafter TF), Pocock (Jack) Memorial Collection, box 14, "Canadian Adjustment of Status Program," folder 18, "Manpower and Immigration Statements."

25 TF, Pocock (Jack) Memorial Collection, box 13, "Lobbying and Public Relations," folder 1, "TADP Statements and Lobbying."

26 LAC, Department of External Affairs fonds, RG 76, vol. 1135, file 5235-6, "Deportation – Appeals Backlog," pt. 1, "Injustice in the Immigration Reform," *Toronto Star,* 12 March 1973.

27 TF, Pocock (Jack) Memorial Collection, box 27 [oversize], folder 2, continued from box 14, "Canadian Adjustment of Status Program," folder 27, "Adjustment of Status Program Clippings," *Toronto Star,* editorial, "Stranded 'Visitors' Deserve Justice," 18, 17 March 1973.

28 TF, Pocock (Jack) Memorial Collection, *box* 14, "Canadian Adjustment of Status Program," folder 10, "Adjustment of Status Program – Correspondence, Press Releases, Notes," letter to Trudeau from Quaker Social Concerns Committee of Vancouver, 8 May 1973.

29 TF, Pocock (Jack) Memorial Collection, box 14, "Canadian Adjustment of Status Program," folder 10, "Adjustment of Status Program – Correspondence, Press Releases, Notes," letter to Andrew Brewin, MP, from Richard Brown, Toronto Anti-Draft Programme (TADP), 8 June 1973.

30 Dalhousie University Archives and Special Collections, Halifax, Nova Scotia, Canada (hereafter DAL), Nova Scotia Committee to Aid American War Objectors fonds, MS-10-7, box 2, folder 6, "Requests for Help or Information on How to Emigrate," correspondence, 1972-73.

31 DAL, Nova Scotia Committee to Aid American War Objectors fonds, MS-10-7, box 2, folder 2, "Counselling Records."

32 LAC, MG 28, I 327, Canadian Council of Churches fonds, box 39, file 39-6, "Commission on Canadian Affairs Minutes – Ministry to Draft-Age US Immigrants – Accountability Committee and Others," 1969-73, minutes, Accountability Committee, 14 December 1972.

33 LAC, MG 28, I 327, Canadian Council of Churches fonds, box 39, file 39-6, "Commission on Canadian Affairs Minutes – Ministry to Draft-Age US Immigrants – Accountability Committee and Others," 1969-73, minutes, Accountability Committee, 29 March 1972.

34 DAL, Nova Scotia Committee to Aid American War Objectors fonds, MS-10-7, box 2, folder 7, "Organizational Correspondence."

35 TF, Pocock (Jack) Memorial Collection, box 14, "Canadian Adjustment of Status Program," folder 3, "November 1972 Immigration Changes," TADP to American Friends Service Committee, 16 November 1972.

36 Some argue the shifts were because of Mackasey's handling of the labour and then immigration portfolios, leading him to resign amid criticism: Knowles, *Strangers at Our Gates,* 163; CBC, *cbcnews.ca,* "Former Liberal Minister Bryce Mackasey Dies," 6 September 1999, http://www.cbc.ca/.

37 For an excellent overview of the debate over multiculturalism from 1960 to 1975, see Howard Palmer, "Reluctant Hosts: Anglo-Canadian Views of Multiculturalism in the Twentieth Century," in *Multiculturalism as State Policy* (Canadian Council of Multiculturalism, Ottawa: Department of Secretary of State for Canada, 1976), reprinted in *Immigration in Canada: Historical Perspectives,* ed. Gerald Tulchisky (Toronto: Copp Clark Longman, 1994), 316-26. See also Michael Dewing, Marc Leman, "Canadian Multiculturalism," Library of Parliament Political and Social Affairs Division, revised 16 March 2006, http://www.parl.gc.ca/.

38 Knowles, *Strangers at Our Gates,* 163; "Metro Death Prompts Immigration Demands," *Globe and Mail,* 8 June 1972, 1.

39 Stanley McDowell, "Angry over Misinformation in Toronto Suicide, Mackasey Warns 'Reactionary' Officials," *Globe and Mail,* 16 June 1972, 1.

40 LAC, Department of External Affairs fonds, RG 76, vol. 1135, file 5235-6, pt. 1, "Deportation – Appeals Backlog," memorandum to the minister, "The Immigration Situation," 26 January 1973; and "Briefing Paper for Minister: Non-Immigrant Control and Non-Immigrant Applicants for Landing in Canada."

41 LAC, Department of External Affairs fonds, RG 76, vol. 996, file 5875-5-1, pt. 1, "Status Adjustment Program – 1973 – Status Adjustment Procedures – General," memo from Assistant Deputy Minister, Operations, to Assistant Deputy Minister, Immigration, 11 April 1973, "Minister's Request for Recommendations from Department"; Memo to J.R. Robillard, Director, Immigration Operations, from V.A. Latour, Manager, Program Forecast Section, "Implementation of 1973 Amendments to the Immigration Appeal Board Act," 22 June 1973.

42 TF, Pocock (Jack) Memorial Collection, box 14, "Canadian Adjustment of Status Program," folder 18, "Manpower and Immigration Statements," release, 18 June 1973.

43 TF, Pocock (Jack) Memorial Collection, box 14, "Canadian Adjustment of Status Program," folder 19, "Manpower and Immigration Statements," "An Address by the Honourable Robert Andras, Minister of Manpower and Immigration, On Second Reading of an Act to Amend the Immigration Appeal Board Act," 20 June 1973.

44 Formerly staff in External Affairs, and deputy minister of communications from 1969 to 1973; later undersecretary of state for external affairs. Department of External Affairs, "Mr. Allan Gotlieb," modified 30 April 2007, http://www.international.gc.ca/.

45 LAC, Department of External Affairs fonds, RG 76, vol. 996, file 5875-5-1, pt. 1, "Status Adjustment Program – 1973 – Status Adjustment Procedures – General," memo to the Minister from A.E. Gotlieb, Deputy Minister, 20 June 1973, "Length of Registration Period of Adjustment Program."

46 LAC, Department of External Affairs fonds, RG 76, vol. 996, file 5875-5-1, pt. 1, "Status Adjustment Program – 1973 – Status Adjustment Procedures – General," copy of "Adjustment of Status Regulations, 1973," 21 June 1973.

47 LAC, Department of External Affairs fonds, RG 76, vol. 996, file 5875-5-1, pt. 1, "Status Adjustment Program – 1973 – Status Adjustment Procedures – General," telex to Manpower Immigration Ottawa from Manpower Immigration Vancouver, 22 June 1973.

48 LAC, Department of External Affairs fonds, RG 76, vol. 996, file 5875-5-1, pt. 1, "Status Adjustment Program – 1973 – Status Adjustment Procedures – General," telex from Director of Operations (Immigration) to all Directors of Immigration Offices, 22 June 1973; LAC, Department of External Affairs fonds, RG 76, vol. 996, file 5875-5-1, pt. 1, "Status Adjustment Program – 1973 – Status Adjustment Procedures – General," memo to J.R. Robillard, Director, Immigration Operations, from V.A. Latour, Manager, Program Forecast Section, "Implementation of 1973 Amendments to the Immigration Appeal Board Act," 22 June 1973.

49 LAC, Department of External Affairs fonds, RG 76, vol. 996, file 5875-5-1, pt. 1, "Status Adjustment Program – 1973 – Status Adjustment Procedures – General," memo from J.R. Robillard, Director of Operations – Immigration, to J.E. McKenna, Director, Home Services Branch, "Implementation of Bill C-197," 19 July 1973.

50 LAC, Department of External Affairs fonds, RG 76, vol. 996, file 5875-5-1, pt. 1, "Status Adjustment Program – 1973 – Status Adjustment Procedures – General," memo from J.E. McKenna, Director, Home Services Branch, to Director, Programs and Procedures Branch, 18 July 1973; Memo to the Deputy Minister from Assistant Deputy Minister (Immigration), "Immigration Adjustment of Status Program," 18 July 1973.

51 LAC, Department of External Affairs fonds, RG 76, vol. 996, file 5875-5-1, pt. 1, "Status Adjustment Program – 1973 – Status Adjustment Procedures – General," memo to the Minister from Gotlieb, n.d. See Steve Hewitt, *Spying 101: The RCMP's Secret Activities*

at Canadian Universities, 1917-1997 (Toronto: University of Toronto Press, 2002) for more on RCMP spying on university professors.

52 The International Students Organization was founded in 1958 "to ease the life of international students while away from their home country." ISO, "About the ISO," accessed 6 July 2008, http://www.isoa.org/.

53 LAC, Department of External Affairs fonds, RG 76, vol. 996, file 5875-5-1, pt. 1, "Status Adjustment Program – 1973 – Status Adjustment Procedures – General," [hand-written] memo from James Cross to "MHB" [Director, Programs and Procedures Branch], 10 July 1973; Memo from J.S. Cross to file, "Position of Students under the Status Adjustment Program," 11 July 1973; Memo from J.E. McKenna, Director, Home Services Branch, to Director, Programs and Procedures Branch, 18 July 1973.

54 LAC, Department of External Affairs fonds, RG 76, vol. 996, file 5875-5-1, pt. 1, "Status Adjustment Program – 1973 – Status Adjustment Procedures – General," memo from J.W. Dobson, Executive Assistant to the Assistant Deputy Minister – Immigration, to Director, Home Services Branch, and Director, Programs and Procedures Branch, "Proclamation Date of Bill C-197 – Effect on University Community," 20 July 1973; Memo from Gotlieb to the Minister, "Immigration Adjustment of Status Regulation," 27 July 1973. The Association of Universities and Colleges of Canada (AUCC) was founded in 1911 and incorporated by Parliament in 1965. AUCC, "About Us," 2013, http://www.aucc.ca/.

55 LAC, Department of External Affairs fonds, RG 76, vol. 996, file 5875-5-1, pt. 1, "Status Adjustment Program – 1973 – Status Adjustment Procedures – General," memo to J.R. Robillard, Director, Immigration Operations, from V.A. Latour, Manager, Program Forecast Section, "Implementation of 1973 Amendments to the Immigration Appeal Board Act," 22 June 1973.

56 TF, Pocock (Jack) Memorial Collection, box 14, "Canadian Adjustment of Status Program," folder 19, "Manpower and Immigration statements," press release, 31 July 1973; Kasinsky, *Refugees from Militarism,* 69; LAC, Department of External Affairs fonds, RG 76, vol. 996, file 5875-5-1, pt. 1, "Status Adjustment Program – 1973 – Status Adjustment Procedures – General," telex from Assistant Deputy Ministers Immigration and Operations to all Regional Directors General, 31 July 1973; copy of proclamation on file, 31 July 1973.

57 LAC, Department of External Affairs fonds, RG 76, vol. 996, file 5875-5-1, pt. 1, "Status Adjustment Program – 1973 – Status Adjustment Procedures – General," memo from J.E. McKenna, Director, Home Services Branch, to Directors of Immigration Offices, 29 August 1973.

58 LAC, Department of External Affairs fonds, RG 76, vol. 1135, file 5235-6, pt. 1, "Deportation – Appeals Backlog," memorandum to the Deputy Minister from the Assistant Deputy Minister (Immigration), 11 December 1973; RG 76, vol. 1030, file 5000-27-1, "Immigration – General Series – Immigration Program (1973),"

memorandum from Deputy Minister to Assistant Deputy Minister (Immigration), "Developments in Immigration Legislation and Policy," 11 December 1973.

59 LAC, Department of External Affairs fonds, RG 76, vol. 996, file 5875-5-1, pt. 1, "Status Adjustment Program – 1973 – Status Adjustment Procedures – General," memo from J.E. McKenna, Director, Home Services Branch, to Directors of Immigration Offices, 29 August 1973.

60 LAC, Department of External Affairs fonds, RG 76, vol. 996, file 5875-5-1, pt. 1, "Status Adjustment Program – 1973 – Status Adjustment Procedures – General," memo to J.A. Hunter, Director of Operations – Manpower, from Oldfield, "Immigration Adjustment of Status Program."

61 DAL, Nova Scotia Committee to Aid American War Objectors fonds, MS-10-7, file 1.1 [Manpower and Immigration publications].

62 Ibid., file 1.2 [Various publications].

63 UBCL, RBSC, Renée Kasinsky fonds, box 6, file 5, "Canadian Publications: *AMEX*," "Immigration 'Grace Period' Ends, No Extension," *AMEX* 4, 5 (November-December 1973), 21.

64 TF, Pocock (Jack) Memorial Collection, box 14, "Canadian Adjustment of Status Program," folder 4, "'Regional Coordinators' and TADP Memo on Canadian Adjustment of Status Program," letter from Dan Zimmerman, Mona Zimmerman, Regional Co-ordinators for Toronto Anti-Draft, to "Friends", n.d. The Department of Immigration did not make estimates based on country of origin.

65 DAL, Nova Scotia Committee to Aid American War Objectors fonds, MS-10-7, file 1.2 [Various publications].

66 TF, Pocock (Jack) Memorial Collection, box 14, "Canadian Adjustment of Status Program," folder 5, "'60 Days of Grace' TADP Information Sheet."

67 TF, Pocock (Jack) Memorial Collection, box 2, "TADP Intake Records, Sales Records, Stationery, and Other Materials," folder 6, *Manual for Draft-Age Immigrants to Canada*, 6th edition corrections.

68 LAC, MG 28, I 327, Canadian Council of Churches fonds, box 39, file 39-6, "Commission on Canadian Affairs Minutes – Ministry to Draft-Age US Immigrants – Accountability Committee and Others," 1969-73; TF, Pocock (Jack) Memorial Collection, box 14, "Canadian Adjustment of Status Program," folder 13, "Correspondence, Press Releases, and Notes," letter to the Members of the Commission on Canadian Affairs, from (Rev. Canon) Maurice Wilkinson, Associate Secretary, 18 July 1973.

69 TF, Pocock (Jack) Memorial Collection, box 14, "Canadian Adjustment of Status Program," folder 13, "Correspondence, Press Releases, and Notes," "US Draft Age Immigrants in Canada – Report on Meeting in Winnipeg," [July 1973]; TF, Pocock (Jack) Memorial Collection, box 14, "Canadian Adjustment of Status Program," folder 2, "Correspondence, Press Releases, and Notes," "CCC Meeting," [July 1973].

70　LAC, Voice of Women fonds, MG 28, I 218, vol. 12, file 3, "Draft Resistance: Correspondence; Printed Material; Clippings," 1966-73, letter to Women Strike for Peace contacts and friends from WSP, 13 July 1973.

71　TF, Pocock (Jack) Memorial Collection, box 14, "Canadian Adjustment of Status Program," folder 10, "Correspondence, Press Releases, and Notes," "News," the United Church of Canada, 1 August 1973.

72　TF, Pocock (Jack) Memorial Collection, box 14, "Canadian Adjustment of Status Program," folder 8, "Press Release, 31 July 1973, 7:30 p.m. and Drafts," "War Resister's Aide [sic] Centres Launch 60 Day Immigration Drive," 31 July 1973; TF, Pocock (Jack) Memorial Collection, box 13, "Lobbying and Public Relations," folder 8, "TADP Statements and Lobbying," Canadian Coalition of War Resisters, press release, "War Resister's Aide [sic] Centres Launch 60 Day Immigration Drive," 31 July 1973.

73　TF, Pocock (Jack) Memorial Collection, box 14, "Canadian Adjustment of Status Program," folder 8, "Press Release, 31 July 1973, 7:30 p.m. and Drafts," "War Resister's Aide [sic] Centres Launch 60 Day Immigration Drive," 31 July 1973.

74　DAL, Nova Scotia Committee to Aid American War Objectors fonds, MS-10-7, file 1.2 [Various publications].

75　TF, Pocock (Jack) Memorial Collection, box 13, "Lobbying and Public Relations," folder 9, "Press Release Aug 6 1973, and Drafts," press release, 6 August 1973.

76　TF, Pocock (Jack) Memorial Collection, box 27 [oversize], folder 2, continued from box 14, "Canadian Adjustment of Status Program," folder 27, "Adjustment of Status Program clippings," *7 News*, 25 August 1973, 4-5; "Notice to All Counsellors"; letter to Don Lumley, Public Service Announcements, CHLO radio, St. Thomas, ON, from Dick Brown, TADP, 12 September 1973.

77　TF, Pocock (Jack) Memorial Collection, box 27 [oversize], folder 2, continued from box 14, "Canadian Adjustment of Status Program," folder 27, "Adjustment of Status Program clippings," *Mountain News*, 15 August 1973, 22; *Dundas Star*, 15 August 1973, 14; *Ancaster News*, 15 August 1973, 8; *Stoney Creek News*, 15 August 1973, 14.

78　DAL, Nova Scotia Committee to Aid American War Objectors fonds, MS-10-7, box 1, folder 5, "Communications with the Press, Community and Affiliated Organizations," letter to "editor" from Eric Stine, Halifax Committee to Aid War Resistors [sic], 1 October 1973.

79　DAL, Nova Scotia Committee to Aid American War Objectors fonds, MS-10-7, box 1, folder 5, "Communications with the Press, Community and Affiliated Organizations," *The Register* (Berwick, Nova Scotia); DAL, Nova Scotia Committee to Aid American War Objectors fonds, MS-10-7, box 2, folder 1, "Financial Documents," *Hants Journal* (Windsor, Nova Scotia), 10 October 1973, 4; *Guardian-Patriot* (Charlottetown), 1 October 1973; *Brunswickan* (Fredericton, New Brunswick), 5 October 1973; *Amherst Daily News* (Amherst, Nova Scotia), 30 September 1973.

80 TF, Pocock (Jack) Memorial Collection, box 14, "Canadian Adjustment of Status Program," folder 15, "Correspondence, Press Releases, and Notes," letter to Ian Laidlaw and Bruce Rogers, CBC Radio, from Dick Brown, TADP, 26 September 1973.

81 TF, Pocock (Jack) Memorial Collection, box 14, "Canadian Adjustment of Status Program," folder 8, "Press Release, 31 July 1973, 7:30 p.m. and Drafts," "War Resister's Aide [sic] Centres Launch 60 Day Immigration Drive," 31 July 1973.

82 TF, Pocock (Jack) Memorial Collection, box 14, "Canadian Adjustment of Status Program," folder 10, "Correspondence, Press Releases, Notes," *Globe and Mail*, "Draft Evaders Fear No-Appeal Deportation," 7 August 1973; *Globe and Mail*, "Offer of Landed Status No Trap, Andras Assures Illegal Immigrants," 11 September 1973.

83 DAL, Nova Scotia Committee to Aid American War Objectors fonds, MS-10-7, box 2, folder 1, "Financial documents," poster, n.d.

84 Ibid., box 1, folder 5, "Communications with the Press, Community and Affiliated Organizations," flyer.

85 TF, Pocock (Jack) Memorial Collection, box 27 [oversize], folder 2, continued from box 14, "Canadian Adjustment of Status Program," folder 27, "Adjustment of Status Program Clippings," poster, n.d.

86 TF, Pocock (Jack) Memorial Collection, box 14, "Canadian Adjustment of Status Program," folder 26, "Bus Promotion," "Canadian Coalition of War Resisters – Personal Service Contract," n.d.

87 TF, Pocock (Jack) Memorial Collection, box 14, "Canadian Adjustment of Status Program," folder 27, Newspaper Clippings, "Anti-Draft Program to Area," *Bancroft, Ont. Weekly,* 8 August 1973.

88 TF, Pocock (Jack) Memorial Collection, box 2, "TADP Intake Records, Sales Records, Stationery, and Other Materials," folders 1-4, "Front Desk Inquiry Records," 1972-73.

89 UBCL, RBSC, Renée Kasinsky fonds, box 6, file 5, "Canadian Publications: *AMEX*," "Fewer Americans Than Expected," *AMEX* 4, 4 (September-October 1973), 32.

90 LAC, Department of External Affairs fonds, RG 76, vol. 996, file 5875-5-1, pt. 1, "Status Adjustment Program – 1973 – Status Adjustment Procedures – General," letter to Prime Minister Pierre Elliott Trudeau from Minister Robert Andras, 30 August 1973.

91 United Nations Treaty Collection, "Convention Relating to the Status of Refugees," accessed 6 July 2008, http://www.unhchr.ch/html/. The convention had existed since 1951. It would not be until 1976 that Canada would adopt legislation allowing refugees to apply for immigrant status. C. Michael Lanphier, "Canada's Response to Refugees," *International Migration Review* 15, 1-2 (1981), 113-30.

92 LAC, Department of External Affairs fonds, RG 76, vol. 996, file 5875-5-1, pt. 1, "Status Adjustment Program – 1973 – Status Adjustment Procedures – General," letter to Prime Minister Pierre Elliott Trudeau from Minister Robert Andras, 30 August 1973.

93 DAL, Nova Scotia Committee to Aid American War Objectors fonds, MS-10-7, file 1.5 [bulletins, posters, publications on amnesty], telex to Robert Andras, 10 October

1973; Halifax Friends Meeting [Quakers], minutes, 7 October 1973, and enclosed press release, [10 October 1973].

94   TF, Pocock (Jack) Memorial Collection, box 13, "Lobbying and Public Relations," folder 1, "TADP Statements and Lobbying," letter from Vancouver Committee to Aid American War Objectors to Robert Andras, Minister of Manpower and Immigration, 1 October 1973.

95   LAC, Department of External Affairs fonds, RG 76, vol. 996, file 5875-5-1, pt. 1, "Status Adjustment Program – 1973 – Status Adjustment Procedures – General," Roger Appleton, "Action Line" [advice column], letter, "Illegal Immigrant's Fear Unjustified," *Ottawa Citizen,* 7 September 1973.

96   LAC, Department of External Affairs fonds, RG 76, vol. 996, file 5875-5-1, pt. 1, "Status Adjustment Program – 1973 – Status Adjustment Procedures – General," memo to the Minister from A.E. Gotlieb, 19 September 1973.

97   Ibid.

98   LAC, Department of External Affairs fonds, RG 76, vol. 996, file 5875-5-1, pt. 1, "Status Adjustment Program – 1973 – Status Adjustment Procedures – General," draft press release, 20 September 1973.

99   TF, Pocock (Jack) Memorial Collection, box 27 [oversize], folder 2, continued from box 14, "Canadian Adjustment of Status Program," folder 27, "Adjustment of Status Program clippings," "Ethnic 'Mediators' Recruited to Encourage More Illegal Immigrants to Seek Landed Status," *Globe and Mail,* 22 September 1973, 1.

100 LAC, Department of External Affairs fonds, RG 76, vol. 996, file 5875-5-1, pt. 1, "Status Adjustment Program – 1973 – Status Adjustment Procedures – General," report on Assistant Directors General Conference – Winnipeg, 1 October 1973.

101 LAC, Department of External Affairs fonds, RG 76, vol. 996, file 5875-5-1, pt. 1, "Status Adjustment Program – 1973 – Status Adjustment Procedures – General," telecommunication message, from A. Duckett, Director, Information Service, to Directors General, all regions, cc. Director, Home Services Branch; Director-General, Foreign Services; Director, Programs and Procedures, "Information Progress for Thursday, 4 October 1973."

102 LAC, Department of External Affairs fonds, RG 76, vol. 996, file 5875-5-1, pt. 1, "Status Adjustment Program – 1973 – Status Adjustment Procedures – General," telecommunication message, from Head, Regional Information Development and Internal Communications, Information Service, to Directors General, all regions, cc. Director, Home Services Branch; Director-General, Foreign Services; Director, Programs and Procedures, "Information Progress for Tuesday, October 9, 1973," 9 October 1973. The Department was also working with ethnic communities such as Chinese, Ceylonese, and Caribbean groups in Toronto. TF, Pocock (Jack) Memorial Collection, box 27 [oversize], folder 2, continued from box 14, "Canadian Adjustment of Status Program," folder 27, "Adjustment of Status Program Clippings," "Ethnic

'Mediators' Recruited to Encourage More Illegal Immigrants to Seek Landed Status," *Globe and Mail,* 22 September 1973, 1.

103 LAC, Department of External Affairs fonds, RG 76, vol. 996, file 5875-5-1, pt. 1, "Status Adjustment Program – 1973 – Status Adjustment Procedures – General," memo to the Minister from Deputy Minister, "Registration under Adjustment Program by Mail or Telegram," 11 October 1973.

104 LAC, Department of External Affairs fonds, RG 76, vol. 996, file 5875-5-1, pt. 1, "Status Adjustment Program – 1973 – Status Adjustment Procedures – General," memo to Assistant Deputy Minister, Immigration, from Director, Home Services Branch, "Adjustment of Status Program – Registrants," 12 October 1973.

105 LAC, Department of External Affairs fonds, RG 76, vol. 996, file 5875-5-1, pt. 1, "Status Adjustment Program – 1973 – Status Adjustment Procedures – General," telecommunication from Director General, Home Branch, to Regional Directors General, 24 October 1973.

106 The statistics reported were 31,879 registrants and 17,893 dependents, of which about 32 percent were illegal. LAC, Department of External Affairs fonds, RG 76, vol. 996, file 5875-5-1, pt. 1, "Status Adjustment Program – 1973 – Status Adjustment Procedures – General," memo to the Minister, "Adjustment of Status Program," 23 October 1973.

107 TF, Pocock (Jack) Memorial Collection, box 14, "Canadian Adjustment of Status Program," folder 10, "Correspondence, Press Releases, Notes," letter from G.D.A. Reid, Director General, Ontario Region, Manpower and Immigration, to Dick Brown, TADP, 19 October 1973.

108 Joseph Jones, interview with the author by email, 21 November 2006.

109 "Daniel," interview with the author by email, 2 November 2006.

110 Paul Copeland, interview with the author, Ottawa, ON, 5 June 2006.

111 Citizenship and Immigration Canada, *Forging Our Legacy: Canadian Citizenship and Immigration, 1900-1977,* Chapter 6, "Trail-Blazing Initiatives," Public Works and Government Services Canada, 2000, http://www.cic.gc.ca/.

112 TF, Pocock (Jack) Memorial Collection, box 27 [oversize], folder 2, continued from box 14, "Canadian Adjustment of Status Program," folder 27, "Adjustment of Status Program Clippings," *Exile* Notes – Newsletter of Vancouver American Exiles Association, n.d.

Conclusion

1 The poem in the epigraph is excerpted from Red Cloud, *Let Freedom Ring,* 2008, Poets Against the War, http://poetsagainstthewar.org.

2 Douglas T. Miller, *On Our Own: Americans in the Sixties* (Toronto: D.C. Heath and Company, 1996), 174.

Bibliography

Archival Sources

Dalhousie University Archives and Special Collections
Nova Scotia Committee to Aid American War Objectors fonds

Joseph Healey Library, University of Massachusetts, Boston
Perrin, Richard: Papers, 1966-2001, Series V, Regina Committee of American
   Deserters (RCAD), 1969

Library and Archives Canada
MG 28, I 218, Voice of Women fonds
MG 28, I 327, Canadian Council of Churches fonds
MG 30, D 326, Judith Merril fonds
MG 31, D 66, Peter Warrian fonds
MG 31, I 4, Goldie Josephy fonds
RG 2, Privy Council Office fonds
RG 25, Department of External Affairs fonds
RG 76, Department of Employment and Immigration fonds
RG 146, Canadian Security Intelligence Service fonds

Records of Yellow Door Coffeehouse, Montreal, QC
Montreal Council/Programme, American Refugee Service

Thomas Fisher Rare Book Library, University of Toronto
Pocock (Jack) Memorial Collection

Université du Québec à Montréal Service des archives
et de gestion des documents
Collection de publications de groupes de gauche et de groupes populaires

University of British Columbia Library Rare Books and Special Collections
Renée Kasinsky fonds
Edward Starkins fonds
Vancouver Vietnam Action Committee fonds

William Ready Division of Archives and Research Collections, McMaster University Library
Canadian student social and political organizations
Doug Ward fonds
Hans Sinn fonds
Quebec social and political organizations

Interviews
"Ben," anti-draft activist, 1978, by email, 4 November 2006
"Daniel," deserter, 1968, by email, 2 November 2006
"James," draft dodger, 1967, by telephone, 10 July 2006
David James Brown, war resister, 1968, by email, 6 November 2006
Paul Copeland, Canadian lawyer, in person, Ottawa, ON, 5 June 2006
Carolyn Egan, war resister, 1969, in person, Toronto, ON, 1 June 2006
Ken Fisher, Canadian activist, in person, Gatineau, QC, 9 June 2006
Michael Goldberg, draft dodger, 1967, by telephone, 11 July 2006
Joseph Jones, draft dodger, 1970, by email, 21 November 2006
Dick Perrin, deserter, unknown arrival date, by email, 12 December 2006
Mark Phillips, draft dodger, 1968, in person, Ottawa, ON, 11 July 2006
Hardy Scott, draft dodger, January 1967, by mail, 31 October 2006
Joan Wilcox, American immigrant, pre-1965, in person, Ottawa, ON, 17 May 2006
Marvin Work, draft dodger, June 1970, by email, 28 November 2006
Lee Zaslovsky, deserter, 1970, by email, 30 October 2006

Other Sources
Abu-Laban, Yasmeen. "Keeping 'Em Out: Gender, Race, and Class Biases in Canadian Immigration Policy." In *Painting the Maple: Essays on Race, Gender, and the Construction of Canada,* edited by Veronica Strong-Boag, Sherrill Grace, Avigail Eisenberg, and Joan Anderson, 69-82. Vancouver: UBC Press, 1998.
Apple, Reuben. "War Resisters Welcome." *Eye Weekly* (Toronto), 5 April 2007.
Appy, Christian. "From Working-Class War: American Combat Soldiers and Vietnam." In *American Identities: An Introductory Textbook,* edited by Lois P. Rudnick, Judith E. Smith, and Rachel Lee Rubin, 138-42. Boston: Blackwell, 1995.
–. *Working-Class War: American Combat Soldiers and Vietnam.* Chapel Hill, NC: University of North Carolina Press, 1993.

Avery, Donald H. "Immigrant Workers and Canada's Changing Immigration Policy, 1952-1980." In *Reluctant Hosts: Canada's Response to Immigrant Workers, 1896-1994*. Toronto: McClelland and Stewart, 1995.

Azzi, Stephen. "Americanism and Anti-Americanism in English Canadian Nationalism, 1965-1975." Paper presented at "The Sixties Canadian-Style: Where Have All the Sixties Gone?" 24th Annual Two Days of Canada conference, Brock University, St. Catharines, ON, 4-5 November 2010.

–. "Foreign Investment and the Paradox of Economic Nationalism." In *Canadas of the Mind: The Making and Unmaking of Canadian Nationalisms in the Twentieth Century,* edited by Norman Hillmer and Adam Chapnick, 63-88. Montreal and Kingston: McGill-Queen's University Press, 2007.

–. *Walter Gordon and the Rise of Canadian Nationalism*. Montreal and Kingston: McGill-Queen's University Press, 1999.

Balcom, Karen Andrea. "The Traffic in Babies: Cross-Border Adoption, Baby-Selling and the Development of Child Welfare Systems in the United States and Canada, 1930-1960." PhD diss., Rutgers State University, 2002.

Ball, Christine. "The History of the Voice of Women/Les Voix des Femmes – The Early Years." PhD diss., University of Toronto, 1994.

Bannerji, Himani. "On the Dark Side of the Nation: Politics of Multiculturalism and the State of 'Canada.'" In *Literary Pluralities,* edited by Crystal Verduyn, 125-51. Peterborough, ON: Broadview Press, 1998.

Bell, Julian, ed. *We Did Not Fight: 1914-18 Experiences of War Resisters*. London: Cobden-Sanderson, 1935.

Black, Conrad. *Richard M. Nixon: A Life in Full*. New York: Public Affairs, 2008.

Boris, Eileen. "The Racialized Gendered State: Constructions of Citizenship in the United States." *Social Politics* 2, 2 (1995): 160-80.

Bothwell, Robert. *Alliance and Illusion: Canada and the World, 1945-1984*. Vancouver: UBC Press, 2007.

–. *The Big Chill: Canada and the Cold War*. Toronto: Canadian Institute of International Affairs, 1998.

–. *Canada and the United States: The Politics of Partnership*. Toronto: University of Toronto Press, 1992.

Bothwell, Robert, Ian Drummond, and John English. *Canada since 1945*. Toronto: University of Toronto Press, 1991.

Breines, Paul, ed. *Critical Interruptions: New Left Perspectives on Herbert Marcuse*. New York: Herder and Herder, 1971.

Briesmaster, Allan, and Steven Michael Berzensky, eds. *Crossing Lines: Poets Who Came to Canada in the Vietnam War Era*. Hamilton, ON: Seraphim Editions, 2008.

Brock, Peter. *The Quaker Peace Testimony, 1660 to 1914*. Syracuse, NY: Syracuse University Press, 1990.

Brock, Peter, ed. *"These Strange Criminals": An Anthology of Prison Memoirs by Conscientious Objectors from the Great War to the Cold War.* Toronto: University of Toronto Press, 2004.

Brock, Peter, and Nigel Young. *Pacifism in the Twentieth Century.* Syracuse, NY: Syracuse University Press, 1999.

Brown, Lorne, and Caroline Brown. *An Unauthorized History of the RCMP.* Toronto: James Lewis and Samuel, 1973.

Brown, Ronnie R. "XIII. Home." Excerpt from "Un-Deferred: A Draft Dodger's Wife Remembers." In *Crossing Lines: Poets Who Came to Canada in the Vietnam War Era,* edited by Allan Briesmaster and Steven Michael Berzensky, 55. Hamilton, ON: Seraphim Editions, 2008.

Bukowczyk, John J., Randy William Widdis, Nora Faires, and David R. Smith. *Permeable Border: The Great Lakes Basin as Transnational Region, 1650-1990.* Pittsburgh: University of Pittsburgh Press, 2005.

Buzzanco, Robert. *Vietnam and the Transformation of American Life,* Malden, MA: Blackwell, 1999.

Campbell, Colin. "The Political Roles of Senior Government Officials in Advanced Democracies." *British Journal of Political Science* 18, 2 (1988): 243-72.

Campbell, Lara. "Women's Liberation and 'US Chauvinism:' Vietnam War Resistance and Feminist Activism." Paper presented at "New World Coming: The Sixties and the Shaping of Global Consciousness," Queen's University, Kingston, ON, 13-16 June 2007.

–. "'Women United Against the War': Gender Politics, Feminism, and Vietnam Draft Resistance in Canada." In *New World Coming: The Sixties and the Shaping of Global Consciousness,* edited by Karen Dubinsky, Catherine Krull, Susan Lord, Sean Mills, and Scott Rutherford, 339-48. Toronto: Between the Lines, 2009.

Canby, Steven L. *Military Manpower Procurement: A Policy Analysis.* Toronto: Lexington Books, 1972.

Carr, Barry. "Globalization from Below: Labour Internationalism under NAFTA." *International Social Science Journal* 51, 1 (1999): 49-59.

Carroll, William K. *Corporate Power and Canadian Capitalism.* Vancouver: UBC Press, 1986.

CBC Radio. "From Naked Man Hill to Skedattle Ridge." *Morningside.* Peter Gzowski/ Canadian Broadcasting Corporation. Broadcast 25 October 1996. http://archives. cbc.ca/.

CBC Television. "Canada Must Be a Just Society." *CBC Archives.* "Pierre Elliott Trudeau: Swinger, Philosopher, Prime Minister." Original air date 9 September 1968. http://archives.cbc.ca.

–. "Safe Haven in Toronto – Yorkville Village." *CBC Archives.* Produced by Larry Bondy. Original air date 10 May 1966. http://archives.cbc.ca/.

–. "Seeking Sanctuary: Draft Dodgers: Trudeau Opens the Door to Draft Dodgers." *CBC Archives.* Original air date 25 March 1969. http://archives.cbc.ca/.

Chambers, John Whiteclay II. *To Raise an Army: The Draft Comes to Modern America.* New York: The Free Press, 1987.

Churchill, David S. "An Ambiguous Welcome: Vietnam Draft Resistance, the Canadian State, and Cold War Containment." *Social History/Histoire sociale* 27, 73 (2004): 1-26.

–. "When Home Became Away: American Expatriates and New Social Movements in Toronto, 1965-1977." PhD diss., University of Chicago, 2001.

Citizenship and Immigration Canada. *Forging Our Legacy: Canadian Citizenship and Immigration, 1900-1977.* Chapter 6, "Trail-Blazing Initiatives." Accessed 31 March 2008. http://www.cic.gc.ca/.

Clarkson, Stephen, ed. *An Independent Foreign Policy for Canada?* Toronto: McClelland and Stewart, 1968.

Clavin, Patricia. "Defining Transnationalism." *Contemporary European History* 14, 4 (2005): 421-39.

Clement, Wallace, and Glen Williams. Introduction to *The New Canadian Political Economy,* edited by Wallace Clement and Glen Williams, 3-15. Montreal and Kingston: McGill-Queen's University Press, 1989.

Cohen, Eliot A. *Citizens and Soldiers: The Dilemmas of Military Service.* Ithaca, NY: Cornell University Press, 1985.

Cohn, Bernard S. *An Anthropologist among Historians and Other Essays.* Delhi and New York: Oxford University Press, 1990.

Comacchio, Cynthia. *The Dominion of Youth: Adolescence and the Making of a Modern Canada, 1920-1950.* Waterloo, ON: Wilfrid Laurier University Press, 2006.

Conrad, Margaret. "2007 Presidential Address of the CHA: Public History and Its Discontents or History in the Age of Wikipedia." *Journal of the Canadian Historical Association* 18, 1 (2007): 1-26.

Cooney, John, and Dana Spitzer. "Hell, No, We Won't Go!" In *The American Military,* edited by Martin Oppenheimer, 117-37. Chicago: Aldine, 1971.

Cordero-Guzmán, Héctor R., Robert C. Smith, and Ramón Grosfoguel, eds. *Migration, Transnationalization, and Race in a Changing New York.* Philadelphia: Temple University Press, 2001.

Cormier, Jeffrey. *The Canadianization Movement: Emergence, Survival, and Success.* Toronto: University of Toronto Press, 2004.

Cortwright, David. *Soldiers in Revolt: GI Resistance during the Vietnam War.* 1975. Reprint, Chicago: Haymarket Books, 2005.

Cox, Robert. "Social Forces, States and World Orders: Beyond International Relations Theory." In *Neorealism and Its Critics,* edited by Robert Keohane, 204-54. New York: Columbia University Press, 1986.

Culhane, Claire. *Why Is Canada in Vietnam? The Truth about Our Foreign Aid.* Toronto: New Canada Press, 1972.

Curry, G. David. *Sunshine Patriots: Punishment and the Vietnam Offender.* Notre Dame, IN: University of Notre Dame Press, 1985.

Curtis, Bruce. *The Politics of Population: State Formation, Statistics, and the Census of Canada, 1849-1875.* Toronto: University of Toronto Press, 2001.

Das Gupta, Tania, and Franca Iacovetta, eds. "Whose Canada Is It? Immigrant Women, Women of Colour and Feminist Critiques of 'Multiculturalism.'" Special issue, *Atlantis: A Women's Studies Journal* 24, 2 (2000): 1-4.

Davidson, Phillip B. *Vietnam at War: The History, 1946-1975.* London: Oxford University Press, 1986.

Davis, Angela. "Preface: Marcuse's Legacies." In *The New Left and the 1960s.* Vol. 3 of *The Collected Papers of Herbert Marcuse,* edited by Douglas Kellner, vii-xiv. New York: Routledge, 2005.

Dean, Joanna. "The Gendered Politics of Nuclear Fallout." Paper presented at Ottawa Historical Association, Ottawa, ON, April 2008.

De Groot, Gerard J. *A Noble Cause? America and the Vietnam War.* Harlow: Longman, 2000.

Dickerson, James. *North to Canada: Men and Women against the Vietnam War.* Westport, CT: Praeger, 1999.

Donaghy, Greg. *Tolerant Allies: Canada and the United States, 1963-1968.* Montreal and Kingston: McGill-Queen's University Press, 2002.

Dubinsky Karen, Catherine Krull, Susan Lord, Sean Mills, and Scott Rutherford, eds. *New World Coming: The Sixties and the Shaping of Global Consciousness.* Toronto: Between the Lines, 2009.

Edwardson, Ryan. "'Kicking Uncle Sam Out of the Peaceable Kingdom': English-Canadian 'New Nationalism' and Americanization." *Journal of Canadian Studies* 37, 4 (2003): 131-52.

Elliott, Bruce S. *Irish Migrants in the Canadas: A New Approach.* Montreal and Kingston: McGill-Queen's University Press, 1988.

Emerick, Kenneth Fred. *War Resisters Canada: The World of the American Military-Political Refugees.* Knox, PA: Knox, Pennsylvania Free Press, 1972.

Epp, Frank H., ed. *I Would Like to Dodge the Draft-Dodgers, But ...* Waterloo and Winnipeg, MB: Conrad Press, 1970.

Epp, Marlene. *Women without Men: Mennonite Refugees of the Second World War.* Toronto: University of Toronto Press, 1999.

Evans, Sara. *Personal Politics: The Roots of Women's Liberation in the Civil Rights Movement and the New Left.* New York: Alfred A. Knopf, 1979.

Faiers, Chris. "draft resister." In *Crossing Lines: Poets Who Came to Canada in the Vietnam War Era,* edited by Allan Briesmaster and Steven Michael Berzensky, 80. Hamilton, ON: Seraphim Editions, 2008.

Finkel, Alvin. *Our Lives: Canada after 1945*. Toronto: James Lorimer, 1997.

Foley, Michael S. *Confronting the War Machine: Draft Resistance during the Vietnam War*. Chapel Hill: University of North Carolina Press, 2003.

Folson, Rose Baaba. "Representation of the Immigrant." In *Calculated Kindness: Global Restructuring, Immigration and Settlement in Canada,* edited by Rose Baaba Folson, 21-32. Halifax: Fernwood Publishing, 2004.

Folvik, Robin. "'They Followed Their Men into Canada?' American Women in Canada during the Vietnam War Era." Paper presented at "New World Coming: The Sixties and the Shaping of Global Consciousness," Queen's University, Kingston, ON, 13-16 June 2007.

Foucault, Michel. "Governmentality." In *The Foucault Effect: Studies in Governmentality,* edited by Graham Burchell, Colin Gordon, and Peter Miller, 87-104. Toronto: Harvester Wheatsheaf, 1991.

Francis, Daniel. *National Dreams: Myth, Memory, and Canadian History*. Vancouver: Arsenal Pulp Press, 1997.

Fuller, C.J. Review of *An Anthropologist among the Historians, and Other Essays,* by Bernard Cohn. *Man* 26, 4 (1991): 762-63.

Garvy, Helen. *Rebels with a Cause*. Los Gatos, CA: Shire Press, 2007.

Gitlin, Todd. *The Sixties: Years of Hope, Days of Rage*. New York: Bantam Books, 1993.

Gramsci, Antonio. "The Intellectuals." In *Selections from the Prison Notebooks of Antonio Gramsci*. Translated and edited by Quintin Hoare and Geoffrey Nowell Smith, 3-23. New York: International Publishers, 1971.

–. "The Modern Prince." In *Selections from the Prison Notebooks of Antonio Gramsci*. Translated and edited by Quintin Hoare and Geoffrey Nowell Smith, 123-205. New York: International Publishers, 1971.

–. *Selections from the Prison Notebooks of Antonio Gramsci*. Edited and translated by Quintin Hoare and Geoffrey Nowell Smith. New York: International Publishers, 1971.

–. "State and Civil Society." In *Selections from the Prison Notebooks of Antonio Gramsci*. Translated and edited by Quintin Hoare and Geoffrey Nowell Smith, 206-76. New York: International Publishers, 1971.

–. "The Study of Philosophy." In *Selections from the Prison Notebooks of Antonio Gramsci*. Translated and edited by Quintin Hoare and Geoffrey Nowell Smith, 321-77. New York: International Publishers, 1971.

Granatstein, J.L. *Canada 1957-1967: The Years of Uncertainty and Innovation*. Toronto: McClelland and Stewart, 1986.

–. *The Ottawa Men: The Civil Service Mandarins, 1935-1957*. Toronto: Oxford University Press. 1982.

–. *Yankee Go Home? Canadians and Anti-Americanism*. Toronto: Harper Collins, 1996.

Granatstein, J.L., and Robert Bothwell. *Pirouette: Pierre Trudeau and Canadian Foreign Policy*. Toronto: University of Toronto Press, 1990.

Granatstein, J.L., and Norman Hillmer. *For Better or For Worse: Canada and the United States to the 1990s.* Toronto: Copp Clark Pitman, 1991.

Grant, George. *Lament for a Nation: The Defeat of Canadian Nationalism.* Toronto: McClelland and Stewart, 1965.

Green, Alan G., and David A. Green. "The Economic Goals of Canada's Immigration Policy: Past and Present." *Canadian Public Policy/Analyse de Politiques* 25, 4 (1999): 425-51.

Greer, Allan. "The Birth of the Police in Canada." In *Colonial Leviathan: State Formation in Mid-Nineteenth Century Canada,* edited by Allan Greer and Ian Radforth, 17-49. Toronto: University of Toronto Press, 1992.

Greer, Allan, and Ian Radforth, eds. *Colonial Leviathan: State Formation in Mid-Nineteenth Century Canada.* Toronto: University of Toronto Press, 1992.

Hagan, John. *Northern Passage: American Vietnam War Resisters in Canada.* Cambridge, MA: Harvard University Press, 2001.

Haig-Brown, Alan. *Hell No We Won't Go: Vietnam Draft Resisters in Canada.* Vancouver: Raincoast Books, 1996.

Hall, Mitchell K. *Because of Their Faith: CALCAV and Religious Opposition to the Vietnam War.* New York: Columbia University Press, 1990.

Hall, Stuart. "Gramsci's Relevance for the Study of Race and Ethnicity." In *Stuart Hall: Critical Dialogues in Cultural Studies,* edited by David Morley and Kuan-Hsing Chen, 411-40. New York: Routledge, 1996.

Halloran, Mary, John Hilliker, and Greg Donaghy, Historical Section, Foreign Affairs Canada. "The White Paper Impulse: Reviewing Foreign Policy under Trudeau and Clark." Paper presented at Canadian Political Science Association conference, Waterloo, Ontario, 3 June 2005. http://www.cpsa-acsp.ca/papers-2005/Halloran.pdf.

Hamilton, Bill. *Place Names of Atlantic Canada.* Toronto: University of Toronto Press, 1996.

Hart, Paul 't. *Groupthink in Government: A Study of Small Groups and Policy Failure.* Rockland, MA: Swets and Zeitlinger, 1990.

Harvey, David D. "Garrison Duty: Canada's Retention of the American Migrant, 1901-1981." *American Review of Canadian Studies* 15, 2 (1985): 169-87.

Hawkins, Freda. *Canada and Immigration: Public Policy and Public Concern.* 2nd ed. Ottawa and Montreal/Kingston: Institute of Public Administration of Canada/McGill-Queen's University Press, 1988.

–. *Critical Years in Immigration: Canada and Australia Compared.* Montreal and Kingston: McGill-Queen's University Press, 1991.

Hayes, Thomas Lee. *American Deserters in Sweden: The Men and Their Challenge.* New York: Association Press, 1971.

Hayward, Robert J. "Federal Access and Privacy Legislation and the Public Archives of Canada." *Archivaria* 18 (Summer 1984): 47-57.

Henderson, Stuart. "Off the Streets and into the Fortress: Experiments in Hip Separatism at Toronto's Rochdale College, 1968-1975." *Canadian Historical Review* 92, 1 (2011): 107-33.

Hewitt, Steve. *Spying 101: The RCMP's Secret Activities at Canadian Universities, 1917-1997.* Toronto: University of Toronto Press, 2002.

Hillmer, Norman, and Adam Chapnick, eds. *Canadas of the Mind: The Making and Unmaking of Canadian Nationalisms in the Twentieth Century.* Montreal and Kingston: McGill-Queen's University Press, 2007.

Iacovetta, Franca. *The Writing of English Canadian Immigrant History.* Ottawa: Canadian Historical Association with the support of Heritage Canada, Government of Canada, 1997.

Jacobson, Matthew Frye. *Whiteness of a Different Color: European Immigrants and the Alchemy of Race.* Cambridge, MA: Harvard University Press, 1999.

Janis, Irving Lester. *Groupthink: Psychological Studies of Policy Decisions and Fiascos.* 2nd ed. Boston: Houghton Mifflin, 1982.

–. *Victims of Groupthink: A Psychological Study of Foreign-Policy Decisions and Fiascos.* Boston: Houghton, Mifflin, 1972.

Janowitz, Morris. "Sociological Theory and Social Control." *American Journal of Sociology* 81, 1 (1975): 82-108.

Janowitz, Morris, and Roger W. Little. *Sociology and the Military Establishment.* Beverly Hills, CA: Sage Publications, 1959.

Jezer, Marty. *Abbie Hoffman: American Rebel.* New Brunswick, NJ: Rutgers University Press, 1992.

Johns, Andrew L. Review of *Northern Passage: American Vietnam War Resisters in Canada* by John Hagan. *Journal of Cold War Studies* 5, 2 (2003): 86-89.

Jones, Joseph. *Contending Statistics: The Numbers for US Vietnam War Resisters in Canada.* Vancouver: Quarter Sheaf, 2005.

–. *Happenstance and Misquotation: Canadian Immigration Policy, 1966-1974, the Arrival of US Vietnam War Resisters, and the Views of Pierre Trudeau.* Vancouver: Quarter Sheaf, 2008.

Kasinsky, Renée G. *Refugees from Militarism: Draft-Age Americans in Canada.* New Brunswick, NJ: Transaction Books, 1976.

Keene, Donald. *Dawn to the West: Japanese Literature of the Modern Era, Poetry, Drama, Criticism.* New York: Columbia University Press, 1999.

Kellner, Douglas, ed. *The New Left and the 1960s.* Vol. 3 of *Collected Papers of Herbert Marcuse.* New York: Routledge, 2005.

Kellogg, Paul. "Kari Levitt and the Long Detour of Canadian Political Economy." *Studies in Political Economy: A Socialist Review* 76 (Autumn 2005): 31-60.

–. "State, Capital and World Economy: Bukharin's Marxism and the Dependency/Class Controversy in Canadian Political Economy." *Canadian Journal of Political Science* 22, 2 (1989): 337-62.

Kelly, Nora, and William Kelly. *The Royal Canadian Mounted Police: A Century of History, 1873-1973.* Edmonton: Hurtig Publishers, 1973.

Kent, Tom. *A Public Purpose: An Experience of Liberal Opposition and Canadian Government.* Montreal and Kingston: McGill-Queen's University Press, 1988.

Kerans, Marion Douglas. *Muriel Duckworth: A Very Active Pacifist.* Halifax: Fernwood Publishing, 1996.

Kinsman, Gary, Dieter K. Buse, and Mercedes Steedman, eds. *Whose National Security? Canadian State Surveillance and the Creation of Enemies.* Toronto: Between the Lines, 2000.

Knowles, Valerie. *Forging Our Legacy: Canadian Citizenship and Immigration, 1900-1977,* Public Works and Government Services Canada, 2000.

–. *Strangers at Our Gates: Canadian Immigration and Immigration Policy, 1540-1990.* 1st ed. Toronto: Dundurn Press, 1992.

Korinek, Valerie J. *Roughing It in the Suburbs: Reading Chatelaine Magazine in the Fifties and Sixties.* Toronto: University of Toronto Press, 2000.

Kusch, Frank. *All American Boys: Draft Dodgers in Canada from the Vietnam War.* Westport, CT: Praeger, 2001.

Lacombe, Dany. "Reforming Foucault: A Critique of the Social Control Thesis." *British Journal of Sociology* 47, 2 (1996): 332-52.

Lanphier, C. Michael. "Canada's Response to Refugees." *International Migration Review* 15, 1-2 (1981): 113-30.

Latour, Bruno. *Science in Action.* Cambridge, MA: Harvard University Press, 1987.

Leacy, F.H., ed. *Historical Statistics of Canada.* 2nd ed. Ottawa: Statistics Canada, 1983.

Legates, Marlene. *In Their Time: A History of Feminism in Western Society.* New York: Routledge, 1991.

Lermer, George. "The Task Force Report: An Economic Notebook." *Canadian Dimension* 5, 4 (1968): 15-20.

Levant, Victor. *Quiet Complicity: Canadian Involvement in the Vietnam War.* Toronto: Between the Lines, 1986.

Levitt, Kari. *Silent Surrender.* Toronto: Macmillan, 1970.

Lexier, Roberta. "'The Backdrop Against Which Everything Happened': English-Canadian Student Movements and Off-Campus Movements for Change." *History of Intellectual Culture* 7, 1 (2007). http://www.ucalgary.ca/hic/.

Little, Roger W., ed. *Selective Service and American Society.* New York: Russell Sage Foundation, 1969.

Loo, Tina, and Carolyn Strange. *Making Good: Law and Moral Regulation in Canada, 1867-1939.* Toronto: University of Toronto Press, 1997.

Lowenthal, David. *The Past Is a Foreign Country.* New York: Cambridge University Press, 1985.

Lumsden, Ian, ed. *Close the 49th Parallel.* Toronto: University of Toronto Press, 1970.

Malleck, Dan. "The Bureaucratization of Moral Regulation: The LCBO and (Not-So) Standard Hotel Licensing in Niagara, 1927-1944." *Social History/Histoire sociale* 38, 75 (2005): 59-77.

–. "Crossing the Line: The American Drinker in Ontario Border Communities, 1927-1944." Paper presented at the British Association of Canadian Studies, Kent, UK, 13 April 2005.

Manning, Erin. *Ephemeral Territories: Representing Nation, Home, and Identity in Canada.* Minneapolis: University of Minnesota Press, 2003.

Marcuse, Herbert. *Repressive Tolerance.* http://www.marcuse.org/.

Marr, William L. "Canadian Immigration Policies since 1962." *Canadian Public Policy/ Analyse de Politiques* 1, 2 (1975): 196-203.

Marshall, Dominique. *The Social Origins of the Welfare State: Quebec Families, Compulsory Education, and Family Allowances, 1940-1955.* Translated by Nicola Doone Danby. Waterloo, ON: Wilfrid Laurier University Press, 2006.

Marx, Karl, and Frederick Engels. *The Communist Manifesto.* 1848. Reprint, New York: International Publishers, 1998.

Massolin, Philip. *Canadian Intellectuals, the Tory Tradition and the Challenge of Modernity, 1939-1970.* Toronto: University of Toronto Press, 2001.

Mathews, Robin. "Economy and Nationhood." *Canadian Dimension* 5, 4 (April-May 1968): 15-20.

Mathews, Robin, and James Steele. "Canadianization Revisited: A Comment on Cormier's 'The Canadianization Movement in Context.'" *Canadian Journal of Sociology* 31 (2006): 491-508.

Maxwell, Donald W. "Religion and Politics at the Border: Canadian Church Support for American Vietnam War Resisters." *Journal of Church and State* 48 (Autumn 2006): 807-30.

McIntyre, Dennis. *International Who's Who in Poetry and Poets' Encyclopaedia.* New York: Routledge, 2001.

McKay, Ian. "The Liberal Order Framework: A Prospectus for a Reconnaissance of Canadian History." *Canadian Historical Review* 81, 4 (2000): 617-45.

–. *Rebels, Reds, Radicals: Rethinking Canada's Left History.* Toronto: Between the Lines, 2005.

McKay, Ian, and Jamie Swift. *Warrior Nation: Rebranding Canada in an Age of Anxiety.* Toronto: Between the Lines, 2012.

McMahon, Patricia I. "The Politics of Canada's Nuclear Policy, 1957-1963." PhD diss., University of Toronto, 1999.

Miliband, Ralph. "The Capitalist State: Reply to Nicos Poulantzas." *New Left Review* 59 (1970): 53-60.

–. *Class Power and State Power.* London: Verso, 1983.

–. "Poulantzas and the Capitalist State." *New Left Review* 82 (1973): 83-93.

Miller, Douglas T. *On Our Own: Americans in the Sixties.* Toronto: D.C. Heath and Company, 1996.

Mills, Sean. *The Empire Within: Postcolonial Thought and Political Activism in Sixties Montreal.* Montreal and Kingston: McGill-Queen's University Press, 2010.

Moore, Steve, and Debi Wells. *Imperialism and the National Question in Canada.* Toronto: S. Moore, 1975.

Nesbitt, Doug. "The 'Radical Trip' of the Canadian Union of Students, 1963-69." MA thesis, Trent University, 2009.

Newman, Jacquetta A. "Continuing Commitment: The Durability of Social Movements – Project Ploughshares in the 1990s." PhD diss., Queen's University, 1998.

Owram, Doug. *Born at the Right Time: A History of the Baby Boom Generation.* Toronto: University of Toronto Press, 1997.

–. *The Government Generation: Canadian Intellectuals and the State, 1900-1945.* Toronto: University of Toronto Press, 1986.

Palmer, Bryan. *Canada's 1960s: The Ironies of Identity in a Rebellious Era.* Toronto: University of Toronto Press, 2009.

–. Review of *The Canadianization Movement,* by Jeffrey Cormier. *Pacific Historical Review* 75, 2 (2006): 369-71.

Palmer, Howard. "Reluctant Hosts: Anglo-Canadian Views of Multiculturalism in the Twentieth Century." From *Multiculturalism as State Policy,* 1976. Reprinted in *Immigration in Canada: Historical Perspectives,* edited by Gerald Tulchisky, 297-333. Toronto: Copp Clark Longman Ltd., 1994.

Parai, Louis. "Canada's Immigration Policy, 1962-74." *International Migration Review* 9, 4 (1975): 449-77.

Paterak, Richard. *Escape from Freedom, Or, I Didn't Raise My Boy to Be a Canadian,* Toronto: Student Union for Peace Action, 1967.

Pendakur, Ravi. *Immigrants and the Labour Force: Policy Regulation, and Impact.* Montreal and Kingston: McGill-Queen's University Press, 2000.

Pennsylvania State University, Dickinson School of Law Library. "Race, Racism, and American Law Bibliography." http://www.dsl.psu.edu/.

Perrin, Dick, and Tim McCarthy. *G.I. Resister: The Story of How One American Soldier and His Family Fought the War in Vietnam.* Victoria, BC: Trafford Publishing, 2001.

Portelli, Alessandro. *The Death of Luigi Trastulli, and Other Stories: Form and Meaning in Oral History.* New York: SUNY Press, 1991.

Poulantzas, Nicos. "Capitalism and the State." *New Left Review* 58 (1969): 67-78.

–. "The Capitalist State: A Reply to Miliband and Laclau." *New Left Review* 95 (1976), 63-83.

Prentice, Alison, Paula Bourne, Gail Cuthbert Brandt, Beth Light, Wendy Mitchinson, and Naomi Black. *Canadian Women: A History.* Toronto: Harcourt Brace Jovanovich, 1988.

Price, Jennifer L. "Fact Sheet: Findings from the National Vietnam Veterans' Readjustment Study." United States Department of Veterans Affairs National Center for Posttraumatic Stress Disorder, 1 January 2007. http://www.ncptsd.va.gov/.

Pross, A. Paul. *Group Politics and Public Policy*. 2nd ed. Toronto: Oxford University Press, 1992.

Raskin, Jonah. *For the Hell of It: The Life and Times of Abbie Hoffman*. Berkeley: University of California Press, 1996.

Rebick, Judy. *Ten Thousand Roses: The Making of a Feminist Revolution*. Toronto: Penguin, 2005.

Reeves, Tom. "A Draft By Any Other Name ... Is Still Wrong: Exposing the Coming Draft." *Counterpunch*, Weekend Edition, 19-21 March 2005, http://www.counterpunch.org.

Resnick, Philip. *Land of Cain: Class and Nationalism in English Canada, 1945-1975*. Vancouver: New Star Books, 1977.

Ritchie, Donald A. *Doing Oral History: A Practical Guide*. New York: Oxford University Press, 2003.

Rodger, Richard, and Joanna Herbert. "Frameworks: Testimony, Representation and Interpretation." In *Testimonies of the City: Identity, Community and Change in a Contemporary Urban World*, edited by Richard Rodger and Joanna Herbert, 1-22. Surrey, UK: Ashgate Publishing, 2007.

Roediger, David R. *Working toward Whiteness: How America's Immigrants Became White: The Strange Journey from Ellis Island to the Suburbs*. New York: Basic Books, 1999.

Ross, Douglas A. *In the Interests of Peace: Canada and Vietnam, 1954-1973*. Toronto: University of Toronto Press, 1984.

Roth, Matthew McKenzie Bryant. "Crossing Borders: The Toronto Anti-Draft Programme and the Canadian Anti-Vietnam War Movement." MA thesis, University of Waterloo, 2008.

Roucek, Joseph S., ed. *Social Control for the 1980s: A Handbook for Order in a Democratic Society*. Westport, CT: Greenwood Press, 1978.

Rudnick, Lois P., Judith E. Smith, and Rachel Lee Rubin, eds. *American Identities: An Introductory Textbook*. Boston: Blackwell, 1995.

Sale, Kirkpatrick. *SDS: Ten Years toward a Revolution*. New York: Random House. 1973.

Satin, Mark, ed. *Manual for Draft-Age Immigrants to Canada*. 1st ed. Toronto: House of Anansi, 1968.

–. *Manual for Draft-Age Immigrants to Canada*. 2nd ed. Toronto: House of Anansi, ca. 1968.

–. *Manual for Draft-Age Immigrants to Canada*. 3rd ed. Toronto: Toronto Anti-Draft Programme, 1969.

–. *Manual for Draft-Age Immigrants to Canada.* 4th ed. Toronto: Toronto Anti-Draft Programme and House of Anansi, 1969.

–. *Manual for Draft-Age Immigrants to Canada.* 4th rev. ed. Toronto: House of Anansi, 1970.

Schwartz, Mildred A. "Cross-Border Ties among Protest Movements: The Great Plains Connection." *Great Plains Quarterly* 17, 2 (1997): 119-30.

Scott, James. *Seeing Like a State: How Certain Schemes to Improve the Human Condition Have Failed.* New Haven, CT: Yale University Press, 1998.

Skocpol, Theda. "Bringing the State Back In: Strategies of Analysis in Current Research." In *Bringing the State Back In,* edited by Peter R. Evans, Dietrich Ruesdchemeyer, and Theda Skocpol, 3-37. Cambridge: Cambridge University Press, 1985.

–. *Diminished Democracy: From Membership to Management in American Civic Life.* Norman: University of Oklahoma Press, 2003.

–. *States and Social Revolutions: A Comparative Analysis of France, Russia and China.* New York: Cambridge University Press, 1979.

–. "Why I Am an Historical Institutionalist." *Polity* 28, 1 (1995): 103-6.

Smart, John. "The Waffle's Impact on the New Democratic Party." *Studies in Political Economy* 32 (Summer 1990): 177-86.

Smith, Miriam. *A Civil Society? Collective Actors in Canadian Political Life.* Peterborough, ON: Broadview Press, 2005.

Snow, David A., Sarah Anne Soule, and Hanspeter Kriesi. *The Blackwell Companion to Social Movements.* Malden, MA: Blackwell Publishing, 2004.

Socknat, Thomas P. *Witness against War: Pacifism in Canada, 1900-1945,* Toronto: University of Toronto Press, 1987.

Squires, Jessica. "The Canadian Anti-Draft Movement, American War Resisters, and the State." In *War Resisters in Retrospect,* edited by Joseph Jones and Lori Olafson, 97-108. Ottawa: National Research Council of Canada, 2009.

–. "Creating Hegemony: Consensus by Exclusion in the Rowell-Sirois Commission." *Studies in Political Economy* 81 (2008): 159-90.

Stillerman, Joel. "Transnational Activist Networks and the Emergence of Labor Internationalism in the NAFTA Countries." *Social Science History* 27, 4 (2003): 577-601.

Strong-Boag, Veronica, Joan Anderson, Sherrill E. Grace, and Avigail Eisenberg, eds. *Painting the Maple: Essays on Race, Gender, and the Construction of Canada.* Vancouver: UBC Press, 1998.

Stuart, Reginald C. "Continentalism Revisited: Recent Narratives on the History of Canadian-American Relations." *Diplomatic History* 18, 3 (1994): 405-14.

–. *Dispersed Relations: Americans and Canadians in Upper North America.* Baltimore: Johns Hopkins University Press, 2007.

Sturman, Susan. "On Black-Boxing Gender: Some Social Questions for Bruno Latour." *Social Epistemology* 20, 2 (2006): 181-84.

Surrey, David Sterling. "The Assimilation of Vietnam-Era Draft Dodgers and Deserters into Canada: A Matter of Class." PhD diss., New School for Social Research, 1980.

–. *Choice of Conscience: Vietnam Era Military and Draft Resisters in Canada*. New York: Praeger, 1982.

Taylor, Charles. *Radical Tories: The Conservative Tradition in Canada*. Toronto: House of Anansi Press, 1982.

Teeple, Gary, ed. *Capitalism and the National Question in Canada*. Toronto: University of Toronto Press, 1972.

Thompson, James D. *Organizations in Action*. New York: McGraw-Hill, 1967.

Thompson, John Herd, and Stephen J. Randall. *Canada and the United States: Ambivalent Allies*. Montreal and Kingston: McGill-Queen's University Press, 1994.

Todd, Jack. *Desertion: In the Time of Vietnam*. New York: Houghton Mifflin Company, 2001.

Toronto Anti-Draft Programme, ed. *Manual for Draft-Age Immigrants to Canada*. 6th ed. Toronto: Toronto Anti-Draft Programme, 1971.

Tough, David. "A Global Introduction to George Grant's *Lament for a Nation*." Paper presented at "New World Coming: The Sixties and the Shaping of Global Consciousness," Queen's University, Kingston, ON, 15 June 2007.

Triandafyllidou, Anna. "Nations, Migrants and Transnational Identifications: An Interactive Approach to Nationalism." In *The Sage Handbook of Nations and Nationalism,* edited by Gerard Delanty and Krishan Kumar, 285-94. London: Sage, 2006.

Underhill, Frank H. *In Search of Canadian Liberalism*. Toronto: Macmillan, 1960.

Wall, Byron. *Manual for Draft-Age Immigrants to Canada*. 5th ed. Toronto: House of Anansi, 1970.

Warnock, John. Review of *An Independent Foreign Policy for Canada,* edited by Stephen Clarkson. *Canadian Dimension* 5, 5 (1968): 36-37.

Watkins, Mel. *Foreign Ownership and the Structure of Canadian Industry: Report of the Task Force on the Structure of Canadian Industry*. Task Force on the Structure of Canadian Industry, Ottawa: Queen's Printer, 1968.

–. "Staples Redux." *Studies in Political Economy: A Socialist Review* 79 (Spring 2007): 213-26.

–. "The Waffle and the National Question." *Studies in Political Economy* 32 (Summer 1990): 173-76.

Weaver, John C. *Crimes, Constables, and Courts: Order and Transgression in a Canadian City, 1816-1970*. Montreal and Kingston: McGill-Queen's University Press, 1995.

Weber, Max. *The Theory of Social and Economic Organization.* Edited by Talcott Parsons. New York: Oxford University Press, 1966.

Whitaker, Reg. *Canadian Immigration Policy since Confederation.* Ottawa: Canadian Historical Association, 1991.

–. *Double Standard: The Secret History of Canadian Immigration.* Toronto: Lester and Orpen Dennys, 1987.

Whitaker, Reg, and Gary Marcuse. *Cold War Canada: The Making of a National Insecurity State, 1945-1957.* Toronto: University of Toronto Press, 1994.

Widdis, Randy William. "Borders, Borderlands and Canadian Identity: A Canadian Perspective." *International Journal of Canadian Studies* 15 (1997): 49-66.

Williams, Roger Neville. *The New Exiles: American War Resisters in Canada.* New York: Liveright Publishers, 1971.

Wood, Patricia K. "Defining 'Canadian': Anti-Americanism and Identity in Sir John A. Macdonald's Nationalism." *Journal of Canadian Studies* 36, 2 (2001): 49-60.

Wyman, Ken. "A Report from the Tip of the Iceberg." *Canadian Dimension* 5, 4 (April-May 1968): 15-20.

Young, Jason. "'To Define a Community in Exile:' Producers, Readers, and War Resister Communication in *AMEX Magazine,* 1968-1977." MA major research paper, York University, 2006.

Index

Printed and bound in Canada by Friesens

Set in Rotis and Minion by Artegraphica Design Co. Ltd.

Copy editor: Joanne Muzak

Proofreader: Lana Okerlund

Indexer: Cheryl Lemmens